JOHN LOCKE

John Locke

ON POLITICS
AND EDUCATION

Introduction by Howard R. Penniman

Published for the Classics Club ® by

WALTER J. BLACK, INC. · ROSLYN, N. Y.

CONTENTS

INTRODUCTION

JOHN LOCKE lived during the exciting years of the English Civil War, the Commonwealth, the return of the Stuarts, and the Glorious Revolution. He advised the Earl of Shaftesbury, twice leader of the government under Charles II. He helped in a minor way to bring about the revolution of 1688, and he again served the government under William and Mary. He took part in or led movements for reform in religion, philosophy, and education. He participated in the great events of his day and yet in his writings he was able to rise above the immediate conflict. Near the end of his life, he published his reflections in each of the fields of his earlier activity. His writings were rooted in the problems of his time, but they emphasized the ever-recurring questions of philosophy, politics, and religion.

Truth for Locke was more important than the transient struggles, but an analysis of immediate issues might aid the quest for truth. The search for truth and certainty in the principles of philosophy and politics bulked so large in his thinking that it sometimes made his works inconsistent. He continued to scrutinize his own principles even when further examination led him to contradict his earlier conclusions. It was this unremitting search and the consequent raising of significant problems, as much as his own solutions to those problems, that has given Locke his enduring position among England's foremost thinkers.

Locke was born in 1632 in Wrington near Bristol. John Locke, senior, a country lawyer of no great wealth or station, brought him up in the Puritan tradition. Early strict obedience and later friendship was the father's formula, and it became Locke's formula when he wrote his *Thoughts Concerning Education*. The elder Locke commanded a few volunteers in the Parliamentary army during the early days of the Civil War, but apparently was not very successful as a soldier. He retired from his command after the siege of Bristol. Little is known of Locke's mother.

Locke studied in grammar school and then was sent to Westminster School in London. After leaving Westminster in 1652, he was given a scholarship at Christ Church, Oxford, where he studied Latin, Greek, rhetoric, logic, mathematics, and Hebrew. During his first years at Oxford Locke found the university dull and uninspiring. Scholarship under the Royalists had been forced into a secondary role by sports and entertainment. Conditions improved only slightly after the defeat and execution of Charles I. Sound religious doctrine, not wide learning, was the chief demand of the Puritans when selecting faculty members. Pedants or worse dominated the university at this period.

In the midst of mediocrity Locke found two men who stimulated his thinking and reflections—Pococke, the Arabic scholar, and Wallis, professor of mathematics. Locke was apparently not an outstanding student, though he performed well enough to be granted a fellowship in 1659, and later was appointed to teach Greek and rhetoric. Lady Masham, from whom we learn much about his early life, says that he preferred the society of a few witty young men to the regular university work. However, he maintained his connection with Oxford until deprived of his fellowship by order of Charles II, in 1684.

Locke's father had wanted him to enter the ministry after his university training. Locke himself was not certain of his fitness for such a career, but it was not until 1666, at the age of 34, that he definitely abandoned all ideas of a post in the church and decided to devote his attention entirely to the study and practice of medicine, a field in which he had been working for some time. Nevertheless, his interest in religion continued until his death. After 1693 most of his published writings were devoted to analyses of the Christian religion or to commentaries on the New Testament.

In 1666 he met Lord Ashley, later Earl of Shaftesbury. Lord Ashley was immediately attracted by the young scholar and asked him to join his household as tutor for his son. Locke agreed and quickly became much more than a tutor. He both advised Ashley in political matters and attended him as a physician. From 1666 until Shaftesbury's death in 1683, Locke's career was closely tied to the political ups and downs of the Earl.

Locke's political ventures did not prevent his continued activity in other fields. He remained particularly interested in medicine. He did not receive a medical degree from Oxford until 1674 because he refused to submit to the university curriculum, which he believed was antiquated and useless. Nevertheless, he gained some reputation by his research and limited practice. Lady Masham tells us that he never received any money for his medical activities.

He was for some years closely associated with Thomas Sydenham, the greatest British physician of his generation. Sydenham, in the preface to one of his books, said that Locke had "amongst the men of our time few equals and no superior." The two men worked together on one research project which sought to determine the cause of small-pox. They each kept careful case histories during the several epidemics of that disease which struck England in the 1660's and 1670's. They did not discover the source of smallpox, but their search for the facts in each case, instead of accepting old theories, helped advance the cause of medical research. Locke and Sydenham both opposed the prevalent, unscientific use of drugs and nostrums, preferring to recommend a good diet and the aid of nature when doctors knew no certain cure.

The most sensational event in Locke's medical career occurred shortly after he moved to Shaftesbury's home. Shaftesbury suffered from a tumor which threatened his life. Locke operated successfully. When the tumor continued to drain, Locke boldly inserted a silver tube to prevent the healing of the wound and allow the poisons to drain off. The success of the operation probably lengthened Shaftesbury's life by more than ten years.

During all the years spent with Shaftesbury, Locke remained interested in science. From 1660 to 1667 he made observations for his friend, the chemist Boyle, which were incorporated in the latter's *General History of the Air,* edited by Locke after Boyle's death. In 1668 he became a member of the famous Royal Society of British scientists and was elected to its executive committee. Ill health and the constant pressure of politics prevented his being active in the Society.

Its records show that Locke was asked to prepare and read papers, but they do not indicate whether he actually wrote them. The experimental methods of the new science influenced all of Locke's later writings.

In 1667 Locke was appointed secretary to Sir Walter Vane, ambassador to the Prussian court in Brandenburg. In 1672 he became Secretary of Presentations under Shaftesbury, who had just become Lord Chancellor. A year later he was appointed Secretary of the Council of Trade and Plantations. When Shaftesbury in 1675 lost favor with the king, Locke went to France for his health and stayed four years. While there he met and talked with many men of science and learning on the Continent. He kept copious notes in his journals of his discussions and personal observations. He returned to England when Shaftesbury regained power. He again acted as his advisor until Shaftesbury became involved in an unsuccessful campaign to prevent the Catholic James II from succeeding his brother, Charles II. Shaftesbury supported the claims of the Protestant Duke of Monmouth and was accordingly arrested in 1681 and tried for treason. He was, however, acquitted and died in exile in Holland in 1683. Locke himself went to Holland late in that year. It was at this time that Locke was deprived of his position at Oxford by command of Charles II. Shortly thereafter James II demanded Locke's extradition from Holland for treasonable conspiracy. The extradition request was not pressed, but Locke felt his position was so dangerous that he lived in hiding, under an assumed name. He was later pardoned by James II but did not return to England until after William and Mary had secured the throne in the Glorious Revolution. Locke, in fact, accompanied Queen Mary to England in February, 1689.

The new regime offered Locke several posts of importance. The king wished to name him ambassador to the court of Frederick the First in Brandenburg, but Locke declined. His ill health, he insisted, would prevent his carrying out the duties of one of the most important positions in the British foreign service. He also declined other positions in the foreign service. Finally he consented to take the job of Commissioner of Appeals, which would not require his living in London. In 1696 he became a member of the Board of Trade and Plantations. Because the work of the Board kept him constantly in

London, he tried for some time unsuccessfully to resign. After 1700 Locke, a bachelor to the end, lived in retirement at the home of his friends, Lord and Lady Masham.

No story of Locke's life would be complete which failed to comment on his personality. He had, as James Gibson puts it, a "genius for friendship." His faculty for making friends aided him in his custom of creating small discussion circles to talk about the varied subjects in which he was interested. Letters and essays of men and women of the period express their admiration for his great ability, but even more they stress his kindliness. Among his friends were men of his own age from Oxford and from public life in England and on the Continent, older men from whom he gained his early inspirations, and young men who turned to him for advice. Letters quoted in Fox Bourne's biography of Locke show that he even worked as a matchmaker and on one occasion selected the wedding clothes for the daughter of one of his friends.

Modest to a fault, quiet and unassuming, he was just the sort of man one might picture as the author of the anti-doctrinaire *Letters Concerning Toleration* or as the proposer of the tentative conclusions of the *Essay Concerning Human Understanding*. In his old age, when fame brought the curious as well as the thoughtful to his door, he wrote to a friend in Holland that he could still "laugh as heartily as ever, and be in pain for the public as much as you . . . (but) I live in fear of the bustlers, and would not have them near me. Such quiet fellows as you are, that come without drum and trumpet, with whom we can talk upon equal terms and receive some benefit by their company, I should be glad to have in my neighborhood, or to see sometimes, though they come from the other side of the water." [1]

Writings

Locke's reputation is based upon his writings. His name would have been relegated to the footnotes of English history books if his fame had depended merely upon his varied activities in politics and science. However, he published nothing in English until 1690, when he was

[1] Quoted in Norman Kemp Smith, *John Locke,* pp. 7-8.

fifty-eight. A few years earlier his *Letter Concerning Toleration* had appeared in Latin in Holland. Though his works were not printed until late in life, Locke had actually projected most of them many years earlier. It is probable that the crucial ideas in his three major works were carefully worked out as early as 1671. In that year he composed the first draft of his most famous book, *An Essay Concerning Human Understanding*. Five years before he had written, but not published, *An Essay on Toleration*, which contained the germinal ideas of his later *Letter Concerning Toleration* and the *Two Treatises on Civil Government*. Notes for these works may be found in the early pages of Locke's commonplace book, which he kept assiduously during most of his adult life.

According to the preface of the *Essay Concerning Human Understanding*, the first draft of this, his great contribution to modern philosophy, grew out of a meeting of five or six friends who had gathered to discuss some philosophical questions. Locke suggested that before taking up any specific problems they ought to consider the extent and limits of man's understanding itself. Accordingly the others asked him to prepare a paper on the subject. Locke says that he set down some "hasty and undigested thoughts" on this subject, which he had not previously considered, and submitted them for discussion. Later he added to his original notes from time to time, until his exile in Holland gave him time to work out the text for the first edition of the book. As we have already indicated, the central ideas of the *Essay* are essentially those of the first draft, extended and slightly modified.

Some Thoughts Concerning Education was written during the 1680's as a series of letters to a friend, advising him of the kind of training that should be given to his son. We know, however, that long before this time Locke had developed many of his very modern ideas on the subject. He had disliked his own schooling and was quite prepared to criticize the educational methods of his day. His experience as tutor of Lord Ashley's son undoubtedly suggested the advice about the early care and training of children.

His religious writings, which began appearing in 1695, followed closely the Latitudinarian thinking of his Oxford days and reflected the influence of discussions with leading theologians on the Continent.

Moreover, they exhibit again his refusal to accept doctrines which he believed to be contrary to the dictates of reason.

Locke's failure to publish anything until late in life was not so much because he had not reached his full powers earlier, but rather because of his modesty and reticence about publishing them at all. We have ample testimony in his journals and in the works of other men that he never intended his writings to be read by any except the small circle of friends interested in the particular problems with which he was then dealing. His friends had to plead with him before he would consent to publication. The classic example of his modesty is to be found in the preface to the *Essay*. After apologizing for his brazenness in publishing the book, Locke gives his estimate of its worth. "Everyone must not hope to be a Boyle or a Sydenham; and in an age that produces such masters as the great Huygens and the incomparable Mr. Newton, with some others of that strain, it is ambition enough to be employed as an under-laborer in clearing the ground a little and removing some of the rubbish that lies in the way of knowledge."

His political activity also no doubt hindered any earlier publication of his works. It was only during the extended visits to Europe, when Shaftesbury was out of power or when Locke himself was in exile, that he took the time to re-write and polish his thoughts. It was on the Continent that he made the acquaintance of leaders in many fields of thought and was able to make new observations to be fitted into the framework of his earlier thinking. There is no evidence that he ever significantly modified his main lines of argument after 1671.

In spite of the catholicity of Locke's interests, all his writings show the influence of the spectacular scientific developments of the sixteenth and seventeenth centuries, and of the new methodology proposed by Descartes. The extraordinary discoveries in astronomy, physics, chemistry, and physiology all emphasized the importance of experiment in testing and confirming hypotheses. Locke early accepted empiricism, and his belief was strengthened by his close association with Boyle and later with the scientists of the Royal Society. He then fitted his experimentalism into the Cartesian system, which called for absolute clarity of statement, the reduction of every problem to its simplest elements, and reasoning from the simple to the more complex. In other matters Locke did not always agree with Descartes, but the Cartesian method, he said, delivered him from the scholastic philosophers' "unintelligible way of talking." In mathematics and morals (including the major principles of politics) Locke insisted that men could reach absolute certainty by combining empiricism with the Cartesian method. In lesser public and private affairs and in physics men could at best attain probable knowledge. In all of his own writings, says C. H. Driver, he attempted to reconcile the scientific method and the Cartesian system with his belief in the simple Christian faith of the Independents.

Influence of Locke

It is difficult to assess accurately the influence of any man upon his own times and upon future generations. The fact of similarity in views does not necessarily mean that a successor has been influenced by the earlier writer. Indeed, men holding distinctly different views from his may have been more deeply influenced by him than those whose views are nearly identical. In the case of Locke, however, we can be fairly sure that his influence touched many fields of thought in England, on the Continent, and in America. We have, for example, the testimony of Voltaire, Diderot, Rousseau, and others that they read and accepted as their guide Locke's *Essay Concerning Human Understanding.* They referred to Locke as the "greatest of all philosophers since Plato," the "sage," a creator of metaphysics comparable to Newton, the creator of physics. This essay unquestionably opened up new fields of contemplation in philosophy and psychology for his successors.

Some Thoughts Concerning Education, emphasizing the need for more practical training at the expense of so much book-learning in Greek and Latin, laid the foundation for a reformation of the British school system. So important were these letters in their influence on British educational methods, that a century and a half later Cardinal Newman, in his famous lectures *On the Idea of a University,* attacked Locke as the forerunner of the modern schools which he so much detested.

In the realm of practical affairs, his influence was greatest in the fields of politics and economics. Both his general theories and specific recommendations were to influence thought and action at home and abroad through the eighteenth and nineteenth centuries. The American Declaration of Independence adopted not only the ideas but the phraseology of the *Second Treatise*. The essential principles of this work are still important to the Anglo-Saxon world of politics and government.

Locke made two major contributions to modern political thought: he secularized the state and he redefined the purpose of the state in terms of individual freedom. Locke was the first English theorist to free the state from the confining shadow of the church. Even the materialist Hobbes, who relegated the church to a secondary role and gave the sovereign complete control of its policy, devoted nearly half of his *Leviathan* to ecclesiastical discussion. A few previous English theorists had separated church and state, but had done so in order to free the church from tyrannical lay domination. Locke, on the other hand, wished to free the state from the religious struggles in which the state had been so embroiled and which were not its primary concern. English theorists after Locke never again distorted the relationship between the state and church.

Locke's second contribution, the redefinition of the purpose of the state in terms of individual freedom, with its allied notion of popular control of government, was perhaps even more important for the thought and action of succeeding generations. The state, said Locke, exists for the good of the individual, not the individual for the good of the state or its rulers. Freedom through law is possible only when the people themselves are sovereign and may express themselves through the will of the majority. The idea of popular consent expressed through the electoral process was not original with Locke, though he broadened the base of participation in the process; but it was significant in Locke's time, in the face of current justifications of absolute monarchy, ruling with what was called the "implied consent" of the people. Locke was not misled by anti-democratic gibberish about ruling "in the name of the people." If the people could not freely give or withhold their consent to men and programs, all nice phrases remained meaningless. Locke's advocacy of popular sovereignty, the electoral process, freedom of expression, and majority rule, marks him, according to Willmoore Kendall, as actually the first modern democratic thinker.

The *Letter Concerning Toleration* supplements the *Second Treatise* with its plea for the protection of the rights of religious minorities (with certain exceptions) to freedom of conviction. Religious freedom is essential, he insists, because no man may know all the answers, nor can he compel acceptance of his views even if he knows he is correct. The same argument clearly holds for freedom of opinion on political issues in a democracy. Force may appear to change men's ideas but it prevents that free expression of preference which alone makes democracy possible.

Particular constitutional devices, such as the separation of the powers of the different branches of the government, were described in the *Second Treatise* as aids to the attainment of freedom in a popularly controlled state. It is, therefore, ironical that some of Locke's "followers" seized upon these devices, tore them out of the context of a democratic system, modified and rearranged them, and produced by their means systems which made difficult, if not impossible, the attainment of the purposes of the very master they professed to acknowledge.

A striking example of this distortion of Locke's views is to be found in the history of the separation of powers. Locke had proposed that there should be a legislative, an executive, and a federative division of government. The latter two were to be combined for convenience in the hands of the executive. The legislature was charged by Locke with the determination of national policy, for "it is in their legislative that the members of a commonwealth are united and combined together into one coherent living body. This is the soul that gives form, life, and unity to the commonwealth; and hence the several members have their mutual influence, sympathy, and connection; and therefore when the legislative is broken, or dissolved, dissolution and death follows. For the essence and union of the society consisting in having one will, the legislative, when once established by the majority, has the declaring and, as it were, keeping of that will."

The legislative would elect the executive, and both were responsible to the people. The separation between the two was not rigid. It was certainly not intended to set up a "do nothing" government, hampered on all sides by a system of checks and balances. There was merely a division of powers for practical convenience. The legislature, for instance, was not always in session. The executive had to have power to act during recesses of Parliament. The federative division, which dealt with foreign policy, was entrusted to the executive for prompt and forceful handling. The nearest modern example of the government Locke wished to erect is the British cabinet system, where the executive is a committee in charge of domestic administration and foreign relations, selected by and responsible to the majority of the House of Commons. Under the cabinet system there is a division of labor but not a complete separation of agencies.

The theory was distorted by Locke's own followers. Montesquieu picked up the doctrine of the separation of powers, developed it in what he thought was a description of the British government of the eighteenth century, but for all his own greatness and his admitted indebtedness to Locke, left it a very different thing from what his predecessor had suggested. He divided the work of the three branches into three sharply separated compartments and destroyed the legislative supremacy. Blackstone, "who should have known better," made the separation even more complete.

In America, the early trend was in the direction of Locke's real position. The first state constitutions, written between 1777 and 1787, sometimes specifically stated that the principle of the separation of powers was to be followed in the organization of the government. But having prescribed in their preamble a rigid separation of the powers of these departments, the constitutions then provided for almost complete legislative control. Some of them granted the legislatures absolute power over state policy, and authorized them to select the governors and judges. In almost all the new states, the executive and the courts were given little or no voice in policy making. The strong democratic movement which accompanied the Revolution entrusted power to the legislatures because its leaders felt that only the legislatures represented the popular will. Locke would have approved the provision for legislative supremacy and the reasoning behind it. Dominant power in legislative hands did not mean a denial of the value of separate executive and judicial agencies to carry out the decisions of the legislature.

But in 1787, less than a century after the publication of the *Second Treatise,* the members of the Federal Constitutional Convention, who opposed the more democratic state documents, wrote into the fundamental law of the new nation a very different kind of separation of powers. The separation provided for in the national constitution made almost impossible the popular sovereignty upon which Locke had insisted, and so checked each of the three branches with the powers of the other two that the whole mechanism would have been nearly unworkable had not the unforeseen advent of political parties provided a way to circumvent in a measure the separation so carefully drawn. Locke, with his insistence on legislative control, would scarcely have recognized the system thus set up in his name. The independence of the legislature from the control of a despotic monarch, which he had advocated, was here turned into an isolation of the three great governmental branches from one another, which made co-operation among them almost impossible and minimized the chances for development of Locke's central idea of popular government.

The marked contrast between the government Locke proposed and the one of which he has sometimes erroneously been called the "godfather," can be explained by the greater confidence which Locke placed in the cautious conservatism of the people. Few at the Constitutional Convention in Philadelphia thought well of his doctrine of the right of revolution. Though they themselves had but recently revolted against the King of England on the principles, and indeed in the very words, which Locke had chosen to justify the Glorious Revolution of his generation, they were profoundly shocked by the more radical agrarians among their own countrymen, who were prepared to carry the revolution still further. Jefferson and Paine, neither of whom was a member of the Constitutional Convention, were among the very few early American thinkers prepared to accept Locke's idea in full. The more conservative members of the Constitutional Convention, who frequently identified democracy with anarchy and mob rule, contended that popular control meant an end to all personal and property rights, and insisted that "transient majorities" would act too often in hasty and ill-considered fashion. In answer to these same objections a hundred years before Locke had argued that on the contrary "the people are not so easily got out of their old forms as some are apt to suggest. They are hardly to be prevailed with to amend the acknowledged faults in the frame they have been accustomed to. And if there be any original defects, or adventitious ones introduced by time and corruption, it is not an easy thing to get them changed, even when all the world sees there is an opportunity for it. This slowness and aversion in the people to quit their old constitutions has . . . still kept us to, or after some interval of fruitless atempts, still brought us back again to our old legislative of kings, lords, and commons. . . ."

Locke recognized, as few conservatives and radicals have done, that most people are not anxious for major changes in policy or institutions, unless driven to them by a prior condition of chaos. Popular inertia and skepticism of all new institutions act as brakes on most demands for revolutionary reforms. The failure of extremists to recognize public opposition to change has been responsible for many unjustified hopes and fears. The radicals (with the exception of the Communists, whose faith is placed in the "advance guard of the proletariat," not in the people at large, whom they recognize as conservative) are constantly surprised by the stubborn refusal of the majority to accept their Utopian formulas. The conservatives are similarly astonished when their dire predictions of popular disorders and the destruction of their favorite institutions fail to materialize.

Locke made one significant contribution to economic thought. His discussion of the origin of private property in the *Second Treatise* had repercussions for two centuries after he published his essay. His labor theory of property rights was expanded and developed by Ricardo into the well-known labor theory of value. A century and a half after Locke, this theory was a pillar of English socialist thought in the hands of Hodgkin, Gray, and Thompson. Still later it became an important part of the economic theories of Karl Marx. A lesser contribution to economic theory was Locke's exposition of mercantilism, which Hecksher, a leading historian of the subject, called the clearest statement of English mercantilist ideas. As always, Locke drew on his own experience. He was a key figure on the old and new Boards of Trade and Plantations, one of the founders of the Bank of England, and a prime mover behind the Coinage Act. During the 1690's he also wrote several essays on money and credit, which the late Lord Keynes considered still valuable in the twentieth century.

Summary

A scant half dozen men in each century influence the thought and action of their own and later generations in dramatic fashion. Perhaps two or three of that number push back the frontiers of knowledge in more than one field of thought. Not many are recognized as leaders in their own generation and two centuries later are still studied to advantage

Locke was more important and more fortunate than most. He participated in the great scientific, political, and philosophical movements of his day. He saw the value of his writings acknowledged by leading thinkers immediately after publication. He both played his own part in a great revolutionary era and through his writings laid the intellectual foundations for greater upheavals abroad in the turbulent eighteenth century. During all that time his influence was deeply felt in religion, politics, education, and philosophy. The Age of Reason looked upon him as its prophet and intellectual master.

In private life he enjoyed a large circle of congenial acquaintances. When ill health or exile prevented face-to-face discussions he carried on an extensive and stimulating correspondence. He was consulted by intellectual giants of his day and asked to advise national leaders on problems of state. Finally, in his old age, he retired to the home of friends who adored him.

Greater philosophers and political theorists are not hard to find, if originality and logical consistency are the only tests of greatness in those fields. Santayana, however, who has pointed out some of Locke's weaknesses as a philosopher, contends that his very weaknesses gave Locke greater influence over his own and the next century. To the ideas he encountered in his reading and conversations, he added his own moderation, his wide experience of affairs, and his remarkable common sense, and so produced works of a practical character, well calculated to influence a century devoted to strenuous activity rather than abstract contemplation.

HOWARD R. PENNIMAN

A Letter Concerning Toleration

LOCKE'S reasonableness, his natural caution, and his "illumined common sense" appear to best advantage in his religious writings. The
Reasonableness of Christianity and *An Essay for the Understanding of
St. Paul's Epistles by Consulting St. Paul Himself* are models of sober
scholarship when contrasted with the wrangling sectarianism of other
writers in an era that produced so many ritualistic formulae for
immortality.

Locke was a deeply religious man. His biographer, Fox Bourne, says
that Locke did not give up plans for entering the ministry until he was
in his thirties. In his early years, he was confronted with the choice
between Anglicanism and Dissent. He chose to remain inside the
established church in spite of his objections to the authority of its
hierarchy of bishops and its connection with the secular government.
He objected even more, however, to the ranting sectarianism of the
Dissenters. He hated their dogmatic insistence that they alone held
the key to salvation and he feared their increase in numbers and power
would be followed by greater national disunity.

In his later years Locke was more and more concerned with religion.
His religious tracts exceed in volume his lengthy *Essay Concerning
Human Understanding*. His *Reasonableness of Christianity* (1695)
and still more his commentary on the Epistles of St. Paul (1705) were
among the earliest examples of modern Biblical criticism produced by
an adherent of Christianity.

The Christian faith to Locke was natural and simple. God had sent
his Son to reveal his true nature as a merciful God rather than the
harshly just God of the Old Testament. A Christian need only believe in Christ as a symbol of immortality and live according to his
moral teachings. Through God's grace immortality was made possible,

even if men occasionally failed to live up to the ethical code of the New Testament. Locke criticized the too frequent emphasis on dogma and ritual. Such an emphasis served only to confuse the real meaning of Christianity and to substitute form for obedience to Christ's teachings. Locke recognized that his own theory could not be proved by reason, but held that it did not conflict with reason.

Locke's interest in religious toleration dated from his days at Oxford. Bourne says that John Owen, director of Oxford and one of the first disinterested advocates of tolerance, influenced Locke's early thinking on this problem.[1] It was at Oxford that Locke first met with the Latitudinarians whose religious ideas and belief in tolerance he shared. In 1665 Locke was appointed secretary to Sir Walter Vane when the latter was sent as ambassador to Brandenburg. There Locke noted with approval that religious freedom actually promoted economic and political unity. Two years later Locke wrote but did not publish his *Essay Concerning Toleration*. In 1669 he helped write the religious sections of the *Fundamental Constitutions of Carolina*.

By the time Locke wrote his *Letter Concerning Toleration* (1685 in Holland, translated from the Latin in 1689) most English thinkers had noted the economic and political value of religious liberty in Holland and had accepted as practical the idea of more toleration at home. Locke was concerned in this letter with a defense of toleration on other than economic and political grounds.

After preliminary observations on the failure of religious persecutors to see weakness in their own members while criticizing others, Locke pointed out that the church as a voluntary association differed from the state. Church members do not give up to a religious association the same rights that they relinquish to the state. They may withdraw from the church of their own free will. If an adherent disagrees with the precepts of the church he may be expelled, but the church has, or should

[1] Others before Owen had argued for tolerance, but their arguments followed more from their being persecuted than from any real belief in tolerance for all religions. They sometimes became intolerant upon gaining control of the state. One need only to look at the intolerance in most of the American colonies of the seventeenth century for examples of changes of mind upon assumption of power.

have, no other power to punish him for failing to abide by its decisions.

The state should not be used by the church to carry out any punishment for the church authorities. The state deals only with civil and temporal affairs and has no right to interfere in religious matters unless the religion can be shown to be subversive of the very foundations of society. Too often, when church and state are tied closely together, the state decides upon the teachings of the church instead of the church guiding the state along a moral path. It seemed to Locke more than a coincidence that the magistrate usually found that the church of which he was a member and which supported his program was good, while the churches which opposed his government were subversive.

No man, Locke argued, can ever know all the truth about religion. The persecutor may be in error and the persecuted correct. Certainly no man has the right to force his religious views on another, when those views cannot be proved by reason. Zeal in forcing others is especially indefensible when the religion is based presumably upon love and charity for others.[2] Even if men could know that their own religion was the correct one, it would be useless to try to compel others to accept their point of view. Religion is a thing of faith and reason and therefore cannot be spread by compulsion. Hypocritical acceptance, not sincere belief, is secured at the point of a gun.

Locke excludes two groups from tolerance. Atheists are not to be allowed civil rights because they have no moral basis for their judgments. Catholics (Locke refers to "Mahometans," but it is clear that he had Catholics in mind) are to be excluded because of their allegiance to a foreign ruler.

The *Letter Concerning Toleration* is of special interest today because of its bearing on the contemporary problems of free speech, press,

[2] That zealously good men are frequently intolerant has been noted by other writers. Zealots with panaceas for mankind are impatient of their failure to secure support from men without the wit to recognize the validity of their programs. Wars and persecutions are not infrequent results of the zeal of good men striving to make others see their point. For an interesting essay on this problem, see Bertrand Russell, "The Harm that Good Men Do," in *Sceptical Essays*.

and assembly, as well as on religious liberty. In the modern world men are more likely to condemn and persecute others for political and economic views than for religious beliefs. We find that unproven and unprovable views on those subjects are insisted upon now with the same fervor as sixteenth and seventeeth century religious beliefs. The fact that a proposition cannot be proved does not detract from the firmness of men's faith in it. Men do not fight about the provable assertion that the sun will rise on the morrow, but they beat each other to death in defense of particular economic and political doctrines that follow logically only from an acceptance on faith in certain undemonstrable premises.

Locke's defense of religious freedom has become in part the classic defense not only for religious tolerance but also for freedom of expression in other matters. The case for free speech, as Justice Holmes so eloquently argued in a dissenting opinion, is based upon a recognition that we can never know that our opinions in many matters are correct ones, and "that the best test of truth is the power of the thought to get itself accepted in the competition of the market." The Supreme Court has now accepted the reasoning of Holmes and Locke. It refuses to uphold limitations upon those freedoms guaranteed in the First Amendment unless particular speeches, written matter, or assemblies and demonstrations constitute a "clear and present danger" to the overthrow of our government, or to an immediate, overt act of lawlessness.

A LETTER CONCERNING TOLERATION

HONORED SIR:

Since you are pleased to inquire what are my thoughts about the mutual toleration of Christians in their different professions of religion, I must needs answer you freely, that I esteem that toleration to be the chief characteristic mark of the true Church. For whatsoever some people boast of the antiquity of places and names, or of the pomp of their outward worship; others, of the reformation of their discipline; all, of the orthodoxy of their faith—for everyone is orthodox to himself—these things, and all others of this nature, are much rather marks of men striving for power and empire over one another than of the Church of Christ. Let anyone have never so true a claim to all these things, yet if he be destitute of charity, meekness, and good will in general towards all mankind, even to those that are not Christians, he is certainly yet short of being a true Christian himself. "The kings of the Gentiles exercise lordship over them," said our Saviour to His disciples, "but ye shall not be so." [Luke 22:25] The business of true religion is quite another thing. It is not instituted in order to the erecting of an external pomp, nor to the obtaining of ecclesiastical dominion, nor to the exercising of compulsive force, but to the regulating of men's lives, according to the rules of virtue and piety. Whosoever will list himself under the banner of Christ must, in the first place, and above all things, make war upon his own lusts and vices. It is in vain for any man to usurp the name of Christian, without holiness of life, purity of manners, benignity and meekness of spirit. "Let everyone that nameth the name of Christ, depart from iniquity." [2 Tim. 2:19] "Thou, when thou art converted, strengthen thy brethren," said our Lord to Peter [Luke 22:32]. It would, indeed, be very hard for one that appears careless about his own salvation to persuade me

21

that he were extremely concerned for mine. For it is impossible that those should sincerely and heartily apply themselves to make other people Christians, who have not really embraced the Christian religion in their own hearts. If the Gospel and the apostles may be credited, no man can be a Christian without charity, and without that faith which works, not by force, but by love. Now, I appeal to the consciences of those that persecute, torment, destroy, and kill other men upon pretense of religion, whether they do it out of friendship and kindness towards them or no? And I shall then indeed, and not until then, believe they do so, when I shall see those fiery zealots correcting in the same manner, their friends and familiar acquaintance for the manifest sins they commit against the precepts of the Gospel; when I shall see them persecute with fire and sword the members of their own communion that are tainted with enormous vices, and without amendment are in danger of eternal perdition; and when I shall see them thus express their love and desire of the salvation of their souls by the infliction of torments, and exercise of all manner of cruelties. For if it be out of a principle of charity, as they pretend, and love to men's souls, that they deprive them of their estates, maim them with corporal punishments, starve and torment them in noisome prisons, and in the end even take away their lives—I say, if all this be done merely to make men Christians and procure their salvation, why then do they suffer whoredom, fraud, malice, and such-like enormities, which, according to the apostle [Rom. 1], manifestly relish of heathenish corruption, to predominate so much and abound amongst their flocks and people? These, and such-like things, are certainly more contrary to the glory of God, to the purity of the Church, and to the salvation of souls, than any conscientious dissent from ecclesiastical decisions, or separation from public worship, whilst accompanied with innocence of life. Why then does this burning zeal for God, for the Church, and for the salvation of souls—burning I say, literally, with fire and faggot—pass by those moral vices and wickednesses, without any chastisement, which are acknowledged by all men to be diametrically opposite to the profession of Christianity, and bend all its nerves either to the introducing of ceremonies, or to the establishment of opinions, which for the most part are about nice and intricate matters that exceed the capacity of ordinary understandings? Which of the parties contending about these things is in the right, which of them is guilty of schism or heresy, whether those that domineer or those that suffer, will then at last be manifest, when the causes of their separation comes to be judged of. He, certainly, that follows Christ, embraces His doctrine, and bears His yoke, though he forsake both father and mother, separate from the public assemblies and ceremonies of his country, or whomsoever or whatsoever else he relinquishes, will not then be judged a heretic.

Now, though the divisions that are amongst sects should be allowed to be never so obstructive of the salvation of souls; yet, nevertheless, adultery, fornication, uncleanliness, lasciviousness, idolatry, and suchlike things, cannot be denied to be works of the flesh, concerning which the apostle has expressly declared [Gal. 5] that "they who do them shall not inherit the kingdom of God." Whosoever, therefore, is sincerely solicitous about the kingdom of God, and thinks it his duty to endeavor the enlargement of it amongst men, ought to apply himself with no less care and industry to the rooting out of these immoralities than to the extirpation of sects. But if anyone do otherwise, and whilst he is cruel and implacable towards those that differ from him in opinion, he be indulgent to such iniquities and immoralities as are unbecoming the name of a Christian, let such a one talk never so much of the Church, he plainly demonstrates by his actions that it is another kingdom he aims at, and not the advancement of the kingdom of God.

That any man should think fit to cause another man—whose salvation he heartily desires—to expire in torments, and that even in an unconverted state, would, I confess, seem very strange to me, and I think, to any other also. But nobody, surely, will ever believe that such a carriage can proceed from charity, love, or good will. If anyone maintain that men ought to be compelled by fire and sword to profess certain doctrines, and conform to this or that exterior worship, without any regard had unto their morals; if anyone endeavor to convert those that are erroneous unto the faith, by forcing them to profess things that they do not believe, and allowing them to practice things that the Gospel does not permit, it cannot be doubted indeed but such a one is desirous to have a numerous assembly joined in the same profession with himself; but that he principally intends by those means to compose a truly Christian Church, is altogether incredible. It is not, therefore, to be wondered at if those who do not really contend for the advancement of the true religion, and of the Church of Christ, make use of arms that do not belong to the Christian warfare. If, like the Captain of our salvation, they sincerely desired the good of souls, they would tread in the steps and follow the perfect example of that Prince of Peace, who sent out His soldiers to the subduing of nations, and gathering them into His Church, not armed with the sword, or other instruments of force, but prepared with the Gospel of peace, and with the exemplary holiness of their conversation. This was His method. Though if infidels were to be converted by force, if those that are either blind or obstinate were to be drawn off from their errors by armed soldiers, we know very well that it was much more easy for Him to do it with armies of heavenly legions, than for any son of the Church, how potent soever, with all his dragoons.

The toleration of those that differ from others in matters of religion is so agreeable to the Gospel of Jesus Christ, and to the genuine reason of mankind, that it seems monstrous for men to be so blind as not to perceive the necessity and advantage of it in so clear a light. I will not here tax the pride and ambition of some, the passion and uncharitable zeal of others. These are faults from which human affairs can perhaps scarce ever be perfectly freed; but yet such as nobody will bear the plain imputation of, without covering them with some specious color; and so pretend to commendation, whilst they are carried away by their own irregular passions. But, however, that some may not color their spirit of persecution and unchristian cruelty with a pretense of care of the public weal and observation of the laws; and that others, under pretense of religion, may not seek impunity for their libertinism and licentiousness; in a word, that none may impose either upon himself or others, by the pretenses of loyalty and obedience to the prince, or of tenderness and sincerity in the worship of God; I esteem it above all things necessary to distinguish exactly the business of civil government from that of religion, and to settle the just bounds that lie between the one and the other. If this be not done, there can be no end put to the controversies that will be always arising between those that have, or at least pretend to have, on the one side, a concernment for the interest of men's souls, and, on the other side, a care of the commonwealth.

The commonwealth seems to me to be a society of men constituted only for the procuring, preserving, and advancing their own civil interests.

Civil interests I call life, liberty, health, and indolency of body; and the possession of outward things, such as money, lands, houses, furniture, and the like.

It is the duty of the civil magistrate, by the impartial execution of equal laws, to secure unto all the people in general and to every one of his subjects in particular the just possession of these things belonging to this life. If anyone presume to violate the laws of public justice and equity, established for the preservation of those things, his presumption is to be checked by the fear of punishment, consisting of the deprivation or diminution of those civil interests, or goods, which otherwise he might and ought to enjoy. But seeing no man does willingly suffer himself to be punished by the deprivation of any part of his goods, and much less of his liberty or life, therefore is the magistrate armed with the force and strength of all his subjects, in order to the punishment of those that violate any other man's rights.

Now that the whole jurisdiction of the magistrate reaches only to these civil concernments, and that all civil power, right and dominion, is bounded and confined to the only care of promoting these things; and that it neither can nor ought in any manner to be extended to the salvation of souls, these following considerations seem unto me abundantly to demonstrate.

First, because the care of souls is not committed to the civil magistrate, any more than to other men. It is not committed unto him, I say, by God, because it appears not that God has ever given any such authority to one man over another, as to compel anyone to his religion. Nor can any such power be vested in the magistrate by the consent of the people, because no man can so far abandon the care of his own salvation as blindly to leave to the choice of any other, whether prince or subject, to prescribe to him what faith or worship he shall embrace.

For no man can, if he would, conform his faith to the dictates of another. All the life and power of true religion consist in the inward and full persuasion of the mind; and faith is not faith without believing. Whatever profession we make, to whatever outward worship we conform, if we are not fully satisfied in our own mind that the one is true, and the other well pleasing unto God, such profession and such practice, far from being any furtherance, are indeed great obstacles to our salvation. For in this manner, instead of expiating other sins by the exercise of religion, I say, in offering thus unto God Almighty such a worship as we esteem to be displeasing unto Him, we add unto the number of our other sins those also of hypocrisy, and contempt of His Divine Majesty.

In the second place, the care of souls cannot belong to the civil magistrate, because his power consists only in outward force; but true and saving religion consists in the inward persuasion of the mind, without which nothing can be acceptable to God. And such is the nature of the understanding that it cannot be compelled to the belief of anything by outward force. Confiscation of estate, imprisonment, torments, nothing of that nature can have any such efficacy as to make men change the inward judgment that they have framed of things.

It may indeed be alleged that the magistrate may make use of arguments, and thereby draw the heterodox into the way of truth, and procure their salvation. I grant it; but this is common to him with other men. In teaching, instructing, and redressing the erroneous by reason, he may certainly do what becomes any good man to do. Magistracy does not oblige him to put off either humanity or Christianity; but it is one thing to persuade, another to command; one thing to press with arguments, another with penalties. This civil power alone has a right to do; to the other good will is authority enough. Every man has commission to admonish, exhort, convince another of error, and, by reasoning, to draw him into truth; but to give laws, receive obedience, and compel with the sword, belongs to none but the magistrate. And upon this ground, I affirm that the magistrate's power extends not to the establishing of any articles of faith, or forms of worship, by the force of his laws. For laws are of no force at all without penalties, and penalties in this case are absolutely impertinent, because they are not proper to convince the mind. Neither the profession of any articles of faith, nor the conformity to any outward form of worship, as has been already said, can be available to the salvation of souls, unless the truth of the one, and the acceptableness of the other unto God, be thoroughly believed by those that so profess and practice. But penalties are no way capable to produce such belief. It is only light and evidence that can work a change in men's opinions; which light can in no manner proceed from corporal sufferings, or any other outward penalties.

In the third place, the care of the salvation of men's souls cannot belong to the magistrate; because, though the rigor of laws and the force of penalties were capable to convince and change men's minds, yet would not that help at all to the salvation of their souls. For there being but one truth, one way to heaven, what hope is there that more men would be led into it if they had no rule but the religion of the court, and were put under the necessity to quit the light of their own reason, and oppose the dictates of their own consciences, and blindly to resign themselves up to the will of their governors, and to the religion which either ignorance, ambition, or superstition had chanced to establish in the countries where they were born? In the variety and contradiction of opinions in religion, wherein the princes of the world are as much divided as in their secular interests, the narrow way would be much straitened; one country alone would be in the right, and all the rest of the world put under an obligation of following their princes in the ways that lead to destruction; and that which heightens the absurdity, and very ill suits the notion of a Deity, men would owe their eternal happiness or misery to the places of their nativity.

These considerations, to omit many others that might have been urged to the same purpose, seem unto me sufficient to conclude that all the power of civil government relates only to men's civil interests, is confined to the care of the things of this world, and hath nothing to do with the world to come.

Let us now consider what a church is. A church, then, I take to be a voluntary society of men, joining themselves together of their own accord in order to the public worshiping of God in such manner as they judge acceptable to Him, and effectual to the salvation of their souls.

I say it is a free and voluntary society. Nobody is born a member of any church; otherwise the religion of parents would descend unto children by the same right of inheritance as their temporal estates, and everyone would hold his faith by the same tenure he does his lands, than which nothing can be imagined more absurd. Thus, therefore, that matter stands. No man by nature is bound unto any particular church or sect, but everyone joins himself voluntarily to that society in which he believes he has found that profession and worship which is truly acceptable to God. The hope of salvation, as it was the only cause of his entrance into that communion, so it can be the only reason of his stay there. For if afterwards he discover anything either erroneous in the doctrine or incongruous in the worship of that society to which he has joined himself, why should it not be as free for him to go out as it was to enter? No member of a religious society can be tied with any other bonds but what proceed from the certain expectation of eternal life. A church, then, is a society of members voluntarily uniting to that end.

It follows now that we consider what is the power of this church, and unto what laws it is subject.

Forasmuch as no society, how free soever, or upon whatsoever slight occasion instituted, whether of philosophers for learning, of merchants for commerce, or of men of leisure for mutual conversation and discourse, no church or company, I say, can in the least subsist and hold together, but will presently dissolve and break in pieces, unless it be regulated by some laws, and the members all consent to observe some order. Place and time of meeting must be agreed on; rules for admitting and excluding members must be established; distinction of officers, and putting things into a regular course, and such-like, cannot be omitted. But since the joining together of several members into this church-society, as has already been demonstrated, is absolutely free and spontaneous, it necessarily follows that the right of making its laws can belong to none but the society itself; or, at least (which is the same thing), to those whom the society by common consent has authorized thereunto.

Some, perhaps, may object that no such society can be said to be a true church unless it have in it a bishop or presbyter, with ruling authority derived from the very Apostles, and continued down to the present times by an uninterrupted succession.

To these I answer: In the first place, let them show me the edict by which Christ has imposed that law upon His Church. And let not any man think me impertinent, if in a thing of this consequence I require that the terms of that edict be very express and positive; for the promise He has made us [Matt. 18:20] that wheresoever two or three are gathered together in His name, He will be in the midst of them, seems to imply the contrary. Whether such an assembly want anything necessary to a true church, pray do you consider. Certain I am that nothing can be there wanting unto the salvation of souls, which is sufficient to our purpose.

Next, pray observe how great have always been the divisions amongst even those who lay so much stress upon the Divine institution and continued succession of a certain order of rulers in the Church. Now, their very dissension unavoidably puts us upon a necessity of deliberating, and, consequently, allows a liberty of choosing that which upon consideration we prefer.

And, in the last place, I consent that these men have a ruler in their church, established by such a long series of succession as they judge necessary, provided I may have liberty at the same time to join myself to that society in which I am persuaded those things are to be found which are necessary to the salvation of my soul. In this manner ecclesiastical liberty will be preserved on all sides, and no man will have a legislator imposed upon him but whom himself has chosen.

But since men are so solicitous about the true church, I would only ask them here, by the way, if it be not more agreeable to the Church of Christ to make the conditions of her communion consist in such things, and such things only, as the Holy Spirit has in the Holy Scriptures declared, in express words, to be necessary to salvation; I ask, I say, whether this be not more agreeable to the Church of Christ than for men to impose their own inventions and interpretations upon others as if they were of Divine authority, and to establish by ecclesiastical laws, as absolutely necessary to the profession of Christianity, such things as the Holy Scriptures do either not mention, or at least not expressly command? Whosoever requires those things in order to ecclesiastical communion, which Christ does not require in order to life eternal, he may, perhaps, indeed constitute a society accommodated to his own opinion and his own advantage; but how that can be called the Church of Christ which is established upon laws that are not His, and which excludes such persons from its communion as He will one day receive into the Kingdom of Heaven, I understand not. But this being not a proper place to inquire into the marks of the true church, I will only mind those that contend so earnestly for the decrees of their own society, and that cry out continually, The Church! the Church! with as much noise, and perhaps upon the same principle, as the Ephesian silversmiths aid for their Diana; this, I say, I desire to mind them of, that the Gospel frequently declares that the true disciples of Christ must suffer persecution; but that the Church of Christ should persecute others, and force others by fire and sword to embrace her faith and doctrine, I could never yet find in any of the books of the New Testament.

The end of a religious society, as has already been said, is the public worship of God, and, by means thereof, the acquisition of eternal life. All discipline ought therefore to tend to that end, and all ecclesiastical laws to be thereunto confined. Nothing ought nor can be transacted in this society relating to the possession of civil and worldly goods. No force is here to be made use of upon any occasion whatsoever. For force belongs wholly to the civil magistrate, and the possession of all outward goods is subject to his jurisdiction.

But, it may be asked, by what means then shall ecclesiastical laws be established, if they must be thus destitute of all compulsive power? I answer: They must be established by means suitable to the nature of such things, whereof the external profession and observation—if not proceeding from a thorough conviction and approbation of the mind —is altogether useless and unprofitable. The arms by which the members of this society are to be kept within their duty are exhortations, admonitions, and advices. If by these means the offenders will not be reclaimed, and the erroneous convinced, there remains nothing further to be done but that such stubborn and obstinate persons, who give no ground to hope for their reformation, should be cast out and separated from the society. This is the last and utmost force of ecclesiastical authority. No other punishment can thereby be inflicted than that, the relation ceasing between the body and the member which is cut off. The person so condemned ceases to be a part of that church.

These things being thus determined, let us inquire, in the next place: How far the duty of toleration extends, and what is required from everyone by it?

And, first, I hold that no church is bound, by the duty of toleration, to retain any such person in her bosom as, after admonition, continues obstinately to offend against the laws of the society. For these being the condition of communion and the bond of the society, if the breach of them were permitted without any animadversion the society would immediately be thereby dissolved. But, nevertheless, in all such cases care is to be taken that the sentence of excommunication, and the execution thereof, carry with it no rough usage of word or action whereby the ejected person may any wise be damnified in body or estate. For all force, as has often been said, belongs only to the magistrate, nor ought any private persons at any time to use force, unless it be in self-defense against unjust violence. Excommunication neither does, nor can, deprive the excommunicated person of any of those civil goods that he formerly possessed. All those things belong to the civil government, and are under the magistrate's protection. The whole force of excommunication consists only in this: that the resolution of the society in that respect being declared, the union that was between the body and some member comes thereby to be dissolved; and that relation ceasing, the participation of some certain things which the society communicated to its members, and unto which no man has any civil right, comes also to cease. For there is no civil injury done unto the excommunicated person by the church minister's refusing him that bread and wine, in the celebration of the Lord's Supper, which was not bought with his but other men's money.

Secondly, no private person has any right in any manner to prejudice another person in his civil enjoyments because he is of another church or religion. All the rights and franchises that belong to him as a man, or as a denizen, are inviolably to be preserved to him. These are not the business of religion. No violence or injury is to be offered him, whether he be Christian or pagan. Nay, we must not content ourselves with the narrow measures of bare justice; charity, bounty, and liberality must be added to it. This the Gospel enjoins, this reason directs, and this that natural fellowship we are born into requires of us. If any man err from the right way, it is his own misfortune, no injury to thee; nor therefore art thou to punish him in the things of this life because thou supposest he will be miserable in that which is to come.

What I say concerning the mutual toleration of private persons differing from one another in religion, I understand also of particular churches which stand, as it were, in the same relation to each other as private persons among themselves: nor has any one of them any manner of jurisdiction over any other; no, not even when the civil magistrate, as it sometimes happens, comes to be of this or the other communion. For the civil government can give no new right to the church, nor the church to the civil government. So that whether the magistrate join himself to any church, or separate from it, the church remains always as it was before—a free and voluntary society. It neither requires the power of the sword by the magistrate's coming to it, nor does it lose the right of instruction and excommunication by his going from it. This is the fundamental and immutable right of a spontaneous society—that it has power to remove any of its members who transgress the rules of its institution; but it cannot, by the accession of any new members, acquire any right of jurisdiction over those that are not joined with it. And therefore peace, equity, and friendship are always mutually to be observed by particular churches, in the same manner as by private persons, without any pretense of superiority or jurisdiction over one another.

That the thing may be made clearer by an example, let us suppose two churches—the one of Arminians,[1] the other of Calvinists—resid-

[1] The Arminians were followers of Arminius, who founded a sect in opposition to several of the main tenets of Calvinism, including predestination. The Arminian theology is represented today by the Wesleyans of Great Britain and the Methodists of the United States.

ing in the city of Constantinople. Will anyone say that either of these churches has right to deprive the members of the other of their estates and liberty, as we see practiced elsewhere, because of their differing from it in some doctrines and ceremonies, whilst the Turks in the meanwhile silently stand by, and laugh to see with what inhuman cruelty Christians thus rage against Christians? But if one of these churches hath this power of treating the other ill, I ask which of them it is to whom that power belongs, and by what right? It will be answered, undoubtedly, that it is the orthodox church which has the right of authority over the erroneous or heretical. This is, in great and specious words, to say just nothing at all. For every church is orthodox to itself; to others, erroneous or heretical. For whatsoever any church believes, it believes to be true; and the contrary unto those things, it pronounces to be error. So that the controversy between these churches about the truth of their doctrines, and the purity of their worship, is on both sides equal; nor is there any judge, either at Constantinople or elsewhere upon earth, by whose sentence it can be determined. The decision of that question belongs only to the Supreme Judge of all men, to whom also alone belongs the punishment of the erroneous. In the meanwhile, let those men consider how heinously they sin, who, adding injustice, if not to their error, yet certainly to their pride, do rashly and arrogantly take upon them to misuse the servants of another master, who are not at all accountable to them.

Nay, further: if it could be manifest which of these two dissenting churches were in the right, there would not accrue thereby unto the orthodox any right of destroying the other. For churches have neither any jurisdiction in worldly matters, nor are fire and sword any proper instruments wherewith to convince men's minds of error, and inform them of the truth. Let us suppose, nevertheless, that the civil magistrate inclined to favor one of them, and to put his sword into their hands, that by his consent they might chastise the dissenters as they pleased. Will any man say that any right can be derived unto a Christian church over its brethren from a Turkish emperor? An infidel, who has himself no authority to punish Christians for the articles of their faith, cannot confer such an authority upon any society of Christians, nor give unto them a right which he has not himself. This would be the case at Constantinople; and the reason of the thing is the same in any Christian kingdom. The civil power is the same in every place. Nor can that power, in the hands of a Christian prince, confer any greater authority upon the Church than in the hands of a heathen; which is to say, just none at all.

Nevertheless, it is worthy to be observed and lamented that the most violent of these defenders of the truth, the opposers of errors, the exclaimers against schism do hardly ever let loose this their zeal for God, with which they are so warmed and inflamed, unless where they have the civil magistrate on their side. But so soon as ever court favor has given them the better end of the staff, and they begin to feel themselves the stronger, then presently peace and charity are to be laid aside. Otherwise they are religiously to be observed. Where they have not the power to carry on persecution and to become masters, there they desire to live upon fair terms, and preach up toleration. When they are not strengthened with the civil power, then they can bear most patiently and unmovedly the contagion of idolatry, superstition, and heresy in their neighborhood; of which on other occasions the interest of religion makes them to be extremely apprehensive. They do not forwardly attack those errors which are in fashion at court or are countenanced by the government. Here they can be content to spare their arguments; which yet, with their leave, is the only right method of propagating truth, which has no such way of prevailing as when strong arguments and good reason are joined with the softness of civility and good usage.

Nobody, therefore, in fine, neither single persons nor churches, nay, nor even commonwealths, have any just title to invade the civil rights and worldly goods of each other upon pretense of religion. Those that are of another opinion would do well to consider with themselves how pernicious a seed of discord and war, how powerful a provocation to endless hatreds, rapines, and slaughters they thereby furnish unto mankind. No peace and security, no, not so much as common friendship, can ever be established or preserved amongst men so long as this opinion prevails, that dominion is founded in grace and that religion is to be propagated by force of arms.

In the third place, let us see what the duty of toleration requires from those who are distinguished from the rest of mankind (from the laity, as they please to call us) by some ecclesiastical character and office; whether they be bishops, priests, presbyters, ministers, or however else dignified or distinguished. It is not my business to inquire here into the original of the power or dignity of the clergy. This only I say, that whencesoever their authority be sprung, since it is ecclesiastical, it ought to be confined within the bounds of the Church, nor can it in any manner be extended to civil affairs, because the Church itself is a thing absolutely separate and distinct from the commonwealth. The boundaries on both sides are fixed and immovable. He jumbles heaven and earth together, the things most remote and opposite, who mixes these two societies, which are in their origin, end, business, and in everything perfectly distinct and infinitely different from each other. No man, therefore, with whatsoever ecclesiastical office he be dignified, can deprive another man that is not of his church and faith either of liberty or of any part of his worldly goods upon the account of that difference between them in religion. For whatsoever is not lawful to the whole Church cannot by any ecclesiastical right become lawful to any of its members.

But this is not all. It is not enough that ecclesiastical men abstain from violence and rapine and all manner of persecution. He that pretends to be a successor of the Apostles, and takes upon him the office of teaching, is obliged also to admonish his hearers of the duties of peace and goodwill towards all men, as well towards the erroneous as the orthodox; towards those that differ from them in faith and worship as well as towards those that agree with them therein. And he ought industriously to exhort all men, whether private persons or magistrates (if any such there be in his church), to charity, meekness, and toleration, and diligently endeavor to allay and temper all that heat and unreasonable averseness of mind which either any man's fiery zeal for his own sect or the craft of others has kindled against dissenters. I will not undertake to represent how happy and how great would be the fruit, both in Church and State, if the pulpits everywhere sounded with this doctrine of peace and toleration, lest I should seem to reflect too severely upon those men whose dignity I desire not to detract from, nor would have it diminished either by others or themselves. But this I say, that thus it ought to be. And if anyone that professes himself to be a minister of the Word of God, a preacher of the gospel of peace, teach otherwise, he either understands not or neglects the business of his calling, and shall one day give account thereof unto the Prince of Peace. If Christians are to be admonished that they abstain from all manner of revenge, even after repeated provocations and multiplied injuries, how much more ought they who suffer nothing, who have had no harm done them, forbear violence and abstain from all manner of ill-usage towards those from whom they have received none! This caution and temper they ought certainly to use towards those who mind only their own business, and are solicitous for nothing but that (whatever men think of them) they may worship God in that manner which they are persuaded is acceptable to Him, and in which they have the strongest hopes of eternal salvation. In private domestic affairs, in the management of estates, in the conservation of bodily health, every man may consider what suits his own convenience, and follow what course he likes best. No man complains of the ill-management of his neighbor's affairs. No man is angry with another for an error committed in sowing his land or in marrying his daughter. Nobody corrects a spendthrift for consuming his substance in taverns. Let any man pull down, or build, or make whatsoever expenses he pleases, nobody murmurs, nobody controls him; he has his liberty. But if any man do not frequent the church, if he do not there conform his behavior exactly to the accustomed ceremonies, or if he brings not his children to be initiated in the sacred mysteries of this or the other congregation, this immediately causes an uproar. The neighborhood is filled with noise and clamor. Everyone is ready to be the avenger of so great a crime, and the zealots hardly have the patience to refrain from violence and rapine so long till the cause be heard, and the poor man be, according to form, condemned to the loss of liberty, goods, or life. Oh, that our ecclesiastical orators of every sect would apply themselves with all the strength of arguments that they are able to the confounding of men's errors! But let them spare their persons. Let them not supply their want of reasons with the instruments of force, which belong to another jurisdiction, and do ill become a churchman's hands. Let them not call in the magistrate's authority to the aid of their eloquence or learning, lest perhaps, whilst they pretend only love for the truth, this their intemperate zeal, breathing nothing but fire and sword, betray their ambition and show that what they desire is temporal dominion. For it will be very difficult to persuade men of sense that he who with dry eyes and satisfaction of mind can deliver his brother to the executioner to be burnt alive, does sincerely and heartily concern himself to save that brother from the flames of hell in the world to come.

In the last place, let us now consider what is the magistrate's duty in the business of toleration, which certainly is very considerable.

We have already proved that the care of souls does not belong to the magistrate. Not a magisterial care, I mean (if I may so call it), which consists in prescribing by laws and compelling by punishments. But a charitable care, which consists in teaching, admonishing, and persuading, cannot be denied unto any man. The care, therefore, of every man's soul belongs unto himself, and is to be left unto himself. But what if he neglect the care of his soul? I answer: What if he neglect the care of his health or of his estate, which things are nearlier related to the government of the magistrate than the other? Will the magistrate provide by an express law that such a one shall not become poor or sick? Laws provide, as much as is possible, that the goods and health of subjects be not injured by the fraud and violence of others; they do not guard them from the negligence or ill-husbandry of the possessors themselves. No man can be forced to be rich or healthful whether he will or no. Nay, God Himself will not save men against their wills.

Let us suppose, however, that some prince were desirous to force his subjects to accumulate riches, or to preserve the health and strength of their bodies. Shall it be provided by law that they must consult none but Roman physicians, and shall everyone be bound to live according to their prescriptions? What, shall no potion, no broth, be taken, but what is prepared either in the Vatican, suppose, or in a Geneva shop? Or, to make these subjects rich, shall they all be obliged by law to become merchants or musicians? Or, shall everyone turn victualer, or smith, because there are some that maintain their families plentifully and grow rich in those professions? But, it may be said, there are a thousand ways to wealth, but one only way to heaven. It is well said, indeed, especially by those that plead for compelling men into this or the other way. For if there were several ways that led thither, there would not be so much as a pretense left for compulsion. But now if I be marching on with my utmost vigor in that way which, according to the sacred geography, leads straight to Jerusalem, why am I beaten and ill-used by others because, perhaps, I wear not buskins; because my hair is not of the right cut; because, perhaps, I have not been dipped in the right fashion; because I eat flesh upon the road, or some other food which agrees with my stomach; because I avoid certain by-ways, which seem unto me to lead into briars or precipices; because, amongst the several paths that are in the same road, I choose that to walk in which seems to be the straightest and cleanest; because I avoid to keep company with some travelers that are less grave, and others that are more sour than they ought to be; or, in fine, because I follow a guide that either is, or is not, clothed in white, or crowned with a mitre? Certainly, if we consider right, we shall find that for the most part they are such frivolous things as these that (without any prejudice to religion or the salvation of souls, if not accompanied with superstition or hypocrisy) might either be observed or omitted. I say, they are such-like things as these which breed implacable enmities amongst Christian brethren, who are all agreed in the substantial and truly fundamental part of religion.

But let us grant unto these zealots, who condemn all things that are not of their mode, that from these circumstances are different ends. What shall we conclude from thence? There is only one of these which is the true way to eternal happiness: but in this great variety of ways that men follow, it is still doubted which is the right one. Now, neither the care of the commonwealth, nor the right enacting of laws, does discover this way that leads to heaven more certainly to the magistrate than every private man's search and study discovers it unto himself. I have a weak body, sunk under a languishing disease, for which, I suppose, there is one only remedy, but that unknown. Does it therefore belong unto the magistrate to prescribe me a remedy, because there is but one, and because it is unknown? Because there is but one way for me to escape death, will it therefore be safe for me to do whatsoever the magistrate ordains? Those things that every man ought sincerely to inquire into himself, and by meditation, study, search, and his own endeavors, attain the knowledge of, cannot be looked upon as the peculiar possession of any sort of men. Princes, indeed, are born superior unto other men in power, but in nature equal. Neither the right nor the art of ruling does necessarily carry along with it the certain knowledge of other things, and least of all of true religion. For if it were so, how could it come to pass that the lords of the earth should differ so vastly as they do in religious matters? But let us grant that it is probable the way to eternal life may be better known by a prince than by his subjects, or at least that in this incertitude of things the safest and most commodious way for private persons is to follow his dictates. You will say, what then? If he should bid you follow merchandise for your livelihood, would you decline that course for fear it should not succeed? I answer: I would turn merchant upon the prince's command, because in case I should have ill-success in trade, he is abundantly able to make up my loss some other way. If it be true, as he pretends, that he desires I should thrive and grow rich, he can set me up again when unsuccessful voyages have broken me. But this is not the case in the things that regard the life to come; if there I take a wrong course, if in that respect I am once undone, it is not in the magistrate's power to repair my loss, to ease my suffering, nor to restore me in any measure, much less entirely to a good estate. What security can be given for the Kingdom of Heaven?

Perhaps some will say that they do not suppose this infallible judgment, that all men are bound to follow in the affairs of religion, to be in the civil magistrate, but in the Church. What the Church has determined, that the civil magistrate orders to be observed; and he provides by his authority that nobody shall either act or believe in the business of religion otherwise than the Church teaches. So that the judgment of those things is in the Church; the magistrate himself yields obedience thereunto, and requires the like obedience from others. I answer: Who sees not how frequently the name of the Church, which was venerable in time of the Apostles, has been made use of to throw dust in the people's eyes, in the following ages? But, however, in the present case it helps us not. The one only narrow way which leads to heaven is not better known to the magistrate than to private persons, and therefore I cannot safely take him for my guide, who may probably be as ignorant of the way as myself, and who certainly is less concerned for my salvation than I myself am. Amongst so many kings of the Jews, how many of them were there whom any Israelite, thus blindly following, had not fallen into idolatry, and thereby into destruction? Yet nevertheless, you bid me be of good courage, and tell me that all is now safe and secure, because the magistrate does not now enjoin the observance of his own decrees in matters of religion, but only the decrees of the Church. Of what Church, I beseech you? Of that, certainly, which likes him best. As if he that compels me by laws and penalties to enter into this or the other Church, did not interpose his own judgment in the matter. What difference is there whether he lead me himself, or deliver me over to be led by others? I depend both ways upon his will, and it is he that determines both ways of my eternal state. Would an Israelite, that had worshiped Baal upon the command of his king, have been in any better condition, because somebody had told him that the king ordered nothing in religion upon his own head, nor commanded anything to be done by his subjects in divine worship but what was approved by the counsel of priests, and declared to be of divine right by the doctors of their Church? If the religion of any Church become, therefore, true and saving, because the head of that sect, the prelates and priests, and those of that tribe, do all of them, with all their might, extol and praise it, what religion can ever be accounted erroneous, false, and destructive? I am doubtful concerning the doctrine of the Socinians,[2] I am suspicious of the way of worship practiced by the Papists, or Lutherans; will it be ever a jot safer for me to join either unto the one or the other of those Churches, upon the magistrate's command, because he commands nothing in religion but by the authority and counsel of the doctors of that Church?

But, to speak the truth, we must acknowledge that the Church

[2] The Socinians were adherents of Socinus, an Italian theologian of the sixteenth century, who denied the divinity of Christ and other tenets of Christianity, but reverenced Christ as a great teacher.

(if a convention of clergymen, making canons, must be called by that name) is for the most part more apt to be influenced by the Court than the Court by the Church. How the Church was under the vicissitude of orthodox and Arian emperors is very well known. Or if those things be too remote, our modern English history affords us fresh examples in the reigns of Henry VIII., Edward VI., Mary, and Elizabeth, how easily and smoothly the clergy changed their decrees, their articles of faith, their form of worship, everything according to the inclination of those kings and queens. Yet were those kings and queens of such different minds in point of religion, and enjoined thereupon such different things, that no man in his wits (I had almost said none but an atheist) will presume to say that any sincere and upright worshiper of God could, with a safe conscience, obey their several decrees. To conclude, it is the same thing whether a king that prescribes laws to another man's religion, pretend to do it by his own judgment, or by the ecclesiastical authority and advice of others. The decisions of churchmen, whose differences and disputes are sufficiently known, cannot be any sounder or safer than his; nor can all their suffrages joined together add a new strength to the civil power. Though this also must be taken notice of—that princes seldom have any regard to the suffrages of ecclesiastics that are not favorers of their own faith and way of worship.

But, after all, the principal consideration, and which absolutely determines this controversy, is this: Although the magistrate's opinion in religion be sound, and the way that he appoints be truly evangelical, yet, if I be not thoroughly persuaded thereof in my own mind, there will be no safety for me in following it. No way whatsoever that I shall walk in against the dictates of my conscience will ever bring me to the mansions of the blessed. I may grow rich by an art that I take not delight in, I may be cured of some disease by remedies that I have not faith in; but I cannot be saved by a religion that I distrust, and by a worship that I abhor. It is in vain for an unbeliever to take up the outward show of another man's profession. Faith only, and inward sincerity, are the things that procure acceptance with God. The most likely and most approved remedy can have no effect upon the patient if his stomach reject it as soon as taken; and you will in vain cram a medicine down a sick man's throat, which his particular constitution will be sure to turn into poison. In a word, whatsoever may be doubtful in religion, yet this at least is certain, that no religion which I believe not to be true can be either true or profitable unto me. In vain, therefore, do princes compel their subjects to come into their Church communion, under pretense of saving their souls. If they believe, they will come of their own accord; if they believe not, their coming will nothing avail them. How great soever, in fine, may be the pretense of good will and charity, and concern for the salvation of men's souls, men cannot be forced to be saved whether they will or no. And therefore, when all is done, they must be left to their own consciences.

Having thus at length freed men from all dominion over one another in matters of religion, let us now consider what they are to do. All men know and acknowledge that God ought to be publicly worshiped; why otherwise do they compel one another unto the public assemblies? Men, therefore, constituted in this liberty are to enter into some religious society, that they meet together, not only for mutual edification, but to own to the world that they worship God, and offer unto His Divine Majesty such service as they themselves are not ashamed of, and such as they think not unworthy of Him, nor unacceptable to Him; and finally, that by the purity of doctrine, holiness of life, and decent form of worship, they may draw others unto the love of the true religion, and perform such other things in religion as cannot be done by each private man apart.

These religious societies I call Churches; and these, I say, the magistrate ought to tolerate, for the business of these assemblies of the people is nothing but what is lawful for every man in particular to take care of—I mean the salvation of their souls; nor in this case is there any difference between the National Church and other separated congregations.

But as in every Church there are two things especially to be considered—the outward form and rites of worship, and the doctrines and articles of faith—these things must be handled each distinctly, that so the whole matter of toleration may the more clearly be understood.

Concerning outward worship, I say, in the first place, that the magistrate has no power to enforce by law, either in his own Church, or much less in another, the use of any rites or ceremonies whatsoever in the worship of God. And this, not only because these Churches are free societies, but because whatsoever is practiced in the worship of God is only so far justifiable as it is believed by those that practice it to be acceptable unto Him. Whatsoever is not done with that assurance of faith is neither well in itself, nor can it be acceptable to God. To impose such things, therefore, upon any people, contrary to their own judgment, is in effect to command them to offend God, which, considering that the end of all religion is to please Him, and that liberty is essentially necessary to that end, appears to be absurd beyond expression.

But perhaps it may be concluded from hence that I deny unto the magistrate all manner of power about indifferent things, which, if it be not granted, the whole subject matter of law making is taken away. No, I readily grant that indifferent things, and perhaps none but such, are subjected to the legislative power. But it does not therefore follow that the magistrate may ordain whatsoever he pleases concerning anything that is indifferent. The public good is the rule and measure of all lawmaking. If a thing be not useful to the commonwealth, though it be never so indifferent, it may not presently be established by law.

And further, things never so indifferent in their own nature, when they are brought into the Church and worship of God, are removed out of the reach of the magistrate's jurisdiction, because in that use they have no connection at all with civil affairs. The only business of the Church is the salvation of souls, and it no way concerns the commonwealth, or any member of it, that this or the other ceremony be there made use of. Neither the use nor the omission of any ceremonies in those religious assemblies does either advantage or prejudice the life, liberty, or estate of any man. For example, let it be granted that the washing of an infant with water is in itself an indifferent thing, let it be granted also that the magistrate understand such washing to be profitable to the curing or preventing of any disease the children are subject unto, and esteem the matter weighty enough to be taken care of by a law. In that case he may order it to be done. But will anyone therefore say that a magistrate has the same right to ordain by law that all children shall be baptized by priests in the sacred font in order to the purification of their souls? The extreme difference of these two cases is visible to everyone at first sight. Or let us apply the last case to the child of a Jew, and the thing speaks itself. For what hinders but a Christian magistrate may have subjects that are Jews? Now, if we acknowledge that such an injury may not be done unto a Jew as to compel him, against his own opinion, to practice in his religion a thing that is in its nature indifferent, how can we maintain that anything of this kind may be done to a Christian?

Again, things in their own nature indifferent cannot, by any human authority, be made any part of the worship of God—for this very reason: because they are indifferent. For, since indifferent things are not capable, by any virtue of their own, to propitiate the Deity, no human power or authority can confer on them so much dignity and excellency as to enable them to do it. In the common affairs of life that use of indifferent things which God has not forbidden is free and lawful, and therefore in those things human authority has place. But it is not so in matters of religion. Things indifferent are not otherwise lawful in the worship of God than as they are instituted by God Himself, and as He, by some positive command, has ordained them to be made a part of that worship which He will vouchsafe to accept at the hands of poor sinful men. Nor, when an incensed Deity shall ask us, "Who has required these, or such-like things at your hands?" will it be enough to answer Him that the magistrate commanded them. If civil jurisdiction extend thus far, what might not lawfully be introduced into religion? What hodgepodge of ceremonies, what superstitious inventions, built upon the magistrate's authority, might not (against conscience) be imposed upon the worshipers of God? For the greatest part of these ceremonies and superstitions consists in the religious use of such things as are in their own nature indifferent; nor are they sinful upon any other account than because God is not the author of them. The sprinkling of water, and the use of bread and wine, are both in their own nature and in the ordinary occasions of life altogether indifferent. Will any man therefore say that these things could have been introduced into religion, and made a part of divine worship, if not by divine institution? If any human authority or civil power could have done this, why might it not also enjoin the eating of fish and drinking of ale in the holy banquet as a part of divine worship? Why not the sprinkling of the blood of beasts in churches, and expiations by water or fire, and abundance more of this kind? But these things, how indifferent soever they be in common uses, when they come to be annexed unto divine worship, without divine authority, they are as abominable to God as the sacrifice of a dog. And why is a dog so abominable? What difference is there between a dog and a goat, in respect of the divine nature, equally and infinitely distant from all affinity with matter, unless it be that God required the use of one in His worship, and not of the other? We see, therefore, that indifferent things, how much soever they be under the power of the civil magistrate, yet cannot, upon that pretense, be introduced into religion, and imposed upon religious assemblies, because, in the worship of God, they wholly cease to be indifferent. He that worships God does it with design to please Him and procure His favor. But that cannot be done by him who, upon the command of another, offers unto God that which he knows will be displeasing to Him, because not commanded by Himself. This is not to please God, or appease his wrath, but willingly and knowingly to provoke Him by a manifest contempt, which is a thing absolutely repugnant to the nature and end of worship.

But it will be here asked: "If nothing belonging to divine worship be left to human discretion, how is it then that Churches themselves have the power of ordering anything about the time and place of worship, and the like? To this I answer, that in religious worship we must distinguish between what is part of the worship itself and what is but a circumstance. That is a part of the worship which is believed to be appointed by God, and to be well-pleasing to Him, and therefore that is necessary. Circumstances are such things which, though in general they cannot be separated from worship, yet the particular instances or modifications of them are not determined, and therefore they are indifferent. Of this sort are the time and place of worship, habit and posture of him that worships. These are circumstances, and perfectly indifferent, where God has not given any express command about them. For example, amongst the Jews the time and place of their worship, and the habits of those that officiated in it, were not mere circumstances, but a part of the worship itself, in which if anything were defective, or different from the institution, they could not hope that it would be accepted by God. But these, to Christians under the liberty of the Gospel, are mere circumstances of worship, which the prudence of every Church may bring into such use as shall be judged most subservient to the end of order, decency, and edification. But, even under the Gospel, those who believe the first or the seventh day to be set apart by God, and consecrated still to His worship, to them that portion of time is not a simple circumstance, but a real part of Divine worship, which can neither be changed nor neglected.

In the next place: As the magistrate has no power to impose by his laws the use of any rites and ceremonies in any Church, so neither has he any power to forbid the use of such rites and ceremonies as are already received, approved, and practiced by any Church; because, if he did so, he would destroy the Church itself: the end of whose institution is only to worship God with freedom after its own manner.

You will say, by this rule, if some congregations should have a mind to sacrifice infants, or (as the primitive Christians were falsely accused) lustfully pollute themselves in promiscuous uncleanness, or practice any other such heinous enormities, is the magistrate obliged to tolerate them, because they are committed in a religious assembly? I answer, No. These things are not lawful in the ordinary course of life, or in any private house; and therefore neither are they so in the worship of God, nor in any religious meeting. But, indeed, if any people congregated upon account of religion should be desirous to sacrifice a calf, I deny that that ought to be prohibited by a law. Meliboeus, whose calf it is, may lawfully kill his calf at home, and burn any part of it that he thinks fit. For no injury is thereby done to anyone, no prejudice to another man's goods. And for the same reason he may kill his calf also in a religious meeting. Whether the doing so be well-pleasing to God or no, it is their part to consider that do it. The part of the magistrate is only to take care that the commonwealth receive no prejudice, and that there be no injury done to any man, either in life or estate. And thus what may be spent on a feast may be spent on a sacrifice. But if peradventure such were the state of things that the interest of the commonwealth required all slaughter of beasts should be forborne for some while, in order to the increasing of the stock of cattle that had been destroyed by some extraordinary murrain, who sees not that the magistrate, in such a case, may forbid all his subjects to kill any calves for any use whatsoever? Only it is to be observed that, in this case, the law is not made about a religious, but a political matter; nor is the sacrifice, but the slaughter of calves, thereby prohibited.

By this we see what difference there is between the Church and the Commonwealth. Whatsoever is lawful in the Commonwealth cannot be prohibited by the magistrate in the Church. Whatsoever is permitted unto any of his subjects for their ordinary use, neither can nor ought to be forbidden by him to any sect of people for their religious uses. If any man may lawfully take bread or wine, either sitting or kneeling in his own house, the law ought not to abridge him of the same liberty in his religious worship; though in the Church the use of bread and wine be very different, and be there applied to the mysteries of faith and rites of Divine worship. But those things that are prejudicial to the commonweal of a people in their ordinary use, and are therefore forbidden by laws, those things ought not to be permitted to Churches in their sacred rites. Only the magistrate ought always to be very careful that he do not misuse his authority to the oppression of any Church, under pretense of public good.

It may be said, what if a Church be idolatrous, is that also to be tolerated by the magistrate? I answer, what power can be given to the magistrate for the suppression of an idolatrous Church, which may not in time and place be made use of to the ruin of an orthodox one? For it must be remembered that the civil power is the same everywhere, and the religion of every prince is orthodox to himself. If, therefore, such a power be granted unto the civil magistrate in spirituals, as that at Geneva, for example, he may extirpate, by violence and blood, the religion which is there reputed idolatrous, by the same rule another magistrate, in some neighboring country, may oppress the reformed religion, and, in India, the Christian. The civil power can either change everything in religion, according to the prince's pleasure, or it can change nothing. If it be once permitted to introduce anything into religion, by the means of laws and penalties, there can be no bounds put to it; but it will in the same manner be lawful to alter everything, according to that rule of truth which the magistrate has framed unto himself. No man whatsoever ought therefore to be deprived of his terrestrial enjoyments upon account of his religion. Not even Americans, subjected unto a Christian prince, are to be punished either in body or goods for not embracing our faith and worship. If they are persuaded that they please God in observing the rites of their own country, and that they shall obtain happiness by that means, they are to be left unto God and themselves. Let us trace this matter to the bottom. Thus it is: an inconsiderable and weak number of Christians, destitute of everything, arrive in a pagan country; these foreigners beseech the inhabitants, by the bowels of humanity, that they would succor them with the necessaries of life; those necessaries are given them, habitations are granted, and they all join together, and grow up into one body of people. The Christian religion by this means takes root in that country, and spreads itself, but does not suddenly grow the strongest. While things are in this condition, peace, friendship, faith, and equal justice are preserved amongst them. At length the magistrate becomes a Christian, and by that means their party becomes the most powerful. Then immediately all compacts are to be broken, all civil rights to be violated, that idolatry may be extirpated; and unless these innocent pagans, strict observers of the rules of equity and the law of Nature, and no ways offending against the laws of the society, I say, unless they will forsake their ancient religion, and embrace a new and strange one, they are to be turned out of the lands and possessions of their forefathers, and perhaps deprived of life itself. Then, at last, it appears what zeal for the Church, joined with the desire of dominion, is capable to produce, and how easily the pretense of religion, and of the care of souls, serves for a cloak to covetousness, rapine, and ambition.

Now whosoever maintains that idolatry is to be rooted out of any place by laws, punishments, fire, and sword, may apply this story to himself. For the reason of the thing is equal, both in America and Europe. And neither pagans there, nor any dissenting Christians here, ian, with any right, be deprived of their worldly goods by the predominating faction of a court-church; nor are any civil rights to be either changed or violated upon account of religion in one place more than another.

But idolatry, say some, is a sin, and therefore not to be tolerated. If they said it were therefore to be avoided, the inference were good. But it does not follow, that because it is a sin it ought therefore to be punished by the magistrate. For it does not belong unto the magistrate to make use of his sword in punishing everything, indifferently, that he takes to be a sin against God. Covetousness, uncharitableness, idleness, and many other things are sins, by the consent of men, which yet no man ever said were to be punished by the magistrate. The reason is, because they are not prejudicial to other men's rights, nor do they break the public peace of societies. Nay, even the sins of lying and perjury are nowhere punishable by laws; unless, in certain cases, in which the real turpitude of the thing and the offense against God are not considered, but only the injury done unto men's neighbors and to the commonwealth. And what if in another country, to a Mahometan or a pagan prince, the Christian religion seem false and offensive to God; may not the Christians for the same reason, and after the same manner, be extirpated there?

But it may be urged farther, that, by the law of Moses, idolaters were to be rooted out. True, indeed, by the law of Moses; but that is not obligatory to us Christians. Nobody pretends that everything generally enjoined by the law of Moses ought to be practiced by Christians; but there is nothing more frivolous than that common distinction of moral, judicial, and ceremonial law, which men ordinarily make use of. For no positive law whatsoever can oblige any people but those to whom it is given. "Hear, O Israel," sufficiently restrains the obligations of the law of Moses only to that people. And this consideration alone is answer enough unto those that urge the authority of the law of Moses for the inflicting of capital punishment upon idolaters. But, however, I will examine this argument a little more particularly.

The case of idolaters, in respect of the Jewish commonwealth, falls under a double consideration. The first is of those who, being initiated in the Mosaical rites and made citizens of that commonwealth, did afterwards apostatize from the worship of the God of Israel. These were proceeded against as traitors and rebels, guilty of no less than high treason. For the commonwealth of the Jews, different in that from all others, was an absolute theocracy; nor was there, or could there be, any difference between that commonwealth and the Church. The laws established there concerning the worship of One Invisible Deity were the civil laws of that people, and a part of their political government, in which God Himself was the legislator. Now, if anyone can show me where there is a commonwealth at this time, constituted upon that foundation, I will acknowledge that the ecclesiastical law do there unavoidably become a part of the civil, and that the subjects of that government both may and ought to be kept in strict conformity with that Church by the civil power. But there is absolutely no such thing under the Gospel as a Christian commonwealth. There are, indeed, many cities and kingdoms that have embraced the faith of Christ, but they have retained their ancient form of government, with which the law of Christ has not at all meddled. He, indeed, has taught men how, by faith and good works, they may obtain eternal life; but He instituted no commonwealth. He prescribed unto His followers no new and peculiar form of government, nor put He the sword into any magistrate's hand, with commission to make use of it in forcing men to forsake their former religion and receive His.

Secondly, foreigners, and such as were strangers to the commonwealth of Israel, were not compelled by force to observe the rites of the Mosaical law; but, on the contrary, in the very same place where it is ordered that an Israelite that was an idolater should be put to death [Exod. 22:20, 21], there it is provided that strangers should not be vexed nor oppressed. I confess that the seven nations that possessed the land which was promised to the Israelites were utterly to be cut off; but this was not singly because they were idolaters. For if that had been the reason, why were the Moabites and other nations to be spared? No: the reason is this: God being in a peculiar manner the King of the Jews, He could not suffer the adoration of any other deity (which was properly an act of high treason against Himself) in the land of Canaan, which was His kingdom. For such a manifest revolt could no ways consist with His dominion, which was perfectly political in that country. All idolatry was therefore to be rooted out of the bounds of His kingdom, because it was an acknowledgment of another god, that is to say, another king, against the laws of Empire. The inhabitants were also to be driven out, that the entire possession of the land might be given to the Israelites. And for the like reason the Emims and the Horims were driven out of their countries by the children of Esau and Lot; and their lands, upon the same grounds, given by God to the invaders [Deut. 2]. But, though all idolatry was thus rooted out of the land of Canaan, yet every idolater was not brought to execution. The whole family of Rahab, the whole nation of the Gibeonites, articled with Joshua, and were allowed by treaty; and there were many captives amongst the Jews who were idolaters. David and Solomon subdued many countries without the confines of the Land of Promise, and carried their conquests as far as Euphrates. Amongst so many captives taken, so many nations reduced under their obedience, we find not one man forced into the Jewish religion and the worship of the true God, and punished for idolatry, though all of them were certainly guilty of it. If anyone indeed, becoming a proselyte, desired to be made a denizen of their commonwealth, he was obliged to submit to their laws; that is, to embrace their religion. But this he did willingly, on his own accord, not by constraint. He did not unwillingly submit, to show his obedience, but he sought and solicited for it as a privilege. And, as soon as he was admitted, he became subject to the laws of the commonwealth, by which all idolatry was forbidden within the borders of the land of Canaan. But that law (as I have said) did not reach to any of those regions, however subjected unto the Jews, that were situated without those bounds.

Thus far concerning outward worship. Let us now consider articles of faith.

The articles of religion are some of them practical and some speculative. Now, though both sorts consist in the knowledge of truth, yet these terminate simply in the understanding, those influence the will and manners. Speculative opinions, therefore, and articles of faith (as they are called) which are required only to be believed, cannot be imposed on any Church by the law of the land. For it is absurd that things should be enjoined by laws which are not in men's power to perform. And to believe this or that to be true, does not depend upon our will. But of this enough has been said already. But (will some say) let men at least profess that they believe. A sweet religion, indeed, that obliges men to dissemble and tell lies, both to God and man, for the salvation of their souls! If the magistrate thinks to save men thus, he seems to understand little of the way of salvation. And if he does it not in order to save them, why is he so solicitous about the articles of faith as to enact them by a law?

Further, the magistrate ought not to forbid the preaching or professing of any speculative opinions in any Church, because they have no manner of relation to the civil rights of the subjects. If a Roman Catholic believe that to be really the body of Christ, which another man calls bread, he does no injury thereby to his neighbor. If a Jew do not believe the New Testament to be the Word of God, he does not thereby alter anything in men's civil rights. If a heathen doubt of both Testaments, he is not therefore to be punished as a pernicious citizen. The power of the magistrate and the estates of the people may be equally secure whether any man believe these things or no. I readily grant that these opinions are false and absurd. But the business of laws is not to provide for the truth of opinions, but for the safety and security of the commonwealth, and of every particular man's goods and person. And so it ought to be. For the truth certainly would do well enough if she were once left to shift for herself. She seldom has received, and I fear never will receive, much assistance from the power of great men, to whom she is but rarely known, and more rarely welcome. She is not taught by laws, nor has she any need of force to procure her entrance into the minds of men. Errors indeed prevail by the assistance of foreign and borrowed succors. But if Truth makes not her way into the understanding by her own light, she will be but the weaker for any borrowed force violence can add to her. Thus much for speculative opinions. Let us now proceed to practical ones.

A good life, in which consists not the least part of religion and true piety, concerns also the civil government; and in it lies the safety both of men's souls and of the commonwealth. Moral actions belong therefore to the jurisdiction both of the outward and inward court; both of the civil and domestic governor; I mean both of the magistrate and conscience. Here, therefore, is great danger, lest one of these jurisdictions intrench upon the other, and discord arise between the keeper of the public peace and the overseers of souls. But if what has been already said concerning the limits of both these governments be rightly considered, it will easily remove all difficulty in this matter.

Every man has an immortal soul, capable of eternal happiness or misery; whose happiness depending upon his believing and doing those things in this life which are necessary to the obtaining of God's favor, and are prescribed by God to that end. It follows from thence, first, that the observance of these things is the highest obligation that lies upon mankind, and that our utmost care, application, and diligence ought to be exercised in the search and performance of them; because there is nothing in this world that is of any consideration in comparison with eternity. Secondly, that seeing one man does not violate the right of another by his erroneous opinions and undue manner of worship, nor is his perdition any prejudice to another man's affairs, therefore, the care of each man's salvation belongs only to himself. But I would not have this understood as if I meant hereby to condemn all charitable admonitions, and affectionate endeavors to reduce men from errors, which are indeed the greatest duty of a Christian. Anyone may employ as many exhortations and arguments as he pleases, towards the promoting of another man's salvation. But all force and compulsion are to be forborne. Nothing is to be done imperiously. Nobody is obliged in that matter to yield obedience unto the admonitions or injunctions of another, further than he himself is persuaded. Every man in that has the supreme and absolute authority of judging for himself. And the reason is because nobody else is concerned in it, nor can receive any prejudice from his conduct therein.

But besides their souls, which are immortal, men have also their temporal lives here upon earth; the state whereof being frail and fleeting, and the duration uncertain, they have need of several outward conveniences to the support thereof, which are to be procured or preserved by pains and industry. For those things that are necessary to the comfortable support of our lives are not the spontaneous products of nature, nor do offer themselves fit and prepared for our use. This part therefore draws on another care, and necessarily gives another employment. But the pravity [3] of mankind being such that they had rather injuriously prey upon the fruits of other men's labors than take pains to provide for themselves, the necessity of preserving men in the possession of what honest industry has already acquired, and also of preserving their liberty and strength, whereby they may acquire what they farther want, obliges men to enter into society with one another, that by mutual assistance and joint force they may secure unto each other their properties, in the things that contribute to the comfort and happiness of this life, leaving in the meanwhile to every man the care of his own eternal happiness, the attainment whereof can neither be facilitated by another man's industry, nor can the loss of it turn to another man's prejudice, nor the hope of it be forced from him by any external violence. But, forasmuch as men thus entering into societies, grounded upon their mutual compacts of assistance for the defense of their temporal goods, may, nevertheless, be deprived of them, either by the rapine and fraud of their fellow citizens, or by the hostile violence of foreigners, the remedy of this evil consists in arms, riches, and multitude of citizens; the remedy of the other in laws; and the care of all things relating both to one and the other is committed by the society to the civil magistrate. This is the original, this is the use, and these are the bounds of the legislative (which is the supreme) power in every commonwealth. I mean, that provision may be made for the security of each man's private possessions; for the peace, riches, and public commodities of the whole people; and, as much as possible, for the increase of their inward strength against foreign invasions.

These things being thus explained, it is easy to understand to what end the legislative power ought to be directed, and by what measures regulated; and that is the temporal good and outward prosperity of the society; which is the sole reason of men's entering into society, and the only thing they seek and aim at in it. And it is also evident what liberty remains to men in reference to their eternal salvation, and that is, that every one should do what he in his conscience is persuaded to be acceptable to the Almighty, on whose good pleasure and acceptance

[3] Depravity.

depends their eternal happiness. For obedience is due, in the first place, to God, and afterwards to the laws.

But some may ask, What if the magistrate should enjoin anything by his authority that appears unlawful to the conscience of a private person? I answer, that if government be faithfully administered, and the counsels of the magistrates be indeed directed to the public good, this will seldom happen. But if, perhaps, it do so fall out, I say, that such a private person is to abstain from the action that he judges unlawful, and he is to undergo the punishment which it is not unlawful for him to bear. For the private judgment of any person concerning a law enacted in political matters, for the public good, does not take away the obligation of that law, nor deserve a dispensation. But if the law indeed be concerning things that lie not within the verge of the magistrate's authority (as for example, that the people, or any party amongst them, should be compelled to embrace a strange religion, and join in the worship and ceremonies of another Church), men are not in these cases obliged by that law, against their consciences. For the political society is instituted for no other end, but only to secure every man's possession of the things of this life. The care of each man's soul, and of the things of heaven, which neither does belong to the commonwealth nor can be subjected to it, is left entirely to every man's self. Thus the safeguard of men's lives, and of the things that belong unto this life, is the business of the commonwealth; and the preserving of those things unto their owners is the duty of the magistrate. And therefore the magistrate cannot take away these worldly things from this man or party, and give them to that; nor change propriety amongst fellow subjects (no, not even by a law), for a cause that has no relation to the end of civil government, I mean for their religion, which whether it be true or false does no prejudice to the worldly concerns of their fellow subjects, which are the things that only belong unto the care of the commonwealth.

But what if the magistrate believe such a law as this to be for the public good? I answer: As the private judgment of any particular person, if erroneous, does not exempt him from the obligation of law, so the private judgment (as I may call it) of the magistrate does not give him any new right of imposing laws upon his subjects, which neither was in the constitution of the government granted him, nor ever was in the power of the people to grant, much less if he make it his business to enrich and advance his followers and fellow-sectaries with the spoils of others. But what if the magistrate believe that he has a right to make such laws, and that they are for the public good, and his subjects believe the contrary? Who shall be judge between them? I answer, God alone. For there is no judge upon earth between the supreme magistrate and the people. God, I say, is the only Judge in this case, who will retribute unto everyone at the last day according to his deserts; that is, according to his sincerity and uprightness in endeavoring to promote piety, and the public weal and peace of mankind. But what shall be done in the meanwhile? I answer: The principal and chief care of everyone ought to be of his own soul first, and, in the next place, of the public peace; though yet there are very few will think it is peace there, where they see all laid waste.

There are two sorts of contests amongst men, the one managed by law, the other by force; and these are of that nature that where the one ends, the other always begins. But it is not my business to inquire into the power of the magistrate in the different constitutions of nations. I only know what usually happens where controversies arise without a judge to determine them. You will say, then, the magistrate being the stronger will have his will, and carry his point. Without doubt; but the question is not here concerning the doubtfulness of the event, but the rule of right.

But to come to particulars. I say, first, no opinions contrary to human society, or to those moral rules which are necessary to the preservation of civil society, are to be tolerated by the magistrate. But of these, indeed, examples in any Church are rare. For no sect can easily arrive to such a degree of madness as that it should think fit to teach, for doctrines of religion, such things as manifestly undermine the foundations of society, and are, therefore, condemned by the judgment of all mankind; because their own interest, peace, reputation, everything would be thereby endangered.

Another more secret evil, but more dangerous to the commonwealth, is when men arrogate to themselves, and to those of their own sect, some peculiar prerogative covered over with a specious show of deceit.

ful words, but in effect opposite to the civil right of the community. For example: we cannot find any sect that teaches, expressly and openly, that men are not obliged to keep their promise; that princes may be dethroned by those that differ from them in religion; or that the dominion of all things belongs only to themselves. For these things, proposed thus nakedly and plainly, would soon draw on them the eye and hand of the magistrate, and awaken all the care of the commonwealth to a watchfulness against the spreading of so dangerous an evil. But, nevertheless, we find those that say the same things in other words. What else do they mean, who teach that faith is not to be kept with heretics? Their meaning, forsooth, is that the privilege of breaking faith belongs unto themselves; for they declare all that are not of their communion to be heretics, or at least may declare them so whensoever they think fit. What can be the meaning of their asserting that kings excommunicated forfeit their crowns and kingdoms? It is evident that they thereby arrogate unto themselves the power of deposing kings, because they challenge the power of excommunication, as the peculiar right of their hierarchy.

That dominion is founded in grace is also an assertion by which those that maintain it do plainly lay claim to the possession of all things. For they are not so wanting to themselves as not to believe, or at least as not to profess themselves to be the truly pious and faithful. These, therefore, and the like, who attribute unto the faithful, religious, and orthodox, that is, in plain terms, unto themselves, any peculiar privilege or power above other mortals, in civil concernments; or who upon pretense of religion do challenge any manner of authority over such as are not associated with them in their ecclesiastical communion, I say these have no right to be tolerated by the magistrate; as neither those that will not own and teach the duty of tolerating all men in matters of mere religion. For what do all these and the like doctrines signify, but that they may, and are ready upon any occasion to seize the government, and possess themselves of the estates and fortunes of their fellow subjects; and that they only ask leave to be tolerated by the magistrate so long until they find themselves strong enough to effect it?

Again: That Church can have no right to be tolerated by the magistrate which is constituted upon such a bottom that all those who enter into it do thereby *ipso facto* deliver themselves up to the protection and service of another prince. For by this means the magistrate would give way to the settling of a foreign jurisdiction in his own country, and suffer his own people to be listed, as it were, for soldiers against his own Government. Nor does the frivolous and fallacious distinction between the Court and the Church afford any remedy to this inconvenience; especially when both the one and the other are equally subject to the absolute authority of the same person, who has not only power to persuade the members of his Church to whatsoever he lists, either as purely religious, or in order thereunto, but can also enjoin it them on pain of eternal fire. It is ridiculous for anyone to profess himself to be a Mahometan only in his religion, but in everything else a faithful subject to a Christian magistrate, whilst at the same time he acknowledges himself bound to yield blind obedience to the Mufti of Constantinople, who himself is entirely obedient to the Ottoman Emperor, and frames the feigned oracles of that religion according to his pleasure. But this Mahometan living amongst Christians would yet more apparently renounce their government if he acknowledged the same person to be head of his Church who is the supreme magistrate in the state.

Lastly, those are not at all to be tolerated who deny the being of a God. Promises, covenants, and oaths, which are the bonds of human society, can have no hold upon an atheist. The taking away of God, though but even in thought, dissolves all; besides also, those that by their atheism undermine and destroy all religion, can have no pretense of religion whereupon to challenge the privilege of a toleration. As for other practical opinions, though not absolutely free from all error, if they do not tend to establish domination over others, or civil impunity to the Church in which they are taught, there can be no reason why they should not be tolerated.

It remains that I say something concerning those assemblies which being vulgarly called, and perhaps having sometimes been conventicles and nurseries of factions and seditions, are thought to afford the strongest matter of objection against this doctrine of toleration. But this has not happened by anything peculiar unto the genius of such assemblies, but by the unhappy circumstances of an oppressed or ill-settled liberty. These accusations would soon cease if the law of toleration were once so settled that all churches were obliged to lay down toleration as the foundation of their own liberty, and teach that liberty of conscience is every man's natural right, equally belonging to dissenters as to themselves; and that nobody ought to be compelled in matters of religion either by law or force. The establishment of this one thing would take away all ground of complaints and tumults upon account of conscience; and these causes of discontents and animosities being once removed, there would remain nothing in these assemblies that were not more peaceable and less apt to produce disturbance of state than in any other meetings whatsoever. But let us examine particularly the heads of these accusations.

You will say that assemblies and meetings endanger the public peace, and threaten the commonwealth. I answer, if this be so, why are there daily such numerous meetings in markets and courts of judicature? Why are crowds upon the Exchange, and a concourse of people in cities suffered? You will reply, those are civil assemblies, but these we object against are ecclesiastical. I answer, it is a likely thing indeed, that such assemblies as are altogether remote from civil affairs should be most apt to embroil them. Oh, but civil assemblies are composed of men that differ from one another in matters of religion, but these ecclesiastical meetings are of persons that are all of one opinion. As if an agreement in matters of religion were in effect a conspiracy against the commonwealth; or as if men would not be so much the more warmly unanimous in religion the less liberty they had of assembling. But it will be urged still, that civil assemblies are open and free for anyone to enter into, whereas religious conventicles are more private, and thereby give opportunity to clandestine machinations. I answer that this is not strictly true, for many civil assemblies are not open to everyone. And if some religious meetings be private, who are they, I beseech you, that are to be blamed for it, those that desire, or those that forbid their being public? Again, you will say that religious communion does exceedingly unite men's minds and affections to one another, and is therefore the more dangerous. But if this be so, why is not the magistrate afraid of his own Church; and why does he not forbid their assemblies as things dangerous to his government? You will say because he himself is a part, and even the head of them. As if he were not also a part of the commonwealth, and the head of the whole people!

Let us therefore deal plainly. The magistrate is afraid of other churches, but not of his own; because he is kind and favorable to the one, but severe and cruel to the other. These he treats like children, and indulges them even to wantonness. Those he uses as slaves, and how blamelessly soever they demean themselves, recompenses them no otherwise than by galleys, prisons, confiscations, and death. These he cherishes and defends; those he continually scourges and oppresses. Let him turn the tables. Or let those dissenters enjoy but the same privileges in civils as his other subjects, and he will quickly find that these religious meetings will be no longer dangerous. For if men enter into seditious conspiracies, it is not religion inspires them to it in their meetings, but their sufferings and oppressions that make them willing to ease themselves. Just and moderate governments are everywhere quiet, everywhere safe; but oppression raises ferments and makes men struggle to cast off an uneasy and tyrannical yoke. I know that seditions are very frequently raised upon pretense of religion, but it is as true that for religion subjects are frequently ill treated, and live miserably. Believe me, the stirs that are made proceed not from any peculiar temper of this or that Church or religious society, but from the common disposition of all mankind, who when they groan under any heavy burden endeavor naturally to shake off the yoke that galls their necks. Suppose this business of religion were let alone, and that there were some other distinction made between men and men upon account of their different complexions, shapes, and features, so that those who have black hair, for example, or gray eyes should not enjoy the same privileges as other citizens; that they should not be permitted either to buy or sell, or live by their callings; that parents should not have the government and education of their own children; that all should either be excluded from the benefit of the laws, or meet with partial judges; can it be doubted but these persons, thus distinguished from others by the color of their hair and eyes, and united together by one common persecution, would be as dangerous to the magistrate as any others that had associated themselves merely upon the account of religion? Some enter into company for trade and profit, others for want of business have their clubs for claret. Neighborhood joins some, and religion others. But there is only one thing which gathers people into seditious commotions, and that is oppression.

You will say, What, will you have people to meet at divine service against the magistrate's will? I answer, Why, I pray, against his will? Is it not both lawful and necessary that they should meet? Against his will, do you say? That is what I complain of; that is the very root of all the mischief. Why are assemblies less sufferable in a church than in a theater or market? Those that meet there are not either more vicious or more turbulent than those that meet elsewhere. The business in that is that they are ill used, and therefore they are not to be suffered. Take away the partiality that is used towards them in matters of common right; change the laws, take away the penalties unto which they are subjected, and all things will immediately become safe and peaceable; nay, those that are averse to the religion of the magistrate will think themselves so much the more bound to maintain the peace of the commonwealth as their condition is better in that place than elsewhere; and all the several separate congregations, like so many guardians of the public peace, will watch one another, that nothing may be innovated or changed in the form of the government, because they can hope for nothing better than what they already enjoy—that is, an equal condition with their fellow-subjects under a just and moderate government. Now if that Church which agrees in religion with the prince be esteemed the chief support of any civil government, and that for no other reason, as has already been shown, than because the prince is kind and the laws are favorable to it, how much greater will be the security of government where all good subjects, of whatsoever Church they be, without any distinction upon account of religion, enjoying the same favor of the prince and the same benefit of the laws, shall become the common support and guard of it, and where none will have any occasion to fear the severity of the laws but those that do injuries to their neighbors and offend against the civil peace?

That we may draw towards a conclusion. The sum of all we drive at is that every man may enjoy the same rights that are granted to others. Is it permitted to worship God in the Roman manner? Let it be permitted to do it in the Geneva form also. Is it permitted to speak Latin in the market place? Let those that have a mind to it be permitted to do it also in the Church. Is it lawful for any man in his own house to kneel, stand, sit, or use any other posture; and to clothe himself in white or black, in short or in long garments? Let it not be made unlawful to eat bread, drink wine, or wash with water in the church. In a word, whatsoever things are left free by law in the common occasions of life, let them remain free unto every Church in divine worship. Let no man's life, or body, or house, or estate, suffer any manner or prejudice upon these accounts. Can you allow of the Presbyterian discipline? Why should not the Episcopal also have what they like? Ecclesiastical authority, whether it be administered by the hands of a single person or many, is everywhere the same; and neither has any jurisdiction in things civil, nor any manner of power of compulsion, nor anything at all to do with riches and revenues.

Ecclesiastical assemblies and sermons are justified by daily experience and public allowance. These are allowed to people of some one persuasion, why not to all? If anything pass in a religious meeting seditiously and contrary to the public peace, it is to be punished in the same manner, and no otherwise than as if it had happened in a fair or market. These meetings ought not to be sanctuaries for factious and flagitious [4] fellows. Nor ought it to be less lawful for men to meet in churches than in halls; nor are one part of the subjects to be esteemed more blamable for their meeting together than others. Everyone is to be accountable for his own actions, and no man is to be laid under a suspicion or odium for the fault of another. Those that are seditious, murderers, thieves, robbers, adulterers, slanderers, etc., of whatsoever Church, whether national or not, ought to be punished and suppressed. But those whose doctrine is peaceable, and whose manners are pure and blameless, ought to be upon equal terms with their fellow-subjects. Thus if solemn assemblies, observations of festivals, public worship be permitted to any one sort of professors, all these things ought to be

[4] Wicked and corrupt.

permitted to the Presbyterians, Independents, Anabaptists, Arminians, Quakers, and others, with the same liberty. Nay, if we may openly speak the truth, and as becomes one man to another, neither pagan nor Mahometan, nor Jew, ought to be excluded from the civil rights of the commonwealth because of his religion. The Gospel commands no such thing. The Church which "judgeth not those that are without" [1 Cor. 5:12, 13] wants it not. And the commonwealth, which embraces indifferently all men that are honest, peaceable, and industrious, requires it not. Shall we suffer a pagan to deal and trade with us, and shall we not suffer him to pray unto and worship God? If we allow the Jews to have private houses and dwellings amongst us, why should we not allow them to have synagogues? Is their doctrine more false, their worship more abominable, or is the civil peace more endangered by their meeting in public than in their private houses? But if these things may be granted to Jews and pagans, surely the condition of any Christians ought not to be worse than theirs in a Christian commonwealth.

You will say, perhaps, Yes, it ought to be; because they are more inclinable to factions, tumults, and civil wars. I answer, Is this the fault of the Christian religion? If it be so, truly the Christian religion is the worst of all religions, and ought neither to be embraced by any particular person, nor tolerated by any commonwealth. For if this be the genius, this the nature of the Christian religion, to be turbulent, and destructive to the civil peace, that Church itself which the magistrate indulges will not always be innocent. But far be it from us to say any such thing of that religion which carries the greatest opposition to covetousness, ambition, discord, contention, and all manner of inordinate desires; and is the most modest and peaceable religion that ever was. We must therefore seek another cause of those evils that are charged upon religion. And if we consider right, we shall find it to consist wholly in the subject that I am treating of. It is not the diversity of opinions, which cannot be avoided, but the refusal of toleration to those that are of different opinions, which might have been granted, that has produced all the bustles and wars that have been in the Christian world upon account of religion. The heads and leaders of the Church, moved by avarice and insatiable desire of dominion, making use of the immoderate ambition of magistrates and the credulous superstition of the giddy multitude, have incensed and animated them against those that dissent from themselves, by preaching unto them, contrary to the laws of the Gospel and to the precepts of charity, that schismatics and heretics are to be outed of their possessions and destroyed. And thus have they mixed together and confounded two things that are in themselves most different, the Church and the commonwealth. Now as it is very difficult for men patiently to suffer themselves to be stripped of the goods which they have got by their honest industry, and, contrary to all the laws of equity, both human and divine, to be delivered up for a prey to other men's violence and rapine; especially when they are otherwise altogether blameless; and that the occasion for which they are thus treated does not at all belong to the jurisdiction of the magistrate, but entirely to the conscience of every particular man, for the conduct of which he is accountable to God only; what else can be expected but that these men, growing weary of the evils under which they labor, should in the end think it lawful for them to resist force with force, and to defend their natural rights (which are not forfeitable upon account of religion) with arms as well as they can? That this has been hitherto the ordinary course of things is abundantly evident in history, and that it will continue to be so hereafter is but too apparent in reason. It cannot, indeed, be otherwise so long as the principle of persecution for religion shall prevail, as it has done hitherto, with magistrate and people, and so long as those that ought to be the preachers of peace and concord shall continue with all their art and strength to excite men to arms and sound the trumpet of war. But that magistrates should thus suffer these incendiaries and disturbers of the public peace might justly be wondered at if it did not appear that they have been invited by them unto a participation of the spoil, and have therefore thought fit to make use of their covetousness and pride as means whereby to increase their own power. For who does not see that these good men are indeed more ministers of the government than ministers of the Gospel, and that by flattering the ambition and favoring the dominion of princes and men in authority, they endeavor with all their might to promote that tyranny in the commonwealth which otherwise they should not be able to establish in the Church? This is the unhappy agreement that we see between the Church and State. Whereas if each of them would contain itself within its own bounds—the one attending to the worldly welfare of the commonwealth, the other to the salvation of souls— it is impossible that any discord should ever have happened between them. *Sed pudet hæc opprobria, etc.* God Almighty grant, I beseech Him, that the gospel of peace may at length be preached, and that civil magistrates, growing more careful to conform their own consciences to the law of God and less solicitous about the binding of other men's consciences by human laws, may, like fathers of their country, direct all their counsels and endeavors to promote universally the civil wel- fare of all their children, except only of such as are arrogant, ungovern- able, and injurious to their brethren; and that all ecclesiastical men, who boast themselves to be the successors of the Apostles, walking peaceably and modestly in the Apostles' steps, without intermeddling with state affairs, may apply themselves wholly to promote the salva- tion of souls.

FAREWELL.

PERHAPS it may not be amiss to add a few things concerning heresy and schism. A Turk is not, nor can be, either heretic or schismatic to a Christian; and if any man fall off from the Christian faith to Ma- hometism, he does not thereby become a heretic or schismatic, but an apostate and an infidel. This nobody doubts of; and by this it appears that men of different religions cannot be heretics or schismatics to one another.

We are to inquire therefore what men are of the same religion. Con- cerning which it is manifest that those who have one and the same rule of faith and worship are of the same religion; and those who have not the same rule of faith and worship are of different religions. For since all things that belong unto that religion are contained in that rule, it follows necessarily that those who agree in one rule are of one and the same religion, and *vice versa*. Thus Turks and Christians are of different religions, because these take the Holy Scriptures to be the rule of their religion, and those the Alcoran. And for the same reason there may be different religions also even amongst Christians. The Papists and Lutherans, though both of them profess faith in Christ, and are therefore called Christians, yet are not both of the same religion, because these acknowledge nothing but the Holy Scriptures to be the rule and foundation of their religion, those take in also traditions and the decrees of Popes, and of these together make the rule of their religion; and thus the Christians of St. John, as they are called, and the Christians of Geneva are of different religions, because these also take only the Scriptures, and those I know not what traditions, for the rule of their religion.

This being settled, it follows, first, that heresy is a separation made in ecclesiastical communion between men of the same religion for some opinions no way contained in the rule itself; and, secondly, that amongst those who acknowledge nothing but the Holy Scriptures to be their rule of faith, heresy is a separation made in their Christian communion for opinions not contained in the express words of Scripture. Now this separation may be made in a twofold manner:

1. When the greater part, or by the magistrate's patronage the stronger part, of the Church separates itself from others by excluding them out of her communion because they will not profess their belief of certain opinions which are not the express words of the Scripture. For it is not the paucity of those that are separated, nor the authority of the magistrate, that can make any man guilty of heresy, but he only is a heretic who divides the Church into parts, introduces names and marks of distinction, and voluntarily makes a separation because of such opinions.

2. When anyone separates himself from the communion of a Church because that Church does not publicly profess some certain opinions which the Holy Scriptures do not expressly teach.

Both these are heretics because they err in fundamentals, and they err obstinately against knowledge; for when they have determined the Holy Scriptures to be the only foundation of faith, they nevertheless lay down certain propositions as fundamental which are not in the Scripture, and because others will not acknowledge these additional opinions of theirs, nor build upon them as if they were necessary and fundamental, they therefore make a separation in the Church, either by withdrawing themselves from others, or expelling the others from them. Nor does it signify anything for them to say that their confessions and symbols are agreeable to Scripture and to the analogy of faith; for if they be conceived in the express words of Scripture, there can be no question about them, because those things are acknowledged by all Christians to be of divine inspiration, and therefore fundamental. But if they say that the articles which they require to be professed are consequences deduced from the Scripture, it is undoubtedly well done of them who believe and profess such things as seem unto them so agreeable to the rule of faith. But it would be very ill done to obtrude those things upon others unto whom they do not seem to be the indubitable doctrines of the Scripture; and to make a separation for such things as these, which neither are nor can be fundamental, is to become heretics; for I do not think there is any man arrived to that degree of madness as that he dare give out his consequences and interpretations of Scripture as divine inspirations, and compare the articles of faith that he has framed according to his own fancy with the authority of Scripture. I know there are some propositions so evidently agreeable to Scripture that nobody can deny them to be drawn from thence, but about those, therefore, there can be no difference. This only I say—that however clearly we may think this or the other doctrine to be deduced from Scripture, we ought not therefore to impose it upon others as a necessary article of faith because we believe it to be agreeable to the rule of faith, unless we would be content also that other doctrines should be imposed upon us in the same manner, and that we should be compelled to receive and profess all the different and contradictory opinions of Lutherans, Calvinists, Remonstrants, Anabaptists, and other sects which the contrivers of symbols, systems, and confessions are accustomed to deliver to their followers as genuine and necessary deductions from the Holy Scripture. I cannot but wonder at the extravagant arrogance of those men who think that they themselves can explain things necessary to salvation more clearly than the Holy Ghost, the eternal and infinite wisdom of God.

Thus much concerning heresy, which word in common use is applied only to the doctrinal part of religion. Let us now consider schism, which is a crime near akin to it; for both these words seem unto me to signify an ill-grounded separation in ecclesiastical communion made about things not necessary. But since use, which is the supreme law in matter of language, has determined that heresy relates to errors in faith, and schism to those in worship or discipline, we must consider them under that distinction.

Schism, then, for the same reasons that have already been alleged, is nothing else but a separation made in the communion of the Church upon account of something in divine worship or ecclesiastical discipline that is not any necessary part of it. Now, nothing in worship or discipline can be necessary to Christian communion but what Christ our legislator, or the Apostles by inspiration of the Holy Spirit, have commanded in express words.

In a word, he that denies not anything that the Holy Scriptures teach in express words, nor makes a separation upon occasion of anything that is not manifestly contained in the sacred text—however he may be nicknamed by any sect of Christians, and declared by some or all of them to be utterly void of true Christianity—yet in deed and in truth this man cannot be either a heretic or schismatic.

These things might have been explained more largely and more advantageously, but it is enough to have hinted at them thus briefly to a person of your parts.

The Second Treatise on
Civil Government

THE TWO ESSAYS on civil government, as Locke said in his preface, were intended "to establish the throne of our Great Restorer, our present King William, and make good his title in the consent of the people." In both essays Locke sought to justify the Glorious Revolution which brought about the abdication of James II and increased the power and prestige of Parliament. In the *Second Treatise* Locke also attempted to answer the theory of absolutism expounded by Thomas Hobbes, his great English predecessor in political theory, and to present the case against the rule of absolute monarchs everywhere. C. H. Driver says that Locke wrote to appeal "to the common sense of humanity and to plead for the spirit of the new world in the face of a triumphant old one. His *Toleration* and *Civil Government* are but two aspects of the same appeal."

Locke conceived of the state as an agent of men's wills to aid them in their quest for freedom and happiness. In Locke's state men were no longer subordinate to the monarch. The positions were reversed and the people determined the ruler. Government was only the agent to carry out their wishes. If it failed to follow the people's instructions, it was in rebellion against them and they were justified in fighting back ("appealing to heaven").

Locke's analysis of the state followed the customary pattern of his day. He used the idea of a primitive "state of nature," as a device for reasoning out the origin and character of the state. He did not assume the historical existence of any pre-state society, although he occasionally referred to American Indian tribes as if they were examples of such a society. Actually, he said to his readers, "To understand the character of the state we must assume first that the state does not exist. We may then see why men need a government and discover the kind of government they would naturally establish."

71

Both Locke and Hobbes used the state of nature as an explanatory
device to show how the state came into being, but their different views
of the character of man made their theories of the state of nature and
of the state very different. Locke did not share his predecessor's belief
that men were completely selfish and that outside the state only lawlessness and anarchy, where every man warred against every other
man, could exist. Neither did he accept Hobbes' contention that men
were forced out of deadly fear to set up a state and to concede all power
to a dictator. Instead, his assumptions about the social nature of man
prevented him from treating men as mere human atoms and led him
to adopt the significantly different point of view that a society could
and did exist independently of the state. This view of the independent
existence of society was important to political philosophers two centuries later. It meant, for example, that one could propose the eventual
disappearance of the state without making anarchy the necessary consequence.

The other characteristics with which Locke endowed men compelled
him to create a democratic state. For Locke's men were rational. They
could discover certain laws of nature which ought to govern mankind,
and as rational beings they were capable of governing themselves
according to those laws. They were free to act upon decisions arrived
at through their search for security and pleasure. And they were
equal in the sense that as men they had equal rights and duties in the
community. Locke did not, of course, suggest that they were equally
talented or of equal ability.

Even in the state of nature, then, men lived in an integrated society
with a vast complex of rights and duties. But in this society they
lacked a common superior, or, as Locke preferred to put it, a common
judge to settle disputes. Each man was obliged to enforce for himself
the laws of nature against those who violated them for their own
selfish ends. Some failed to discover these laws because they were too
lazy or careless in their thinking; some, because they allowed their
own interest in particular cases to sway their judgments. So, because
they needed an impartial judge, men, being rational, decided to set
up a state. They contracted with each other to give up their individual
power of judgment to the whole society, whose will was to be ex-

pressed in laws and institutions of government approved by the majority. The decision of the majority was to be binding upon all members of the state.

The laws of nature under which mankind lived before setting up the state, were still discoverable by deductive reasoning, as in mathematics, or by the experimental methods of science. The law of nature which Locke discussed most thoroughly was that which conferred on men the right to private property. According to him, all property was at first held in common. But when a man mixed his labor with the land he gained a special right to the produce of that land because he had mixed a portion of himself with it. Man's right to property in the earliest state of nature, however, was strictly circumscribed. He could claim land only if there were enough left from which others might secure their livelihood; and he had no right to more goods than he could use before they spoiled. After the introduction of money, it was possible for a man to own more than he could use because he could exchange his perishable goods for coins that did not spoil. Locke did not say that the introduction of money relieved a man of the responsibility of leaving a share for others. He made very clear his view that the unregulated accumulation of property through money continued only while men still lived without a state, i.e., "outside the bounds of society and the compact; for in governments, the laws regulate it."

Inside the state, he said, "no one can enclose or appropriate any part (of the common land) without the consent of all his fellow-commoners; because this is left common by the compact—i.e., by the law of the land, which is not to be violated." The state may tax or regulate a man's property as public need requires. Still it must have "his own consent—i.e., the consent of the majority, giving it either by themselves or their representatives chosen by them."

Elsewhere in the *Second Treatise* there are lines which suggest that Locke wished to prevent even the majority from regulating property, but it is difficult to believe that he would have committed himself to the severe limitations on government control of property advocated by the *laissez-faire* economists of the next two centuries. As a thorough-going mercantilist, Locke must have automatically assumed some government regulation. There is no doubt that he meant to limit the power of government regulation always to the execution of mandates from the majority, but he apparently did not intend to limit the majority, whose will he frequently identified with the will of the individual or of the whole society. It must be always remembered that Locke's majority was a majority in a free society, where minorities could express themselves and could seek to build up their own numbers to a majority.

Locke could reconcile his doctrine of majority rule with the idea of an absolute and just law of nature, as Willmoore Kendall has suggested, as long as he accepted the "latent premise" that the majority has the right to rule, because it will, in the long run, rule rightly, i.e., in accordance with this natural law. Locke never explicitly committed himself to this notion, but some of his arguments are meaningless on any other basis.

The *Second Treatise*, as we have indicated, is not without its occasional ambiguities, inconsistencies and tendency to accept basic assumptions without much critical examination. For these reasons, its contribution to political thought has sometimes been underestimated. Professor Laski once wrote that Locke was one of the "political classics who are taken for granted rather than read." This is not strange, for Locke's proposed reforms have become so commonplace in the Anglo-Saxon world that it is hard for the modern reader to realize the tremendous influence of his work in eighteenth century France and America, as well as in England. More than the writings of any other English political theorist, Locke's *Toleration* and *Civil Government* exemplify that search for a practical, if not always logically consistent, way to freedom which the world has come to look upon as typical of British democratic development.

THE SECOND TREATISE
ON CIVIL GOVERNMENT

CHAPTER I

1. IT having been shown in the foregoing discourse: [1]

Firstly, That Adam had not, either by natural right of fatherhood or by positive donation from God, any such authority over his children, nor dominion over the world, as is pretended.

Secondly, That if he had, his heirs yet had no right to it.

Thirdly, That if his heirs had, there being no law of Nature nor positive law of God that determines which is the right heir in all cases that may arise, the right of succession, and consequently of bearing rule, could not have been certainly determined.

Fourthly, That if even that had been determined, yet the knowledge of which is the eldest line of Adam's posterity being so long since utterly lost, that in the races of mankind and families of the world, there remains not to one above another the least pretense to be the eldest house, and to have the right of inheritance.

All these promises having, as I think, been clearly made out, it is impossible that the rulers now on earth should make any benefit, or derive any the least shadow of authority from that which is held to be the fountain of all power, "Adam's private dominion and paternal jurisdiction"; so that he that will not give just occasion to think that all government in the world is the product only of force and violence, and that men live together by no other rules but that of beasts, where the strongest carries it, and so lay a foundation for perpetual disorder

[1] See Introduction to this section.

and mischief, tumult, sedition, and rebellion (things that the followers of that hypothesis so loudly cry out against), must of necessity
find out another rise of government, another original of political
power, and another way of designing and knowing the persons that
have it than what Sir Robert Filmer [2] hath taught us.

2. To this purpose, I think it may not be amiss to set down what I
take to be political power. That the power of a magistrate over a subject may be distinguished from that of a father over his children, a
master over his servant, a husband over his wife, and a lord over his
slave. All which distinct powers happening sometimes together in
the same man, if he be considered under these different relations, it
may help us to distinguish these powers one from another, and show
the difference betwixt a ruler of a commonwealth, a father of a family,
and a captain of a galley.

3. Political power, then, I take to be a right of making laws, with
penalties of death, and consequently all less penalties for the regulating
and preserving of property, and of employing the force of the community in the execution of such laws, and in the defense of the commonwealth from foreign injury, and all this only for the public good.

CHAPTER II

Of the State of Nature

4. To understand political power aright, and derive it from its original,
we must consider what estate all men are naturally in, and that is,
a state of perfect freedom to order their actions, and dispose of their
possessions and persons as they think fit, within the bounds of the law
of Nature, without asking leave or depending upon the will of any
other man.

A state also of equality, wherein all the power and jurisdiction is

[2] Sir Robert Filmer had published in 1680 his *Patriarchia,* an exposition of
his theory of absolutism in government.

reciprocal, no one having more than another, there being nothing more evident than that creatures of the same species and rank, promiscuously born to all the same advantages of Nature, and the use of the same faculties, should also be equal one amongst another, without subordination or subjection, unless the lord and master of them all should, by any manifest declaration of his will, set one above another, and confer on him, by an evident and clear appointment, an undoubted right to dominion and sovereignty.

5. This equality of men by Nature, the judicious Hooker [3] looks upon as so evident in itself, and beyond all question, that he makes it the foundation of that obligation to mutual love amongst men on which he builds the duties they owe one another, and from whence he derives the great maxims of justice and charity. His words are:

"The like natural inducement hath brought men to know that it is no less their duty to love others than themselves, for seeing those things which are equal, must needs all have one measure; if I cannot but wish to receive good, even as much at every man's hands, as any man can wish unto his own soul, how should I look to have any part of my desire herein satisfied, unless myself be careful to satisfy the like desire, which is undoubtedly in other men weak, being of one and the same nature: to have anything offered them repugnant to this desire must needs, in all respects, grieve them as much as me; so that if I do harm, I must look to suffer, there being no reason that others should show greater measure of love to me than they have by me showed unto them; my desire, therefore, to be loved of my equals in Nature, as much as possible may be, imposeth upon me a natural duty of bearing to themward fully the like affection. From which relation of equality between ourselves and them that are as ourselves, what several rules and canons natural reason hath drawn for direction of life no man is ignorant." (*Eccl. Pol.* i.)

6. But though this be a state of liberty, yet it is not a state of license; though man in that state have an uncontrollable liberty to dispose of his person or possessions, yet he has not liberty to destroy himself,

---

[3] The Rev. Richard Hooker, author of *The Laws of Ecclesiastical Polity*, is frequently quoted in the following pages.

or so much as any creature in his possession, but where some nobler use than its bare preservation calls for it. The state of Nature has a law of Nature to govern it, which obliges everyone, and reason, which is that law, teaches all mankind who will but consult it, that being all equal and independent, no one ought to harm another in his life, health, liberty or possessions; for men being all the workmanship of one omnipotent and infinitely wise Maker; all the servants of one sovereign Master, sent into the world by His order and about His business; they are His property, whose workmanship they are made to last during His, not one another's pleasure. And, being furnished with like faculties, sharing all in one community of Nature, there cannot be supposed any such subordination among us that may authorize us to destroy one another, as if we were made for one another's uses, as the inferior ranks of creatures are for ours. Everyone as he is bound to preserve himself, and not to quit his station willfully, so by the like reason, when his own preservation comes not in competition, ought he as much as he can to preserve the rest of mankind, and not unless it be to do justice on an offender, take away or impair the life, or what tends to the preservation of the life, the liberty, health, limb, or goods of another.

7. And that all men may be restrained from invading others' rights, and from doing hurt to one another, and the law of Nature be observed, which willeth the peace and preservation of all mankind, the execution of the law of Nature is in that state put into every man's hands, whereby everyone has a right to punish the transgressors of that law to such a degree as may hinder its violation. For the law of Nature would, as all other laws that concern men in this world, be in vain if there were nobody that in the state of Nature had a power to execute that law, and thereby preserve the innocent and restrain offenders; and if anyone in the state of Nature may punish another for any evil he has done, everyone may do so. For in that state of perfect equality, where naturally there is no superiority or jurisdiction of one over another, what any may do in prosecution of that law, everyone must needs have a right to do.

8. And thus, in the state of Nature, one man comes by a power over another, but yet no absolute or arbitrary power to use a criminal,

when he has got him in his hands, according to the passionate heats or boundless extravagancy of his own will, but only to retribute to him so far as calm reason and conscience dictate, what is proportionate to his transgression, which is so much as may serve for reparation and restraint. For these two are the only reasons why one man may lawfully do harm to another, which is that we call punishment. In transgressing the law of Nature, the offender declares himself to live by another rule than that of reason and common equity, which is that measure God has set to the actions of men for their mutual security, and so he becomes dangerous to mankind; the tie which is to secure them from injury and violence being slighted and broken by him, which being a trespass against the whole species, and the peace and safety of it, provided for by the law of Nature, every man upon this score, by the right he hath to preserve mankind in general, may restrain, or where it is necessary, destroy things noxious to them, and so may bring such evil on anyone who hath transgressed that law, as may make him repent the doing of it, and thereby deter him, and, by his example, others from doing the like mischief. And in this case, and upon this ground, every man hath a right to punish the offender, and be executioner of the law of Nature.

9. I doubt not but this will seem a very strange doctrine to some men; but before they condemn it, I desire them to resolve me by what right any prince or state can put to death or punish an alien for any crime he commits in their country? It is certain their laws, by virtue of any sanction they receive from the promulgated will of the legislature, reach not a stranger. They speak not to him, nor, if they did, is he bound to hearken to them. The legislative authority by which they are in force over the subjects of that commonwealth hath no power over him. Those who have the supreme power of making laws in England, France, or Holland are, to an Indian, but like the rest of the world—men without authority. And therefore, if by the law of Nature every man hath not a power to punish offenses against it, as he soberly judges the case to require, I see not how the magistrates of any community can punish an alien of another country, since, in reference to him, they can have no more power than what every man naturally may have over another.

10. Besides the crime which consists in violating the laws, and varying from the right rule of reason, whereby a man so far becomes degenerate, and declares himself to quit the principles of human nature and to be a noxious creature, there is commonly injury done, and some person or other, some other man, receives damage by his transgression; in which case, he who hath received any damage has (besides the right of punishment common to him, with other men) a particular right to seek reparation from him that hath done it. And any other person who finds it just may also join with him that is injured, and assist him in recovering from the offender so much as may make satisfaction for the harm he hath suffered.

11. From these two distinct rights (the one of punishing the crime, for restraint and preventing the like offense, which right of punishing is in everybody, the other of taking reparation, which belongs only to the injured party) comes it to pass that the magistrate, who by being magistrate hath the common right of punishing put into his hands, can often, where the public good demands not the execution of the law, remit the punishment of criminal offenses by his own authority, but yet cannot remit the satisfaction due to any private man for the damage he has received. That he who hath suffered the damage has a right to demand in his own name, and he alone can remit. The damnified person has this power of appropriating to himself the goods or service of the offender by right of self-preservation, as every man has a power to punish the crime to prevent its being committed again, by the right he has of preserving all mankind, and doing all reasonable things he can in order to that end.

And thus it is that every man in the state of Nature has a power to kill a murderer, both to deter others from doing the like injury (which no reparation can compensate) by the example of the punishment that attends it from everybody, and also to secure men from the attempts of a criminal who, having renounced reason, the common rule and measure God hath given to mankind, hath, by the unjust violence and slaughter he hath committed upon one, declared war against all mankind, and therefore may be destroyed as a lion or a tiger, one of those wild savage beasts with whom men can have no society nor security. And upon this is grounded that great law of Nature, "Whoso sheddeth man's blood, by man shall his blood be shed." And Cain was so fully convinced that everyone had a right to destroy such a criminal, that, after the murder of his brother, he cries out, "Everyone that findeth me shall slay me," so plain was it writ in the hearts of all mankind.

12. By the same reason may a man in the state of Nature punish the lesser breaches of that law, it will, perhaps, be demanded, with death? I answer: Each transgression may be punished to that degree, and with so much severity, as will suffice to make it an ill bargain to the offender, give him cause to repent, and terrify others from doing the like. Every offense that can be committed in the state of Nature may, in the state of Nature, be also punished equally, and as far forth, as it may, in a commonwealth. For though it would be beside my present purpose to enter here into the particulars of the law of Nature, or its measures of punishment, yet it is certain there is such a law, and that too as intelligible and plain to a rational creature and a studier of that law as the positive laws of commonwealths, nay, possibly plainer; as much as reason is easier to be understood than the fancies and intricate contrivances of men, following contrary and hidden interests put into words; for truly so are a great part of the municipal laws of countries, which are only so far right as they are founded on the law of Nature, by which they are to be regulated and interpreted.

13. To this strange doctrine—viz., That in the state of Nature everyone has the executive power of the law of Nature—I doubt not but it will be objected that it is unreasonable for men to be judges in their own cases, that self-love will make men partial to themselves and their friends; and, on the other side, ill-nature, passion, and revenge will carry them too far in punishing others, and hence nothing but confusion and disorder will follow, and that therefore God hath certainly appointed government to restrain the partiality and violence of men. I easily grant that civil government is the proper remedy for the inconveniences of the state of Nature, which must certainly be great where men may be judges in their own case, since it is easy to be imagined that he who was so unjust as to do his brother an injury will scarce be so just as to condemn himself for it. But I shall desire those who make this objection to remember that absolute monarchs are but men; and if government is to be the remedy of those evils which necessarily fol-

low from men being judges in their own cases, and the state of Nature is therefore not to be endured, I desire to know what kind of govern· ment that is, and how much better it is than the state of Nature, where one man commanding a multitude has the liberty to be judge in his own case, and may do to all his subjects whatever he pleases without the least question or control of those who execute his pleasure? and in whatsoever he doth, whether led by reason, mistake, or passion, must be submitted to? which men in the state of Nature are not bound to do one to another. And if he that judges, judges amiss in his own or any other case, he is answerable for it to the rest of mankind.

14. It is often asked as a mighty objection, where are, or ever were, there any men in such a state of Nature? To which it may suffice as an answer at present, that since all princes and rulers of "independent" governments all through the world are in a state of Nature, it is plain the world never was, nor never will be, without numbers of men in that state. I have named all govenors of "independent" communities, whether they are, or are not, in league with others; for it is not every compact that puts an end to the state of Nature between men, but only this one of agreeing together mutually to enter into one community, and make one body politic; other promises and compacts men may make one with another, and yet still be in the state of Nature. The promises and bargains for truck, etc., between the two men in Soldania, in or between a Swiss and an Indian, in the woods of America, are binding to them, though they are perfectly in a state of Nature in reference to one another for truth, and keeping of faith belongs to men as men, and not as members of society.

15. To those that say there were never any men in the state of Nature, I will not only oppose the authority of the judicious Hooker (*Eccl. Pol.* i. 10), where he says, "the laws which have been hitherto mentioned"—i.e., the laws of Nature—"do bind men absolutely, even as they are men, although they have never any settled fellowship, never any solemn agreement amongst themselves what to do or not to do; but for as much as we are not by ourselves sufficient to furnish our-selves with competent store of things needful for such a life as our Nature doth desire, a life fit for the dignity of man, therefore to supply those defects and imperfections which are in us, as living single and

solely by ourselves, we are naturally induced to seek communion and fellowship with others; this was the cause of men uniting themselves at first in politic societies." But I, moreover, affirm that all men are naturally in that state, and remain so till, by their own consents, they make themselves members of some politic society, and I doubt not, in the sequel of this discourse, to make it very clear.

CHAPTER III

Of the State of War

16. THE state of war is a state of enmity and destruction; and therefore declaring by word or action, not a passionate and hasty, but sedate, settled design upon another man's life puts him in a state of war with him against whom he has declared such an intention, and so has exposed his life to the other's power to be taken away by him, or anyone that joins with him in his defense, and espouses his quarrel; it being reasonable and just I should have a right to destroy that which threatens me with destruction; for by the fundamental law of Nature, man being to be preserved as much as possible, when all cannot be preserved, the safety of the innocent is to be preferred, and one may destroy a man who makes war upon him, or has discovered an enmity to his being, for the same reason that he may kill a wolf or a lion, because they are not under the ties of the common law of reason, have no other rule but that of force and violence, and so may be treated as a beast of prey, those dangerous and noxious creatures that will be sure to destroy him whenever he falls into their power.

17. And hence it is that he who attempts to get another man into his absolute power does thereby put himself into a state of war with him; it being to be understood as a declaration of a design upon his life. For I have reason to conclude that he who would get me into his power without my consent would use me as he pleased when he had got me there, and destroy me too when he had a fancy to it; for nobody can desire to have me in his absolute power unless it be to compel me

by force to that which is against the right of my freedom—i.e., make me a slave. To be free from such force is the only security of my preservation, and reason bids me look on him as an enemy to my preservation who would take away that freedom which is the fence to it; so that he who makes an attempt to enslave me thereby puts himself into a state of war with me. He that in the state of Nature would take away the freedom that belongs to anyone in that state must necessarily be supposed to have a design to take away everything else, that freedom being the foundation of all the rest; as he that in the state of society would take away the freedom belonging to those of that society or commonwealth must be supposed to design to take away from them everything else, and so be looked on as in a state of war.

18. This makes it lawful for a man to kill a thief who has not in the least hurt him, or declared any design upon his life, any farther than by the use of force, so to get him in his power as to take away his money, or what he pleases, from him; because using force, where he has no right to get me into his power, let his pretense be what it will, I have no reason to suppose that he who would take away my liberty would not, when he had me in his power, take away everything else. And, therefore, it is lawful for me to treat him as one who has put himself into a state of war with me—i.e., kill him if I can; for to that hazard does he justly expose himself whoever introduces a state of war, and is aggressor in it.

19. And here we have the plain difference between the state of Nature and the state of war, which however some men have confounded, are as far distant as a state of peace, goodwill, mutual assistance, and preservation; and a state of enmity, malice, violence and mutual destruction are one from another. Men living together according to reason without a common superior on earth, with authority to judge between them, is properly the state of Nature. But force, or a declared design of force upon the person of another, where there is no common superior on earth to appeal to for relief, is the state of war; and it is the want of such an appeal gives a man the right of war even against an aggressor, though he be in society and a fellow-subject. Thus, a thief whom I cannot harm, but by appeal to the law, for having

stolen all that I am worth, I may kill when he sets on me to rob me but of my horse or coat, because the law, which was made for my preservation, where it cannot interpose to secure my life from present force, which if lost is capable of no reparation, permits me my own defense and the right of war, a liberty to kill the aggressor, because the aggressor allows not time to appeal to our common judge, nor the decision of the law, for remedy in a case where the mischief may be irreparable. Want of a common judge with authority puts all men in a state of Nature; force without right upon a man's person makes a state of war both where there is, and is not, a common judge.

20. But when the actual force is over, the state of war ceases between those that are in society and are equally on both sides subject to the judge; and, therefore, in such controversies, where the question is put, "Who shall be judge?" it cannot be meant who shall decide the controversy; everyone knows what Jephtha here tells us, that "the Lord the Judge" shall judge. Where there is no judge on earth the appeal lies to God in Heaven. That question then cannot mean who shall judge, whether another hath put himself in a state of war with me, and whether I may, as Jephtha did, appeal to Heaven in it? Of that I myself can only judge in my own conscience, as I will answer it at the great day to the Supreme Judge of all men.

CHAPTER IV

Of Slavery

21. THE natural liberty of man is to be free from any superior power on earth, and not to be under the will or legislative authority of man, but to have only the law of Nature for his rule. The liberty of man in society is to be under no other legislative power but that established by consent in the commonwealth, nor under the dominion of any will, or restraint of any law, but what that legislative shall enact according to the trust put in it. Freedom, then, is not what Sir Robert

Filmer tells us: "A liberty for everyone to do what he lists, to live as he pleases, and not to be tied by any laws"; but freedom of men under government is to have a standing rule to live by, common to everyone of that society, and made by the legislative power erected in it. A liberty to follow my own will in all things where that rule prescribes not, not to be subject to the inconstant, uncertain, unknown, arbitrary will of another man, as freedom of nature is to be under no other restraint but the law of Nature.

22. This freedom from absolute, arbitrary power is so necessary to, and closely joined with, a man's preservation, that he cannot part with it but by what forfeits his preservation and life together. For a man, not having the power of his own life, cannot by compact or his own consent enslave himself to anyone, nor put himself under the absolute, arbitrary power of another to take away his life when he pleases. Nobody can give more power than he has himself, and he that cannot take away his own life cannot give another power over it. Indeed, having by his fault forfeited his own life by some act that deserves death, he to whom he has forfeited it may, when he has him in his power, delay to take it, and make use of him to his own service; and he does him no injury by it. For, whenever he finds the hardship of his slavery outweigh the value of his life, it is in his power, by resisting the will of his master, to draw on himself the death he desires.

23. This is the perfect condition of slavery, which is nothing else but the state of war continued between a lawful conqueror and a captive, for if once compact enter between them, and make an agreement for a limited power on the one side, and obedience on the other, the state of war and slavery ceases as long as the compact endures; for, as has been said, no man can by agreement pass over to another that which he hath not in himself—a power over his own life.

I confess, we find among the Jews, as well as other nations, that men did sell themselves; but it is plain this was only to drudgery, not to slavery; for it is evident the person sold was not under an absolute, arbitrary, despotical power, for the master could not have power to kill him at any time, whom at a certain time he was obliged to let go free out of his service; and the master of such a servant was so far from having an arbitrary power over his life that he could not at pleasure so much as maim him, but the loss of an eye or tooth set him free (Exod. xxi.).

CHAPTER V

Of Property

24. WHETHER we consider natural reason, which tells us that men, being once born, have a right to their preservation, and consequently to meat and drink and such other things as Nature affords for their subsistence, or "revelation," which gives us an account of those grants God made of the world to Adam, and to Noah and his sons, it is very clear that God, as King David says (Psalm cxv. 16), "has given the earth to the children of men," given it to mankind in common. But, this being supposed, it seems to some a very great difficulty how anyone should ever come to have a property in anything, I will not content myself to answer, that, if it be difficult to make out "property" upon a supposition that God gave the world to Adam and his posterity in common, it is impossible that any man but one universal monarch should have any "property" upon a supposition that God gave the world to Adam and his heirs in succession, exclusive of all the rest of his posterity; but I shall endeavor to show how men might come to have a property in several parts of that which God gave to mankind in common, and that without any express compact of all the commoners.

25. God, who hath given the world to men in common, hath also given them reason to make use of it to the best advantage of life and convenience. The earth and all that is therein is given to men for the support and comfort of their being. And though all the fruits it naturally produces, and beasts it feeds, belong to mankind in common, as they are produced by the spontaneous hand of Nature, and nobody has originally a private dominion exclusive of the rest of mankind in any of them, as they are thus in their natural state, yet being given for

the use of men, there must of necessity be a means to appropriate them some way or other before they can be of any use, or at all beneficial, to any particular men. The fruit or venison which nourishes the wild Indian, who knows no enclosure, and is still a tenant in common, must be his, and so his—i.e., a part of him, that another can no longer have any right to it before it can do him any good for the support of his life.

26. Though the earth and all inferior creatures be common to all men, yet every man has a "property" in his own "person." This nobody has any right to but himself. The "labor" of his body and the "work" of his hands, we may say, are properly his. Whatsoever, then, he removes out of the state that Nature hath provided and left it in, he hath mixed his labor with it, and joined to it something that is his own, and thereby makes it his property. It being by him removed from the common state Nature placed it in, it hath by this labor something annexed to it that excludes the common right of other men. For this "labor" being the unquestionable property of the laborer, no man but he can have a right to what that is once joined to, at least where there is enough, and as good left in common for others.

27. He that is nourished by the acorns he picked up under an oak, or the apples he gathered from the trees in the wood, has certainly appropriated them to himself. Nobody can deny but the nourishment is his. I ask, then, when did they begin to be his? when he digested? or when he ate? or when he boiled? or when he brought them home? or when he picked them up? And it is plain, if the first gathering made them not his, nothing else could. That labor put a distinction between them and common. That added something to them more than Nature, the common mother of all, had done, and so they became his private right. And will anyone say he had no right to those acorns or apples he thus appropriated because he had not the consent of all mankind to make them his? Was it a robbery thus to assume to himself what belonged to all in common? If such a consent as that was necessary, man had starved, notwithstanding the plenty God had given him. We see in commons, which remain so by compact, that it is the taking any part of what is common, and removing it out of the state Nature leaves it in, which begins the property, without which the common is of no use. And the taking of this or that part does not depend on the express

consent of all the commoners. Thus, the grass my horse has bit, the turfs my servant has cut, and the ore I have digged in any place, where I have a right to them in common with others, become my property without the assignation or consent of anybody. The labor that was mine, removing them out of that common state they were in, hath fixed my property in them.

28. By making an explicit consent of every commoner necessary to anyone's appropriating to himself any part of what is given in common. Children or servants could not cut the meat which their father or master had provided for them in common without assigning to everyone his peculiar part. Though the water running in the fountain be everyone's, yet who can doubt but that in the pitcher is his only who drew it out? His labor hath taken it out of the hands of Nature where it was common, and belonged equally to all her children, and hath thereby appropriated it to himself.

29. Thus this law of reason makes the deer that Indian's who hath killed it; it is allowed to be his goods who hath bestowed his labor upon it, though, before, it was the common right of everyone. And amongst those who are counted the civilized part of mankind, who have made and multiplied positive laws to determine property, this original law of Nature for the beginning of property, in what was before common, still takes place, and by virtue thereof, what fish anyone catches in the ocean, that great and still remaining common of mankind; or what ambergris anyone takes up here is by the labor that removes it out of that common state Nature left it in, made his property who takes that pains about it. And even amongst us, the hare that anyone is hunting is thought his who pursues her during the chase. For being a beast that is still looked upon as common, and no man's private possession, whoever has employed so much labor about any of that kind as to find and pursue her has thereby removed her from the state of Nature wherein she was common, and hath begun a property.

30. It will, perhaps, be objected to this, that if gathering the acorns or other fruits of the earth, etc., makes a right to them, then anyone may engross as much as he will. To which I answer, Not so. The same law of Nature that does by this means give us property, does also

bound that property too. "God has given us all things richly." Is the voice of reason confirmed by inspiration? But how far has He given it us "to enjoy"? As much as anyone can make use of to any advantage of life before it spoils, so much he may by his labor fix a property in. Whatever is beyond this is more than his share, and belongs to others. Nothing was made by God for man to spoil or destroy. And thus considering the plenty of natural provisions there was a long time in the world, and the few spenders, and to how small a part of that provision the industry of one man could extend itself and engross it to the prejudice of others, especially keeping within the bounds set by reason of what might serve for his use, there could be then little room for quarrels or contentions about property so established.

31. But the chief matter of property being now not the fruits of the earth and the beasts that subsist on it, but the earth itself, as that which takes in and carries with it all the rest, I think it is plain that property in that too is acquired as the former. As much land as a man tills, plants, improves, cultivates, and can use the product of, so much is his property. He by his labor does, as it were, enclose it from the common. Nor will it invalidate his right to say everybody else has an equal title to it, and therefore he cannot appropriate, he cannot enclose, without the consent of all his fellow-commoners, all mankind. God, when He gave the world in common to all mankind, commanded man also to labor, and the penury of his condition required it of him. God and his reason commanded him to subdue the earth—i.e., improve it for the benefit of life and therein lay out something upon it that was his own, his labor. He that, in obedience to this command of God, subdued, tilled, and sowed any part of it, thereby annexed to it something that was his property, which another had no title to, nor could without injury take from him.

32. Nor was this appropriation of any parcel of land, by improving it, any prejudice to any other man, since there was still enough and as good left, and more than the yet unprovided could use. So that, in effect, there was never the less left for others because of his enclosure for himself. For he that leaves as much as another can make use of does as good as take nothing at all. Nobody could think himself injured by the drinking of another man, though he took a good

draught, who had a whole river of the same water left him to quench his thirst. And the case of land and water, where there is enough of both, is perfectly the same.

33. God gave the world to men in common, but since He gave it them for their benefit and the greatest conveniencies of life they were capable to draw from it, it cannot be supposed He meant it should always remain common and uncultivated. He gave it to the use of the industrious and rational (and labor was to be his title to it) ; not to the fancy or covetousness of the quarrelsome and contentious. He that had as good left for his improvement as was already taken up needed not complain, ought not to meddle with what was already improved by another's labor; if he did it is plain he desired the benefit of an-other's pains, which he had no right to, and not the ground which God had given him, in common with others, to labor on, and whereof there was as good left as that already possessed, and more than he knew what to do with, or his industry could reach to.

34. It is true, in land that is common in England or any other country, where there are plenty of people under government who have money and commerce, no one can enclose or appropriate any part without the consent of all his fellow-commoners; because this is left common by compact—i.e., by the law of the land, which is not to be violated. And, though it be common in respect of some men, it is not so to all mankind, but is the joint propriety of this country, or this parish. Besides, the remainder, after such enclosure, would not be as good to the rest of the commoners as the whole was, when they could all make use of the whole; whereas in the beginning and first peopling of the great common of the world it was quite otherwise. The law man was under was rather for appropriating. God commanded, and his wants forced him to labor. That was his property, which could not be taken from him wherever he had fixed it. And hence subduing or cultivating the earth and having dominion, we see, are joined together. The one gave title to the other. So that God, by commanding to subdue, gave authority so far to appropriate. And the condition of human life, which requires labor and materials to work on, neces-sarily introduce private possessions.

35. The measure of property Nature well set, by the extent of

men's labor and the conveniency of life. No man's labor could subdue or appropriate all, nor could his enjoyment consume more than a small part; so that it was impossible for any man, this way, to entrench upon the right of another or acquire to himself a property to the prejudice of his neighbor, who would still have room for as good and as large a possession (after the other had taken out his) as before it was appropriated. Which measure did confine every man's possession to a very moderate proportion, and such as he might appropriate to himself without injury to anybody in the first ages of the world, when men were more in danger to be lost, by wandering from their company, in the then vast wilderness of the earth than to be straitened for want of room to plant in.

36. The same measure may be allowed still, without prejudice to anybody, full as the world seems. For, supposing a man or family, in the state they were at first, peopling of the world by the children of Adam or Noah, let him plant in some inland vacant places of America. We shall find that the possessions he could make himself, upon the measures we have given, would not be very large, nor, even to this day, prejudice the rest of mankind or give them reason to complain or think themselves injured by this man's encroachment, though the race of men have now spread themselves to all the corners of the world, and do infinitely exceed the small number at the beginning. Nay, the extent of ground is of so little value without labor that I have heard it affirmed that in Spain itself a man may be permitted to plow, sow, and reap, without being disturbed, upon land he has no other title to, but only his making use of it. But, on the contrary, the inhabitants think themselves beholden to him who, by his industry on neglected, and consequently waste land, has increased the stock of corn, which they wanted. But be this as it will, which I lay no stress on, this I dare boldly affirm, that the same rule of propriety—viz., that every man should have as much as he could make use of, would hold still in the world, without straitening anybody, since there is land enough in the world to suffice double the inhabitants, had not the invention of money, and the tacit agreement of men to put a value on it, introduced (by consent) larger possessions and a right to them; which, how it has done, I shall by and by show more at large.

37. This is certain, that in the beginning, before the desire of having more than men needed had altered the intrinsic value of things, which depends only on their usefulness to the life of man, or had agreed that a little piece of yellow metal, which would keep without wasting or decay, should be worth a great piece of flesh or a whole heap of corn, though men had a right to appropriate by their labor, each one to himself, as much of the things of Nature as he could use, yet this could not be much, nor to the prejudice of others, where the same plenty was still left, to those who would use the same industry.

Before the appropriation of land, he who gathered as much of the wild fruit, killed, caught, or tamed as many of the beasts as he could —he that so employed his pains about any of the spontaneous products of Nature as any way to alter them from the state Nature put them in, by placing any of his labor on them, did thereby acquire a propriety in them; but if they perished in his possession without their due use—if the fruits rotted or the venison putrefied before he could spend it, he offended against the common law of Nature, and was liable to be punished: he invaded his neighbor's share, for he had no right farther than his use called for any of them, and they might serve to afford him conveniencies of life.

38. The same measures governed the possession of land, too. Whatsoever he tilled and reaped, laid up and made use of before it spoiled, that was his peculiar right; whatsoever he enclosed, and could feed and make use of, the cattle and product was also his. But if either the grass of his enclosure rotted on the ground, or the fruit of his planting perished without gathering and laying up, this part of the earth, notwithstanding his enclosure, was still to be looked on as waste, and might be the possession of any other. Thus, at the beginning, Cain might take as much ground as he could till and make it his own land, and yet leave enough to Abel's sheep to feed on: a few acres would serve for both their possessions. But as families increased and industry enlarged their stocks, their possessions enlarged with the need of them; but yet it was commonly without any fixed property in the ground they made use of till they incorporated, settled themselves together, and built cities, and then, by consent, they came in

time to set out the bounds of their distinct territories and agree on limits between them and their neighbors, and by laws within themselves settled the properties of those of the same society. For we see that in that part of the world which was first inhabited, and therefore like to be best peopled, even as low down as Abraham's time, they wandered with their flocks and their herds, which was their substance, freely up and down—and this Abraham did in a country where he was a stranger; whence it is plain that, at least, a great part of the land lay in common, that the inhabitants valued it not, nor claimed property in any more than they made use of; but when there was not room enough in the same place for their herds to feed together, they, by consent, as Abraham and Lot did (Gen. xiii. 5), separated and enlarged their pasture where it best liked them. And for the same reason, Esau went from his father and his brother, and planted in Mount Seir (Gen. xxxvi. 6).

39. And thus, without supposing any private dominion and property in Adam over all the world, exclusive of all other men, which can no way be proved, nor anyone's property be made out from it, but supposing the world, given as it was to the children of men in common, we see how labor could make men distinct titles to several parcels of it for their private uses, wherein there could be no doubt of right, no room for quarrel.

40. Nor is it so strange as, perhaps, before consideration, it may appear, that the property of labor should be able to overbalance the community of land, for it is labor indeed that puts the difference of value on everything; and let anyone consider what the difference is between an acre of land planted with tobacco or sugar, sown with wheat or barley, and an acre of the same land lying in common without any husbandry upon it, and he will find that the improvement of labor makes the far greater part of the value. I think it will be but a very modest computation to say, that of the products of the earth useful to the life of man, nine-tenths are the effects of labor. Nay, if we will rightly estimate things as they come to our use, and cast up the several expenses about them—what in them is purely owing to Nature and what to labor—we shall find that in most of them ninety-nine hundredths are wholly to be put on the account of labor.

41. There cannot be a clearer demonstration of anything than several nations of the Americans are of this, who are rich in land and poor in all the comforts of life; whom Nature, having furnished as liberally as any other people with the materials of plenty—i.e., a fruitful soil, apt to produce in abundance what might serve for food, raiment, and delight; yet, for want of improving it by labor, have not one hundredth part of the conveniencies we enjoy, and a king of a large and fruitful territory there feeds, lodges, and is clad worse than a day laborer in England.

42. To make this a little clearer, let us but trace some of the ordinary provisions of life, through their several progresses, before they come to our use, and see how much they receive of their value from human industry. Bread, wine, and cloth are things of daily use and great plenty; yet notwithstanding acorns, water, and leaves, or skins must be our bread, drink and clothing, did not labor furnish us with these more useful commodities. For whatever bread is more worth than acorns, wine than water, and cloth or silk than leaves, skins or moss, that is wholly owing to labor and industry. The one of these being the food and raiment which unassisted Nature furnishes us with; the other provisions which our industry and pains prepare for us, which how much they exceed the other in value, when anyone hath computed, he will then see how much labor makes the far greatest part of the value of things we enjoy in this world; and the ground which produces the materials is scarce to be reckoned in as any, or at most, but a very small part of it; so little, that even amongst us, land that is left wholly to nature, that hath no improvement of pasturage, tillage, or planting, is called, as indeed it is, waste; and we shall find the benefit of it amount to little more than nothing.

43. An acre of land that bears here twenty bushels of wheat, and another in America, which, with the same husbandry, would do the like, are, without doubt, of the same natural, intrinsic value. But yet the benefit mankind receives from one in a year is worth five pounds, and the other possibly not worth a penny; if all the profit an Indian received from it were to be valued and sold here, at least I may truly say, not one thousandth. It is labor, then, which puts the greatest part of value upon land, without which it would scarcely be worth any·

thing; it is to that we owe the greatest part of all its useful products; for all that the straw, bran, bread, of that acre of wheat, is more worth than the product of an acre of as good land which lies waste is all the effect of labor. For it is not barely the plowman's pains, the reaper's and thresher's toil, and the baker's sweat, is to be counted into the bread we eat; the labor of those who broke the oxen, who digged and wrought the iron and stones, who felled and framed the timber employed about the plow, mill, oven, or any other utensils, which are a vast number, requisite to this corn, from its sowing to its being made bread, must all be charged on the account of labor, and received as an effect of that; Nature and the earth furnished only the almost worthless materials as in themselves. It would be a strange catalogue of things that industry provided and made use of about every loaf of bread before it came to our use if we could trace them; iron, wood, leather, bark, timber, stone, bricks, coals, lime, cloth, dyeing-drugs, pitch, tar, masts, ropes, and all the materials made use of in the ship that brought any of the commodities made use of by any of the workmen, to any part of the work, all which it would be almost impossible, at least too long, to reckon up.

44. From all which it is evident, that though the things of Nature are given in common, man (by being master of himself, and proprietor of his own person, and the actions or labor of it) had still in himself the great foundation of property; and that which made up the great part of what he applied to the support or comfort of his being, when invention and arts had improved the conveniences of life, was perfectly his own, and did not belong in common to others.

45. Thus labor, in the beginning, gave a right of property, wherever anyone was pleased to employ it, upon what was common, which remained a long while, the far greater part, and is yet more than mankind makes use of. Men at first, for the most part, contented themselves with what unassisted Nature offered to their necessities; and though afterwards, in some parts of the world, where the increase of people and stock, with the use of money, had made land scarce, and so of some value, the several communities settled the bounds of their distinct territories, and, by laws, within themselves, regulated the properties of the private men of their society, and so, by compact and

agreement, settled the property which labor and industry began. And the leagues that have been made between several states and kingdoms, either expressly or tacitly disowning all claim and right to the land in the other's possession, have, by common consent, given up their pretenses to their natural common right, which originally they had to those countries; and so have, by positive agreement, settled a property amongst themselves, in distinct parts of the world; yet there are still great tracts of ground to be found, which the inhabitants thereof, not having joined with the rest of mankind in the consent of the use of their common money, lie waste, and are more than the people who dwell on it, do, or can make use of, and so still lie in common; though this can scarce happen amongst that part of mankind that have consented to the use of money.

46. The greatest part of things really useful to the life of man, and such as the necessity of subsisting made the first commoners of the world look after—as it doth the Americans now—are generally things of short duration, such as—if they are not consumed by use—will decay and perish of themselves. Gold, silver, and diamonds are things that fancy or agreement hath put the value on, more than real use and the necessary support of life. Now of those good things which Nature hath provided in common, everyone has a right (as has been said) to as much as he could use, and had a property in all he could effect with his labor; all that his industry could extend to, to alter from the state Nature had put it in, was his. He that gathered a hundred bushels of acorns or apples had thereby a property in them; they were his goods as soon as gathered. He was only to look that he used them before they spoiled, else he took more than his share, and robbed others. And, indeed, it was a foolish thing, as well as dishonest, to hoard up more than he could make use of. If he gave away a part to anybody else, so that it perished not uselessly in his possession, these he also made use of. And if he also bartered away plums that would have rotted in a week, for nuts that would last good for his eating a whole year, he did no injury; he wasted not the common stock; destroyed no part of the portion of goods that belonged to others, so long as nothing perished uselessly in his hands. Again, if he would give his nuts for a piece of metal, pleased with its color, or exchange

his sheep for shells, or wool for a sparkling pebble or a diamond, and keep those by him all his life, he invaded not the right of others; he might heap up as much of these durable things as he pleased; the exceeding of the bounds of his just property not lying in the largeness of his possession, but the perishing of anything uselessly in it.

47. And thus came in the use of money; some lasting thing that men might keep without spoiling, and that, by mutual consent, men would take in exchange for the truly useful but perishable supports of life.

48. And as different degrees of industry were apt to give men possessions in different proportions, so this invention of money gave them the opportunity to continue and enlarge them. For supposing an island, separate from all possible commerce with the rest of the world, wherein there were but a hundred families, but there were sheep, horses, and cows, with other useful animals, wholesome fruits, and land enough for corn for a hundred thousand times as many, but nothing in the island, either because of its commonness or perishableness, fit to supply the place of money. What reason could anyone have there to enlarge his possessions beyond the use of his family, and a plentiful supply to its consumption, either in what their own industry produced, or they could barter for like perishable, useful commodities with others? Where there is not something both lasting and scarce, and so valuable to be hoarded up, there men will not be apt to enlarge their possessions of land, were it never so rich, never so free for them to take. For I ask, what would a man value ten thousand or a hundred thousand acres of excellent land, ready cultivated and well stocked, too, with cattle, in the middle of the inland parts of America, where he had no hopes of commerce with other parts of the world, to draw money to him by the sale of the product? It would not be worth the enclosing, and we should see him give up again to the wild common of Nature whatever was more than would supply the conveniences of life, to be had there for him and his family.

49. Thus, in the beginning, all the world was America, and more so than that is now; for no such thing as money was anywhere known. Find out something that hath the use and value of money amongst

his neighbors, you shall see the same man will begin presently to enlarge his possessions.

50. But since gold and silver, being little useful to the life of man, in proportion to food, raiment, and carriage, has its value only from the consent of men—whereof labor yet makes in great part the measure—it is plain that the consent of men have agreed to a disproportionate and unequal possession of the earth—I mean out of the bounds of society and compact; for in governments the laws regulate it; they having, by consent, found out and agreed in a way how a man may, rightfully and without injury, possess more than he himself can make use of by receiving gold and silver, which may continue long in a man's possession without decaying for the overplus, and agreeing those metals should have a value.

51. And thus, I think, it is very easy to conceive, without any difficulty, how labor could at first begin a title of property in the common things of Nature, and how the spending it upon our uses bounded it; so that there could then be no reason of quarreling about title, nor any doubt about the largeness of possession it gave. Right and conveniency went together. For as a man had a right to all he could employ his labor upon, so he had no temptation to labor for more than he could make use of. This left no room for controversy about the title, nor for encroachment on the right of others. What portion a man carved to himself was easily seen; and it was useless, as well as dishonest, to carve himself too much, or take more than he needed.

CHAPTER VI

Of Paternal Power

52. It may perhaps be censured as impertinent criticism in a discourse of this nature to find fault with words and names that have obtained in the world. And yet possibly it may not be amiss to offer new ones when the old are apt to lead men into mistakes, as this of paternal power probably has done, which seems so to place the power

of parents over their children wholly in the father, as if the mother had no share in it; whereas if we consult reason or revelation, we shall find she has an equal title, which may give one reason to ask whether this might not be more properly called parental power? For whatever obligation Nature and the right of generation lays on children, it must certainly bind them equal to both the concurrent causes of it. And accordingly we see the positive law of God everywhere joins them together without distinction, when it commands the obedience of children: "Honor thy father and thy mother" (Exod. xx. 12); "Whosoever curseth his father or his mother" (Lev. xx. 9); "Ye shall fear every man his mother and his father" (Lev. xix. 3); "Children, obey your parents" (Eph. vi. 1), etc., is the style of the Old and New Testament.

53. Had but this one thing been well considered without looking any deeper into the matter, it might perhaps have kept men from running into those gross mistakes they have made about this power of parents, which however it might without any great harshness bear the name of absolute dominion and regal authority, when under the title of "paternal" power, it seemed appropriated to the father; would yet have sounded but oddly, and in the very name shown the absurdity, if this supposed absolute power over children had been called parental, and thereby discovered that it belonged to the mother too. For it will but very ill serve the turn of those men who contend so much for the absolute power and authority of the fatherhood, as they call it, that the mother should have any share in it. And it would have but ill supported the monarchy they contend for, when by the very name it appeared that that fundamental authority from whence they would derive their government of a single person only was not placed in one, but two persons jointly. But to let this of names pass.

54. Though I have said above (2) "That all men by nature are equal," I cannot be supposed to understand all sorts of "equality." Age or virtue may give men a just precedency. Excellency of parts and merit may place others above the common level. Birth may subject some, and alliance or benefits others, to pay an observance to those to whom Nature, gratitude, or other respects, may have made it due; and yet all this consists with the equality which all men are in in

respect of jurisdiction or dominion one over another, which was the equality I there spoke of as proper to the business in hand, being that equal right that every man hath to his natural freedom, without being subjected to the will or authority of any other man.

55. Children, I confess, are not born in this full state of equality, though they are born to it. Their parents have a sort of rule and jurisdiction over them when they come into the world, and for some time after, but it is but a temporary one. The bonds of this subjection are like the swaddling clothes they are wrapped up in and supported by in the weakness of their infancy. Age and reason as they grow up loosen them, till at length they drop quite off, and leave a man at his own free disposal.

56. Adam was created a perfect man, his body and mind in full possession of their strength and reason, and so was capable from the first instance of his being to provide for his own support and preservation, and govern his actions according to the dictates of the law of reason God had implanted in him. From him the world is peopled with his descendants, who are all born infants, weak and helpless, without knowledge or understanding. But to supply the defects of this imperfect state till the improvement of growth and age had re-moved them, Adam and Eve, and after them all parents were, by the law of Nature, under an obligation to preserve, nourish, and educate the children they had begotten, not as their own workmanship, but the workmanship of their own Maker, the Almighty, to whom they were to be accountable for them.

57. The law that was to govern Adam was the same that was to govern all his posterity, the law of reason. But his offspring having another way of entrance into the world, different from him, by a natural birth, that produced them ignorant, and without the use of reason, they were not presently under that law. For nobody can be under a law that is not promulgated to him; and this law being pro-mulgated or made known by reason only, he that is not come to the use of his reason cannot be said to be under this law; and Adam's children being not presently as soon as born under this law of reason, were not presently free. For law, in its true notion, is not so much the limitation as the direction of a free and intelligent agent to his

proper interest, and prescribes no farther than is for the general good of those under that law. Could they be happier without it, the law, as a useless thing, would of itself vanish; and that ill deserves the name of confinement which hedges us in only from bogs and precipices. So that however it may be mistaken, the end of law is not to abolish or restrain, but to preserve and enlarge freedom. For in all the states of created beings, capable of laws, where there is no law there is no freedom. For liberty is to be free from restraint and violence from others, which cannot be where there is no law; and is not, as we are told, "a liberty for every man to do what he lists." For who could be free, when every other man's humor might domineer over him? But a liberty to dispose and order freely as he lists his person, actions, possessions, and his whole property within the allowance of those laws under which he is, and therein not to be subject to the arbitrary will of another, but freely follow his own.

58. The power, then, that parents have over their children arises from that duty which is incumbent on them, to take care of their offspring during the imperfect state of childhood. To inform the mind, and govern the actions of their yet ignorant nonage, till reason shall take its place and ease them of that trouble, is what the children want, and the parents are bound to. For God having given man an understanding to direct his actions, has allowed him a freedom of will and liberty of acting, as properly belonging thereunto within the bounds of that law he is under. But whilst he is in an estate wherein he has no understanding of his own to direct his will, he is not to have any will of his own to follow. He that understands for him must will for him too; he must prescribe to his will, and regulate his actions, but when he comes to the estate that made his father a free man, the son is a free man too.

59. This holds in all the laws a man is under, whether natural or civil. Is a man under the law of Nature? What made him free of that law? What gave him a free disposing of his property, according to his own will, within the compass of that law? I answer, an estate wherein he might be supposed capable to know that law, that so he might keep his actions within the bounds of it. When he has acquired that state, he is presumed to know how far that law is to be his

guide, and how far he may make use of his freedom, and so comes to have it; till then, somebody else must guide him, who is presumed to know how far the law allows a liberty. If such a state of reason, such an age of discretion made him free, the same shall make his son free too. Is a man under the law of England? What made him free of that law—that is, to have the liberty to dispose of his actions and posses-sions, according to his own will, within the permission of that law? A capacity of knowing that law. Which is supposed, by that law, at the age of twenty-one, and in some cases sooner. If this made the father free, it shall make the son free too. Till then, we see the law allows the son to have no will, but he is to be guided by the will of his father or guardian, who is to understand for him. And if the father die and fail to substitute a deputy in this trust, if he hath not provided a tutor to govern his son during his minority, during his want of under-standing, the law takes care to do it: some other must govern him and be a will to him till he has attained to a state of freedom, and his understanding be fit to take the government of his will. But after that the father and son are equally free, as much as tutor and pupil, after nonage, equally subjects of the same law together, without any dominion left in the father over the life, liberty, or estate of his son, whether they be only in the state and under the law of Nature, or under the positive laws of an established government.

60. But if through defects that may happen out of the ordinary course of Nature, anyone comes not to such a degree of reason wherein he might be supposed capable of knowing the law, and so living within the rules of it, he is never capable of being a free man, he is never let loose to the disposure of his own will; because he knows no bounds to it, has not understanding, its proper guide, but is continued under the tuition and government of others all the time his own under-standing is incapable of that charge. And so lunatics and idiots are never set free from the government of their parents: "Children who are not as yet come unto those years whereat they may have, and inno-cents, which are excluded by a natural defect from ever having." Thirdly, "Madmen, which, for the present, cannot possibly have the use of right reason to guide themselves, have, for their guide, the reason that guideth other men which are tutors over them, to seek

and procure their good for them," says Hooker (*Eccl. Pol.*, lib. i., s. 7). All which seems no more than that duty which God and Nature has laid on man, as well as other creatures, to preserve their offspring till they can be able to shift for themselves, and will scarce amount to an instance or proof of parents' regal authority.

61. Thus we are born free as we are born rational; not that we have actually the exercise of either: age that brings one, brings with it the other too. And thus we see how natural freedom and subjection to parents may consist together, and are both founded on the same principle. A child is free by his father's title, by his father's understanding, which is to govern him till he hath it of his own. The freedom of a man at years of discretion, and the subjection of a child to his parents, whilst yet short of it, are so consistent and so distinguishable that the most blinded contenders for monarchy, "by right of fatherhood," cannot miss of it; the most obstinate cannot but allow of it. For were their doctrine all true, were the right heir of Adam now known, and, by that title, settled a monarch in his throne, invested with all the absolute unlimited power Sir Robert Filmer talks of, if he should die as soon as his heir were born, must not the child, notwithstanding he were never so free, never so much sovereign, be in subjection to his mother and nurse, to tutors and governors, till age and education brought him reason and ability to govern himself and others? The necessities of his life, the health of his body, and the information of his mind would require him to be directed by the will of others and not his own; and yet will anyone think that this restraint and subjection were inconsistent with, or spoiled him of, that liberty or sovereignty he had a right to, or gave away his empire to those who had the government of his nonage? This government over him only prepared him the better and sooner for it. If anybody should ask me when my son is of age to be free, I shall answer, just when his monarch is of age to govern. "But at what time," says the judicious Hooker (*Eccl. Pol.*, lib. i., s. 6), "a man may be said to have attained so far forth the use of reason as sufficeth to make him capable of those laws whereby he is then bound to guide his actions; this is a great deal more easy for sense to discern than for anyone, by skill and learning, to determine."

62. Commonwealths themselves take notice of, and allow that there is a time when men are to begin to act like free men, and therefore, till that time, require not oaths of fealty or allegiance, or other public owning of, or submission to, the government of their countries.

63. The freedom then of man, and liberty of acting according to his own will, is grounded on his having reason, which is able to instruct him in that law he is to govern himself by, and make him know how far he is left to the freedom of his own will. To turn him loose to an unrestrained liberty, before he has reason to guide him, is not the allowing him the privilege of his nature to be free, but to thrust him out amongst brutes, and abandon him to a state as wretched and as much beneath that of a man as theirs. This is that which puts the authority into the parents' hands to govern the minority of their children. God has made it their business to employ this care on their offspring, and has placed in them suitable inclinations of tenderness and concern to temper this power, to apply it as His wisdom designed it, to the children's good as long as they should need to be under it.

64. But what reason can hence advance this care of the parents due to their offspring into an absolute, arbitrary dominion of the father, whose power reaches no farther than by such a discipline as he finds most effectual to give such strength and health to their bodies, such vigor and rectitude to their minds, as may best fit his children to be most useful to themselves and others, and, if it be necessary to his condition, to make them work when they are able for their own subsistence; but in this power the mother, too, has her share with the father.

65. Nay, this power so little belongs to the father by any peculiar right of Nature, but only as he is guardian of his children, that when he quits his care of them he loses his power over them, which goes along with their nourishment and education, to which it is inseparably annexed, and belongs as much to the foster-father of an exposed child as to the natural father of another. So little power does the bare act of begetting give a man over his issue, if all his care ends there, and this be all the title he has to the name and authority of a father. And what will become of this paternal power in that part of the world where one woman hath more than one husband at a

time? or in those parts of America where, when the husband and wife part, which happens frequently, the children are all left to the mother, follow her, and are wholly under her care and provision? And if the father die whilst the children are young, do they not naturally everywhere owe the same obedience to their mother, during their minority, as to their father, were he alive? And will anyone say that the mother has a legislative power over her children that she can make standing rules which shall be of perpetual obligation, by which they ought to regulate all the concerns of their property, and bound their liberty all the course of their lives, and enforce the observation of them with capital punishments? For this is the proper power of the magistrate, of which the father has not so much as the shadow. His command over his children is but temporary, and reaches not their life or property. It is but a help to the weakness and imperfection of their nonage, a discipline necessary to their education. And though a father may dispose of his own possessions as he pleases when his children are out of danger of perishing for want, yet his power extends not to the lives or goods which either their own industry, or another's bounty, has made theirs, nor to their liberty neither, when they are once arrived to the enfranchisement of the years of discretion. The father's empire then ceases, and he can from thenceforward no more dispose of the liberty of his son than that of any other man. And it must be far from an absolute or perpetual jurisdiction from which a man may withdraw himself, having license from Divine authority to "leave father and mother and cleave to his wife."

66. But though there be a time when a child comes to be as free from subjection to the will and command of his father as he himself is free from subjection to the will of anybody else, and they are both under no other restraint but that which is common to them both, whether it be the law of Nature or municipal law of their country, yet this freedom exempts not a son from that honor which he ought, by the law of God and Nature, to pay his parents, God having made the parents instruments in His great design of continuing the race of mankind and the occasions of life to their children. As He has laid on them an obligation to nourish, preserve, and bring up their offspring, so He has laid on the children a perpetual obligation of honoring their

parents, which, containing in it an inward esteem and reverence to be shown by all outward expressions, ties up the child from anything that may ever injure or affront, disturb or endanger the happiness or life of those from whom he received his, and engages him in all actions of defense, relief, assistance, and comfort of those by whose means he entered into being and has been made capable of any enjoyments of life. From this obligation no state, no freedom, can absolve children. But this is very far from giving parents a power of command over their children, or an authority to make laws and dispose as they please of their lives or liberties. It is one thing to owe honor, respect, gratitude, and assistance; another to require an absolute obedience and submission. The honor due to parents a monarch on his throne owes his mother, and yet this lessens not his authority nor subjects him to her government.

67. The subjection of a minor places in the father a temporary government which terminates with the minority of the child; and the honor due from a child places in the parents a perpetual right to respect, reverence, support, and compliance, to more or less, as the father's care, cost, and kindness in his education has been more or less, and this ends not with minority, but holds in all parts and conditions of a man's life. The want of distinguishing these two powers which the father has, in the right of tuition, during minority, and the right of honor all his life, may perhaps have caused a great part of the mistakes about this matter. For, to speak properly of them, the first of these is rather the privilege of children and duty of parents than any prerogative of paternal power. The nourishment and education of their children is a charge so incumbent on parents for their children's good, that nothing can absolve them from taking care of it. And though the power of commanding and chastising them go along with it, yet God hath woven into the principles of human nature such a tenderness for their offspring, that there is little fear that parents should use their power with too much rigor; the excess is seldom on the severe side, the strong bias of nature drawing the other way. And therefore God Almighty, when He would express His gentle dealing with the Israelites, He tells them that though He chastened them, "He chastened them as a man chastens his son"

(Deut. viii. 5)—i.e., with tenderness and affection, and kept them under no severer discipline than what was absolutely best for them, and had been less kindness to have slackened. This is that power to which children are commanded obedience, that the pains and care of their parents may not be increased or ill-rewarded.

68. On the other side, honor and support all that which gratitude requires to return; for the benefits received by and from them is the indispensable duty of the child and the proper privilege of the parents. This is intended for the parents' advantage, as the other is for the child's; though education, the parents' duty, seems to have most power, because the ignorance and infirmities of childhood stand in need of restraint and correction, which is a visible exercise of rule and a kind of dominion. And that duty which is comprehended in the word "honor" requires less obedience, though the obligation be stronger on grown than younger children. For who can think the command, "Children, obey your parents," requires in a man that has children of his own the same submission to his father as it does in his yet young children to him, and that by this precept he were bound to obey all his father's commands, if, out of a conceit of authority, he should have the indiscretion to treat him still as a boy?

69. The first part, then, of paternal power, or rather duty, which is education, belongs so to the father that it terminates at a certain season. When the business of education is over it ceases of itself, and is also alienable before. For a man may put the tuition of his son in other hands; and he that has made his son an apprentice to another has discharged him, during that time, of a great part of his obedience, both to himself and to his mother. But all the duty of honor, the other part, remains nevertheless entire to them; nothing can cancel that. It is so inseparable from them both, that the father's authority cannot dispossess the mother of this right, nor can any man discharge his son from honoring her that bore him. But both these are very far from a power to make laws, and enforcing them with penalties that may reach estate, liberty, limbs, and life. The power of commanding ends with nonage, and though after that honor and respect, support and defense, and whatsoever gratitude can oblige a man to, for the highest benefits he is naturally capable of be always

due from a son to his parents, yet all this puts no scepter into the father's hand, no sovereign power of commanding. He has no dominion over his son's property or actions, nor any right that his will should prescribe to his son's in all things; however, it may become his son in many things, not very inconvenient to him and his family, to pay a deference to it.

70. A man may owe honor and respect to an ancient or wise man, defense to his child or friend, relief and support to the distressed, and gratitude to a benefactor, to such a degree that all he has, all he can do, cannot sufficiently pay it. But all these give no authority, no right of making laws to anyone over him from whom they are owing. And it is plain all this is due, not to the bare title of father, not only because, as has been said, it is owing to the mother too, but because these obligations to parents, and the degrees of what is required of children, may be varied by the different care and kindness, trouble and expense, is often employed upon one child more than another.

71. This shows the reason how it comes to pass that parents in societies, where they themselves are subjects, retain a power over their children and have as much right to their subjection as those who are in the state of Nature, which could not possibly be if all political power were only paternal, and that, in truth, they were one and the same thing; for then, all paternal power being in the prince, the subject could naturally have none of it. But these two powers, political and paternal, are so perfectly distinct and separate, and built upon so different foundations, and given to so different ends, that every subject that is a father has as much a paternal power over his children as the prince has over his. And every prince that has parents owes them as much filial duty and obedience as the meanest of his subjects do to theirs, and can therefore contain not any part or degree of that kind of dominion which a prince or magistrate has over his subjects.

72. Though the obligation on the parents to bring up their children, and the obligation on children to honor their parents, contain all the power, on the one hand, and submission on the other, which are proper to this relation, yet there is another power ordinarily in the

father, whereby he has a tie on the obedience of his children, which, though it be common to him with other men, yet the occasions of showing it, almost constantly happening to fathers in their private families and in instances of it elsewhere being rare, and less taken notice of, it passes in the world for a part of "paternal jurisdiction." And this is the power men generally have to bestow their estates on those who please them best. The possessions of the father being the expectation and inheritance of the children ordinarily, in certain proportions, according to the law and custom of each country, yet it is commonly in the father's power to bestow it with a more sparing or liberal hand, according as the behavior of this or that child hath comported with his will and humor.

73. This is no small tie to the obedience of children; and there being always annexed to the enjoyment of land a submission to the government of the country of which that land is a part, it has been commonly supposed that a father could oblige his posterity to that government of which he himself was a subject, that his compact held them; whereas, it being only a necessary condition annexed to the land which is under that government, reaches only those who will take it on that condition, and so is no natural tie or engagement, but a voluntary submission; for every man's children being, by Nature, as free as himself or any of his ancestors ever were, may, whilst they are in that freedom, choose what society they will join themselves to, what commonwealth they will put themselves under. But if they will enjoy the inheritance of their ancestors, they must take it on the same terms their ancestors had it, and submit to all the conditions annexed to such a possession. By this power, indeed, fathers oblige their children to obedience to themselves even when they are past minority, and most commonly, too, subject them to this or that political power. But neither of these by any peculiar right of father-hood, but by the reward they have in their hands to enforce and recompense such a compliance, and is no more power than what a Frenchman has over an Englishman, who, by the hopes of an estate he will leave him, will certainly have a strong tie on his obedience; and if when it is left him, he will enjoy it, he must certainly take it

upon the conditions annexed to the possession of land in that country where it lies, whether it be France or England.

74. To conclude, then, though the father's power of commanding extends no farther than the minority of his children, and to a degree only fit for the discipline and government of that age; and though that honor and respect, and all that which the Latins called piety, which they indispensably owe to their parents all their lifetime, and in all estates, with all that support and defense, is due to them, gives the father no power of governing—i.e., making laws and exacting penalties on his children; though by this he has no dominion over the property or actions of his son, yet it is obvious to conceive how easy it was, in the first ages of the world, and in places still where the thinness of people gives families leave to separate into unpossessed quarters, and they have room to remove and plant themselves in yet vacant habitations, for the father of the family to become the prince of it; [4] he had been a ruler from the beginning of the infancy of his children; and when they were grown up, since without some government it would be hard for them to live together, it was likeliest it should, by the express or tacit consent of the children, be in the father, where it seemed, without any change, barely to continue. And when, indeed, nothing more was required to it than the

[4] "It is no improbable opinion, therefore, which the arch-philosopher was of, That the chief person in every household was always, as it were, a king; so when numbers of households joined themselves in civil societies together, kings were the first kind of governors among them, which is also, as it seemeth, the reason why the name of fathers continued still in them, who of fathers were made rulers; as also the ancient custom of governors to do as Melchizedec; and being kings, to exercise the office of priests, which fathers did, at the first, grew, perhaps, by the same occasion. Howbeit, this is not the only kind of regimen that has been received in the world. The inconveniencies of one kind have caused sundry others to be devised, so that, in a word, all public regimen, of what kind soever, seemeth evidently to have risen from the deliberate advice, consultation and composition between men, judging it convenient and behoveful, there being no impossibility in Nature, considered by itself, but that man might have lived without any public regimen."—Hooker, *Eccl. Pol.,* lib. i. s. 10. (L.)

permitting the father to exercise alone in his family that executive power of the law of Nature which every free man naturally hath, and by that permission resigning up to him a monarchical power whilst they remained in it. But that this was not by any paternal right, but only by the consent of his children, is evident from hence, that nobody doubts but if a stranger, whom chance or business had brought to his family, had there killed any of his children, or committed any other act, he might condemn and put him to death, or otherwise have punished him as well as any of his children, which was impossible he should do by virtue of any paternal authority over one who was not his child, but by virtue of that executive power of the law of Nature which, as a man, he had a right to; and he alone could punish him in his family where the respect of his children had laid by the exercise of such a power, to give way to the dignity and authority they were willing should remain in him above the rest of his family.

75. Thus it was easy and almost natural for children, by a tacit and almost natural consent, to make way for the father's authority and government. They had been accustomed in their childhood to follow his direction, and to refer their little differences to him; and when they were men, who was fitter to rule them? Their little properties and less covetousness seldom afforded greater controversies; and when any should arise, where could they have a fitter umpire than he, by whose care they had every one been sustained and brought up, and who had a tenderness for them all? It is no wonder that they made no distinction betwixt minority and full age, nor looked after one-and-twenty, or any other age, that might make them the free disposers of themselves and fortunes, when they could have no desire to be out of their pupilage. The government they had been under during it continued still to be more their protection than restraint; and they could nowhere find a greater security to their peace, liberties, and fortunes than in the rule of a father.

76. Thus the natural fathers of families, by an insensible change, became the politic monarchs of them too; and as they chanced to live long, and leave able and worthy heirs for several successions or otherwise, so they laid the foundations of hereditary or elective kingdoms under several constitutions and manors, according as chance,

contrivance, or occasions happened to mold them. But if princes have their titles in the father's right, and it be a sufficient proof of the natural right of fathers to political authority, because they commonly were those in whose hands we find, *de facto,* the exercise or government, I say, if this argument be good, it will as strongly prove that all princes, nay, princes only, ought to be priests, since it is as certain that in the beginning "the father of the family was priest, as that he was ruler in his own household."

CHAPTER VII

Of Political or Civil Society

77. GOD, having made man such a creature that, in His own judgment, it was not good for him to be alone, put him under strong obligations of necessity, convenience, and inclination, to drive him into society, as well as fitted him with understanding and language to continue and enjoy it. The first society was between man and wife, which gave beginning to that between parents and children, to which, in time, that between master and servant came to be added. And though all these might, and commonly did, meet together, and make up but one family, wherein the master or mistress of it had some sort of rule proper to a family, each of these, or all together, came short of "political society," as we shall see if we consider the different ends, ties, and bounds of each of these.

78. Conjugal society is made by a voluntary compact between man and woman, and though it consist chiefly in such a communion and right in one another's bodies as is necessary to its chief end, procreation, yet it draws with it mutual support and assistance, and a communion of interests too, as necessary not only to unite their care and affection, but also necessary to their common offspring, who have a right to be nourished and maintained by them till they are able to provide for themselves.

79. For the end of conjunction between male and female being not barely procreation, but the continuation of the species, this con-

junction betwixt male and female ought to last, even after procreation, so long as is necessary to the nourishment and support of the young ones, who are to be sustained by those that got them till they are able to shift and provide for themselves. This rule, which the infinite wise Maker hath set to the works of His hands, we find the inferior creatures steadily obey. In those viviparous animals which feed on grass the conjunction between male and female lasts no longer than the very act of copulation, because the teat of the dam being sufficient to nourish the young till it be able to feed on grass, the male only begets, but concerns not himself for the female or young, to whose sustenance he can contribute nothing. But in beasts of prey the conjunction lasts longer, because the dam, not being able well to subsist herself and nourish her numerous offspring by her own prey alone (a more laborious as well as more dangerous way of living than by feeding on grass), the assistance of the male is necessary to the maintenance of their common family, which cannot subsist till they are able to prey for themselves, but by the joint care of male and female. The same is observed in all birds (except some domestic ones, where plenty of food excuses the cock from feeding and taking care of the young brood), whose young, needing food in the nest, the cock and hen continue mates till the young are able to use their wings and provide for themselves.

80. And herein, I think, lies the chief, if not the only reason, why the male and female in mankind are tied to a longer conjunction than other creatures—viz., because the female is capable of conceiving, and, *de facto,* is commonly with child again, and brings forth too a new birth, long before the former is out of a dependency for support on his parents' help and able to shift for himself, and has all the assistance due to him from his parents, whereby the father, who is bound to take care for those he has begot, is under an obligation to continue in conjugal society with the same woman longer than other creatures, whose young, being able to subsist of themselves before the time of procreation returns again, the conjugal bond dissolves of itself, and they are at liberty till Hymen, at his usual anniversary season, summons them again to choose new mates. Wherein one cannot but admire the wisdom of the great Creator, who, having given

to man an ability to lay up for the future as well as supply the present necessity, hath made it necessary that society of man and wife should be more lasting than of male and female amongst other creatures, that so their industry might be encouraged, and their interest better united, to make provision and lay up goods for their common issue, which uncertain mixture, or easy and frequent solutions of conjugal society, would mightily disturb.

81. But though these are ties upon mankind which make the conjugal bonds more firm and lasting in a man than the other species of animals, yet it would give one reason to inquire why this compact, where procreation and education are secured and inheritance taken care for, may not be made determinable, either by consent, or at a certain time, or upon certain conditions, as well as any other voluntary compacts, there being no necessity, in the nature of the thing, nor to the ends of it, that it should always be for life—I mean, to such as are under no restraint of any positive law which ordains all such contracts to be perpetual.

82. But the husband and wife, though they have but one common concern, yet having different understandings, will unavoidably sometimes have different wills too. It therefore being necessary that the last determination (i.e., the rule) should be placed somewhere, it naturally falls to the man's share as the abler and the stronger. But this, reaching but to the things of their common interest and property, leaves the wife in the full and true possession of what by contract is her peculiar right, and at least gives the husband no more power over her than she has over his life; the power of the husband being so far from that of an absolute monarch that the wife has, in many cases, a liberty to separate from him where natural right or their contract allows it, whether that contract be made by themselves in the state of Nature or by the customs or laws of the country they live in, and the children, upon such separation, fall to the father or mother's lot as such contract does determine.

83. For all the ends of marriage being to be obtained under politic government, as well as in the state of Nature, the civil magistrate doth not abridge the right or power of either, naturally necessary to those ends—viz., procreation and mutual support and as

sistance whilst they are together, but only decides any controversy that may arise between man and wife about them. If it were otherwise, and that absolute sovereignty and power of life and death naturally belonged to the husband, and were necessary to the society between man and wife, there could be no matrimony in any of these countries where the husband is allowed no such absolute authority. But the ends of matrimony requiring no such power in the husband, it was not at all necessary to it. The condition of conjugal society put it not in him; but whatsoever might consist with procreation and support of the children till they could shift for themselves—mutual assistance, comfort, and maintenance—might be varied and regulated by that contract which first united them in that society, nothing being necessary to any society that is not necessary to the ends for which it is made.

84. The society betwixt parents and children, and the distinct rights and powers belonging respectively to them, I have treated of so largely in the foregoing chapter that I shall not here need to say anything of it; and I think it is plain that it is far different from a politic society.

85. Master and servant are names as old as history, but given to those of far different condition; for a free man makes himself a servant to another by selling him for a certain time the service he undertakes to do in exchange for wages he is to receive; and though this commonly puts him into the family of his master, and under the ordinary discipline thereof, yet it gives the master but a temporary power over him, and no greater than what is contained in the contract between them. But there is another sort of servant which by a peculiar name we call slaves, who being captives taken in a just war are, by the right of Nature, subjected to the absolute dominion and arbitrary power of their masters. These men having, as I say, forfeited their lives and, with it, their liberties, and lost their estates, and being in the state of slavery, not capable of any property, cannot in that state be considered as any part of civil society, the chief end whereof is the preservation of property.

86. Let us therefore consider a master of a family with all these subordinate relations of wife, children, servants and slaves, united

under the domestic rule of a family, with what resemblance soever it may have in its order, offices, and number too, with a little commonwealth, yet is very far from it both in its constitution, power, and end; or if it must be thought a monarchy, and the paterfamilias the absolute monarch in it, absolute monarchy will have but a very shattered and short power, when it is plain by what has been said before, that the master of the family has a very distinct and differently limited power both as to time and extent over those several persons that are in it; for excepting the slave (and the family is as much a family, and his power as paterfamilias as great, whether there be any slaves in his family or no) he has no legislative power of life and death over any of them, and none too but what a mistress of a family may have as well as he. And he certainly can have no absolute power over the whole family who has but a very limited one over every individual in it. But how a family, or any other society of men, differ from that which is properly political society, we shall best see by considering wherein political society itself consists.

87. Man being born, as has been proved, with a title to perfect freedom and an uncontrolled enjoyment of all the rights and privileges of the law of Nature, equally with any other man, or number of men in the world, has by nature a power not only to preserve his property—that is, his life, liberty, and estate, against the injuries and attempts of other men, but to judge of and punish the breaches of that law in others, as he is persuaded the offense deserves, even with death itself, in crimes where the heinousness of the fact, in his opinion, requires it. But because no political society can be, nor subsist, without having in itself the power to preserve the property, and in order thereunto punish the offenses of all those of that society, there, and there only, is political society where every one of the members has quitted this natural power, resigned it up into the hands of the community in all cases that exclude him not from appealing for protection to the law established by it. And thus all private judgment of every particular member being excluded, the community comes to be umpire, and by understanding indifferent rules and men authorized by the community for their execution, decides all the differences that may happen between any members of that society con-

cerning any matter of right, and punishes those offenses which any member hath committed against the society with such penalties as the law has established; whereby it is easy to discern who are, and are not, in political society together. Those who are united into one body, and have a common established law and judicature to appeal to, with authority to decide controversies between them and punish offenders, are in civil society one with another; but those who have no such common appeal, I mean on earth, are still in the state of Nature, each being where there is no other, judge for himself and executioner; which is, as I have before showed it, the perfect state of Nature.

88. And thus the commonwealth comes by a power to set down what punishment shall belong to the several transgressions they think worthy of it, committed amongst the members of that society (which is the power of making laws), as well as it has the power to punish any injury done unto any of its members by anyone that is not of it (which is the power of war and peace) ; and all this for the preservation of the property of all the members of that society, as far as is possible. But though every man entered into society has quitted his power to punish offenses against the law of Nature in prosecution of his own private judgment, yet with the judgment of offenses which he has given up to the legislative, in all cases where he can appeal to the magistrate, he has given up a right to the commonwealth to employ his force for the execution of the judgments of the commonwealth whenever he shall be called to it, which, indeed, are his own judgments, they being made by himself or his representative. And herein we have the original of the legislative and executive power of civil society, which is to judge by standing laws how far offenses are to be punished when committed within the commonwealth; and also by occasional judgments founded on the present circumstances of the fact, how far injuries from without are to be vindicated, and in both these to employ all the force of all the members when there shall be need.

89. Wherever, therefore, any number of men so unite into one society as to quit every one his executive power of the law of Nature, and to resign it to the public, there and there only is a political or civil society. And this is done wherever any number of men, in the

state of Nature, enter into society to make one people one body politic under one supreme government: or else when anyone joins himself to, and incorporates with any government already made. For hereby he authorizes the society, or which is all one, the legislative thereof, to make laws for him as the public good of the society shall require, to the execution whereof his own assistance (as to his own decrees) is due. And this puts men out of a state of Nature into that of a commonwealth, by setting up a judge on earth with authority to determine all the controversies and redress the injuries that may happen to any member of the commonwealth, which judge is the legislative or magistrates appointed by it. And wherever there are any number of men, however associated, that have no such decisive power to appeal to, there they are still in the state of Nature.

90. And hence it is evident that absolute monarchy, which by some men is counted for the only government in the world, is indeed inconsistent with civil society, and so can be no form of civil government at all. For the end of civil society being to avoid and remedy those inconveniencies of the state of Nature which necessarily follow from every man's being judge in his own case, by setting up a known authority to which every one of that society may appeal upon any injury received, or controversy that may arise, and which every one of the society ought to obey.[5] Wherever any persons are who have not such an authority to appeal to, and decide any difference between them there, those persons are still in the state of Nature. And so is every absolute prince in respect of those who are under his dominion.

91. For he being supposed to have all, both legislative and executive, power in himself alone, there is no judge to be found, no appeal lies open to anyone, who may fairly and indifferently, and with authority decide, and from whence relief and redress may be expected of any injury or inconveniency that may be suffered from him, or by his order. So that such a man, however entitled, Czar, or

[5] "The public power of all society is above every soul contained in the same society, and the principal use of that power is to give laws unto all that are under it, which laws in such cases we must obey, unless there be reason showed which may necessarily enforce that the law of reason or of God doth enjoin the contrary."—Hooker, *Eccl. Pol.*, lib. i., s. 16. (L.)

Grand Signior, or how you please, is as much in the state of Nature, with all under his dominion, as he is with the rest of mankind. For wherever any two men are, who have no standing rule and common judge to appeal to on earth, for the determination of controversies of right betwixt them, there they are still in the state of Nature, and under all the inconveniencies of it, with only this woeful difference to the subject, or rather slave of an absolute prince.[6] That whereas, in the ordinary state of Nature, he has a liberty to judge of his right, according to the best of his power to maintain it; but whenever his property is invaded by the will and order of his monarch, he has not only no appeal, as those in society ought to have, but, as if he were degraded from the common state of rational creatures, is denied a liberty to judge of, or defend his right, and so is exposed to all the misery and inconveniencies that a man can fear from one, who being in the unrestrained state of Nature, is yet corrupted with flattery and armed with power.

92. For he that thinks absolute power purifies men's blood, and corrects the baseness of human nature, need read but the history of this, or any other age, to be convinced to the contrary. He that would

[6] "To take away all such mutual grievances, injuries, and wrongs—i.e., such as attend men in the state of Nature, there was no way but only by growing into composition and agreement amongst themselves by ordaining some kind of government public, and by yielding themselves subject thereunto, that unto whom they granted authority to rule and govern, by them the peace, tranquillity, and happy estate of the rest might be procured. Men always knew that where force and injury was offered, they might be defenders of themselves. They knew that, however men may seek their own commodity, yet if this were done with injury unto others, it was not to be suffered, but by all men and all good means to be withstood. Finally, they knew that no man might, in reason, take upon him to determine his own right, and according to his own determination proceed in maintenance thereof, in as much as every man is towards himself, and them whom he greatly affects, partial; and therefore, that strifes and troubles would be endless, except they gave their common consent, all to be ordered by some whom they should agree upon, without which consent there would be no reason that one man should take upon him to be lord or judge over another."—Hooker, *ibid.*, s. 10. (L)

have been insolent and injurious in the woods of America would not probably be much better on a throne, where perhaps learning and religion shall be found out to justify all that he shall do to his subjects, and the sword presently silence all those that dare question it. For what the protection of absolute monarchy is, what kind of fathers of their countries it makes princes to be, and to what a degree of happiness and security it carries civil society, where this sort of government is grown to perfection, he that will look into the late relation of Ceylon may easily see.

93. In absolute monarchies, indeed, as well as other governments of the world, the subjects have an appeal to the law, and judges to decide any controversies, and restrain any violence that may happen betwixt the subjects themselves, one amongst another. This everyone thinks necessary, and believes; he deserves to be thought a declared enemy to society and mankind who should go about to take it away. But whether this be from a true love of mankind and society, and such a charity as we owe all one to another, there is reason to doubt. For this is no more than what every man, who loves his own power, profit, or greatness, may, and naturally must do, keep those animals from hurting or destroying one another who labor and drudge only for his pleasure and advantage; and so are taken care of, not out of any love the master has for them, but love of himself, and the profit they bring him. For if it be asked what security, what fence is there in such a state against the violence and oppression of this absolute ruler, the very question can scarce be borne. They are ready to tell you that it deserves death only to ask after safety. Betwixt subject and subject, they will grant, there must be measures, laws, and judges for their mutual peace and security. But as for the ruler, he ought to be absolute, and is above all such circumstances; because he has a power to do more hurt and wrong, it is right when he does it. To ask how you may be guarded from harm or injury on that side, where the strongest hand is to do it, is presently the voice of faction and rebellion. As if when men, quitting the state of Nature, entered into society, they agreed that all of them but one should be under the restraint of laws; but that he should still retain all the liberty of the state of Nature, increased with power, and made licentious by im-

punity. This is to think that men are so foolish that they take care to avoid what mischiefs may be done them by polecats or foxes, but are content, nay, think it safety, to be devoured by lions.

94. But, whatever flatterers may talk to amuse people's understandings, it never hinders men from feeling; and when they perceive that any man, in what station soever, is out of the bounds of the civil society they are of, and that they have no appeal, on earth, against any harm they may receive from him, they are apt to think themselves in the state of Nature, in respect of him whom they find to be so; and to take care, as soon as they can, to have that safety and security, in civil society, for which it was first instituted, and for which only they entered into it. And therefore, though perhaps at first, as shall be showed more at large hereafter, in the following part of this discourse, some one good and excellent man having got a pre-eminency amongst the rest, had this deference paid to his goodness and virtue, as to a kind of natural authority, that the chief rule, with arbitration of their differences, by a tacit consent devolved into his hands, without any other caution but the assurance they had of his uprightness and wisdom; yet when time giving authority, and, as some men would persuade us, sacredness to customs, which the negligent and unforeseeing innocence of the first ages began, had brought in successors of another stamp, the people finding their properties not secure under the government as then it was [7] (whereas government has no other end but the preservation of property), could never be safe, nor at rest, nor think themselves in civil society, till the legislative was so placed in collective bodies of men, call them senate, parliament, or what you please, by which means every single person became subject equally,

[7] "At the first, when some certain kind of regimen was once appointed, it may be that nothing was then further thought upon for the manner of governing, but all permitted unto their wisdom and discretion which were to rule till, by experience, they found this for all parts very inconvenient, so as the thing which they had devised for a remedy did indeed but increase the sore which it should have cured. They saw that to live by one man's will became the cause of all men's misery. This constrained them to come unto laws wherein all men might see their duty beforehand, and know the penalties of transgressing them."—Hooker, *Eccl. Pol.*, lib. i., s. 10. (L.)

with other the meanest men, to those laws, which he himself, as part of the legislative, had established; nor could anyone, by his own authority, avoid the force of the law, when once made, nor by any pretense of superiority plead exemption, thereby to license his own, or the miscarriages of any of his dependents. No man in civil society can be exempted from the laws of it. For if any man may do what he thinks fit and there be no appeal on earth for redress or security against any harm he shall do, I ask whether he be not perfectly still in the state of Nature, and so can be no part or member of that civil society, unless anyone will say the state of Nature and civil society are one and the same thing, which I have never yet found anyone so great a patron of anarchy as to affirm.[8]

CHAPTER VIII

Of the Beginning of Political Societies

95. MEN being, as has been said, by nature all free, equal, and independent, no one can be put out of this estate and subjected to the political power of another without his own consent, which is done by agreeing with other men, to join and unite into a community for their comfortable, safe, and peaceable living, one amongst another, in a secure enjoyment of their properties, and a greater security against any that are not of it. This any number of men may do, because it injures not the freedom of the rest; they are left, as they were, in the liberty of the state of Nature. When any number of men have so consented to make one community or government, they are thereby presently incorporated, and make one body politic, wherein the majority have a right to act and conclude the rest.

96. For, when any number of men have, by the consent of every individual, made a community, they have thereby made that community one body, with a power to act as one body, which is only by

[8] "Civil law, being the act of the whole body politic, doth therefore overrule each several part of the same body."—Hooker, *ibid.* (L.)

the will and determination of the majority. For that which acts any community, being only the consent of the individuals of it, and it being one body, must move one way, it is necessary the body should move that way whither the greater force carries it, which is the consent of the majority, or else it is impossible it should act or continue one body, one community, which the consent of every individual that united into it agreed that it should; and so everyone is bound by that consent to be concluded by the majority. And therefore we see that in assemblies empowered to act by positive laws where no number is set by that positive law which empowers them, the act of the majority passes for the act of the whole, and of course determines as having, by the law of Nature and reason, the power of the whole.

97. And thus every man, by consenting with others to make one body politic under one government, puts himself under an obligation to everyone of that society to submit to the determination of the majority, and to be concluded by it; or else this original compact, whereby he with others incorporates into one society, would signify nothing, and be no compact if he be left free and under no other ties than he was in before in the state of Nature. For what appearance would there be of any compact? What new engagement if he were no farther tied by any decrees of the society than he himself thought fit and did actually consent to? This would be still as great a liberty as he himself had before his compact, or anyone else in the state of Nature, who may submit himself and consent to any acts of it if he thinks fit.

98. For if the consent of the majority shall not in reason be received as the act of the whole, and conclude every individual, nothing but the consent of every individual can make anything to be the act of the whole, which, considering the infirmities of health and avocations of business, which in a number though much less than that of a commonwealth, will necessarily keep many away from the public assembly; and the variety of opinions and contrariety of interests which unavoidably happen in all collections of men, it is next impossible ever to be had. And, therefore, if coming into society be upon such terms, it will be only like Cato's coming into the theater, *tantum ut exiret*.[9] Such a

[9] Merely to go out again

constitution as this would make the mighty leviathan of a shorter duration than the feeblest creatures, and not let it outlast the day it was born in, which cannot be supposed till we can think that rational creatures should desire and constitute societies only to be dissolved. For where the majority cannot conclude the rest, there they cannot act as one body, and consequently will be immediately dissolved again.

99. Whosoever, therefore, out of a state of Nature unite into a community, must be understood to give up all the power necessary to the ends for which they unite into society to the majority of the community, unless they expressly agreed in any number greater than the majority. And this is done by barely agreeing to unite into one political society, which is all the compact that is, or needs be, between the individuals that enter into or make up a commonwealth. And thus, that which begins and actually constitutes any political society is nothing but the consent of any number of freemen capable of majority, to unite and incorporate into such a society. And this is that, and that only, which did or could give beginning to any lawful government in the world.

100. To this I find two objections made: 1. That there are no instances to be found in story of a company of men, independent and equal one amongst another, that met together, and in this way began and set up a government. 2. It is impossible of right that men should do so, because all men, being born under government, they are to submit to that, and are not at liberty to begin a new one.

101. To the first there is this to answer: That it is not at all to be wondered that history gives us but a very little account of men that lived together in the state of Nature. The inconveniencies of that condition, and the love and want of society, no sooner brought any number of them together, but they presently united and incorporated if they designed to continue together. And if we may not suppose men ever to have been in the state of Nature, because we hear not much of them in such a state, we may as well suppose the armies of Salmanasser or Xerxes were never children, because we hear little of them till they were men and embodied in armies. Government is everywhere antecedent to records, and letters seldom come in amongst a people till a long continuation of civil society has, by other more necessary arts,

provided for their safety, ease, and plenty. And then they begin to look after the history of their founders, and search into their original when they have outlived the memory of it. For it is with commonwealths as with particular persons, they are commonly ignorant of their own births and infancies; and if they know anything of it, they are beholding for it to the accidental records that others have kept of it. And those that we have of the beginning of any polities in the world, excepting that of the Jews, where God Himself immediately interposed, and which favors not at all paternal dominion, are all either plain instances of such a beginning as I have mentioned, or at least have manifest footsteps of it.

102. He must show a strange inclination to deny evident matter of fact, when it agrees not with his hypothesis, who will not allow that the beginning of Rome and Venice were by the uniting together of several men, free and independent one of another, amongst whom there was no natural superiority or subjection. And if Josephus Acosta's [10] word may be taken, he tells us that in many parts of America there was no government at all. "There are great and apparent conjectures," says he, "that these men (speaking of those of Peru) for a long time had neither kings nor commonwealths, but lived in troops, as they do this day in Florida—the Cheriquanas, those of Brazil, and many other nations, which have no certain kings, but, as occasion is offered in peace or war, they choose their captains as they please" (lib. i. cap. 25). If it be said that every man there was born subject to his father, or the head of his family, that the subjection due from a child to a father took not away his freedom of uniting into what political society he thought fit, has been already proved; but be that as it will, these men, it is evident, were actually free; and whatever superiority some politicians now would place in any of them, they themselves claimed it not; but, by consent, were all equal, till, by the same consent, they set rulers over themselves. So that their politic societies all began from a voluntary union, and the mutual agreement of men freely acting in the choice of their governors and forms of government.

[10] José de Acosta was a Spanish missionary and writer.

103. And I hope those who went away from Sparta, with Palantus, mentioned by Justin, will be allowed to have been freemen independent one of another, and to have set up a government over themselves by their own consent. Thus I have given several examples out of history of people, free and in the state of Nature, that, being met together, incorporated and began a commonwealth. And if the want of such instances be an argument to prove that government were not nor could not be so begun, I suppose the contenders for paternal empire were better let it alone than urge it against natural liberty; for if they can give so many instances out of history of governments begun upon paternal right, I think (though at least an argument from what has been to what should of right be of no great force) one might, without any great danger, yield them the cause. But if I might advise them in the case, they would do well not to search too much into the original of governments as they have begun *de facto,* lest they should find at the foundation of most of them something very little favorable to the design they promote, and such a power as they contend for.

104. But, to conclude: Reason being plain on our side that men are naturally free; and the examples of history showing that the governments of the world, that were begun in peace, had their beginning laid on that foundation, and were made by the consent of the people; there can be little room for doubt, either where the right is, or what has been the opinion or practice of mankind about the first erecting of governments.

105. I will not deny that if we look back, as far as history will direct us, towards the original of commonwealths, we shall generally find them under the government and administration of one man. And I am also apt to believe that where a family was numerous enough to subsist by itself, and continue entire together, without mixing with others, as it often happens, where there is much land and few people, the government commonly began in the father. For the father having, by the law of Nature, the same power, with every man else, to punish, as he thought fit, any offenses against that law, might thereby punish his transgressing children, even when they were men, and out of their pupilage; and they were very likely to submit to his punishment, and all join with him against the offender in their turns, giving him

thereby power to execute his sentence against any transgression, and so, in effect, make him the law-maker and governor over all that remained in conjunction with his family. He was fittest to be trusted; paternal affection secured their property and interest under his care, and the custom of obeying him in their childhood made it easier to submit to him rather than any other.

If, therefore, they must have one to rule them, as government is hardly to be avoided amongst men that live together, who so likely to be the man as he that was their common father, unless negligence, cruelty, or any other defect of mind or body, made him unfit for it? But when either the father died, and left his next heir—for want of age, wisdom, courage, or any other qualities—less fit for rule, or where several families met and consented to continue together, there, it is not to be doubted, but they used their natural freedom to set up him whom they judged the ablest and most likely to rule well over them. Conformable hereunto we find the people of America, who—living out of the reach of the conquering swords and spreading domination of the two great empires of Peru and Mexico—enjoyed their own natural freedom, though, *cæteris paribus*,[11] they commonly prefer the heir of their deceased king; yet, if they find him any way weak or incapable, they pass him by, and set up the stoutest and bravest man for their ruler.

106. Thus, though looking back as far as records give us any account of peopling the world, and the history of nations, we commonly find the government to be in one hand, yet it destroys not that which I affirm—viz., that the beginning of politic society depends upon the consent of the individuals to join into and make one society, who, when they are thus incorporated, might set up what form of government they thought fit. But this having given occasion to men to mistake and think that, by Nature, government was monarchical, and belonged to the father, it may not be amiss here to consider why people, in the beginning, generally pitched upon this form, which, though perhaps the father's preeminency might, in the first institution of some commonwealths, give a rise to and place in the beginning the

[11] Other things being equal.

power in one hand, yet it is plain that the reason that continued the form of government in a single person was not any regard or respect to paternal authority, since all petty monarchies—that is, almost all monarchies, near their original, have been commonly, at least upon occasion, elective.

107. First, then, in the beginning of things, the father's government of the childhood of those sprung from him having accustomed them to the rule of one man, and taught them that where it was exercised with care and skill, with affection and love to those under it, it was sufficient to procure and preserve men (all the political happiness they sought for in society), it was no wonder that they should pitch upon and naturally run into that form of government which, from their infancy, they had been all accustomed to, and which, by experience, they had found both easy and safe. To which if we add, that monarchy being simple and most obvious to men, whom neither experience had instructed in forms of government, nor the ambition or insolence of empire had taught to beware of the encroachments of prerogative or the inconveniencies of absolute power, which monarchy, in succession, was apt to lay claim to and bring upon them; it was not at all strange that they should not much trouble themselves to think of methods of restraining any exorbitances of those to whom they had given the authority over them, and of balancing the power of government by placing several parts of it in different hands. They had neither felt the oppression of tyrannical dominion, nor did the fashion of the age, nor their possessions or way of living, which afforded little matter for covetousness or ambition, give them any reason to apprehend or provide against it; and, therefore, it is no wonder they put themselves into such a frame of government as was not only, as I said, most obvious and simple, but also best suited to their present state and condition, which stood more in need of defense against foreign invasions and injuries than of multiplicity of laws where there was but very little property, and wanted not variety of rulers and abundance of officers to direct and look after their execution where there were but few trespassers and few offenders.

Since, then, those who liked one another so well as to join into society cannot but be supposed to have some acquaintance and friendship together, and some trust one in another, they could not but have greater apprehensions of others than of one another; and, therefore, their first care and thought cannot but be supposed to be, how to secure themselves against foreign force. It was natural for them to put themselves under a frame of government which might best serve to that end, and choose the wisest and bravest man to conduct them in their wars and lead them out against their enemies, and in this chiefly be their ruler.

108. Thus we see that the kings of the Indians, in America, which is still a pattern of the first ages in Asia and Europe, whilst the inhabitants were too few for the country, and want of people and money gave men no temptation to enlarge their possessions of land or contest for wider extent of ground, are little more than generals of their armies; and though they command absolutely in war, yet at home, and in time of peace, they exercise very little dominion, and have but a very moderate sovereignty, the resolutions of peace and war being ordinarily either in the people or in a council, though the war itself, which admits not of pluralities of governors, naturally evolves the command into the king's sole authority.

109. And thus, in Israel itself, the chief business of their judges and first kings seems to have been to be captains in war and leaders of their armies, which (besides what is signified by "going out and in before the people," which was, to march forth to war and home again at the heads of their forces) appears plainly in the story of Jephtha. The Ammonites making war upon Israel, the Gileadites, in fear, send to Jephtha, a bastard of their family, whom they had cast off, and article with him, if he will assist them against the Ammonites, to make him their ruler, which they do in these words: "And the people made him head and captain over them" (Judges xi. 11), which was, as it seems, all one as to be judge. "And he judged Israel" (Judges xii. 7)—that is, was their captain-general—"six years." So when Jotham upbraids the Shechemites with the obligation they had to Gideon, who had been their judge and ruler, he tells them: "He fought for you, and adventured his life for, and delivered you out of the hands of Midian" (Judges ix. 17). Nothing mentioned of him but what he did as a general, and, indeed, that is all is found in his

history, or in any of the rest of the judges. And Abimelech particularly is called king, though at most he was but their general. And when, being weary of the ill-conduct of Samuel's sons, the children of Israel desired a king, "like all the nations, to judge them, and to go out before them, and to fight their battles" (1 Sam. viii. 20), God, granting their desire, says to Samuel, "I will send thee a man, and thou shalt anoint him to be captain over my people Israel, that he may save my people out of the hands of the Philistines" (ch. ix. 16). As if the only business of a king had been to lead out their armies and fight in their defense; and, accordingly, at his inauguration, pouring a vial of oil upon him, declares to Saul that "the Lord had anointed him to be captain over his inheritance" (ch. x. 1). And therefore those who, after Saul being solemnly chosen and saluted king by the tribes at Mispah, were unwilling to have him their king, make no other objection but this, "How shall this man save us?" (ch. x. 27), as if they should have said: "This man is unfit to be our king, not having skill and conduct enough in war to be able to defend us." And when God resolved to transfer the government to David, it is in these words: "But now thy kingdom shall not continue: the Lord hath sought Him a man after His own heart, and the Lord hath commanded him to be captain over His people" (ch. xiii. 14). As if the whole kingly authority were nothing else but to be their general; and therefore the tribes who had stuck to Saul's family, and opposed David's reign, when they came to Hebron with terms of submission to him, they tell him, amongst other arguments, they had to submit to him as to their king, that he was, in effect, their king in Saul's time, and therefore they had no reason but to receive him as their king now. "Also," say they, "in time past, when Saul was king over us, thou wast he that ledest out and broughtest in Israel, and the Lord said unto thee, Thou shalt feed my people Israel, and thou shalt be a captain over Israel."

110. Thus, whether a family, by degrees, grew up into a commonwealth, and the fatherly authority being continued on to the elder son, everyone in his turn growing up under it tacitly submitted to it, and the easiness and equality of it not offending anyone, everyone acquiesced till time seemed to have confirmed it and settled a right

of succession by prescription; or whether several families, or the descendants of several families, whom chance, neighborhood, or business brought together, united into society; the need of a general whose conduct might defend them against their enemies in war, and the great confidence the innocence and sincerity of that poor but virtuous age, such as are almost all those which begin governments that ever come to last in the world, gave men one of another, made the first beginners of commonwealths generally put the rule into one man's hand, without any other express limitation or restraint but what the nature of the thing and the end of government required. It was given them for the public good and safety, and to those ends, in the infancies of commonwealths, they commonly used it; and unless they had done so, young societies could not have subsisted. Without such nursing fathers, without this care of the governors, all governments would have sunk under the weakness and infirmities of their infancy, the prince and the people had soon perished together.

111. But the golden age (though before vain ambition and *amor sceleratus habendi*, evil concupiscence, had corrupted men's minds into a mistake of true power and honor) had more virtue, and consequently better governors, as well as less vicious subjects; and there was then no stretching prerogative on the one side to oppress the people, nor, consequently, on the other, any dispute about privilege, to lessen or restrain the power of the magistrate; and so no contest betwixt rulers and people about governors or government.[12] Yet, when ambition and luxury, in future ages, would retain and increase the power, without doing the business for which it was given, and aided by flattery, taught princes to have distinct and separate interests from

[12] "At the first, when some certain kind of regimen was once approved, it may be that nothing was then further thought upon for the manner of governing, but all permitted unto their wisdom and discretion, which were to rule till, by experience, they found this for all parts very inconvenient, so as the thing which they had devised for a remedy did indeed but increase the sore which it should have cured. They saw that to live by one man's will became the cause of all men's misery. This constrained them to come unto laws wherein all men might see their duty beforehand, and know the penalties of transgressing them."—Hooker, *Eccl. Pol.*, lib. i., s. 10. (L.)

their people, men found it necessary to examine more carefully the original and rights of government, and to find out ways to restrain the exorbitances and prevent the abuses of that power, which they having entrusted in another's hands, only for their own good, they found was made use of to hurt them.

112. Thus we may see how probable it is that people that were naturally free, and, by their own consent, either submitted to the government of their father, or united together, out of different families, to make a government, should generally put the rule into one man's hands, and choose to be under the conduct of a single person, without so much, as by express conditions, limiting or regulating his power, which they thought safe enough in his honesty and prudence; though they never dreamed of monarchy being *jure Divino*,[13] which we never heard of among mankind till it was revealed to us by the divinity of this last age, nor ever allowed paternal power to have a right to dominion or to be the foundation of all government. And thus much may suffice to show that, as far as we have any light from history, we have reason to conclude that all peaceful beginnings of government have been laid in the consent of the people. I say "peaceful," because I shall have occasion, in another place, to speak of conquest, which some esteem a way of beginning of governments.

The other objection, I find, urged against the beginning of polities, in the way I have mentioned, is this, viz.:

113. "That all men being born under government, some or other, it is impossible any of them should ever be free and at liberty to unite together and begin a new one, or ever be able to erect a lawful government." If this argument be good, I ask, How came so many lawful monarchies into the world? For if anybody, upon this supposition, can show me any one man, in any age of the world, free to begin a lawful monarchy, I will be bound to show him ten other free men at liberty, at the same time, to unite and begin a new government under a regal or any other form. It being demonstration that if anyone born under the dominion of another may be so free as to have a right to command others in a new and distinct empire, everyone that is born under the

13 By divine law.

dominion of another may be so free too, and may become a ruler or subject of a distinct separate government. And so, by this their own principle, either all men, however born, are free, or else there is but one lawful prince, one lawful government in the world; and then they have nothing to do but barely to show us which that is, which, when they have done, I doubt not but all mankind will easily agree to pay obedience to him.

114. Though it be a sufficient answer to their objection to show that it involves them in the same difficulties that it doth those they use it against, yet I shall endeavor to discover the weakness of this argument a little farther.

"All men," say they, "are born under government, and therefore they cannot be at liberty to begin a new one. Everyone is born a subject to his father or his prince, and is therefore under the perpetual tie of subjection and allegiance." It is plain mankind never owned nor considered any such natural subjection that they were born in, to one or to the other, that tied them, without their own consents, to a subjection to them and their heirs.

115. For there are no examples so frequent in history, both sacred and profane, as those of men withdrawing themselves and their obedience from the jurisdiction they were born under, and the family or community they were bred up in, and setting up new governments in other places, from whence sprang all that number of petty commonwealths in the beginning of ages, and which always multiplied as long as there was room enough, till the stronger or more fortunate swallowed the weaker; and those great ones, again breaking to pieces, dissolved into lesser dominions; all which are so many testimonies against paternal sovereignty, and plainly prove that it was not the natural right of the father descending to his heirs that made governments in the beginning; since it was impossible, upon that ground, there should have been so many little kingdoms but only one universal monarchy if men had not been at liberty to separate themselves from their families and their government, be it what it will that was set up in it, and go and make distinct commonwealths and other governments as they thought fit.

116. This has been the practice of the world from its first begin-

ning to this day; nor is it now any more hindrance to the freedom of mankind, that they are born under constituted and ancient polities that have established laws and set forms of government, than if they were born in the woods amongst the unconfined inhabitants that run loose in them. For those who would persuade us that by being born under any government we are naturally subject to it, and have no more any title or pretense to the freedom of the state of Nature, have no other reason (bating that of paternal power, which we have already answered) to produce for it, but only because our fathers or progenitors passed away their natural liberty, and thereby bound up themselves and their posterity to a perpetual subjection to the government which they themselves submitted to. It is true that whatever engagements or promises anyone made for himself, he is under the obligation of them, but cannot by any compact whatsoever bind his children or posterity. For his son, when a man, being altogether as free as the father, any act of the father can no more give away the liberty of the son than it can of anybody else. He may, indeed, annex such conditions to the land he enjoyed, as a subject of any commonwealth, as may oblige his son to be of that community, if he will enjoy those possessions which were his father's, because that estate being his father's property, he may dispose or settle it as he pleases.

117. And this has generally given the occasion to the mistake in this matter; because commonwealths not permitting any part of their dominions to be dismembered, nor to be enjoyed by any but those of their community, the son cannot ordinarily enjoy the possessions of his father but under the same terms his father did, by becoming a member of the society, whereby he puts himself presently under the government he finds there established, as much as any other subject of that commonweal. And thus the consent of free men, born under government, which only makes them members of it, being given separately in their turns, as each comes to be of age, and not in a multitude together, people take no notice of it, and thinking it not done at all, or not necessary, conclude they are naturally subjects as they are men.

118. But it is plain governments themselves understand it otherwise; they claim no power over the son because of that they had over

the father; nor look on children as being their subjects, by their fathers being so. If a subject of England have a child by an English-woman in France, whose subject is he? Not the King of England's; for he must have leave to be admitted to the privileges of it. Nor the King of France's, for how then has his father a liberty to bring him away, and breed him as he pleases; and whoever was judged as a traitor or deserter, if he left, or warred against a country, for being barely born in it of parents that were aliens there? It is plain, then, by the practice of governments themselves, as well as by the law of right reason, that a child is born a subject of no country nor government. He is under his father's tuition and authority till he come to age of discretion, and then he is a free man, at liberty what government he will put himself under, what body politic he will unite himself to. For if an Englishman's son born in France be at liberty, and may do so, it is evident there is no tie upon him by his father being a subject of that kingdom, nor is he bound up by any compact of his ancestors; and why then hath not his son, by the same reason, the same liberty, though he be born anywhere else? Since the power that a father hath naturally over his children is the same wherever they be born, and the ties of natural obligations are not bounded by the positive limits of kingdoms and commonwealths.

119. Every man being, as has been showed, naturally free, and nothing being able to put him into subjection to any earthly power, but only his own consent, it is to be considered what shall be under-stood to be a sufficient declaration of a man's consent to make him subject to the laws of any government. There is a common distinction of an express and a tacit consent, which will concern our present case. Nobody doubts but an express consent of any man, entering into any society, makes him a perfect member of that society, a subject of that government. The difficulty is, what ought to be looked upon as a tacit consent, and how far it binds—i.e., how far anyone shall be looked on to have consented, and thereby submitted to any government, where he has made no expressions of it at all. And to this I say, that every man that hath any possession or enjoyment of any part of the do-minions of any government doth hereby give his tacit consent, and is as far forth obliged to obedience to the laws of that government,

during such enjoyment, as anyone under it, whether this his possession be of land to him and his heirs forever, or a lodging only for a
week; or whether it be barely traveling freely on the highway; and,
in effect, it reaches as far as the very being of anyone within the territories of that government.

120. To understand this the better, it is fit to consider that every
man, when he at first incorporates himself into any commonwealth,
he, by his uniting himself thereunto, annexes also, and submits to the
community those possessions which he has, or shall acquire, that do
not already belong to any other government. For it would be a direct
contradiction for anyone to enter into society with others for the
securing and regulating of property, and yet to suppose his land,
whose property is to be regulated by the laws of the society, should be
exempt from the jurisdiction of that government to which he himself,
and the property of the land, is a subject. By the same act, therefore,
whereby anyone unites his person, which was before free, to any
commonwealth, by the same he unites his possessions, which were
before free, to it also; and they become, both of them, person and
possession, subject to the government and dominion of that commonwealth as long as it has a being. Whoever therefore, from thenceforth,
by inheritance, purchases permission, or otherwise enjoys any part of
the land so annexed to, and under the government of that commonweal, must take it with the condition it is under—that is, of submitting to the government of the commonwealth, under whose jurisdiction it is, as far forth as any subject of it.

121. But since the government has a direct jurisdiction only over
the land and reaches the possessor of it (before he has actually incorporated himself in the society) only as he dwells upon and enjoys
that, the obligation anyone is under by virtue of such enjoyment to
submit to the government begins and ends with the enjoyment; so
that whenever the owner, who has given nothing but such a tacit consent to the government will, by donation, sale or otherwise, quit the
said possession, he is at liberty to go and incorporate himself into
any other commonwealth, or agree with others to begin a new one
in vacuis locis,[14] in any part of the world they can find free and un-

[14] In an empty place.

possessed; whereas he that has once, by actual agreement and any express declaration, given his consent to be of any commonweal, is perpetually and indispensably obliged to be, and remain unalterably a subject to it, and can never be again in the liberty of the state of Nature, unless by any calamity the government he was under comes to be dissolved.

122. But submitting to the laws of any country, living quietly and enjoying privileges and protection under them, makes not a man a member of that society; it is only a local protection and homage due to and from all those who, not being in a state of war, come within the territories belonging to any government, to all parts whereof the force of its law extends. But this no more makes a man a member of that society, a perpetual subject of that commonwealth, than it would make a man a subject to another in whose family he found it convenient to abide for some time, though, whilst he continued in it, he were obliged to comply with the laws and submit to the government he found there. And thus we see that foreigners, by living all their lives under another government, and enjoying the privileges and protection of it, though they are bound, even in conscience, to submit to its administration as far forth as any denizen, yet do not thereby come to be subjects or members of that commonwealth. Nothing can make any man so but his actually entering into it by positive engagement and express promise and compact. This is that which, I think, concerning the beginning of political societies, and that consent which makes anyone a member of any commonwealth.

CHAPTER IX

Of the Ends of Political Society and Government

123. If man in the state of Nature be so free as has been said, if he be absolute lord of his own person and possessions, equal to the greatest and subject to nobody, why will he part with his freedom, this empire, and subject himself to the dominion and control of any other

power? To which it is obvious to answer, that though in the state of Nature he has such a right, yet the enjoyment of it is very uncertain and constantly exposed to the invasion of others; for all being kings as much as he, every man his equal, and the greater part no strict observers of equity and justice, the enjoyment of the property he has in this state is very unsafe, very insecure. This makes him willing to quit this condition which, however free, is full of fears and continual dangers; and it is not without reason that he seeks out and is willing to join in society with others who are already united, or have a mind to unite for the mutual preservation of their lives, liberties and estates, which I call by the general name—property.

124. The great and chief end, therefore, of men uniting into commonwealths, and putting themselves under government, is the preservation of their property; to which in the state of Nature there are many things wanting.

Firstly, there wants an established, settled, known law, received and allowed by common consent to be the standard of right and wrong, and the common measure to decide all controversies between them. For though the law of Nature be plain and intelligible to all rational creatures, yet men, being biased by their interest, as well as ignorant for want of study of it, are not apt to allow of it as a law binding to them in the application of it to their particular cases.

125. Secondly, in the state of Nature there wants a known and indifferent judge, with authority to determine all differences according to the established law. For everyone in that state being both judge and executioner of the law of Nature, men being partial to themselves, passion and revenge is very apt to carry them too far, and with too much heat in their own cases, as well as negligence and unconcernedness, make them too remiss in other men's.

126. Thirdly, in the state of Nature there often wants power to back and support the sentence when right, and to give it due execution. They who by any injustice offended will seldom fail where they are able by force to make good their injustice. Such resistance many times makes the punishment dangerous, and frequently destructive to those who attempt it.

127. Thus mankind, notwithstanding all the privileges of the state

of Nature, being but in an ill condition while they remain in it are quickly driven into society. Hence it comes to pass, that we seldom find any number of men live any time together in this state. The inconveniences that they are therein exposed to by the irregular and uncertain exercise of the power every man has of punishing the transgressions of others, make them take sanctuary under the established laws of government, and therein seek the preservation of their property. It is this makes them so willingly give up everyone his single power of punishing to be exercised by such alone as shall be appointed to it amongst them, and by such rules as the community, or those authorized by them to that purpose, shall agree on. And in this we have the original right and rise of both the legislative and executive power as well as of the governments and societies themselves.

128. For in the state of Nature to omit the liberty he has of innocent delights, a man has two powers. The first is to do whatsoever he thinks fit for the preservation of himself and others within the permission of the law of Nature; by which law, common to them all, he and all the rest of mankind are one community, make up one society distinct from all other creatures, and were it not for the corruption and viciousness of degenerate men, there would be no need of any other, no necessity that men should separate from this great and natural community, and associate into lesser combinations. The other power a man has in the state of Nature is the power to punish the crimes committed against that law. Both these he gives up when he joins in a private, if I may so call it, or particular political society, and incorporates into any commonwealth separate from the rest of mankind.

129. The first power—viz., of doing whatsoever he thought fit for the preservation of himself and the rest of mankind, he gives up to be regulated by laws made by the society, so far forth as the preservation of himself and the rest of that society shall require; which laws of the society in many things confine the liberty he had by the law of Nature.

130. Secondly, the power of punishing he wholly gives up, and engages his natural force, which he might before employ in the execution of the law of Nature, by his own single authority, as he thought fit, to assist the executive power of the society as the law thereof shall

require. For being now in a new state, wherein he is to enjoy many conveniencies from the labor, assistance, and society of others in the same community, as well as protection from its whole strength, he is to part also with as much of his natural liberty, in providing for himself, as the good, prosperity, and safety of the society shall require, which is not only necessary but just, since the other members of the society do the like.

131. But though men when they enter into society give up the equality, liberty, and executive power they had in the state of Nature into the hands of the society, to be so far disposed of by the legislative as the good of the society shall require, yet it being only with an intention in everyone the better to preserve himself, his liberty and property (for no rational creature can be supposed to change his condition with an intention to be worse), the power of the society or legislative constituted by them can never be supposed to extend farther than the common good, but is obliged to secure everyone's property by providing against those three defects above mentioned that made the state of Nature so unsafe and uneasy. And so, whoever has the legislative or supreme power of any commonwealth, is bound to govern by established standing laws, promulgated and known to the people, and not by extemporary decrees, by indifferent and upright judges, who are to decide controversies by those laws; and to employ the force of the community at home only in the execution of such laws, or abroad to prevent or redress foreign injuries and secure the community from inroads and invasion. And all this to be directed to no other end but the peace, safety, and public good of the people.

CHAPTER X

Of the Forms of a Commonwealth

132. THE majority having, as has been showed, upon men's first uniting into society, the whole power of the community naturally in them, may employ all that power in making laws for the community from time to time, and executing those laws by officers of their own

appointing, and then the form of the government is a perfect democracy; or else may put the power of making laws into the hands of a few select men, and their heirs or successors, and then it is an oligarchy; or else into the hands of one man, and then it is a monarchy; if to him and his heirs, it is a hereditary monarchy; if to him only for life, but upon his death the power only of nominating a successor, to return to them, an elective monarchy. And so accordingly of these make compounded and mixed forms of government, as they think good. And if the legislative power be at first given by the majority to one or more persons only for their lives, or any limited time, and then the supreme power to revert to them again, when it is so reverted the community may dispose of it again anew into what hands they please, and so constitute a new form of government; for the form of government depending upon the placing the supreme power, which is the legislative, it being impossible to conceive that an inferior power should prescribe to a superior, or any but the supreme make laws, according as the power of making laws is placed, such is the form of the commonwealth.

133. By "commonwealth" I must be understood all along to mean not a democracy, or any form of government, but any independent community which the Latins signified by the word *civitas,* to which the word which best answers in our language is "commonwealth," and most properly expresses such a society of men which "community" does not (for there may be subordinate communities in a government), and "city" much less. And therefore, to avoid ambiguity, I crave leave to use the word "commonwealth" in that sense, in which sense I find the word used by King James himself, which I think to be its genuine signification, which, if anybody dislike, I consent with him to change it for a better.

CHAPTER XI

Of the Extent of the Legislative Power

134. THE great end of men's entering into society being the enjoyment of their properties in peace and safety, and the great instrument

and means of that being the laws established in that society, the first and fundamental positive law of all commonwealths is the establishing of the legislative power, as the first and fundamental natural law which is to govern even the legislative. Itself is the preservation of the society and (as far as will consist with the public good) of every person in it. This legislative is not only the supreme power of the commonwealth, but sacred and unalterable in the hands where the community have once placed it. Nor can any edict of anybody else, in what form soever conceived, or by what power soever backed, have the force and obligation of a law which has not its sanction from that legislative which the public has chosen and appointed; for without this the law could not have that which is absolutely necessary to its being a law, the consent of the society, over whom nobody can have a power to make laws [15] but by their own consent and by authority received from them; and therefore all the obedience, which by the most solemn ties anyone can be obliged to pay, ultimately terminates in this supreme power, and is directed by those laws which it enacts. Nor can any oaths to any foreign power whatsoever, or any domestic subordinate power, discharge any member of the society from his obedience to the legislative, acting pursuant to their trust, nor oblige him to any obedience contrary to the laws so enacted or farther than they

[15] "The lawful power of making laws to command whole politic societies of men, belonging so properly unto the same entire societies, that for any prince or potentate, of what kind soever upon earth, to exercise the same of himself, and not by express commission immediately and personally received from God, or else by authority derived at the first from their consent, upon whose persons they impose laws, it is no better than mere tyranny. Laws they are not, therefore, which public approbation hath not made so."— Hooker (*Eccl. Pol.,* lib. i., s. 10). "Of this point, therefore, we are to note that such men naturally have no full and perfect power to command whole politic multitudes of men, therefore utterly without our consent we could in such sort be at no man's commandment living. And to be commanded, we do consent when that society, whereof we be a part, hath at any time before consented, without revoking the same after by the like universal agreement.

"Laws therefore human, of what kind soever, are available by consent." —Hooker, *Eccl. Pol.* (L.)

do allow, it being ridiculous to imagine one can be tied ultimately to obey any power in the society which is not the supreme.

135. Though the legislative, whether placed in one or more, whether it be always in being or only by intervals, though it be the supreme power in every commonwealth, yet, first, it is not, nor can possibly be, absolutely arbitrary over the lives and fortunes of the people. For it being but the joint power of every member of the society given up to that person or assembly which is legislator, it can be no more than those persons had in a state of Nature before they entered into society, and gave it up to the community. For nobody can transfer to another more power than he has in himself, and nobody has an absolute arbitrary power over himself, or over any other, to destroy his own life, or take away the life or property of another. A man, as has been proved, cannot subject himself to the arbitrary power of another; and having, in the state of Nature, no arbitrary power over the life, liberty, or possession of another, but only so much as the law of Nature gave him for the preservation of himself and the rest of mankind, this is all he does, or can give up to the commonwealth, and by it to the legislative power, so that the legislative can have no more than this. Their power in the utmost bounds of it is limited to the public good of the society.[16] It is a power

[16] "Two foundations there are which bear up public societies; the one a natural inclination whereby all men desire sociable life and fellowship; the other an order, expressly or secretly agreed upon, touching the manner of their union in living together. The latter is that which we call the law of a commonweal, the very soul of a politic body, the parts whereof are by law animated, held together, and set on work in such actions as the common good requireth. Laws politic, ordained for external order and regimen amongst men, are never framed as they should be, unless presuming the will of man to be inwardly obstinate, rebellious, and averse from all obedience to the sacred laws of his nature; in a word, unless presuming man to be in regard of his depraved mind little better than a wild beast, they do accordingly provide notwithstanding, so to frame his outward actions, that they be no hindrance unto the common good, for which societies are instituted. Unless they do this they are not perfect."—Hooker, *Eccl. Pol.,* lib. i., s. 10. (L.)

that has no other end but preservation, and therefore can never have a right to destroy, enslave, or designedly to impoverish the subjects; the obligations of the law of Nature cease not in society, but only in many cases are drawn closer, and have, by human laws, known penalties annexed to them to enforce their observation. Thus the law of Nature stands as an eternal rule to all men, legislators as well as others. The rules that they make for other men's actions must, as well as their own and other men's actions, be conformable to the law of Nature—i.e., to the will of God, of which that is a declaration, and the fundamental law of Nature being the preservation of mankind, no human sanction can be good or valid against it.

136. Secondly, the legislative or supreme authority cannot assume to itself a power to rule by extemporary arbitrary decrees, but is bound to dispense justice and decide the rights of the subject by promulgated standing laws,[17] and known authorized judges. For the law of Nature being unwritten, and so nowhere to be found but in the minds of men, they who, through passion or interest, shall miscite or misapply it, cannot so easily be convinced of their mistake where there is no established judge; and so it serves not as it ought, to determine the rights and fence the properties of those that live under it, especially where everyone is judge, interpreter, and executioner of it too, and that in his own case; and he that has right on his side, having ordinarily but his own single strength, hath not force enough to defend himself from injuries or punish delinquents. To avoid these inconveniencies which disorder men's properties in the state of Nature, men unite into societies that they may have the united strength of the whole society to secure and defend their properties, and may have standing rules to bound it by which everyone may know what is his. To this end

[17] "Human laws are measures in respect of men whose actions they must direct, howbeit such measures they are as have also their higher rules to be measured by, which rules are two—the law of God and the law of Nature; so that laws human must be made according to the general laws of Nature, and without contradiction to any positive law of Scripture, otherwise they are ill made."—Hooker, *Eccl. Pol.,* lib. iii., s. 9.

"To constrain men to anything inconvenient doth seem unreasonable."—*Ibid.,* i., 10. (L.)

it is that men give up all their natural power to the society they enter into, and the community put the legislative power into such hands as they think fit, with this trust, that they shall be governed by declared laws, or else their peace, quiet, and property will still be at the same uncertainty as it was in the state of Nature.

137. Absolute arbitrary power, or governing without settled standing laws, can neither of them consist with the ends of society and government, which men would not quit the freedom of the state of Nature for, and tie themselves up under, were it not to preserve their lives, liberties, and fortunes, and by stated rules of right and property to secure their peace and quiet. It cannot be supposed that they should intend, had they a power so to do, to give anyone or more an absolute arbitrary power over their persons and estates, and put a force into the magistrate's hand to execute his unlimited will arbitrarily upon them; this were to put themselves into a worse condition than the state of Nature, wherein they had a liberty to defend their right against the injuries of others, and were upon equal terms of force to maintain it, whether invaded by a single man or many in combination. Whereas by supposing they have given up themselves to the absolute arbitrary power and will of a legislator, they have disarmed themselves, and armed him to make a prey of them when he pleases; he being in a much worse condition that is exposed to the arbitrary power of one man who has the command of a hundred thousand than he that is exposed to the arbitrary power of a hundred thousand single men, nobody being secure, that his will who has such a command is better than that of other men, though his force be a hundred thousand times stronger. And, therefore, whatever form the commonwealth is under, the ruling power ought to govern by declared and received laws, and not by extemporary dictates and undetermined resolutions, for then mankind will be in a far worse condition than in the state of Nature if they shall have armed one or a few men with the joint power of a multitude, to force them to obey at pleasure the exorbitant and unlimited decrees of their sudden thoughts, or unrestrained, and till that moment, unknown wills, without having any measures set down which may guide and justify their actions. For all the power the government has, being only for the good of the society, as it ought

not to be arbitrary and at pleasure, so it ought to be exercised by established and promulgated laws, that both the people may know their duty, and be safe and secure within the limits of the law, and the rulers, too, kept within their due bounds, and not be tempted by the power they have in their hands to employ it to purposes, and by such measures as they would not have known, and own not willingly.

138. Thirdly, the supreme power cannot take from any man any part of his property without his own consent. For the preservation of property being the end of government, and that for which men enter into society, it necessarily supposes and requires that the people should have property, without which they must be supposed to lose that by entering into society which was the end for which they entered into it; too gross an absurdity for any man to own. Men, therefore, in society having property, they have such a right to the goods, which by the law of the community are theirs, that nobody has a right to take them, or any part of them, from them without their own consent; without this they have no property at all. For I have truly no property in that which another can by right take from me when he pleases against my consent. Hence it is a mistake to think that the supreme or legislative power of any commonwealth can do what it will, and dispose of the estates of the subject arbitrarily, or take any part of them at pleasure. This is not much to be feared in governments where the legislative consists wholly or in part in assemblies which are variable, whose members upon the dissolution of the assembly are subjects under the common laws of their country, equally with the rest. But in governments where the legislative is in one lasting assembly, always in being, or in one man as in absolute monarchies, there is danger still, that they will think themselves to have a distinct interest from the rest of the community, and so will be apt to increase their own riches and power by taking what they think fit from the people. For a man's property is not at all secure, though there be good and equitable laws to set the bounds of it between him and his fellow-subjects, if he who commands those subjects have power to take from any private man what part he pleases of his property, and use and dispose of it as he thinks good.

139. But government, into whosesoever hands it is put, being as I

have before showed, entrusted with this condition, and for this end, that men might have and secure their properties, the prince or senate, however it may have power to make laws for the regulating of property between the subjects one amongst another, yet can never have a power to take to themselves the whole, or any part of the subjects' property, without their own consent; for this would be in effect to leave them no property at all. And to let us see that even absolute power, where it is necessary, is not arbitrary by being absolute, but is still limited by that reason, and confined to those ends which required it in some cases to be absolute, we need look no farther than the common practice of martial discipline. For the preservation of the army, and in it of the whole commonwealth, requires an absolute obedience to the command of every superior officer, and it is justly death to disobey or dispute the most dangerous or unreasonable of them; but yet we see that neither the sergeant that could command a soldier to march up to the mouth of a cannon, or stand in a breach where he is almost sure to perish, can command that soldier to give him one penny of his money; nor the general that can condemn him to death for deserting his post, or not obeying the most desperate orders, cannot yet with all his absolute power of life and death dispose of one farthing of that soldier's estate, or seize one jot of his goods; whom yet he can command anything, and hang for the least disobedience. Because such a blind obedience is necessary to that end for which the commander has his power—viz., the preservation of the rest, but the disposing of his goods has nothing to do with it.

140. It is true governments cannot be supported without great charge, and it is fit everyone who enjoys his share of the protection should pay out of his estate his proportion for the maintenance of it. But still it must be with his own consent—i.e., the consent of the majority, giving it either by themselves or their representatives chosen by them; for if anyone shall claim a power to lay and levy taxes on the people by his own authority, and without such consent of the people, he thereby invades the fundamental law of property, and subverts the end of government. For what property have I in that which another may by right take when he pleases to himself?

141. Fourthly, the legislative cannot transfer the power of making

laws to any other hands, for it being but a delegated power from the people, they who have it cannot pass it over to others. The people alone can appoint the form of the commonwealth, which is by constituting the legislative, and appointing in whose hands that shall be. And when the people have said, "We will submit, and be governed by laws made by such men, and in such forms," nobody else can say other men shall make laws for them; nor can they be bound by any laws but such as are enacted by those whom they have chosen and authorized to make laws for them.

142. These are the bounds which the trust that is put in them by the society and the law of God and Nature have set to the legislative power of every commonwealth, in all forms of government. First, they are to govern by promulgated established laws, not to be varied in particular cases, but to have one rule for rich and poor, for the favorite at Court, and the countryman at plow. Secondly, these laws also ought to be designed for no other end ultimately but the good of the people. Thirdly, they must not raise taxes on the property of the people without the consent of the people given by themselves or their deputies. And this properly concerns only such governments where the legislative is always in being, or at least where the people have not reserved any part of the legislative to deputies, to be from time to time chosen by themselves. Fourthly, legislative neither must nor can transfer the power of making laws to anybody else, or place it anywhere but where the people have.

CHAPTER XII

The Legislative, Executive, and Federative Power of the Commonwealth

143. THE legislative power is that which has a right to direct how the force of the commonwealth shall be employed for preserving the community and the members of it. Because those laws which are constantly to be executed, and whose force is always to continue, may

be made in a little time, therefore there is no need that the legislative should be always in being, not having always business to do. And because it may be too great temptation to human frailty, apt to grasp at power, for the same persons who have the power of making laws to have also in their hands the power to execute them, whereby they may exempt themselves from obedience to the laws they make, and suit the law, both in its making and execution, to their own private advantage, and thereby come to have a distinct interest from the rest of the community, contrary to the end of society and government. Therefore in well-ordered commonwealths, where the good of the whole is so considered as it ought, the legislative power is put into the hands of divers persons who, duly assembled, have by themselves, or jointly with others, a power to make laws, which when they have done, being separated again, they are themselves subject to the laws they have made; which is a new and near tie upon them to take care that they make them for the public good.

144. But because the laws that are at once, and in a short time made, have a constant and lasting force, and need a perpetual execution, or an attendance thereunto, therefore it is necessary there should be a power always in being which should see to the execution of the laws that are made, and remain in force. And thus the legislative and executive power come often to be separated.

145. There is another power in every commonwealth which one may call natural, because it is that which answers to the power every man naturally had before he entered into society. For though in a commonwealth the members of it are distinct persons, still, in reference to one another, and, as such, are governed by the laws of the society, yet, in reference to the rest of mankind, they make one body, which is, as every member of it before was, still in the state of Nature with the rest of mankind, so that the controversies that happen between any man of the society with those that are out of it are managed by the public, and an injury done to a member of their body engages the whole in the reparation of it. So that under this consideration the whole community is one body in the state of Nature in respect of all other states or persons out of its community.

146. This, therefore, contains the power of war and peace, leagues

and alliances, and all the transactions with all persons and communities without the commonwealth, and may be called federative if anyone pleases. So the thing be understood, I am indifferent as to the name.

147. These two powers, executive and federative, though they be really distinct in themselves, yet one comprehending the execution of the municipal laws of the society within itself upon all that are parts of it, the other the management of the security and interest of the public without with all those that it may receive benefit or damage from, yet they are always almost united. And though this federative power in the well or ill management of it be of great moment to the commonwealth, yet it is much less capable to be directed by antecedent, standing, positive laws than the executive, and so must necessarily be left to the prudence and wisdom of those whose hands it is in, to be managed for the public good. For the laws that concern subjects one amongst another, being to direct their actions, may well enough precede them. But what is to be done in reference to foreigners depending much upon their actions, and the variation of designs and interests, must be left in great part to the prudence of those who have this power committed to them, to be managed by the best of their skill for the advantage of the commonwealth.

148. Though, as I said, the executive and federative power of every community be really distinct in themselves, yet they are hardly to be separated and placed at the same time in the hands of distinct persons. For both of them requiring the force of the society for their exercise, it is almost impracticable to place the force of the commonwealth in distinct and not subordinate hands, or that the executive and federative power should be placed in persons that might act separately, whereby the force of the public would be under different commands, which would be apt some time or other to cause disorder and ruin.

CHAPTER XIII

Of the Subordination of the Powers of the Commonwealth

149. **THOUGH** in a constituted commonwealth standing upon its own basis and acting according to its own nature—that is, acting for the preservation of the community, there can be but one supreme power, which is the legislative, to which all the rest are and must be subordinate, yet the legislative being only a fiduciary power to act for certain ends, there remains still in the people a supreme power to remove or alter the legislative, when they find the legislative act contrary to the trust reposed in them. For all power given with trust for the attaining and end being limited by that end, whenever that end is manifestly neglected or opposed, the trust must necessarily be forfeited, and the power devolve into the hands of those that gave it, who may place it anew where they shall think best for their safety and security. And thus the community perpetually retains a supreme power of saving themselves from the attempts and designs of anybody, even of their legislators, whenever they shall be so foolish or so wicked as to lay and carry on designs against the liberties and properties of the subject. For no man or society of men having a power to deliver up their preservation, or consequently the means of it, to the absolute will and arbitrary dominion of another, whenever anyone shall go about to bring them into such a slavish condition, they will always have a right to preserve what they have not a power to part with, and to rid themselves of those who invade this fundamental, sacred, and unalterable law of self-preservation for which they entered into society. And thus the community may be said in this respect to be always the supreme power, but not as considered under any form of government, because this power of the people can never take place till the government be dissolved.

150. In all cases whilst the government subsists, the legislative is the supreme power. For what can give laws to another must needs be superior to him, and since the legislative is not otherwise legislative

The Second Treatise on Civil Government

of the society but by the right it has to make laws for all the parts, and every member of the society prescribing rules to their actions, and giving power of execution where they are transgressed, the legislative must needs be the supreme, and all other powers in any members or parts of the society derived from and subordinate to it.

151. In some commonwealths where the legislative is not always in being, and the executive is vested in a single person who has also a share in the legislative, there that single person, in a very tolerable sense, may also be called supreme; not that he has in himself all the supreme power, which is that of lawmaking, but because he has in him the supreme execution from whom all inferior magistrates derive all their several subordinate powers, or, at least, the greatest part of them; having also no legislative superior to him, there being no law to be made without his consent, which cannot be expected should ever subject him to the other part of the legislative, he is properly enough in this sense supreme. But yet it is to be observed that though oaths of allegiance and fealty are taken to him, it is not to him as supreme legislator, but as supreme executor of the law made by a joint power of him with others, allegiance being nothing but an obedience according to law, which, when he violates, he has no right to obedience, nor can claim it otherwise than as the public person vested with the power of the law, and so is to be considered as the image, phantom, or representative of the commonwealth, acted by the will of the society declared in its laws, and thus he has no will, no power, but that of the law. But when he quits this representation, this public will, and acts by his own private will, he degrades himself, and is but a single private person without power and without will; the members owing no obedience but to the public will of the society.

152. The executive power placed anywhere but in a person that has also a share in the legislative is visibly subordinate and accountable to it, and may be at pleasure changed and displaced; so that it is not the supreme executive power that is exempt from subordination, but the supreme executive power vested in one, who having a share in the legislative, has no distinct superior legislative to be subordinate and accountable to, farther than he himself shall join and consent, so that he is no more subordinate than he himself shall think fit, which

one may certainly conclude will be but very little. Of other ministerial and subordinate powers in a commonwealth we need not speak, they being so multiplied with infinite variety in the different customs and constitutions of distinct commonwealths, that it is impossible to give a particular account of them all. Only thus much which is necessary to our present purpose we may take notice of concerning them, that they have no manner of authority, any of them, beyond what is by positive grant and commission delegated to them, and are all of them accountable to some other power in the commonwealth.

153. It is not necessary—no, nor so much as convenient—that the legislative should be always in being; but absolutely necessary that the executive power should, because there is not always need of new laws to be made, but always need of execution of the laws that are made. When the legislative hath put the execution of the laws they make into other hands, they have a power still to resume it out of those hands when they find cause, and to punish for any maladministration against the laws. The same holds also in regard of the federative power, that and the executive being both ministerial and subordinate to the legislative, which, as has been shown, in a constituted commonwealth is the supreme, the legislative also in this case being supposed to consist of several persons; for if it be a single person it cannot but be always in being, and so will, as supreme, naturally have the supreme executive power, together with the legislative, may assemble and exercise their legislative at the times that either their original constitution or their own adjournment appoints, or when they please, if neither of these has appointed any time, or there be no other way prescribed to convoke them. For the supreme power being placed in them by the people, it is always in them, and they may exercise it when they please, unless by their original constitution they are limited to certain seasons, or by an act of their supreme power they have adjourned to a certain time, and when that time comes they have a right to assemble and act again.

154. If the legislative, or any part of it, be of representatives, chosen for that time by the people, which afterwards return into the ordinary state of subjects, and have no share in the legislative but upon a new choice, this power of choosing must also be exercised by

the people, either at certain appointed seasons, or else when they are summoned to it; and, in this latter case, the power of convoking the legislative is ordinarily placed in the executive, and has one of these two limitations in respect of time:—that either the original constitution requires their assembling and acting at certain intervals; and then the executive power does nothing but ministerially issue directions for their electing and assembling according to due forms; or else it is left to his prudence to call them by new elections when the occasions or exigencies of the public require the amendment of old or making of new laws, or the redress or prevention of any inconveniencies that lie on or threaten the people.

155. It may be demanded here, what if the executive power, being possessed of the force of the commonwealth, shall make use of that force to hinder the meeting and acting of the legislative, when the original constitution or the public exigencies require it? I say, using force upon the people, without authority, and contrary to the trust put in him that does so, is a state of war with the people, who have a right to reinstate their legislative in the exercise of their power. For having erected a legislative with an intent they should exercise the power of making laws, either at certain set times, or when there is need of it, when they are hindered by any force from what is so necessary to the society, and wherein the safety and preservation of the people consists, the people have a right to remove it by force. In all states and conditions the true remedy of force without authority is to oppose force to it. The use of force without authority always puts him that uses it into a state of war as the aggressor, and renders him liable to be treated accordingly.

156. The power of assembling and dismissing the legislative, placed in the executive, gives not the executive a superiority over it, but is a fiduciary trust placed in him for the safety of the people in a case where the uncertainty and variableness of human affairs could not bear a steady fixed rule. For it not being possible that the first framers of the government should by any foresight be so much masters of future events as to be able to prefix so just periods of return and duration to the assemblies of the legislative, in all times to come, that might exactly answer all the exigencies of the commonwealth, the

best remedy could be found for this defect was to trust this to the prudence of one who was always to be present, and whose business it was to watch over the public good. Constant, frequent meetings of the legislative, and long continuations of their assemblies, without necessary occasion, could not but be burdensome to the people, and must necessarily in time produce more dangerous inconveniencies, and yet the quick turn of affairs might be sometimes such as to need their present help; any delay of their convening might endanger the public; and sometimes, too, their business might be so great that the limited time of their sitting might be too short for their work, and rob the public of that benefit which could be had only from their mature deliberation.

What, then, could be done in this case to prevent the community from being exposed some time or other to imminent hazard on one side or the other, by fixed intervals and periods set to the meeting and acting of the legislative, but to entrust it to the prudence of some who, being present and acquainted with the state of public affairs, might make use of this prerogative for the public good? And where else could this be so well placed as in his hands who was entrusted with the execution of the laws for the same end? Thus, supposing the regulation of times for the assembling and sitting of the legislative not settled by the original constitution, it naturally fell into the hands of the executive; not as an arbitrary power depending on his good pleasure, but with this trust always to have it exercised only for the public weal, as the occurrences of times and change of affairs might require. Whether settled periods of their convening, or a liberty left to the prince for convoking the legislative, or perhaps a mixture of both, has the least inconvenience attending it, it is not my business here to inquire, but only to show that, though the executive power may have the prerogative of convoking and dissolving such conventions of the legislative, yet it is not thereby superior to it.

157. Things of this world are in so constant a flux that nothing remains long in the same state. Thus people, riches, trade, power, change their stations; flourishing mighty cities come to ruin, and prove in time neglected desolate corners, whilst other unfrequented places grow into populous countries filled with wealth and inhabitants. But

things not always changing equally, and private interest often keeping up customs and privileges when the reasons of them are ceased, it often comes to pass that in governments where part of the legislative consists of representatives chosen by the people, that in tract of time this representation becomes very unequal and disproportionate to the reasons it was at first established upon. To what gross absurdities the following of custom when reason has left it may lead, we may be satisfied when we see the bare name of a town, of which there remains not so much as the ruins, where scarce so much housing as a sheepcote, or more inhabitants than a shepherd is to be found, send as many representatives to the grand assembly of lawmakers as a whole county numerous in people and powerful in riches. This strangers stand amazed at, and everyone must confess needs a remedy; though most think it hard to find one, because the constitution of the legislative being the original and supreme act of the society, antecedent to all positive laws in it, and depending wholly on the people, no inferior power can alter it. And, therefore, the people when the legislative is once constituted, having in such a government as we have been speaking of no power to act as long as the government stands, this inconvenience is thought incapable of a remedy.

158. *Salus populi suprema lex* [18] is certainly so just and fundamental a rule, that he who sincerely follows it cannot dangerously err. If, therefore, the executive who has the power of convoking the legislative, observing rather the true proportion than fashion of representation, regulates not by old custom, but true reason, the number of members in all places, that have a right to be distinctly represented, which no part of the people, however incorporated, can pretend to, but in proportion to the assistance which it affords to the public, it cannot be judged to have set up a new legislative, but to have restored the old and true one, and to have rectified the disorders which succession of time had insensibly as well as inevitably introduced; for it being the interest as well as intestion of the people to have a fair and equal representative, whoever brings it nearest to that is an undoubted friend to and establisher of the government, and cannot miss

[18] The health of the people is the highest law.

the consent and approbation of the community; prerogative being nothing but a power in the hands of the prince to provide for the public good in such cases which, depending upon unforeseen and uncertain occurrences, certain and unalterable laws could not safely direct. Whatsoever shall be done manifestly for the good of the people, and establishing the government upon its true foundations is, and always will be, just prerogative. The power of erecting new corporations, and therewith new representatives, carries with it a supposition that in time the measures of representation might vary, and those have a just right to be represented which before had none; and by the same reason, those cease to have a right, and be too inconsiderable for such a privilege, which before had it. It is not a change from the present state which, perhaps, corruption or decay has introduced, that makes an inroad upon the government, but the tendency of it to injure or oppress the people, and to set up one part or party with a distinction from and an unequal subjection of the rest. Whatsoever cannot but be acknowledged to be of advantage to the society and people in general, upon just and lasting measures, will always, when done, justify itself; and whenever the people shall choose their representatives upon just and undeniably equal measures, suitable to the original frame of the government, it cannot be doubted to be the will and act of the society, whoever permitted or proposed to them so to do.

CHAPTER XIV

Of Prerogative

159. WHERE the legislative and executive power are in distinct hands, as they are in all moderated monarchies and well-framed governments, there the good of the society requires that several things should be left to the discretion of him that has the executive power. For the legislators not being able to foresee and provide by laws for all that may be useful to the community, the executor of the laws, having the power in his hands, has by the common law of Nature a right to make use of it for the good of the society, in many cases where the

municipal law has given no direction, till the legislative can conveniently be assembled to provide for it; nay, many things there are which the law can by no means provide for, and those must necessarily be left to the discretion of him that has the executive power in his hands, to be ordered by him as the public good and advantage shall require; nay, it is fit that the laws themselves should in some cases give way to the executive power, or rather to this fundamental law of Nature and government—viz., that as much as may be all the members of the society are to be preserved. For since many accidents may happen wherein a strict and rigid observation of the laws may do harm, as not to pull down an innocent man's house to stop the fire when the next to it is burning; and a man may come sometimes within the reach of the law, which makes no distinction of persons, by an action that may deserve reward and pardon; it is fit the ruler should have a power in many cases to mitigate the severity of the law, and pardon some offenders, since the end of government being the preservation of all as much as may be, even the guilty are to be spared where it can prove no prejudice to the innocent.

160. This power to act according to discretion for the public good, without the prescription of the law and sometimes even against it, is that which is called prerogative; for since in some governments the lawmaking power is not always in being and is usually too numerous, and so too slow for the dispatch requisite to execution, and because, also, it is impossible to foresee and so by laws to provide for all accidents and necessities that may concern the public, or make such laws as will do no harm, if they are executed with an inflexible rigor on all occasions and upon all persons that may come in their way, therefore there is a latitude left to the executive power to do many things of choice which the laws do not prescribe.

161. This power, whilst employed for the benefit of the community and suitably to the trust and ends of the government, is undoubted prerogative, and never is questioned. For the people are very seldom or never scrupulous or nice in the point or questioning of prerogative whilst it is in any tolerable degree employed for the use it was meant—that is, the good of the people, and not manifestly against it. But if there comes to be a question between the executive

power and the people about a thing claimed as a prerogative, the
tendency of the exercise of such prerogative, to the good or hurt of
the people, will easily decide that question.

162. It is easy to conceive that in the infancy of governments,
when commonwealths differed little from families in number of
people, they differed from them too but little in number of laws; and
the governors being as the fathers of them, watching over them for
their good, the government was almost all prerogative. A few established laws served the turn, and the discretion and care of the ruler
supplied the rest. But when mistake or flattery prevailed with weak
princes, to make use of this power for private ends of their own and
not for the public good, the people were fain, by express laws, to
get prerogative determined in those points wherein they found disadvantage from it, and declared limitations of prerogative in those cases
which they and their ancestors had left in the utmost latitude to the
wisdom of those princes who made no other but a right use of it—that
is, for the good of their people.

163. And therefore they have a very wrong notion of government
who say that the people have encroached upon the prerogative when
they have got any part of it to be defined by positive laws. For in so
doing they have not pulled from the prince anything that of right
belonged to him, but only declared that that power which they indefi-
nitely left in his or his ancestors' hands, to be exercised for their
good, was not a thing they intended him, when he used it otherwise.
For the end of government being the good of the community, whatsoever alterations are made in it tending to that end cannot be an
encroachment upon anybody; since nobody in government can have
a right tending to any other end; and those only are encroachments
which prejudice or hinder the public good. Those who say otherwise
speak as if the prince had a distinct and separate interest from the
good of the community, and was not made for it; the root and source
from which spring almost all those evils and disorders which happen
in kingly governments. And, indeed, if that be so, the people under
his government are not a society of rational creatures, entered into
a community for their mutual good, such as have set rulers over themselves, to guard and promote that good; but are to be looked on as a

herd of inferior creatures under the dominion of a master, who keeps them and works them for his own pleasure or profit. If men were so void of reason and brutish as to enter into society upon such terms, prerogative might indeed be, what some men would have it, an arbitrary power to do things hurtful to the people.

164. But since a rational creature cannot be supposed, when free, to put himself into subjection to another for his own harm (though where he finds a good and a wise ruler he may not, perhaps, think it either necessary or useful to set precise bounds to his power in all things), prerogative can be nothing but the people's permitting their rulers to do several things of their own free choice where the law was silent, and sometimes too against the direct letter of the law, for the public good and their acquiescing in it when so done. For as a good prince, who is mindful of the trust put into his hands and careful of the good of his people, cannot have too much prerogative—that is, power to do good, so a weak and ill prince, who would claim that power his predecessors exercised, without the direction of the law, as a prerogative belonging to him by right of his office, which he may exercise at his pleasure to make or promote an interest distinct from that of the public, gives the people an occasion to claim their right and limit that power, which, whilst it was exercised for their good, they were content should be tacitly allowed.

165. And therefore he that will look into the history of England will find that prerogative was always largest in the hands of our wisest and best princes, because the people observing the whole tendency of their actions to be the public good, or if any human frailty or mistake (for princes are but men, made as others) appeared in some small declinations from that end, yet it was visible the main of their conduct tended to nothing but the care of the public. The people, therefore, finding reason to be satisfied with these princes, whenever they acted without, or contrary to the letter of the law, acquiesced in what they did, and without the least complaint, let them enlarge their prerogative as they pleased, judging rightly that they did nothing herein to the prejudice of their laws, since they acted conformably to the foundation and end of all laws—the public good.

166. Such godlike princes, indeed, had some title to arbitrary

power by that argument that would prove absolute monarchy the best government, as that which God Himself governs the universe by, because such kings partake of His wisdom and goodness. Upon this is founded that saying, "That the reigns of good princes have been always most dangerous to the liberties of their people." For when their successors, managing the government with different thoughts, would draw the actions of those good rulers into precedent and make them the standard of their prerogative—as if what had been done only for the good of the people was a right in them to do for the harm of the people, if they so pleased—it has often occasioned contest, and sometimes public disorders, before the people could recover their original right and get that to be declared not to be prerogative which truly was never so; since it is impossible anybody in the society should ever have a right to do the people harm, though it be very possible and reasonable that the people should not go about to set any bounds to the prerogative of those kings or rulers who themselves transgressed not the bounds of the public good. For "prerogative is nothing but the power of doing public good without a rule."

167. The power of calling parliaments in England, as to precise time, place, and duration, is certainly a prerogative of the king, but still with this trust, that it shall be made use of for the good of the nation as the exigencies of the times and variety of occasion shall require. For it being impossible to foresee which should always be the fittest place for them to assemble in, and what the best season, the choice of these was left with the executive power, as might be best subservient to the public good and best suit the ends of parliament.

168. The old question will be asked in this matter of prerogative, "But who shall be judge when this power is made a right use of?" I answer: Between an executive power in being, with such a prerogative, and a legislative that depends upon his will for their convening, there can be no judge on earth. As there can be none between the legislative and the people, should either the executive or the legislative, when they have got the power in their hands, design, or go about to enslave or destroy them, the people have no other remedy in this, as in all other cases where they have no judge on earth, but to appeal to Heaven; for the rulers in such attempts, exercising

power the people never put into their hands, who can never be supposed to consent that anybody should rule over them for their harm, do that which they have not a right to do.

And where the body of the people, or any single man, are deprived of their right, or are under the exercise of a power without right, having no appeal on earth they have a liberty to appeal to Heaven whenever they judge the cause of sufficient moment. And therefore, though the people cannot be judge, so as to have, by the constitution of that society, any superior power to determine and give effective sentence in the case, yet they have reserved that ultimate determination to themselves which belongs to all mankind, where there lies no appeal on earth, by a law antecedent and paramount to all positive laws of men, whether they have just cause to make their appeal to Heaven. And this judgment they cannot part with, it being out of a man's power so to submit himself to another as to give him a liberty to destroy him; God and Nature never allowing a man so to abandon himself as to neglect his own preservation. And since he cannot take away his own life, neither can he give another power to take it. Nor let anyone think this lays a perpetual foundation for disorder; for this operates not till the inconvenience is so great that the majority feel it, and are weary of it, and find a necessity to have it amended. And this the executive power, or wise princes, never need come in the danger of; and it is the thing of all others they have most need to avoid, as, of all others, the most perilous.

CHAPTER XV

Of Paternal, Political and Despotical Power, Considered Together

169. THOUGH I have had occasion to speak of these separately before, yet the great mistakes of late about government having, as I suppose, arisen from confounding these distinct powers one with another, it may not perhaps be amiss to consider them here together.

170. First, then, paternal or parental power is nothing but that which parents have over their children to govern them, for the children's good, till they come to the use of reason, or a state of knowledge, wherein they may be supposed capable to understand that rule, whether it be the law of Nature or the municipal law of their country, they are to govern themselves by—capable, I say, to know it, as well as several others, who live as free men under that law. The affection and tenderness God hath planted in the breasts of parents towards their children makes it evident that this is not intended to be a severe arbitrary government, but only for the help, instruction, and preservation of their offspring. But happen as it will, there is, as I have proved, no reason why it should be thought to extend to life and death, at any time, over their children, more than over anybody else, or keep the child in subjection to the will of his parents when grown to a man and the perfect use of reason, any farther than as having received life and education from his parents obliges him to respect, honor, gratitude, assistance, and support, all his life, to both father and mother. And thus, it is true, the paternal is a natural government, but not at all extending itself to the ends and jurisdictions of that which is political. The power of the father doth not reach at all to the property of the child, which is only in his own disposing.

171. Secondly, political power is that power which every man having in the state of Nature has given up into the hands of the society, and therein to the governors whom the society hath set over itself, with this express or tacit trust, that it shall be employed for their good and the preservation of their property. Now this power, which every man has in the state of Nature, and which he parts with to the society in all such cases where the society can secure him, is to use such means for the preserving of his own property as he thinks good and Nature allows him; and to punish the breach of the law of Nature in others so as (according to the best of his reason) may most conduce to the preservation of himself and the rest of mankind; so that the end and measure of this power, when in every man's hands, in the state of Nature, being the preservation of all of his society—that is, all mankind in general—it can have no other end or measure, when in the hands of the magistrate, but to preserve the members of

that society in their lives, liberties, and possessions, and so cannot be an absolute, arbitrary power over their lives and fortunes, which are as much as possible to be preserved; but a power to make laws, and annex such penalties to them as may tend to the preservation of the whole, by cutting off those parts, and those only, which are so corrupt that they threaten the sound and healthy, without which no severity is lawful. And this power has its original only from compact and agreement and the mutual consent of those who make up the community.

172. Thirdly, despotical power is an absolute, arbitrary power one man has over another, to take away his life whenever he pleases; and this is a power which neither Nature gives, for it has made no such distinction between one man and another, nor compact can convey. For man, not having such an arbitrary power over his own life, cannot give another man such a power over it, but it is the effect only of forfeiture which the aggressor makes of his own life when he puts himself into the state of war with another. For having quitted reason, which God hath given to be the rule betwixt man and man, and the peaceable ways which that teaches, and made use of force to compass his unjust ends upon another where he has no right, he renders himself liable to be destroyed by his adversary whenever he can, as any other noxious and brutish creature that is destructive to his being. And thus captives, taken in a just and lawful war, and such only, are subject to a despotical power, which, as it arises not from compact, so neither is it capable of any, but is the state of war continued. For what compact can be made with a man that is not master of his own life? What condition can he perform? And if he be once allowed to be master of his own life, the despotical, arbitrary power of his master ceases. He that is master of himself and his own life has a right, too, to the means of preserving it; so that as soon as compact enters, slavery ceases, and he so far quits his absolute power and puts an end to the state of war who enters into conditions with his captive.

173. Nature gives the first of these—viz., paternal power to parents for the benefit of their children during their minority, to supply their want of ability and understanding how to manage their property. (By property I must be understood here, as in other places, to mean that

property which men have in their persons as well as goods.) Voluntary agreement gives the second—viz., political power to governors, for the benefit of their subjects, to secure them in the possession and use of their properties. And forfeiture gives the third—despotical power to lords for their own benefit over those who are stripped of all property.

174. He that shall consider the distinct rise and extent, and the different ends of these several powers, will plainly see that paternal power comes as far short of that of the magistrate as despotical exceeds it; and that absolute dominion, however placed, is so far from being one kind of civil society that it is as inconsistent with it as slavery is with property. Paternal power is only where minority makes the child incapable to manage his property; political where men have property in their own disposal; and despotical over such as have no property at all.

CHAPTER XVI

Of Conquest

175. THOUGH governments can originally have no other rise than that before mentioned, nor polities be founded on anything but the consent of the people, yet such have been the disorders ambition has filled the world with, that in the noise of war, which makes so great a part of the history of mankind, this consent is little taken notice of; and, therefore, many have mistaken the force of arms for the consent of the people, and reckon conquest as one of the originals of government. But conquest is as far from setting up any government as demolishing a house is from building a new one in the place. Indeed, it often makes way for a new frame of a commonwealth by destroying the former; but, without the consent of the people, can never erect a new one.

176. That the aggressor, who puts himself into the state of war with another, and unjustly invades another man's right, can, by such an unjust war, never come to have a right over the conquered, will be

easily agreed by all men, who will not think that robbers and pirates have a right of empire over whomsoever they have force enough to master, or that men are bound by promises which unlawful force extorts from them. Should a robber break into my house, and, with a dagger at my throat, make me seal deeds to convey my estate to him, would this give him any title? Just such a title by his sword has an unjust conqueror who forces me into submission. The injury and the crime is equal, whether committed by the wearer of a crown or some petty villain. The title of the offender and the number of his followers make no difference in the offense, unless it be to aggravate it. The only difference is, great robbers punish little ones to keep them in their obedience; but the great ones are rewarded with laurels and triumphs, because they are too big for the weak hands of justice in this world, and have the power in their own possession which should punish offenders. What is my remedy against a robber that so broke into my house? Appeal to the law for justice. But perhaps justice is denied, or I am crippled and cannot stir; robbed, and have not the means to do it. If God has taken away all means of seeking remedy, there is nothing left but patience. But my son, when able, may seek the relief of the law, which I am denied; he or his son may renew his appeal till he recover his right. But the conquered, or their children, have no court—no arbitrator on earth to appeal to. Then they may appeal, as Jephtha did, to Heaven, and repeat their appeal till they have recovered the native right of their ancestors, which was to have such a legislative over them as the majority should approve and freely acquiesce in. If it be objected this would cause endless trouble, I answer, no more than justice does, where she lies open to all that appeal to her. He that troubles his neighbor without a cause is punished for it by the justice of the court he appeals to. And he that appeals to Heaven must be sure he has right on his side, and a right, too, that is worth the trouble and cost of the appeal, as he will answer at a tribunal that cannot be deceived, and will be sure to retribute to everyone according to the mischiefs he hath created to his fellow-subjects—that is, any part of mankind. From whence it is plain that he that conquers in an unjust war can thereby have no title to the subjection and obedience of the conquered.

177. But supposing victory favors the right side, let us consider a conqueror in a lawful war, and see what power he gets, and over whom.

First, it is plain he gets no power by his conquest over those that conquered with him. They that fought on his side cannot suffer by the conquest, but must, at least, be as much free men as they were before. And most commonly they serve upon terms, and on condition to share with their leader, and enjoy a part of the spoil and other advantages that attend the conquering sword, or, at least, have a part of the subdued country bestowed upon them. And the conquering people are not, I hope, to be slaves by conquest, and wear their laurels only to show they are sacrifices to their leader's triumph. They that found absolute monarchy upon the title of the sword make their heroes, who are the founders of such monarchies, arrant "draw-can-sirs," and forget they had any officers and soldiers that fought on their side in the battles they won, or assisted them in the sub-duing, or shared in possessing the countries they mastered. We are told by some that the English monarchy is founded in the Norman Conquest, and that our princes have thereby a title to absolute do-minion, which, if it were true (as by the history it appears other-wise), and that William had a right to make war on this island, yet his dominion by conquest could reach no farther than to the Saxons and Britons that were then inhabitants of this country. The Normans that came with him and helped to conquer, and all descended from them, are free men and no subjects by conquest, let that give what dominion it will. And if I or anybody else shall claim freedom as derived from them, it will be very hard to prove the contrary; and it is plain, the law that has made no distinction between the one and the other intends not there should be any difference in their freedom or privileges.

178. But supposing, which seldom happens, that the conquerors and conquered never incorporate into one people under the same laws and freedom; let us see next what power a lawful conqueror has over the subdued, and that I say is purely despotical. He has an abso-lute power over the lives of those who, by an unjust war, have for-feited them, but not over the lives or fortunes of those who engaged

not in the war, nor over the possessions even of those who were actually engaged in it.

179. Secondly, I say, then, the conqueror gets no power but only over those who have actually assisted, concurred, or consented to that unjust force that is used against him. For the people having given to their governors no power to do an unjust thing, such as is to make an unjust war (for they never had such a power in themselves), they ought not to be charged as guilty of the violence and injustice that is committed in an unjust war any farther than they actually abet it, no more than they are to be thought guilty of any violence or oppression their governors should use upon the people themselves or any part of their fellow-subjects, they having empowered them no more to the one than to the other. Conquerors, it is true, seldom trouble themselves to make the distinction, but they willingly permit the confusion of war to sweep all together; but yet this alters not the right; for the conqueror's power over the lives of the conquered being only because they have used force to do or maintain an injustice, he can have that power only over those who have concurred in that force; all the rest are innocent, and he has no more title over the people of that country who have done him no injury, and so have made no forfeiture of their lives, than he has over any other who, without any injuries or provocations, have lived upon fair terms with him.

180. Thirdly, the power a conqueror gets over those he overcomes in a just war is perfectly despotical; he has an absolute power over the lives of those who, by putting themselves in a state of war, have forfeited them, but he has not thereby a right and title to their possessions. This I doubt not but at first sight will seem a strange doctrine, it being so quite contrary to the practice of the world; there being nothing more familiar in speaking of the dominion of countries than to say such a one conquered it, as if conquest, without any more ado, conveyed a right of possession. But when we consider that the practice of the strong and powerful, how universal soever it may be, is seldom the rule of right, however it be one part of the subjection of the conquered not to argue against the conditions cut out to them by the conquering swords.

181. Though in all war there be usually a complication of force

and damage, and the aggressor seldom fails to harm the estate when he uses force against the persons of those he makes war upon, yet it is the use of force only that puts a man into the state of war. For whether by force he begins the injury, or else having quietly and by fraud done the injury, he refuses to make reparation, and by force maintains it, which is the same thing as at first to have done it by force; it is the unjust use of force that makes the war. For he that breaks open my house and violently turns me out of doors, or having peaceably got in, by force keeps me out, does, in effect, the same thing; supposing we are in such a state that we have no common judge on earth whom I may appeal to, and to whom we are both obliged to submit, for of such I am now speaking. It is the unjust use of force, then, that puts a man into the state of war with another, and thereby he that is guilty of it makes a forfeiture of his life. For quitting reason, which is the rule given between man and man, and using force, the way of beasts, he becomes liable to be destroyed by him he uses force against, as any savage ravenous beast that is dangerous to his being.

182. But because the miscarriages of the father are no faults of the children, who may be rational and peaceable, notwithstanding the brutishness and injustice of the father, the father, by his miscarriages and violence, can forfeit but his own life, and involves not his children in his guilt or destruction. His goods which Nature, that willeth the preservation of all mankind as much as is possible, hath made to belong to the children to keep them from perishing, do still continue to belong to his children. For supposing them not to have joined in the war either through infancy or choice, they have done nothing to forfeit them, nor has the conqueror any right to take them away by the bare right of having subdued him that by force attempted his destruction, though perhaps he may have some right to them to repair the damages he has sustained by the war, and the defense of his own right, which how far it reaches to the possessions of the conquered we shall see by and by; so that he that by conquest has a right over a man's person, to destroy him if he pleases, has not thereby a right over his estate to possess and enjoy it. For it is the brutal force the aggressor has used that gives his adversary a right to take away his life and destroy

him, if he pleases, as a noxious creature; but it is damage sustained that alone gives him title to another man's goods; for though I may kill a thief that sets on me in the highway, yet I may not (which seems less) take away his money and let him go; this would be robbery on my side. His force, and the state of war he put himself in, made him forfeit his life, but gave me no title to his goods. The right, then, of conquest extends only to the lives of those who joined in the war, but not to their estates, but only in order to make reparation for the damages received and the charges of the war, and that, too, with reservation of the right of the innocent wife and children.

183. Let the conqueror have as much justice on his side as could be supposed, he has no right to seize more than the vanquished could forfeit; his life is at the victor's mercy, and his service and goods he may appropriate to make himself reparation; but he cannot take the goods of his wife and children, they too had a title to the goods he enjoyed, and their shares in the estate he possessed. For example, I in the state of Nature (and all commonwealths are in the state of Nature one with another) have injured another man, and refusing to give satisfaction, it is come to a state of war wherein my defending by force what I had gotten unjustly makes me the aggressor. I am conquered; my life, it is true, as forfeit, is at mercy, but not my wife's and children's. They made not the war, nor assisted in it. I could not forfeit their lives, they were not mine to forfeit. My wife had a share in my estate, that neither could I forfeit. And my children also, being born of me, had a right to be maintained out of my labor or substance. Here then is the case: The conqueror has a title to reparation for damages received, and the children have a title to their father's estate for their subsistence. For as to the wife's share, whether her own labor or compact gave her a title to it, it is plain her husband could not forfeit what was hers. What must be done in the case? I answer: the fundamental law of Nature being that all, as much as may be, should be preserved, it follows that if there be not enough fully to satisfy both—viz., for the conqueror's losses and children's maintenance, he that hath and to spare must remit something of his full satisfaction, and give way to the pressing and preferable title of those who are in danger to perish without it.

184. But supposing the charge and damages of the war are to be made up to the conqueror to the utmost farthing, and that the children of the vanquished, spoiled of all their father's goods, are to be left to starve and perish, yet the satisfying of what shall, on this score, be due to the conqueror will scarce give him a title to any country he shall conquer. For the damages of war can scarce amount to the value of any considerable tract of land in any part of the world, where all the land is possessed, and none lies waste. And if I have not taken away the conqueror's land which, being vanquished, it is impossible I should, scarce any other spoil I have done him can amount to the value of mine, supposing it of an extent any way coming near what I had overrun of his, and equally cultivated too. The destruction of a year's product or two (for it seldom reaches four or five) is the utmost spoil that usually can be done. For as to money, and such riches and treasure taken away, these are none of Nature's goods, they have but a phantastical imaginary value; Nature has put no such upon them. They are of no more account by her standard than the Wampompeke of the Americans to an European prince, or the silver money of Europe would have been formerly to an American. And five years' product is not worth the perpetual inheritance of land, where all is possessed and none remains waste, to be taken up by him that is disseized, which will be easily granted, if one do but take away the imaginary value of money, the disproportion being more than between five and five thousand; though, at the same time, half a year's product is more worth than the inheritance where, there being more land than the inhabitants possess and make use of, anyone has liberty to make use of the waste. But their conquerors take little care to possess themselves of the lands of the vanquished. No damage therefore that men in the state of Nature (as all princes and governments are in reference to one another) suffer from one another can give a conqueror power to dispossess the posterity of the vanquished, and turn them out of that inheritance which ought to be the possession of them and their descendants to all generations. The conqueror indeed will be apt to think himself master; and it is the very condition of the subdued not to be able to dispute their right. But, if that be all, it gives no other title than what bare force gives to the stronger over the weaker; and,

by this reason, he that is strongest will have a right to whatever he pleases to seize on.

185. Over those, then, that joined with him in the war, and over those of the subdued country that opposed him not, and the posterity even of those that did, the conqueror, even in a just war, hath, by his conquest, no right of dominion. They are free from any subjection to him, and if their former government be dissolved, they are at liberty to begin and erect another to themselves.

186. The conqueror, it is true, usually by the force he has over them, compels them, with a sword at their breasts, to stoop to his conditions, and submit to such a government as he pleases to afford them; but the inquiry is, what right he has to do so? If it be said they submit by their own consent, then this allows their own consent to be necessary to give the conqueror a title to rule over them. It remains only to be considered whether promises, extorted by force, without right, can be thought consent, and how far they bind. To which I shall say, they bind not at all; because whatsoever another gets from me by force, I still retain the right of, and he is obliged presently to restore. He that forces my horse from me ought presently to restore him, and I have still a right to retake him. By the same reason, he that forced a promise from me ought presently to restore it—i.e., quit me of the obligation of it; or I may resume it myself—i.e., choose whether I will perform it. For the law of Nature laying an obligation on me, only by the rules she prescribes, cannot oblige me by the violation of her rules; such is the extorting anything from me by force. Nor does it at all alter the case, to say I gave my promise, no more than it excuses the force, and passes the right, when I put my hand in my pocket and deliver my purse myself to a thief who demands it with a pistol at my breast.

187. From all which, it follows that the government of a conqueror, imposed by force on the subdued, against whom he had no right of war, or who joined not in the war against him, where he had right, has no obligation upon them.

188. But let us suppose that all the men of that community being all members of the same body politic, may be taken to have joined

in that unjust war, wherein they are subdued, and so their lives are at the mercy of the conqueror.

189. I say this concerns not their children who are in their minority. For since a father hath not, in himself, a power over the life or liberty of his child, no act of his can possibly forfeit it; so that the children, whatever may have happened to the fathers, are free men, and the absolute power of the conqueror reaches no farther than the persons of the men that were subdued by him, and dies with them; and should he govern them as slaves, subjected to his absolute, arbitrary power, he has no such right of dominion over their children. He can have no power over them but by their own consent, whatever he may drive them to say or do, and he has no lawful authority, whilst force, and not choice, compels them to submission.

190. Every man is born with a double right. First, a right of freedom to his person, which no other man has a power over, but the free disposal of it lies in himself. Secondly, a right before any other man, to inherit, with his brethren, his father's goods.

191. By the first of these, a man is naturally free from subjection to any government, though he be born in a place under its jurisdiction. But if he disclaim the lawful government of the country he was born in, he must also quit the right that belonged to him, by the laws of it, and the possessions there descending to him from his ancestors, if it were a government made by their consent.

192. By the second, the inhabitants of any country, who are descended and derive a title to their estates from those who are subdued, and had a government forced upon them, against their free consents, retain a right to the possession of their ancestors, though they consent not freely to the government, whose hard conditions were, by force, imposed on the possessors of that country. For the first conqueror never having had a title to the land of that country, the people, who are the descendants of, or claim under those who were forced to submit to the yoke of a government by constraint, have always a right to shake it off, and free themselves from the usurpation or tyranny the sword hath brought in upon them, till their rulers put them under such a frame of government as they willingly and of choice consent to (which they can never be supposed to do, till

either they are put in a full state of liberty to choose their government and governors, or at least till they have such standing laws to which they have, by themselves or their representatives, given their free consent, and also till they are allowed their due property, which is so to be proprietors of what they have that nobody can take away any part of it without their own consent, without which, men under any government are not in the state of free men, but are direct slaves under the force of war). And who doubts but the Grecian Christians, descendants of the ancient possessors of that country, may justly cast off the Turkish yoke they have so long groaned under, whenever they have a power to do it?

193. But granting that the conqueror, in a just war, has a right to the estates, as well as power over the persons of the conquered, which, it is plain, he hath not, nothing of absolute power will follow from hence in the continuance of the government. Because the descendants of these being all free men, if he grants them estates and possessions to inhabit his country, without which it would be worth nothing, whatsoever he grants them they have so far as it is granted property in; the nature whereof is, that, without a man's own consent, it cannot be taken from him.

194. Their persons are free by a native right, and their properties, be they more or less, are their own, and at their own dispose, and not at his; or else it is no property. Supposing the conqueror gives to one man a thousand acres, to him and his heirs for ever; to another he lets a thousand acres, for his life, under the rent of £50 or £500 per annum. Has not the one of these a right to his thousand acres for ever, and the other during his life, paying the said rent? And hath not the tenant for life a property in all that he gets over and above his rent, by his labor and industry, during the said term, supposing it be double the rent? Can anyone say, the king, or conqueror, after his grant, may, by his power of conqueror, take away all, or part of the land, from the heirs of one, or from the other during his life, he paying the rent? Or, can he take away from either the goods or money they have got upon the said land at his pleasure? If he can, then all free and voluntary contracts cease, and are void in the world; there needs nothing but power enough to dissolve them at any time, and all

the grants and promises of men in power are but mockery and collusion. For can there be anything more ridiculous than to say, I give you and yours this forever, and that in the surest and most solemn way of conveyance can be devised, and yet it is to be understood that I have right, if I please, to take it away from you again tomorrow?

195. I will not dispute now whether princes are exempt from the laws of their country, but this I am sure, they owe subjection to the laws of God and Nature. Nobody, no power can exempt them from the obligations of that eternal law. Those are so great and so strong in the case of promises, that Omnipotency itself can be tied by them. Grants, promises, and oaths are bonds that hold the Almighty, whatever some flatterers say to princes of the world, who, all together, with all their people joined to them, are, in comparison of the great God, but as a drop of the bucket, or a dust on the balance—inconsiderable, nothing!

196. The short of the case in conquest, is this: The conqueror, if he have a just cause, has a despotical right over the persons of all that actually aided and concurred in the war against him, and a right to make up his damage and cost out of their labor and estates, so he injure not the right of any other. Over the rest of the people, if there were any that consented not to the war, and over the children of the captives themselves or the possessions of either he has no power, and so can have, by virtue of conquest, no lawful title himself to dominion over them, or derive it to his posterity; but is an aggressor, and puts himself in a state of war against them, and has no better a right of principality, he, nor any of his successors, than Hingar, or Hubba, the Danes, had here in England, or Spartacus, had he conquered Italy, which is to have their yoke cast off as soon as God shall give those under their subjection courage and opportunity to do it. Thus, notwithstanding whatever title the kings of Assyria had over Judah, by the sword, God assisted Hezekiah to throw off the dominion of that conquering empire. "And the Lord was with Hezekiah, and he prospered; wherefore he went forth, and he rebelled against the king of Assyria, and served him not" (2 Kings xviii. 7). Whence it is plain that shaking off a power which force, and not right, hath set over anyone, though it hath the name of rebellion, yet is no offense before

God, but that which He allows and countenances, though even promises and covenants, when obtained by force, have intervened. For it is very probable, to anyone that reads the story of Ahaz and Hezekiah attentively, that the Assyrians subdued Ahaz, and deposed him, and made Hezekiah king in his father's lifetime, and that Hezekiah, by agreement, had done him homage, and paid him tribute till this time.

CHAPTER XVII

Of Usurpation

197. As conquest may be called a foreign usurpation, so usurpation is a kind of domestic conquest, with this difference—that an usurper can never have right on his side, it being no usurpation but where one is got into the possession of what another has right to. This, so far as it is usurpation, is a change only of persons, but not of the forms and rules of the government; for if the usurper extend his power beyond what, of right, belonged to the lawful princes or governors of the commonwealth, it is tyranny added to usurpation.

198. In all lawful governments the designation of the persons who are to bear rule being as natural and necessary a part as the form of the government itself, and that which had its establishment originally from the people—the anarchy being much alike, to have no form of government at all, or to agree that it shall be monarchical, yet appoint no way to design the person that shall have the power and be the monarch—all commonwealths, therefore, with the form of government established, have rules also of appointing and conveying the right to those who are to have any share in the public authority; and whoever gets into the exercise of any part of the power by other ways than what the laws of the community have prescribed hath no right to be obeyed, though the form of the commonwealth be still preserved, since he is not the person the laws have appointed, and, consequently, not the person the people have consented to. Nor can such an usurper,

or any deriving from him, ever have a title till the people are both at liberty to consent, and have actually consented, to allow and confirm in him the power he hath till then usurped.

CHAPTER XVIII

Of Tyranny

199. As usurpation is the exercise of power which another hath a right to, so tyranny is the exercise of power beyond right, which nobody can have a right to; and this is making use of the power anyone has in his hands, not for the good of those who are under it, but for his own private, separate advantage. When the governor, however entitled, makes not the law, but his will, the rule, and his commands and actions are not directed to the preservation of the properties of his people, but the satisfaction of his own ambition, revenge, covetousness, or any other irregular passion.

200. If one can doubt this to be truth or reason because it comes from the obscure hand of a subject, I hope the authority of a king will make it pass with him. King James, in his speech to the Parliament, 1603, tells them thus: "I will ever prefer the weal of the public and of the whole commonwealth, in making of good laws and constitutions, to any particular and private ends of mine, thinking ever the wealth and weal of the commonwealth to be my greatest weal and worldly felicity—a point wherein a lawful king doth directly differ from a tyrant; for I do acknowledge that the special and greatest point of difference that is between a rightful king and an usurping tyrant is this—that whereas the proud and ambitious tyrant doth think his kingdom and people are only ordained for satisfaction of his desires and unreasonable appetites, the righteous and just king doth, by the contrary, acknowledge himself to be ordained for the procuring of the wealth and property of his people." And again, in his speech to the Parliament, 1609, he hath these words: "The king binds himself, by a double oath, to the observation of the fundamental laws of his

kingdom—tacitly, as by being a king, and so bound to protect, as well the people as the laws of his kingdom; and expressly by his oath at his coronation; so as every just king, in a settled kingdom, is bound to observe that paction made to his people, by his laws, in framing his government agreeable thereunto, according to that paction which God made with Noah after the deluge: 'Hereafter, seed-time, and harvest, and cold, and heat, and summer, and winter, and day, and night, shall not cease while the earth remaineth.' And therefore a king, governing in a settled kingdom, leaves to be a king, and degenerates into a tyrant, as soon as he leaves off to rule according to his laws." And a little after: "Therefore, all kings that are not tyrants, or perjured, will be glad to bound themselves within the limits of their laws, and they that persuade them the contrary are vipers, pests, both against them and the commonwealth." Thus, that learned king, who well understood the notions of things, makes the difference betwixt a king and a tyrant to consist only in this: that one makes the laws the bounds of his power and the good of the public the end of his government; the other makes all give way to his own will and appetite.

201. It is a mistake to think this fault is proper only to monarchies. Other forms of government are liable to it as well as that; for wherever the power that is put in any hands for the government of the people and the preservation of their properties is applied to other ends, and made use of to impoverish, harass, or subdue them to the arbitrary and irregular commands of those that have it, there it presently becomes tyranny, whether those that thus use it are one or many. Thus we read of the thirty tyrants at Athens, as well as one at Syracuse; and the intolerable dominion of the Decemviri at Rome was nothing better.

202. Wherever law ends, tyranny begins, if the law be transgressed to another's harm; and whosoever in authority exceeds the power given him by the law, and makes use of the force he has under his command to compass that upon the subject which the law allows not, ceases in that to be a magistrate, and acting without authority may be opposed, as any other man who by force invades the right of another. This is acknowledged in subordinate magistrates. He that

hath authority to seize my person in the street may be opposed as a thief and a robber if he endeavors to break into my house to execute a writ, notwithstanding that I know he has such a warrant and such a legal authority as will empower him to arrest me abroad. And why this should not hold in the highest, as well as in the most inferior magistrate, I would gladly be informed. Is it reasonable that the eldest brother, because he has the greatest part of his father's estate, should thereby have a right to take away any of his younger brothers' portions? Or that a rich man, who possessed a whole country, should from thence have a right to seize, when he pleased, the cottage and garden of his poor neighbor? The being rightfully possessed of great power and riches, exceedingly beyond the greatest part of the sons of Adam, is so far from being an excuse, much less a reason for rapine and oppression, which the endamaging another without authority is, that it is a great aggravation of it. For exceeding the bounds of authority is no more a right in a great than a petty officer, no more justifiable in a king than a constable. But so much the worse in him as that he has more trust put in him, is supposed, from the advantage of education and counsellors, to have better knowledge and less reason to do it, having already a greater share than the rest of his brethren.

203. May the commands, then, of a prince be opposed? May he be resisted, as often as anyone shall find himself aggrieved, and but imagine he has not right done him? This will unhinge and overturn all polities, and instead of government and order, leave nothing but anarchy and confusion.

204. To this I answer: That force is to be opposed to nothing but to unjust and unlawful force. Whoever makes any opposition in any other case draws on himself a just condemnation, both from God and man; and so no such danger or confusion will follow, as is often suggested. For—

205. First, as in some countries the person of the prince by the law is sacred, and so whatever he commands or does, his person is still free from all question or violence, not liable to force, or any judicial censure or condemnation. But yet opposition may be made to the illegal acts of any inferior officer or other commissioned by him, unless he will, by actually putting himself into a state of war with his people,

dissolve the government, and leave them to that defense, which belongs to everyone in the state of Nature. For of such things, who can tell what the end will be? And a neighbor kingdom has showed the world an odd example. In all other cases the sacredness of the person exempts him from all inconveniencies, whereby he is secure, whilst the government stands, from all violence and harm whatsoever, than which there cannot be a wiser constitution. For the harm he can do in his own person not being likely to happen often, nor to extend itself far, nor being able by his single strength to subvert the laws nor oppress the body of the people, should any prince have so much weakness and ill-nature as to be willing to do it. The inconveniency of some particular mischiefs that may happen sometimes when a heady prince comes to the throne are well recompensed by the peace of the public and security of the government in the person of the chief magistrate, thus set out of the reach of danger; it being safer for the body that some few private men should be sometimes in danger to suffer than that the head of the republic should be easily and upon slight occasions exposed.

206. Secondly, but this privilege, belonging only to the king's person, hinders not but they may be questioned, opposed, and resisted, who use unjust force, though they pretend a commission from him which the law authorizes not; as is plain in the case of him that has the king's writ to arrest a man which is a full commission from the king, and yet he that has it cannot break open a man's house to do it, nor execute this command of the king upon certain days nor in certain places, though this commission have no such exception in it; but they are the limitations of the law, which, if anyone transgress, the king's commission excuses him not. For the king's authority being given him only by the law, he cannot empower anyone to act against the law, or justify him by his commission in so doing. The commission or command of any magistrate where he has no authority, being as void and insignificant as that of any private man, the difference between the one and the other being that the magistrate has some authority so far and to such ends, and the private man has none at all; for it is not the commission but the authority that gives the right of acting, and against the laws there can be no authority. But notwithstanding such

resistance, the king's person and authority are still both secured. and so no danger to governor or government.

207. Thirdly, supposing a government wherein the person of the chief magistrate is not thus sacred, yet this doctrine of the lawfulness of resisting all unlawful exercises of his power will not, upon every slight occasion, endanger him or embroil the government; for where the injured party may be relieved and his damages repaired by appeal to the law, there can be no pretense for force, which is only to be used where a man is intercepted from appealing to the law. For nothing is to be accounted hostile force but where it leaves not the remedy of such an appeal, and it is such force alone that puts him that uses it into a state of war, and makes it lawful to resist him. A man with a sword in his hand demands my purse on the highway, when perhaps I have not 12d. in my pocket. This man I may lawfully kill. To another I deliver £100 to hold only whilst I alight, which he refuses to restore me when I am got up again, but draws his sword to defend the possession of it by force. I endeavor to retake it. The mischief this man does me is a hundred, or possibly a thousand times more than the other perhaps intended me (whom I killed before he really did me any) ; and yet I might lawfully kill the one and cannot so much as hurt the other lawfully. The reason whereof is plain; because the one using force which threatened my life, I could not have time to appeal to the law to secure it, and when it was gone it was too late to appeal. The law could not restore life to my dead carcass. The loss was irreparable; which to prevent the law of Nature gave me a right to destroy him who had put himself into a state of war with me and threatened my destruction. But in the other case, my life not being in danger, I might have the benefit of appealing to the law, and have reparation for my £100 that way.

208. Fourthly, but if the unlawful acts done by the magistrate be maintained (by the power he has got), and the remedy, which is due by law, be by the same power obstructed, yet the right of resisting, even in such manifest acts of tyranny, will not suddenly, or on slight occasions, disturb the government. For if it reach no farther than some private men's cases, though they have a right to defend themselves, and to recover by force what by unlawful force is taken from

them, yet the right to do so will not easily engage them in a contest wherein they are sure to perish; it being as impossible for one or a few oppressed men to disturb the government where the body of the people do not think themselves concerned in it, as for a raving madman or heady malcontent to overturn a well-settled state, the people being as little apt to follow the one as the other.

209. But if either these illegal acts have extended to the majority of the people, or if the mischief and oppression has light only on some few, but in such cases as the precedent and consequences seem to threaten all, and they are persuaded in their consciences that their laws, and with them, their estates, liberties, and lives are in danger, and perhaps their religion too, how they will be hindered from resisting illegal force used against them I cannot tell. This is an inconvenience, I confess, that attends all governments whatsoever, when the governors have brought it to this pass, to be generally suspected of their people, the most dangerous state they can possibly put themselves in; wherein they are the less to be pitied, because it is so easy to be avoided. It being as impossible for a governor, if he really means the good of his people, and the preservation of them and their laws together, not to make them see and feel it, as it is for the father of a family not to let his children see he loves and takes care of them.

210. But if all the world shall observe pretenses of one kind, and actions of another, arts used to elude the law, and the trust of prerogative (which is an arbitrary power in some things left in the prince's hand to do good, not harm, to the people) employed contrary to the end for which it was given; if the people shall find the ministers and subordinate magistrates chosen, suitable to such ends, and favored or laid by proportionably as they promote or oppose them; if they see several experiments made of arbitrary power, and that religion underhand favored, though publicly proclaimed against, which is readiest to introduce it, and the operators in it supported as much as may be; and when that cannot be done, yet approved still, and liked the better, and a long train of acting show the counsels all tending that way, how can a man any more hinder himself from being persuaded in his own mind which way things are going; or, from casting about how to save himself, than he could from believing the captain of a ship he was in

was carrying him and the rest of the company to Algiers, when he found him always steering that course, though cross winds, leaks in his ship, and want of men and provisions did often force him to turn his course another way for some time, which he steadily returned to again as soon as the wind, weather, and other circumstances would let him?

CHAPTER XIX

Of the Dissolution of Government

211. HE that will, with any clearness, speak of the dissolution of government, ought in the first place to distinguish between the dissolution of the society and the dissolution of the government. That which makes the community, and brings men out of the loose state of Nature into one politic society, is the agreement which everyone has with the rest to incorporate and act as one body, and so be one distinct commonwealth. The usual, and almost only way whereby this union is dissolved, is the inroad of foreign force making a conquest upon them. For in that case (not being able to maintain and support themselves as one entire and independent body) the union belonging to that body, which consisted therein, must necessarily cease, and so everyone return to the state he was in before, with a liberty to shift for himself and provide for his own safety, as he thinks fit, in some other society. Whenever the society is dissolved, it is certain the government of that society cannot remain. Thus conquerors' swords often cut up governments by the roots, and mangle societies to pieces, separating the subdued or scattered multitude from the protection of and dependence on that society which ought to have preserved them from violence. The world is too well instructed in, and too forward to allow of this way of dissolving of governments, to need any more to be said of it; and there wants not much argument to prove that where the society is dissolved, the government cannot remain; that being as impossible as for the frame of a house to subsist when the materials

of it are scattered and displaced by a whirlwind, or jumbled into a confused heap by an earthquake.

212. Besides this overturning from without, governments are dissolved from within:

First, when the legislative is altered, civil society being a state of peace amongst those who are of it, from whom the state of war is excluded by the umpirage which they have provided in their legislative for the ending all differences that may arise amongst any of them; it is in their legislative that the members of a commonwealth are united and combined together into one coherent living body. This is the soul that gives form, life, and unity to the commonwealth; from hence the several members have their mutual influence, sympathy, and connection; and therefore when the legislative is broken, or dissolved, dissolution and death follows. For the essence and union of the society consisting in having one will, the legislative, when once established by the majority, has the declaring and, as it were, keeping of that will. The constitution of the legislative is the first and fundamental act of society, whereby provision is made for the continuation of their union under the direction of persons and bonds of laws, made by persons authorized thereunto, by the consent and appointment of the people, without which no one man, or number of men, amongst them can have authority of making laws that shall be binding to the rest. When any one, or more, shall take upon them to make laws whom the people have not appointed so to do, they make laws without authority, which the people are not therefore bound to obey; by which means they come again to be out of subjection, and may constitute to themselves a new legislative, as they think best, being in full liberty to resist the force of those who, without authority, would impose anything upon them. Everyone is at the disposure of his own will, when those who had, by the delegation of the society, the declaring of the public will, are excluded from it, and others usurp the place who have no such authority or delegation.

213. This being usually brought about by such in the commonwealth who misuse the power they have, it is hard to consider it aright, and know at whose door to lay it, without knowing the form of government in which it happens. Let us suppose, then, the legislative

placed in the concurrence of three distinct persons: First, a single hereditary person having the constant, supreme, executive power, and with it the power of convoking and dissolving the other two within certain periods of time. Secondly, an assembly of hereditary nobility. Thirdly, an assembly of representatives chosen, *pro tempore,* by the people. Such a form of government supposed, it is evident:

214. First, that when such a single person or prince sets up his own arbitrary will in place of the laws which are the will of the society declared by the legislative, then the legislative is changed. For that being, in effect, the legislative whose rules and laws are put in execution, and required to be obeyed, when other laws are set up, and other rules pretended and enforced than what the legislative, constituted by the society, have enacted, it is plain that the legislative is changed. Whoever introduces new laws, not being thereunto authorized, by the fundamental appointment of the society, or subverts the old, disowns and overturns the power by which they were made, and so sets up a new legislative.

215. Secondly, when the prince hinders the legislative from assembling in its due time, or from acting freely, pursuant to those ends for which it was constituted, the legislative is altered. For it is not a certain number of men—no, nor their meeting, unless they have also freedom of debating and leisure of perfecting what is for the good of the society, wherein the legislative consists; when these are taken away, or altered, so as to deprive the society of the due exercise of their power, the legislative is truly altered. For it is not names that constitute governments, but the use and exercise of those powers that were intended to accompany them; so that he who takes away the freedom, or hinders the acting of the legislative in its due seasons, in effect takes away the legislative, and puts an end to the government.

216. Thirdly, when, by the arbitrary power of the prince, the electors or ways of election are altered without the consent and contrary to the common interest of the people, there also the legislative is altered. For if others than those whom the society hath authorized thereunto do choose, or in another way than what the society hath prescribed, those chosen are not the legislative appointed by the people.

217. Fourthly, the delivery also of the people into the subjection of a foreign power, either by the prince or by the legislative, is certainly a change of the legislative, and so a dissolution of the government. For the end why people entered into society being to be preserved one entire, free, independent society, to be governed by its own laws, this is lost whenever they are given up into the power of another.

218. Why, in such a constitution as this, the dissolution of the government in these cases is to be imputed to the prince is evident, because he, having the force, treasure, and offices of the State to employ, and often persuading himself or being flattered by others, that, as supreme magistrate, he is incapable of control; he alone is in a condition to make great advances towards such changes under pretense of lawful authority, and has it in his hands to terrify or suppress opposers as factious, seditious, and enemies to the government; whereas no other part of the legislative, or people, is capable by themselves to attempt any alteration of the legislative without open and visible rebellion, apt enough to be taken notice of, which, when it prevails, produces effects very little different from foreign conquest. Besides, the prince, in such a form of government, having the power of dissolving the other parts of the legislative, and thereby rendering them private persons, they can never, in opposition to him, or without his concurrence, alter the legislative by a law, his consent being necessary to give any of their decrees that sanction. But yet so far as the other parts of the legislative any way contribute to any attempt upon the government, and do either promote, or not, what lies in them, hinder such designs, they are guilty, and partake in this, which is certainly the greatest crime men can be guilty of one towards another.

219. There is one way more whereby such a government may be dissolved, and that is: When he who has the supreme executive power neglects and abandons that charge, so that the laws already made can no longer be put in execution; this is demonstratively to reduce all to anarchy, and so effectively to dissolve the government. For laws not being made for themselves, but to be, by their execution, the bonds of the society to keep every part of the body politic in its due place and function. When that totally ceases, the government visibly ceases,

and the people become a confused multitude without order or connection. Where there is no longer the administration of justice for the securing of men's rights, nor any remaining power within the community to direct the force, or provide for the necessities of the public, there certainly is no government left. Where the laws cannot be executed it is all one as if there were no laws, and a government without laws is, I suppose, a mystery in politics inconceivable to human capacity, and inconsistent with human society.

220. In these, and the like cases, when the government is dissolved, the people are at liberty to provide for themselves by erecting a new legislative differing from the other by the change of persons, or form, or both, as they shall find it most for their safety and good. For the society can never, by the fault of another, lose the native and original right it has to preserve itself, which can only be done by a settled legislative and a fair and impartial execution of the laws made by it. But the state of mankind is not so miserable that they are not capable of using this remedy till it be too late to look for any. To tell people they may provide for themselves by erecting a new legislative, when, by oppression, artifice, or being delivered over to a foreign power, their old one is gone, is only to tell them they may expect relief when it is too late, and the evil is past cure. This is, in effect, no more than to bid them first be slaves, and then to take care of their liberty, and, when their chains are on, tell them they may act like free men. This, if barely so, is rather mockery than relief, and men can never be secure from tyranny if there be no means to escape it till they are perfectly under it; and, therefore, it is that they have not only a right to get out of it, but to prevent it.

221. There is, therefore, secondly, another way whereby governments are dissolved, and that is, when the legislative, or the prince, either of them act contrary to their trust.

For the legislative acts against the trust reposed in them when they endeavor to invade the property of the subject, and to make themselves, or any part of the community, masters or arbitrary disposers of the lives, liberties, or fortunes of the people.

222. The reason why men enter into society is the preservation of their property; and the end while they choose and authorize a legis-

lative is that there may be laws made, and rules set, as guards and fences to the properties of all the society, to limit the power and moderate the dominion of every part and member of the society. For since it can never be supposed to be the will of the society that the legislative should have a power to destroy that which everyone designs to secure by entering into society, and for which the people submitted themselves to legislators of their own making: whenever the legislators endeavor to take away and destroy the property of the people, or to reduce them to slavery under arbitrary power, they put themselves into a state of war with the people, who are thereupon absolved from any farther obedience, and are left to the common refuge which God hath provided for all men against force and violence. Whensoever, therefore, the legislative shall transgress this fundamental rule of society, and either by ambition, fear, folly, or corruption, endeavor to grasp themselves, or put into the hands of any other, an absolute power over the lives, liberties, and estates of the people, by this breach of trust they forfeit the power the people had put into their hands for quite contrary ends, and it devolves to the people, who have a right to resume their original liberty, and by the establishment of a new legislative (such as they shall think fit), provide for their own safety and security, which is the end for which they are in society.

What I have said here concerning the legislative in general holds true also concerning the supreme executor, who having a double trust put in him, both to have a part in the legislative and the supreme execution of the law, acts against both, when he goes about to set up his own arbitrary will as the law of the society. He acts also contrary to his trust when he employs the force, treasure, and offices of the society to corrupt the representatives and gain them to his purposes, when he openly pre-engages the electors, and prescribes, to their choice, such whom he has, by solicitation, threats, promises, or otherwise, won to his designs, and employs them to bring in such who have promised beforehand what to vote and what to enact. Thus to regulate candidates and electors, and new model the ways of election, what is it but to cut up the government by the roots, and poison the very fountain of public security? For the people having reserved to themselves the choice of their representatives as the fence to their properties, could do it for no other end but that they might always be freely chosen, and so chosen, freely act and advise as the necessity of the commonwealth and the public good should, upon examination and mature debate, be judged to require. This, those who give their votes before they hear the debate, and have weighed the reasons on all sides, are not capable of doing. To prepare such an assembly as this, and endeavor to set up the declared abettors of his own will, for the true representatives of the people, and the law-makers of the society, is certainly as great a breach of trust, and as perfect a declaration of a design to subvert the government, as is possible to be met with. To which, if one shall add rewards and punishments visibly employed to the same end, and all the arts of perverted law made use of to take off and destroy all that stand in the way of such a design, and will not comply and consent to betray the liberties of their country, it will be past doubt what is doing. What power they ought to have in the society who thus employ it contrary to the trust went along with it in its first institution, is easy to determine; and one cannot but see that he who has once attempted any such thing as this cannot any longer be trusted.

223. To this, perhaps, it will be said that the people being ignorant and always discontented, to lay the foundation of government in the unsteady opinion and uncertain humor of the people, is to expose it to certain ruin; and no government will be able long to subsist if the people may set up a new legislative whenever they take offense at the old one. To this I answer, quite the contrary. People are not so easily got out of their old forms as some are apt to suggest. They are hardly to be prevailed with to amend the acknowledged faults in the frame they have been accustomed to. And if there be any original defects, or adventitious ones introduced by time or corruption, it is not an easy thing to get them changed, even when all the world sees there is an opportunity for it. This slowness and aversion in the people to quit their old constitutions has in the many revolutions we have seen in this kingdom, in this and former ages, still kept us to, or after some interval of fruitless attempts, still brought us back again to our old legislative of king, lords and commons; and whatever provocations have made the crown be taken from some of our princes' heads, they never carried the people so far as to place it in another line.

224. But it will be said this hypothesis lays a ferment for frequent rebellion. To which I answer:

First, no more than any other hypothesis. For when the people are made miserable, and find themselves exposed to the ill usage of arbitrary power, cry up their governors as much as you will for sons of Jupiter, let them be sacred and divine, descended or authorized from Heaven; give them out for whom or what you please, the same will happen. The people generally ill treated, and contrary to right, will be ready upon any occasion to ease themselves of a burden that sits heavy upon them. They will wish and seek for the opportunity, which in the change, weakness, and accidents of human affairs, seldom delays long to offer itself. He must have lived but a little while in the world, who has not seen examples of this in his time; and he must have read very little who cannot produce examples of it in all sorts of governments in the world.

225. Secondly, I answer, such revolutions happen not upon every little mismanagement in public affairs. Great mistakes in the ruling part, many wrong and inconvenient laws, and all the slips of human frailty will be borne by the people without mutiny or murmur. But if a long train of abuses, prevarications, and artifices, all tending the same way, make the design visible to the people, and they cannot but feel what they lie under, and see whither they are going, it is not to be wondered that they should then rouse themselves, and endeavor to put the rule into such hands which may secure to them the ends for which government was at first erected, and without which, ancient names and specious forms are so far from being better, that they are much worse than the state of Nature or pure anarchy; the inconveniences being all as great and as near, but the remedy farther off and more difficult.

226. Thirdly, I answer, that this power in the people of providing for their safety anew by a new legislative when their legislators have acted contrary to their trust by invading their property, is the best fence against rebellion, and the probablest means to hinder it. For rebellion being an opposition, not to persons, but authority, which is founded only in the constitutions and laws of the government: those, whoever they be, who, by force, break through, and, by force, justify

their violation of them, are truly and properly rebels. For when men, by entering into society and civil government, have excluded force, and introduced laws for the preservation of property, peace, and unity amongst themselves, those who set up force again in opposition to the laws, do *rebellare*—that is, bring back again the state of war, and are properly rebels, which they who are in power, by the pretense they have to authority, the temptation of force they have in their hands, and the flattery of those about them being likeliest to do, the properest way to prevent the evil is to show them the danger and injustice of it who are under the greatest temptation to run into it.

227. In both the forementioned cases, when either the legislative is changed, or the legislators act contrary to the end for which they were constituted, those who are guilty are guilty of rebellion. For if anyone by force takes away the established legislative of any society, and the laws by them made, pursuant to their trust, he thereby takes away the umpirage which everyone had consented to for a peaceable decision of all their controversies, and a bar to the state of war amongst them. They who remove or change the legislative take away this decisive power, which nobody can have but by the appointment and consent of the people, and so destroying the authority which the people did, and nobody else can set up, and introducing a power which the people hath not authorized, actually introduce a state of war, which is that of force without authority; and thus by removing the legislative established by the society, in whose decisions the people acquiesced and united as to that of their own will, they untie the knot, and expose the people anew to the state of war. And if those, who by force take away the legislative, are rebels, the legislators themselves, as has been shown, can be no less esteemed so, when they who were set up for the protection and preservation of the people, their liberties and properties shall by force invade and endeavor to take them away; and so they putting themselves into a state of war with those who made them the protectors and guardians of their peace, are properly, and with the greatest aggravation, *rebellantes*, rebels.

228. But if they who say it lays a foundation for rebellion mean that it may occasion civil wars or intestine broils to tell the people they are absolved from obedience when illegal attempts are made upon their

liberties or properties, and may oppose the unlawful violence of those who were their magistrates when they invade their properties, contrary to the trust put in them, and that, therefore, this doctrine is not to be allowed, being so destructive to the peace of the world; they may as well say, upon the same ground, that honest men may not oppose robbers or pirates, because this may occasion disorder or bloodshed. If any mischief come in such cases, it is not to be charged upon him who defends his own right, but on him that invades his neighbor's. If the innocent honest man must quietly quit all he has for peace sake to him who will lay violent hands upon it, I desire it may be considered what a kind of peace there will be in the world which consists only in violence and rapine, and which is to be maintained only for the benefit of robbers and oppressors. Who would not think it an admirable peace betwixt the mighty and the mean, when the lamb, without resistance, yielded his throat to be torn by the imperious wolf? Polyphemus' den gives us a perfect pattern of such a peace. Such a government wherein Ulysses and his companions had nothing to do but quietly to suffer themselves to be devoured. And no doubt Ulysses, who was a prudent man, preached up passive obedience, and exhorted them to a quiet submission by representing to them of what concernment peace was to mankind, and by showing the inconveniencies that might happen if they should offer to resist Polyphemus, who had now the power over them.

229. The end of government is the good of mankind; and which is best for mankind, that the people should be always exposed to the boundless will of tyranny, or that the rulers should be sometimes liable to be opposed when they grow exorbitant in the use of their power, and employ it for the destruction, and not the preservation, of the properties of their people?

230. Nor let anyone say that mischief can arise from hence as often as it shall please a busy head or turbulent spirit to desire the alteration of the government. It is true such men may stir whenever they please, but it will be only to their own just ruin and perdition. For till the mischief be grown general, and the ill designs of the rulers become visible, or their attempts sensible to the greater part, the people, who are more disposed to suffer than right themselves by resistance, are

not apt to stir. The examples of particular injustice or oppression of here and there an unfortunate man moves them not. But if they universally have a persuasion grounded upon manifest evidence that designs are carrying on against their liberties, and the general course and tendency of things cannot but give them strong suspicions of the evil intention of their governors, who is to be blamed for it? Who can help it if they, who might avoid it, bring themselves into this suspicion? Are the people to be blamed if they have the sense of rational creatures, and can think of things no otherwise than as they find and feel them? And is it not rather their fault who put things in such a posture that they would not have them thought as they are? I grant that the pride, ambition, and turbulency of private men have sometimes caused great disorders in commonwealths, and factions have been fatal to states and kingdoms. But whether the mischief hath oftener begun in the people's wantonness, and a desire to cast off the lawful authority of their rulers, or in the rulers' insolence and endeavors to get and exercise an arbitrary power over their people, whether oppression or disobedience gave the first rise to the disorder, I leave it to impartial history to determine.

This I am sure, whoever, either ruler or subject, by force goes about to invade the rights of either prince or people, and lays the foundation for overturning the constitution and frame of any just government, he is guilty of the greatest crime I think a man is capable of, being to answer for all those mischiefs of blood, rapine, and desolation, which the breaking to pieces of governments bring on a country; and he who does it is justly to be esteemed the common enemy and pest of mankind, and is to be treated accordingly.

231. That subjects or foreigners attempting by force on the properties of any people may be resisted with force is agreed on all hands; but that magistrates doing the same thing may be resisted, hath of late been denied; as if those who had the greatest privileges and advantages by the law had thereby a power to break those laws by which alone they were set in a better place than their brethren; whereas their offense is thereby the greater, both as being ungrateful for the greater share they have by the law, and breaking also that trust which is put into their hands by their brethren.

232. Whosoever uses force without right—as everyone does in society who does it without law—puts himself into a state of war with those against whom he so uses it, and in that state all former ties are canceled, all other rights cease, and everyone has a right to defend himself, and to resist the aggressor. This is so evident that Barclay [19] himself—that great assertor of the power and sacredness of kings—is forced to confess that it is lawful for the people, in some cases, to resist their king, and that, too, in a chapter wherein he pretends to show that the Divine law shuts up the people from all manner of rebellion. Whereby it is evident, even by his own doctrine, that since they may, in some cases, resist, all resisting of princes is not rebellion. His words are these: "Quod siquis dicat, Ergone populus tyrannicæ crudelitati et furori jugulum semper præbebit? Ergone multitudo civitates suas fame, ferro, et flammâ vastari, seque, conjuges, et liberos fortunæ ludibrio et tyranni libidini exponi, inque omnia vitæ pericula omnesque miserias et molestias à rege deduci patientur? Num illis quod omni animantium generi est à naturâ tributum, dene-gari debet, ut sc. vim vi repellant, seseque ab injuriâ tueantur? Huic breviter responsum sit, populo universo negari defensionem, quæ juris naturalis est, neque ultionem quæ præter naturam est adversus regem concedi debere. Quapropter si rex non in singulares tantum personas aliquot privatum odium exerceat, sed corpus etiam reipublicæ, cujus ipse caput est—i.e., totum populum, vel insignem aliquam ejus partem immani et intolerandâ sævitiâ seu tyrannide divexet; populo, quidem hoc casu resistendi ac tuendi se ab injuriâ potestas competit, sed tuendi se tantum, non enim in principem invadendi: et restituendæ injuriæ illatæ, non recedendi à debitâ reverentiâ propter acceptam injuriam. Præsentem denique impetum propulsandi non vim præteritam ul-ciscendi jus habet. Horum enim alterum à naturâ est, ut vitam scilicet corpusque tueamur. Alterum vero contra naturam, ut inferior de superiori supplicium sumat. Quod itaque populus malum, antequam factum sit, impedire potest, ne fiat, id postquam factum est, in regem authorem sceleris vindicare non potest, populus igitur hoc ampliùs quam privatus quispiam habet: Quod huic, vel ipsis adversariis judi-

[19] William Barclay, Scottish jurist.

cibus, excepto Buchanano, nullum nisi in patientia remedium superest. Cum ille si intolerabilis tyrannis est (modicum enim ferre omnino debet) resistere cum reverentiâ possit."—Barclay, *Contra Monarchomachos,* l. iii., c. 8.

In English thus:

233. "But if anyone should ask: Must the people, then, always lay, themselves open to the cruelty and rage of tyranny—must they see their cities pillaged and laid in ashes, their wives and children exposed to the tyrant's lust and fury, and themselves and families reduced by their king to ruin and all the miseries of want and oppression, and yet sit still—must men alone be debarred the common privilege of opposing force with force, which Nature allows so freely to all other creatures for their preservation from injury? I answer: Self-defense is a part of the law of Nature; nor can it be denied the community, even against the king himself; but to revenge themselves upon him must, by no means, be allowed them, it being not agreeable to that law. Wherefore, if the king shall show an hatred, not only to some particular persons, but sets himself against the body of the commonwealth, whereof he is the head, and shall, with intolerable ill-usage, cruelly tyrannize over the whole, or a considerable part of the people; in this case the people have a right to resist and defend themselves from injury; but it must be with this caution, that they only defend themselves, but do not attack their prince. They may repair the damages received, but must not, for any provocation, exceed the bounds of due reverence and respect. They may repulse the present attempt, but must not revenge past violences. For it is natural for us to defend life and limb, but that an inferior should punish a superior is against nature. The mischief which is designed them the people may prevent before it be done, but, when it is done, they must not revenge it on the king, though author of the villainy. This, therefore, is the privilege of the people in general above what any private person hath: That particular men are allowed, by our adversaries themselves (Buchanan only excepted), to have no other remedy but patience; but the body of the people may, with respect, resist intolerable tyranny, for when it is but moderate they ought to endure it."

234. Thus far that great advocate of monarchical power allows of resistance.

235. It is true, he has annexed two limitations to it, to no purpose: First, he says it must be with reverence.

Secondly, it must be without retribution or punishment; and the reason he gives is, "because an inferior cannot punish a superior."

First. How to resist force without striking again, or how to strike with reverence, will need some skill to make intelligible. He that shall oppose an assault only with a shield to receive the blows, or in any more respectful posture, without a sword in his hand to abate the confidence and force of the assailant, will quickly be at an end of his resistance, and will find such a defense serve only to draw on himself the worse usage. This is as ridiculous a way of resisting as Juvenal thought it of fighting: *Ubi tu pulsas, ego vapulo tantum.*[20] And the success of the combat will be unavoidably the same he there describes it:

> *Libertas pauperis hæc est;*
> *Pulsatus rogat, et pugnis concisus, adorat,*
> *Ut liceat paucis cum dentibus inde reverti.*[21]

This will always be the event of such an imaginary resistance, where men may not strike again. He, therefore, who may resist must be allowed to strike. And then let our author, or anybody else, join a knock on the head or a cut on the face with as much reverence and respect as he thinks fit. He that can reconcile blows and reverence may, for aught I know, deserve for his pains a civil, respectful cudgeling wherever he can meet with it.

Secondly. As to his second—"An inferior cannot punish a superior" —that is true, generally speaking, whilst he is his superior. But to resist force with force, being the state of war that levels the parties, cancels all former relation of reverence, respect, and superiority; and then the odds that remains is—that he who opposes the unjust aggres-

---

[20] While you hit out, I simply take the beating.
[21] The poor man's freedom consists of this:
When struck to entreat, and when battered with fists to implore
Permission to go with a few teeth left him still.

sor has this superiority over him, that he has a right, when he prevails, to punish the offender, both for the breach of the peace and all the evils that followed upon it. Barclay, therefore, in another place, more coherently to himself, denies it to be lawful to resist a king in any case. But he there assigns two cases whereby a king may unking himself. His words are:

"Quid ergo, nulline casus incidere possunt quibus populo sese erigere atque in regem impotentius dominantem arma capere et invadere jure suo suâque authoritate liceat? Nulli certe quamdiu rex manet. Semper enim ex divinis id obstat, Regem honorificato, et qui potestati resistit, Dei ordinationi resistit; non aliàs igitur in eum populo potestas est quam si id committat propter quod ipso jure rex esse desinat. Tunc enim se ipse principatu exuit atque in privatis constituit liber; hoc modo populus et superior efficitur, reverso ad eum scilicet jure illo quod ante regem inauguratum in interregno habuit. At sunt paucorum generum commissa ejusmodi quæ hunc effectum pariunt. At ego cum plurima animo perlustrem, duo tantum invenio, duos, inquam, casus quibus rex ipso facto ex rege non regem se facit et omni honore et dignitate regali atque in subditos potestate destituit; quorum etiam meminit Winzerus. Horum unus est, si regnum disperdat, quemadmodum de Nerone fertur, quod is nempe senatum populumque Romanum atque adeo urbem ipsam ferro flammaque vastare, ac novas sibi sedes quærere decrevisset. Et de Caligula, quod palam denunciarit se neque civem neque principem senatui amplius fore, inque animo habuerit, interempto utriusque ordinis electissimo, quoque Alexandriam commigrare, ac ut populum uno ictu interimeret, unam ei cervicem optavit. Talia cum rex aliquis meditatur et molitur serio, omnem regnandi curam et animum ilico abjicit, ac proinde imperium in subditos amittit, ut dominus servi pro derelicto habiti, dominium.

236. "Alter casus est, si rex in alicujus clientelam se contulit, ac regnum quod liberum à majoribus et populo traditum accepit, alienæ ditioni mancipavit. Nam tunc quamvis forte non eâ mente id agit populo plane ut incommodet; tamen quia quod præcipuum est regiæ dignitatis amisit, ut summus scilicet in regno secundum Deum sit, et solo Deo inferior, atque populum etiam totum ignorantem vel in-

vitum, cujus libertatem sartam et tectam conservare debuit, in alterius gentis ditionem et potestatem dedidit; hâc velut quadam rengi abalienatione effecit, ut nec quod ipse in regno imperium habuit retineat, nec in eum cui collatum voluit, juris quicquam transferat. atque ita eo facto liberum jam et suæ potestatis populum relinquit, cujus rei exemplum unum annales Scotici suppeditant."—Barclay, *Contra Monarchomachos,* l. iii., c. 16.

Which may be thus Englished:

237. "What, then, can there no case happen wherein the people may of right, and by their own authority, help themselves, take arms, and set upon their king, imperiously domineering over them? None at all whilst he remains a king. 'Honor the king,' and 'he that resists the power, resists the ordinance of God,' are Divine oracles that will never permit it. The people, therefore, can never come by a power over him unless he does something that makes him cease to be a king; for then he divests himself of his crown and dignity, and returns to the state of a private man, and the people become free and superior; the power which they had in the interregnum, before they crowned him king, devolving to them again. But there are but few miscarriages which bring the matter to this state. After considering it well on all sides, I can find but two. Two cases there are, I say, whereby a king, *ipso facto,* becomes no king, and loses all power and regal authority over his people, which are also taken notice of by Winzerus. The first is, if he endeavor to overturn the government—that is, if he have a purpose and design to ruin the kingdom and commonwealth, as it is recorded of Nero that he resolved to cut off the senate and people of Rome, lay the city waste with fire and sword, and then remove to some other place; and of Caligula, that he openly declared that he would be no longer a head to the people or senate, and that he had it in his thoughts to cut off the worthiest men of both ranks, and then retire to Alexandria; and he wished that the people had but one neck that he might dispatch them all at a blow. Such designs as these, when any king harbors in his thoughts, and seriously promotes, he immediately gives up all care and thought of the commonwealth, and, consequently, forfeits the power of governing his subjects, as a master does the dominion over his slaves whom he hath abandoned.

238. "The other case is, when a king makes himself the dependent of another, and subjects his kingdom, which his ancestors left him, and the people put free into his hands, to the dominion of another. For however, perhaps, it may not be his intention to prejudice the people, yet because he has hereby lost the principal part of regal dignity— viz., to be next and immediately under God, supreme in his kingdom; and also because he betrayed or forced his people, whose liberty he ought to have carefully preserved, into the power and dominion of a foreign nation. By this, as it were, alienation of his kingdom, he himself loses the power he had in it before, without transferring any the least right to those on whom he would have bestowed it; and so by this act sets the people free, and leaves them at their own disposal. One example of this is to be found in the Scotch annals."

239. In these cases Barclay, the great champion of absolute monarchy, is forced to allow that a king may be resisted, and ceases to be a king. That is in short—not to multiply cases—in whatsoever he has no authority, there he is no king, and may be resisted: for wheresoever the authority ceases, the king ceases too, and becomes like other men who have no authority. And these two cases that he instances differ little from those above mentioned, to be destructive to governments, only that he has omitted the principle from which his doctrine flows, and that is the breach of trust in not preserving the form of government agreed on, and in not intending the end of government itself, which is the public good and preservation of property. When a king has dethroned himself, and put himself in a state of war with his people, what shall hinder them from prosecuting him who is no king, as they would any other man, who has put himself into a state of war with them, Barclay, and those of his opinion, would do well to tell us. Bilson, a bishop of our Church, and a great stickler for the power and prerogative of princes, does, if I mistake not, in his treatise of *Christian Subjection,* acknowledge that princes may forfeit their power and their title to the obedience of their subjects; and if there needed authority in a case where reason is so plain, I could send my reader to Bracton, Fortescue, and the author of the *Mirror,* and others, writers that cannot be suspected to be ignorant of our government, or enemies to it. But I thought Hooker alone might be enough to satisfy

those men who, relying on him for their ecclesiastical polity, are by a strange fate carried to deny those principles upon which he builds it. Whether they are herein made the tools of cunninger workmen, to pull down their own fabric, they were best look. This I am sure, their civil policy is so new, so dangerous, and so destructive to both rulers and people, that as former ages never could bear the broaching of it, so it may be hoped those to come, redeemed from the impositions of these Egyptian under-taskmasters, will abhor the memory of such servile flatterers, who, whilst it seemed to serve their turn, resolved all government into absolute tyranny, and would have all men born to what their mean souls fitted them—slavery.

240. Here it is like the common question will be made: Who shall be judge whether the prince or legislative act contrary to their trust? This, perhaps, ill-affected and factious men may spread amongst the people, when the prince only makes use of his due prerogative. To this I reply, The people shall be judge; for who shall be judge whether his trustee or deputy acts well and according to the trust reposed in him, but he who deputes him and must, by having deputed him, have still a power to discard him when he fails in his trust? If this be reasonable in particular cases of private men, why should it be otherwise in that of the greatest moment, where the welfare of millions is concerned and also where the evil, if not prevented, is greater, and the redress very difficult, dear, and dangerous?

241. But, farther, this question, Who shall be judge? cannot mean that there is no judge at all. For where there is no judicature on earth to decide controversies amongst men, God in heaven is judge. He alone, it is true, is judge of the right. But every man is judge for himself, as in all other cases so in this, whether another hath put himself into a state of war with him, and whether he should appeal to the supreme Judge, as Jephtha did.

242. If a controversy arise betwixt a prince and some of the people in a matter where the law is silent or doubtful, and the thing be of great consequence, I should think the proper umpire in such a case should be the body of the people. For in such cases where the prince hath a trust reposed in him, and is dispensed from the common, ordinary rules of the law, there, if any men find themselves aggrieved,

and think the prince acts contrary to, or beyond that trust, who so proper to judge as the body of the people (who at first lodged that trust in him) how far they meant it should extend? But if the prince, or whoever they be in the administration, decline that way of determination, the appeal then lies nowhere but to Heaven. Force between either persons who have no known superior on earth, or which permits no appeal to a judge on earth, being properly a state of war, wherein the appeal lies only to Heaven; and in that state the injured party must judge for himself when he will think fit to make use of that appeal and put himself upon it.

243. To conclude. The power that every individual gave the society when he entered into it can never revert to the individuals again, as long as the society lasts, but will always remain in the community; because without this there can be no community—no commonwealth, which is contrary to the original agreement; so also when the society hath placed the legislative in any assembly of men, to continue in them and their successors, with direction and authority for providing such successors, the legislative can never revert to the people whilst that government lasts; because, having provided a legislative with power to continue forever, they have given up their political power to the legislative, and cannot resume it. But if they have set limits to the duration of their legislative, and made this supreme power in any person or assembly only temporary; or else when, by the miscarriages of those in authority, it is forfeited; upon the forfeiture of their rulers, or at the determination of the time set, it reverts to the society, and the people have a right to act as supreme, and continue the legislative in themselves or place it in a new form, or new hands, as they think good.

Some Thoughts Concerning Education

LOCKE HAS been called the father of modern education in England. Most of the reforms he advocated in *Some Thoughts Concerning Education* were adopted in the century and a half that followed its publication. To his contemporaries, accustomed to the educational rituals inherited from the Middle Ages, Locke's proposals must have been shocking. He attacked the schools of his day where "Latin and learning make all the noise," and where "education fits us rather for the university than the world." He objected to the teaching of Greek and Latin, grammar, rhetoric, and logic to the exclusion of practical training that would fit a man for his place in the community.

Some Thoughts Concerning Education was originally a series of letters written to Edward Clarke about the training of Clarke's son, a youth of no great intellectual promise. When Locke edited his letters for publication he sought to fit his advice to the needs of other boys whose capacities and birth destined them, as they did young Clarke, for the life of average English gentlemen. He probably would have applied many of his proposals to the training of other young men, of different backgrounds and talents, though he always insisted that education should be varied with the individual child.

The essay may be roughly divided into two sections. The first section deals with the care and training of the child; the second, with the education of the youth and young man. No exact line, however, separates the two subjects of the essay. Locke wrote his letters while Clarke's son was still young, a fact which perhaps accounts for his constant reference to the problems of childhood, even while discussing the boy's later schooling. In any case, he considered education a continuous process extending from an early age to maturity. Children, he thought, should never be considered merely as youngsters but rather as adults in the making.

Much of Locke's advice concerning the child's care and training seems as modern as the latest book on the subject. Random samples will be enough to indicate how "up-to-date" was Locke's thinking. A sound body is necessary for a healthy mind. Children should play out-of-doors a good deal and should get plenty of sleep. Their diet should consist mainly of coarse food with little meat and no strong drink. They should be dressed in loose fitting clothes, a rule especially intended for girls whose tight clothes might make them ill-shapen and unhealthy on the excuse of greater beauty. Children should not be dressed too warmly in either summer or winter, but should become accustomed to the cold. Locke even suggested, though he admitted it would horrify mothers, that a child should wear leaky shoes in cold wet weather. While still very young a child should be taught two things—to be civil to his "inferiors" and kind to animals. It is, he said, but a short step from cruelty to animals to inhumanity to men.

Locke anticipated modern progressive educators with his argument that a child learns best by doing. If parents and teachers make studying a game, the child's interest in his work increases and his learning is hastened. Pictorial aids should supplement the printed page. Instructors ought to note and encourage particular aptitudes in the child rather than insist upon a set training formula for all children. The child cannot be made to learn by beatings.

The problem of discipline receives considerable attention in the essay. Locke restricts the use of corporal punishment to persistent cases of "stubbornness, lying, and ill-natured actions." Other disciplinary cases he would handle by shaming the child for his misbehavior. Contrariwise, he would praise the child for good behavior. The example of parents and teachers is of greater importance in the child's development than any beatings. In his early years, a child should be taught absolute obedience and awe for his parents, but when he has learned to reason, discipline should be relaxed and he should be treated more and more like an adult. Friendship should replace authority. "The sooner *you treat him as a man,* the sooner he will be one." (Italics are Locke's.) Even as a child he should be encouraged to join in the conversation of adults, and parents should discuss some of their own problems with him so that he may see the confidence they place in him.

Four things are wanted in a son—virtue, wisdom (i.e., worldly wisdom that will help him in his daily life), breeding, and learning. The first three are primary requisites. Learning or schooling is secondary. Learning is important only if it contributes to a pleasant and useful life in the community.

Such education as the child is given should be made palatable to him. The boring and useless should not be forced upon him. While the child is young he should learn one foreign language, preferably French, by conversation and not by mastering rules of grammar.[1] Any careful study of grammar should be confined to English. Latin should be taught later by the same method as French; Greek should be taught only to those who show promise of becoming scholars. Latin grammar, the memorizing of Latin poetry and the writing of themes on subjects with which the student has little acquaintance, should be discarded.

Locke's objection to the usual curriculum of his day may be traced to his own boredom at Westminster School and to a dislike of his courses at Oxford. Lady Masham tells us that Locke was sorry that he had come to Oxford at the end of his first year there. He had been forced to study logic, moral philosophy, rhetoric, mathematics, grammar, and Greek. In his later advice on curriculum Locke eliminates logic (which makes men "disputatious," not thoughtful), as well as rhetoric, Greek and much grammar. He argues that logic and rhetoric, and perhaps Greek, are of little value even to scholars.

Particular bits of advice in the essay may seem curious and antiquated, but many of the suggestions are both sound and modern. In spite of (or because of) being a bachelor, Locke was more observant and practical than most parents about the problems of rearing children. *Some Thoughts Concerning Education* is perhaps the most interesting and fruitful of all Locke's writings for the average twentieth century reader.

[1] It is interesting that during World War II the American Army, with its demand for quickly trained linguists, followed almost exactly the pattern laid down by Locke. Since the war a number of universities have adopted similar methods.

DEDICATION

To EDWARD CLARKE, of Chipley, Esq.[1]
  SIR:

THESE thoughts concerning education, which now come abroad into the world, do of right belong to you, being written several years since for your sake, and are no other than what you have already by you in my letters. I have so little varied anything, but only the order of what was sent you at different times, and on several occasions, that the reader will easily find, in the familiarity and fashion of the style, that they were rather the private conversation of two friends than a discourse designed for public view.

The importunity of friends is the common apology for publications men are afraid to own themselves forward to. But you know I can truly say that if some, who having heard of these papers of mine, had not pressed to see them, and afterwards to have them printed, they had lain dormant still in that privacy they were designed for. But those, whose judgment I defer much to, telling me that they were persuaded that this rough draft of mine might be of some use if made more public, touched upon what will always be very prevalent with me: for I think it every man's indispensable duty to do all the service he can to his country; and I see not what difference he puts between himself and his cattle, who lives without that thought. This subject is of so great concernment, and a right way of education is of so general advantage, that did I find my abilities answer my wishes, I should not have needed exhortations or importunities from others. However, the meanness of these papers, and my just distrust of them, shall not keep me, by the shame of doing so little, from contributing my mite, when there is no more required of me than my throwing it into the public receptacle. And if there be any more of their size and notions, who liked them so

[1] Edward Clarke was a member of William's second parliament.

well that they thought them worth printing, I may flatter myself they will not be lost labor to everybody.

I myself have been consulted of late by so many who profess themselves at a loss how to breed their children, and the early corruption of youth is now become so general a complaint that he cannot be thought wholly impertinent who brings the consideration of this matter on the stage, and offers something, if it be but to excite others, or afford matter of correction: for errors in education should be less indulged than any. These, like faults in the first concoction, that are never mended in the second or third, carry their afterwards incorrigible taint with them through all the parts and stations of life.

I am so far from being conceited of anything I have here offered, that I should not be sorry, even for your sake, if someone abler and fitter for such a task would in a just treatise of education, suited to our English gentry, rectify the mistakes I have made in this; it being much more desirable to me that young gentlemen should be put into (that which everyone ought to be solicitous about) the best way of being formed and instructed, than that my opinion should be received concerning it. You will, however, in the meantime bear me witness that the method here proposed has had no ordinary effects upon a gentleman's son it was not designed for. I will not say the good temper of the child did not very much contribute to it; but this I think you and the parents are satisfied of, that a contrary usage, according to the ordinary disciplining of children, would not have mended that temper, nor have brought him to be in love with his book, to take a pleasure in learning, and to desire, as he does, to be taught more than those about him think fit always to teach him.

But my business is not to recommend this treatise to you, whose opinion of it I know already; nor it to the world, either by your opinion or patronage. The well educating of their children is so much the duty and concern of parents, and the welfare and prosperity of the nation so much depends on it, that I would have everyone lay it seriously to heart; and after having well examined and distinguished what fancy, custom, or reason advises in the case, set his helping hand to promote everywhere that way of training up youth, with regard to their several conditions, which is the easiest, shortest, and likeliest to produce virtuous, useful, and able men in their distinct callings; though that most to be taken care of is the gentleman's calling. For if those of that rank are by their education once set right, they will quickly bring all the rest into order.

I know not whether I have done more than shown my good wishes towards it in this short discourse; such as it is, the world now has it, and if there be anything in it worth their acceptance, they owe their thanks to you for it. My affection to you gave the first rise to it, and I am pleased that I can leave to posterity this mark of the friendship that has been between us. For I know no greater pleasure in this life, nor a better remembrance to be left behind one, than a long continued friendship with an honest, useful, and worthy man, and lover of his country. I am, Sir,

Your most humble and most faithful servant,

JOHN LOCKE.

March 7, 1692.

SOME THOUGHTS CONCERNING EDUCATION

1. A SOUND mind in a sound body is a short but full description of a happy state in this world. He that has these two has little more to wish for; and he that wants either of them will be but little the better for anything else. Men's happiness or misery is most part of their own making. He whose mind directs not wisely will never take the right way; and he whose body is crazy and feeble will never be able to advance in it. I confess there are some men's constitutions of body and mind so vigorous and well framed by nature that they need not much assistance from others; but by the strength of their natural genius they are from their cradles carried towards what is excellent; and by the privilege of their happy constitutions are able to do wonders. But examples of this kind are but few; and I think I may say that of all the men we meet with, nine parts of ten are what they are, good or evil, useful or not, by their education. 'Tis that which makes the great difference in mankind. The little or almost insensible impressions on

our tender infancies have very important and lasting consequences: and there 'tis, as in the fountains of some rivers, where a gentle application of the hand turns the flexible waters in channels, that make them take quite contrary courses; and by this direction given them at first in the source, they receive different tendencies, and arrive at last at very remote and distant places.

2. I imagine the minds of children as easily turned this or that way as water itself: and though this be the principal part, and our main care should be about the inside, yet the clay cottage is not to be neglected. I shall therefore begin with the case, and consider first the health of the body, as that which perhaps you may rather expect from that study I have been thought more peculiarly to have applied myself to; and that also which will be soonest dispatched, as lying, if I guess not amiss, in a very little compass.

3. How necessary health is to our business and happiness, and how requisite a strong constitution, able to endure hardships and fatigue, is to one that will make any figure in the world, is too obvious to need any proof.

4. The consideration I shall here have of health, shall be, not what a physician ought to do with a sick and crazy child, but what the parents, without the help of physic, should do for the preservation and improvement of a healthy, or at least not sickly constitution in their children. And this perhaps might be all dispatched in this one short rule, viz., that gentlemen should use their children as the honest farmers and substantial yeomen do theirs. But because the mothers possibly may think this a little too hard, and the fathers too short, I shall explain myself more particularly; only laying down this as a general and certain observation for the women to consider, viz., that most children's constitutions are either spoiled, or at least harmed, by cockering [2] and tenderness.

5. The first thing to be taken care of, is, that children be not too warmly clad or covered, winter or summer. The face when we are born is no less tender than any other part of the body. 'Tis use alone hardens it, and makes it more able to endure the cold. And there

[2] Coddling or pampering.

fore the Scythian philosopher gave a very significant answer to the Athenian, who wondered how he could go naked in frost and snow. "How," said the Scythian, "can you endure your face exposed to the sharp winter air?" "My face is used to it," said the Athenian. "Think me all face," replied the Scythian. Our bodies will endure anything, that from the beginning they are accustomed to.

An eminent instance of this, though in the contrary excess of heat, being to our present purpose, to show what use can do, I shall set down in the author's words, as I met with it in a late ingenious voyage.

> The heats, says he, are more violent in Malta, than in any part of Europe: they exceed those of Rome itself, and are perfectly stifling; and so much the more, because there are seldom any cooling breezes here. This makes the common people as black as gypsies: but yet the peasants defy the sun; they work on in the hottest part of the day, without intermission, or sheltering themselves from his scorching rays. This has convinced me, that nature can bring itself to many things, which seem impossible, provided we accustom ourselves from our infancy. The Malteses do so, who harden the bodies of their children, and reconcile them to the heat, by making them go stark naked, without shirt, drawers, or anything on their heads, from their cradles till they are ten years old.

Give me leave therefore to advise you not to fence too carefully against the cold of this our climate. There are those in England, who wear the same clothes winter and summer, and that without any inconvenience, or more sense of cold than others find. But if the mother will needs have an allowance for frost and snow, for fear of harm, and the father, for fear of censure, be sure let not his winter clothing be too warm: And amongst other things, remember, that when nature has so well covered his head with hair, and strengthened it with a year or two's age, that he can run about by day without a cap, it is best that by night a child should also lie without one; there being nothing that more exposes to headaches, colds, catarrhs, coughs, and several other diseases, than keeping the head warm.

6. I have said *he* here, because the principal aim of my discourse

is, how a young gentleman should be brought up from his infancy, which in all things will not so perfectly suit the education of daughters; though where the difference of sex requires different treatment, 'twill be no hard matter to distinguish.

7. I will also advise his feet to be washed every day in cold water, and to have his shoes so thin that they might leak and let in water, whenever he comes near it. Here, I fear I shall have the mistress and maids too against me. One will think it too filthy, and the other perhaps too much pains, to make clean his stockings. But yet truth will have it that his health is much more worth than all such considerations, and ten times as much more. And he that considers how mischievous and mortal a thing taking wet in the feet is, to those who have been bred nicely, will wish he had, with the poor people's children, gone barefoot, who, by that means, come to be so reconciled by custom to wet in their feet that they take no more cold or harm by it than if they were wet in their hands. And what is it, I pray, that makes this great difference between the hands and the feet in others, but only custom? I doubt not, but if a man from his cradle had been always used to go barefoot, whilst his hands were constantly wrapped up in warm mittens, and covered with *hand-shoes,* as the Dutch call gloves; I doubt not, I say, but such a custom would make taking wet in his hands as dangerous to him as now taking wet in their feet is to a great many others. The way to prevent this is to have his shoes made so as to leak water, and his feet washed constantly every day in cold water. It is recommendable for its cleanliness, but that which I aim at in it, is health; and therefore I limit it not precisely to any time of day. I have known it used every night with very good success, and that all the winter, without the omitting it so much as one night in extreme cold weather; when thick ice covered the water, the child bathed his legs and feet in it, though he was of an age not big enough to rub and wipe them himself, and when he began this custom was puling and very tender. But the great end being to harden those parts by a frequent and familiar use of cold water, and thereby to prevent the mischiefs that usually attend accidental taking wet in the feet in those who are bred otherwise, I think it may be left to the prudence and convenience of the parents, to choose either night or morning. The time

I deem indifferent, so the thing be effectually done. The health and hardiness procured by it would be a good purchase at a much dearer rate. To which if I add the preventing of corns, that to some men would be a very valuable consideration. But begin first in the spring with luke-warm, and so colder and colder every time, till in a few days you come to perfectly cold water, and then continue it so winter and summer. For it is to be observed in this, as in all other alterations from our ordinary way of living, the changes must be made by gentle and insensible degrees; and so we may bring our bodies to anything, without pain, and without danger.

How fond mothers are like to receive this doctrine is not hard to foresee. What can it be less than to murder their tender babes, to use them thus? What! put their feet in cold water in frost and snow, when all one can do is little enough to keep them warm? A little to remove their fears by examples, without which the plainest reason is seldom hearkened to: Seneca tells us of himself, *Epistles* 53, and 83, that he used to bathe himself in cold spring water in the midst of winter. This, if he had not thought it not only tolerable but healthy too, he would scarce have done, in an exorbitant fortune that could well have borne the expense of a warm bath, and in an age (for he was then old) that would have excused greater indulgence. If we think his stoical principles led him to this severity, let it be so, that this sect reconciled cold water to his sufferance. What made it agreeable to his health? For that was not impaired by this hard usage. But what shall we say to Horace, who warmed not himself with the reputation of any sect, and least of all affected stoical austerities? Yet he assures us, he was wont in the winter season to bathe himself in cold water. But, perhaps, Italy will be thought much warmer than England, and the chillness of their waters not to come near ours in winter. If the rivers of Italy are warmer, those of Germany and Poland are much colder, than any in this our country, and yet in these, the Jews, both men and women, bathe all over, at all seasons of the year, without any prejudice to their health. And everyone is not apt to believe it is miracle, or any peculiar virtue of St. Winifred's Well, that makes the cold waters of that famous spring do no harm to the tender bodies that bathe in it. Everyone is now full of the miracles done by cold baths on decayed and weak constitutions, for the recovery of health and strength; and therefore they cannot be impracticable or intolerable for the improving and hardening the bodies of those who are in better circumstances.

If these examples of grown men be not thought yet to reach the case of children, but that they may be judged still to be too tender, and unable to bear such usage, let them examine what the Germans of old, and the Irish now, do to them, and they will find that infants too, as tender as they are thought, may, without any danger, endure bathing, not only of their feet, but of their whole bodies, in cold water. And there are, at this day, ladies in the Highlands of Scotland who use this discipline to their children in the midst of winter, and find that cold water does them no harm, even when there is ice in it.

8. I shall not need here to mention swimming, when he is of an age able to learn, and has anyone to teach him. 'Tis that saves many a man's life; and the Romans thought it so necessary, that they ranked it with letters; and it was the common phrase to mark one ill-educated, and good for nothing, that he had neither learnt to read nor to swim: *Nec literas didicit nec natare*. But, besides the gaining a skill which may serve him at need, the advantages to health by often bathing in cold water during the heat of summer are so many that I think nothing need be said to encourage it; provided this one caution be used, that he never go into the water when exercise has at all warmed him, or left any emotion in his blood or pulse.

9. Another thing that is of great advantage to everyone's health, but especially children's, is to be much in the open air and as little as may be by the fire, even in winter. By this he will accustom himself also to heat and cold, shine and rain; all which if a man's body will not endure, it will serve him to very little purpose in this world; and when he is grown up, it is too late to begin to use him to it. It must be got early, and by degrees. Thus the body may be brought to bear almost anything. If I should advise him to play in the wind and sun without a hat, I doubt whether it could be borne. There would a thousand objections be made against it, which at last would amount to no more, in truth, than being sunburnt. And if my young master be to be kept always in the shade, and never exposed to the sun and

wind for fear of his complexion, it may be a good way to make him a *beau,* but not a man of business. And although greater regard be to be had to beauty in the daughters; yet I will take the liberty to say that the more they are in the air, without prejudice to their faces, the stronger and healthier they will be; and the nearer they come to the hardships of their brothers in their education, the greater advantage will they receive from it all the remaining part of their lives.

10. Playing in the open air has but this one danger in it that I know; and that is, that when he is hot with running up and down, he should sit or lie down on the cold or moist earth. This I grant; and drinking cold drink, when they are hot with labor or exercise, brings more people to the grave or to the brink of it, by fevers and other diseases, than anything I know. These mischiefs are easily enough prevented whilst he is little, being then seldom out of sight. And if, during his childhood, he be constantly and rigorously kept from sitting on the ground, or drinking any cold liquor whilst he is hot, the custom of forbearing, growing into habit, will help much to preserve him, when he is no longer under his maid's or tutor's eye. This is all I think can be done in the case: for, as years increase, liberty must come with them; and in a great many things he must be trusted to his own conduct, since there cannot always be a guard upon him, except what you have put into his own mind by good principles and established habits, which is the best and surest, and therefore most to be taken care of. For, from repeated cautions and rules never so often inculcated, you are not to expect anything either in this, or any other case, farther than practice has established them into habits.

11. One thing the mention of the girls brings into my mind, which must not be forgot; and that is, that your son's clothes be never made strait, especially about the breast. Let nature have scope to fashion the body as she thinks best. She works herself a great deal better and exacter than we can direct her. And if women were themselves to frame the bodies of their children in their wombs, as they often endeavor to mend their shapes when they are out, we should as certainly have no perfect children born, as we have few well-shaped that are strait-laced, or much tampered with. This consideration should, methinks, keep busy people (I will not say ignorant nurses and bodice-

makers) from meddling in a matter they understand not; and they should be afraid to put nature out of her way in fashioning the parts, when they know not how the least and meanest is made. And yet I have seen so many instances of children receiving great harm from strait-lacing, that I cannot but conclude there are other creatures as well as monkeys, who, little wiser than they, destroy their young ones by senseless fondness, and too much embracing.

12. Narrow breasts, short and stinking breath, ill lungs, and crook-edness, are natural and almost constant effects of hard bodice, and clothes that pinch. That way of making slender waists and fine shapes serves but the more effectually to spoil them. Nor can there indeed but be disproportion in the parts, when the nourishment prepared in the several offices of the body cannot be distributed as nature de-signs. And therefore what wonder is it, if, it being laid where it can, on some part not so braced, it often makes a shoulder or hip higher or bigger than its just proportion? 'Tis generally known that the women of China (imagining I know not what kind of beauty in it) by bracing and binding them hard from their infancy, have very little feet. I saw lately a pair of China shoes, which I was told were for a grown woman: they were so exceedingly disproportioned to the feet of one of the same age among us, that they would scarce have been big enough for one of our little girls. Besides this, 'tis observed that their women are also very little and short-lived; whereas the men are of the ordinary stature of other men, and live to a propor-tionable age. These defects in the female sex in that country are by some imputed to the unreasonable binding of their feet, whereby the free circulation of the blood is hindered, and the growth and health of the whole body suffers. And how often do we see that some small part of the foot being injured by a wrench or a blow, the whole leg or thigh thereby lose their strength and nourishment, and dwindle away? How much greater inconveniences may we expect, when the thorax, wherein is placed the heart and seat of life, is unnaturally compressed, and hindered from its due expansion?

13. As for his diet, it ought to be very plain and simple; and, it I might advise, flesh should be forborne as long as he is in coats, or at least till he is two or three years old. But whatever advantage this

may be to his present and future health and strength, I fear it will hardly be consented to by parents, misled by the custom of eating too much flesh themselves, who will be apt to think their children, as they do themselves, in danger to be starved, if they have not flesh at least twice a day. This I am sure, children would breed their teeth with much less danger, be freer from diseases whilst they were little, and lay the foundations of an healthy and strong constitution much surer, if they were not crammed so much as they are by fond mothers and foolish servants, and were kept wholly from flesh the first three or four years of their lives.

But if my young master must needs have flesh, let it be but once a day, and of one sort at a meal. Plain beef, mutton, veal, etc., without other sauce than hunger, is best; and great care should be used that he eat bread plentifully, both alone and with everything else; and whatever he eats that is solid, make him chew it well. We English are often negligent herein; from whence follow indigestion and other great inconveniences.

14. For breakfast and supper, milk, milk-pottage, water-gruel, flummery, and twenty other things that we are wont to make in England, are very fit for children; only, in all these, let care be taken that they be plain, and without much mixture, and very sparingly seasoned with sugar, or rather none at all; especially all spice, and other things that may heat the blood, are carefully to be avoided. Be sparing also of salt in the seasoning of all his victuals, and use him not to high-seasoned meats. Our palates grow into a relish and liking of the seasoning and cookery which by custom they are set to; and an over-much use of salt, besides that it occasions thirst and over-much drinking, has other ill effects upon the body. I should think that a good piece of well-made and well-baked brown bread, sometimes with, and sometimes without butter or cheese, would be often the best breakfast for my young master. I am sure 'tis as wholesome and will make him as strong a man as greater delicacies; and if he be used to it, it will be as pleasant to him. If he at any time calls for victuals between meals, use him to nothing but dry bread. If he be hungry more than wanton, bread alone will down; and if he be not hungry, 'tis not fit he should eat. By this you will obtain two

good effects: 1. That by custom he will come to be in love with bread; for, as I said, our palates and stomachs too are pleased with the things we are used to. 2. Another good you will gain hereby is, that you will not teach him to eat more nor oftener than nature requires. I do not think that all people's appetites are alike; some have naturally stronger and some weaker stomachs. But this I think, that many are made gourmands and gluttons by custom, that were not so by nature: and I see in some countries men as lusty and strong that eat but two meals a day, as others that have set their stomachs by a constant usage, like alarums, to call on them for four or five. The Romans usually fasted till supper, the only set meal even of those who eat more than once a day; and those who used breakfast, as some did, at eight, some at ten, others at twelve of the clock, and some later, neither eat flesh, nor had anything made ready for them. Augustus, when the greatest monarch on the earth, tells us he took a bit of dry bread in his chariot. And Seneca, in his 83rd Epistle, giving an account how he managed himself, even when he was old, and his age permitted indulgence, says that he used to eat a piece of dry bread for his dinner, without the formality of sitting to it, though his estate would as well have paid for a better meal (had health required it) as any subject's in England, were it doubled. The masters of the world were bred up with this spare diet; and the young gentlemen of Rome felt no want of strength or spirit because they eat but once a day. Or if it happened by chance that anyone could not fast so long as till supper, their only set meal, he took nothing but a bit of dry bread, or at most a few raisins, or some such slight thing with it, to stay his stomach. This part of temperance was found so necessary, both for health and business, that the custom of only one meal a day held out against that prevailing luxury which their Eastern conquests and spoils had brought in amongst them; and those who had given up their old frugal eating, and made feasts, yet began them not till the evening. And more than one set meal a day was thought so monstrous that it was a reproach as low down as Caesar's time, to make an entertainment or sit down to a full table, till towards sunset; and therefore, if it would not be thought too severe, I should judge it most convenient that my young master should have nothing but bread too for breakfast. You cannot imagine of what force custom is; and I impute a great part of our diseases in England to our eating too much flesh and too little bread.

15. As to his meals, I should think it best that as much as it can be conveniently avoided they should not be kept constantly to an hour: for when custom has fixed his eating to certain stated periods, his stomach will expect victuals at the usual hour, and grow peevish if he passes it; either fretting itself into a troublesome excess, or flagging into a downright want of appetite. Therefore I would have no time kept constantly to for his breakfast, dinner, and supper, but rather varied almost every day. And if betwixt these, which I call *meals,* he will eat, let him have, as often as he calls for it, good dry bread. If anyone think this too hard and sparing a diet for a child, let them know that a child will never starve nor dwindle for want of nourishment, who, besides flesh at dinner, and spoon-meat, or some such other thing, at supper, may have good bread and beer as often as he has a stomach. For thus, upon second thoughts, I should judge it best for children to be ordered. The morning is generally designed for study, to which a full stomach is but an ill preparation. Dry bread, though the best nourishment, has the least temptation; and nobody would have a child crammed at breakfast, who has any regard to his mind or body, and would not have him dull and unhealthy. Nor let anyone think this unsuitable to one of estate and condition. A gentleman in any age ought to be so bred as to be fitted to bear arms and be a soldier. But he that in this breeds his son so, as if he designed him to sleep over his life in the plenty and ease of a full fortune he intends to leave him, little considers the examples he has seen, or the age he lives in.

16. His drink should be only small beer; and that too he should never be suffered to have between meals, but after he had eat a piece of bread. The reasons why I say this are these.

17. 1. More fevers and surfeits are got by people's drinking when they are hot than by any one thing I know. Therefore, if by play he be hot and dry, bread will ill go down; and so if he cannot have drink but upon that condition, he will be forced to forbear; for, if he be very hot, he should by no means drink; at least a good piece

of bread first to be eaten, will gain time to warm the beer blood-hot, which then he may drink safely. If he be very dry, it will go down so warmed, and quench his thirst better; and if he will not drink it so warmed, abstaining will not hurt him. Besides, this will teach him to forbear, which is a habit of greatest use for health of body and mind too.

18. 2. Not being permitted to drink without eating, will prevent the custom of having the cup often at his nose; a dangerous beginning, and preparation to good-fellowship. Men often bring habitual hunger and thirst on themselves by custom. And if you please to try, you may, though he be weaned from it, bring him by use to such a necessity again of drinking in the night that he will not be able to sleep without it. It being the lullaby used by nurses to still crying children, I believe mothers generally find some difficulty to wean their children from drinking in the night, when they first take them home. Believe it, custom prevails as much by day as by night; and you may, if you please, bring anyone to be thirsty every hour.

I once lived in a house where, to appease a froward child, they gave him drink as often as he cried; so that he was constantly bibbing. And though he could not speak, yet he drank more in twenty-four hours than I did. Try it when you please, you may with small, as well as with strong beer, drink yourself into a drought. The great thing to be minded in education is, what *habits* you settle; and therefore in this, as all other things, do not begin to make anything customary, the practice whereof you would not have continue and increase. It is convenient for health and sobriety to drink no more than natural thirst requires; and he that eats not salt meats, nor drinks strong drink, will seldom thirst between meals, unless he has been accustomed to such unseasonable drinking.

19. Above all, take great care that he seldom, if ever, taste any wine or strong drink. There is nothing so ordinarily given children in England, and nothing so destructive to them. They ought never to drink any strong liquor but when they need it as a cordial, and the doctor prescribes it. And in this case it is that servants are most narrowly to be watched and most severely to be reprehended when they transgress. Those mean sort of people, placing a great part of

their happiness in strong drink, are always forward to make court
to my young master by offering him that which they love best themselves; and finding themselves made merry by it, they foolishly think
'twill do the child no harm. This you are carefully to have your eye
upon, and restrain with all the skill and industry you can, there being
nothing that lays a surer foundation of mischief, both to body and
mind, than children's being used to strong drink, especially to drink
in private with the servants.

20. Fruit makes one of the most difficult chapters in the government of health, especially that of children. Our first parents ventured
Paradise for it; and 'tis no wonder our children cannot stand the
temptation, though it cost them their health. The regulation of this
cannot come under any one general rule; for I am by no means of their
mind, who would keep children almost wholly from fruit, as a thing
totally unwholesome for them: by which strict way, they make them
but the more ravenous after it, and to eat good or bad, ripe or unripe,
all that they can get, whenever they come at it. Melons, peaches,
most sorts of plums, and all sorts of grapes in England, I think
children should be wholly kept from, as having a very tempting
taste, in a very unwholesome juice; so that if it were possible, they
should never so much as see them or know there were any such
thing. But strawberries, cherries, gooseberries, or currants, when
thorough ripe, I think may be very safely allowed them, and that
with a pretty liberal hand, if they be eaten with these cautions: 1.
Not after meals, as we usually do, when the stomach is already full
of other food, but I think they should be eaten rather before or between meals, and children should have them for their breakfast.
2. Bread eaten with them. 3. Perfectly ripe. If they are thus eaten,
I imagine them rather conducing than hurtful to our health. Sum-
mer-fruits, being suited to the hot season of the year they come in,
refresh our stomachs, languishing and fainting under it; and therefore I should not be altogether so strict in this point as some are
to their children; who being kept so very short, instead of a moderate
quantity of well-chosen fruit, which being allowed them would content them, whenever they can get loose, or bribe a servant to supply

them, satisfy their longing with any trash they can get, and eat to a surfeit.

Apples and pears too, which are thorough ripe, and have been gathered some time, I think may be safely eaten at any time, and in pretty large quantities, especially apples; which never did anybody hurt, that I have heard, after October.

Fruits also dried without sugar, I think very wholesome. But sweet-meats of all kinds are to be avoided; which whether they do more harm to the maker or eater, is not easy to tell. This I am sure, it is one of the most inconvenient [3] ways of expense that vanity has yet found out; and so I leave them to the ladies.

21. Of all that looks soft and effeminate, nothing is more to be indulged children than sleep. In this alone they are to be permitted to have their full satisfaction; nothing contributing more to the growth and health of children than sleep. All that is to be regulated in it, is, in what part of the twenty-four hours they should take it; which will easily be resolved, by only saying that it is of great use to accustom 'em to rise early in the morning. It is best so to do, for health; and he that from his childhood has by a settled custom made rising betimes easy and familiar to him, will not, when he is a man, waste the best and most useful part of his life in drowsiness and lying a-bed. If children therefore are to be called up early in the morning, it will follow of course that they must go to bed betimes; whereby they will be accustomed to avoid the unhealthy and unsafe hours of de-bauchery, which are those of the evenings; and they who keep good hours, seldom are guilty of any great disorders. I do not say this as if your son, when grown up, should never be in company past eight, nor ever chat over a glass of wine till midnight. You are now, by the accustoming of his tender years, to indispose him to those in-conveniences as much as you can; and it will be no small advantage, that contrary practice having made sitting up uneasy to him it will make him often avoid and very seldom propose midnight revels. But if it should not reach so far, but fashion and company should prevail, and make him live as others do above twenty, 'tis worth the

[3] Improper (obsolete).

while to accustom him to early rising and early going to bed, between this and that, for the present improvement of his health and other advantages.

Though I have said a large allowance of sleep, even as much as they will take, should be made to children when they are little; yet I do not mean that it should always be continued to them in so large a proportion, and they suffered to indulge a drowsy laziness in their bed, as they grow up bigger. But whether they should begin to be restrained at seven or ten years old, or any other time, is impossible to be precisely determined. Their tempers, strength, and constitutions, must be considered. But some time between seven and fourteen, if they are too great lovers of their beds, I think it may be seasonable to begin to reduce them by degrees to about eight hours, which is generally rest enough for healthy grown people. If you have accustomed him, as you should do, to rise constantly very early in the morning, this fault of being too long in bed will easily be reformed, and most children will be forward enough to shorten that time themselves, by coveting to sit up with the company at night; though if they be not looked after, they will be apt to take it out in the morning, which should by no means be permitted. They should constantly be called up and made to rise at their early hour; but great care should be taken in waking them that it be not done hastily, nor with a loud or shrill voice, or any other sudden violent noise. This often affrights children and does them great harm; and sound sleep thus broke off, with sudden alarms, is apt enough to discompose anyone. When children are to be wakened out of their sleep, be sure to begin with a low call, and some gentle motion, and so draw them out of it by degrees, and give them none but kind words and usage, till they are come perfectly to themselves, and being quite dressed, you are sure they are thoroughly awake. The being forced from their sleep, how gently so ever you do it, is pain enough to them; and care should be taken not to add any other uneasiness to it, especially such that may terrify them.

22. Let his bed be hard, and rather quilts than feathers. Hard lodging strengthens the parts; whereas being buried every night in feathers melts and dissolves the body, is often the cause of weakness,

and forerunner of an early grave. And, besides the stone, which has often its rise from this warm wrapping of the reins,[4] several other indispositions, and that which is the root of them all, a tender weakly constitution, is very much owing to down-beds. Besides, he that is used to hard lodging at home will not miss his sleep (where he has most need of it) in his travels abroad, for want of his soft bed and his pillows laid in order. And therefore, I think it would not be amiss to make his bed after different fashions, sometimes lay his head higher, sometimes lower, that he may not feel every little change he must be sure to meet with, who is not designed to lie always in my young master's bed at home, and to have his maid lay all things in print, and tuck him in warm. The great cordial of nature is sleep. He that misses that will suffer by it; and he is very unfortunate who can take his cordial only in his mother's fine gilt cup, and not in a wooden dish. He that can sleep soundly takes the cordial; and it matters not whether it be on a soft bed or the hard boards. 'Tis sleep only that is the thing necessary.

23. One thing more there is which has a great influence upon the health, and that is, going to stool regularly; people that are very loose have seldom strong thoughts or strong bodies. But the cure of this, both by diet and medicine, being much more easy than the contrary evil, there needs not much to be said about it: for if it come to threaten, either by its violence or duration, it will soon enough, and sometimes too soon, make a physician be sent for; and if it be moderate or short, it is commonly best to leave it to nature. On the other side, costiveness has too its ill effects, and is much harder to be dealt with by physic; purging medicines, which seem to give relief, rather increasing them than removing the evil.

24. It being an indisposition I had a particular reason to inquire into, and not finding the cure of it in books, I set my thoughts on work, believing that greater changes than that might be made in our bodies, if we took the right course and proceeded by rational steps.

1. Then I considered that going to stool was the effect of certain motions of the body; especially of the peristaltic motion of the guts.

[4] Kidneys.

2. I considered, that several motions that were not perfectly voluntary might yet, by use and constant application, be brought to be habitual, if by an unintermitted custom they were at certain seasons endeavored to be constantly produced.

3. I had observed some men who, by taking after supper a pipe of tobacco, never failed of a stool, and began to doubt with myself whether it were not more custom than the tobacco, that gave them the benefit of nature; or at least, if the tobacco did it, it was rather by exciting a vigorous motion in the guts than by any purging quality; for then it would have had other effects.

Having thus once got the opinion that it was possible to make it habitual, the next thing was to consider what way and means was the likeliest to obtain it.

4. Then I guessed that if a man, after his first eating in the morning, would presently solicit nature and try whether he could strain himself so as to obtain a stool, he might in time, by constant application, bring it to be habitual.

25. The reasons that made me choose this time, were,

1. Because the stomach being then empty, if it received anything grateful to it (for I would never but in case of necessity have anyone eat but what he likes, and when he has an appetite) it was apt to embrace it close by a strong constriction of its fibers; which constriction, I supposed, might probably be continued on in the guts, and so increase their peristaltic motion, as we see in the ileus, that an inverted motion, being begun anywhere below, continues itself all the whole length, and makes even the stomach obey that irregular motion.

2. Because when men eat, they usually relax their thoughts, and the spirits then, free from other employments, are more vigorously distributed into the lower belly, which thereby contribute to the same effect.

3. Because, whenever men have leisure to eat, they have leisure enough also to make so much court to Madam Cloacina, as would be necessary to our present purpose; but else, in the variety of human affairs and accidents, it was impossible to affix it to any hour certain, whereby the custom would be interrupted. Whereas men in health

seldom failing to eat once a day, though the hour changed, the custom might still be preserved.

26. Upon these grounds the experiment began to be tried, and I have known none who have been steady in the prosecution of it, and taken care to go constantly to the necessary-house, after their first eating, whenever that happened, whether they found themselves called on or no, and there endeavored to put nature upon her duty, but in a few months they obtained the desired success, and brought themselves to so regular a habit that they seldom ever failed of a stool after their first eating, unless it were by their own neglect: for, whether they have any motion or no, if they go to the place, and do their part, they are sure to have nature very obedient.

27. I would therefore advise that this course should be taken with a child every day presently after he has eaten his breakfast. Let him be set upon the stool, as if disburdening were as much in his power as filling his belly; and let not him or his maid know anything to the contrary, but that it is so; and if he be forced to endeavor, by being hindered from his play or eating again till he has been effectually at stool, or at least done his utmost, I doubt not but in a little while it will become natural to him. For there is reason to suspect that children being usually intent on their play and very heedless of anything else, often let pass those motions of nature, when she calls them but gently; and so they, neglecting the seasonable offers, do by degrees bring themselves into an habitual costiveness. That by this method costiveness may be prevented, I do more than guess; having known by the constant practice of it for some time, a child brought to have a stool regularly after his breakfast every morning.

28. How far any grown people will think fit to make trial of it, must be left to them; though I cannot but say, that considering the many evils that come from that defect, of a requisite easing of nature, I scarce know anything more conducing to the preservation of health than this is. Once in four and twenty hours I think is enough; and nobody, I guess, will think it too much. And by this means it is to be obtained without physic, which commonly proves very ineffectual in the cure of a settled and habitual costiveness.

29. This is all I have to trouble you with concerning his manage-

ment in the ordinary course of his health. Perhaps it will be expected from me, that I should give some directions of physic, to prevent diseases; for which I have only this one, very sacredly to be observed, never to give children any physic for prevention. The observation of what I have already advised, will, I suppose, do that better than the ladies' diet-drinks or apothecaries' medicines. Have a great care of tampering that way, lest, instead of preventing, you draw on diseases. Nor even upon every little indisposition is physic to be given, or the physician to be called to children, especially if he be a busy man, that will presently fill their windows with gally-pots,[5] and their stomachs with drugs. It is safer to leave them wholly to nature than to put 'em into the hands of one forward to tamper, or that thinks children are to be cured, in ordinary distempers, by anything but diet, or by a method very little distant from it: it seeming suitable both to my reason and experience that the tender constitutions of children should have as little done to them as is possible, and as the absolute necessity of the case requires. A little cold-stilled red poppy-water, which is the true surfeit-water with ease, and abstinence from flesh, often puts an end to several distempers in the beginning, which, by too forward applications, might have been made lusty diseases. When such a gentle treatment will not stop the growing mischief, nor hinder it from turning into a formed disease, it will be time to seek the advice of some sober and discreet physician. In this part, I hope, I shall find an easy belief; and nobody can have a pretense to doubt the advice of one who has spent some time in the study of physic, when he counsels you not to be too forward in making use of physic and physicians.

30. And thus I have done with what concerns the body and health, which reduces itself to these few and easy observable rules: plenty of open air, exercise, and sleep, plain diet, no wine or strong drink, and very little or no physic, not too warm and strait clothing, especially the head and feet kept cold, and the feet often used to cold water, and exposed to wet.

31. Due care being had to keep the body in strength and vigor,

[5] A small vessel used by apothecaries.

so that it may be able to obey and execute the orders of the mind; the next and principal business is to set the mind right, that on all occasions it may be disposed to consent to nothing but what may be suitable to the dignity and excellency of a rational creature.

32. If what I have said in the beginning of this discourse be true, as I do not doubt but it is, viz., that the difference to be found in the manners and abilities of men is owing more to their education than to anything else, we have reason to conclude that great care is to be had of the forming children's minds, and giving them that seasoning early, which shall influence their lives always after: for when they do well or ill, the praise and blame will be laid there; and when anything is done awkwardly, the common saying will pass upon them, that it's suitable to their breeding.

33. As the strength of the body lies chiefly in being able to endure hardships, so also does that of the mind. And the great principle and foundation of all virtue and worth is placed in this: that a man is able to deny himself of his own desires, cross his own inclinations, and purely follow what reason directs as best, though the appetite lean the other way.

34. The great mistake I have observed in people's breeding their children has been, that this has not been taken care enough of in its due season: that the mind has not been made obedient to discipline and pliant to reason, when at first it was most tender, most easy to be bowed. Parents being wisely ordained by nature to love their children, are very apt, if reason watch not that natural affection very warily, are apt, I say, to let it run into fondness. They loved their little ones and it is their duty; but they often, with them, cherish their faults too. They must not be crossed, forsooth; they must be permitted to have their wills in all things; and they being in their infancies not capable of great vices, their parents think they may safe enough indulge their irregularities, and make themselves sport with that pretty perverseness which they think well enough becomes that innocent age. But to a fond parent that would not have his child corrected for a perverse trick, but excused it, saying it was a small matter, Solon very well replied, "Aye, but custom is a great one."

35. The fondling must be taught to strike and call names, must

have what he cries for, and do what he pleases. Thus parents, by
humoring and cockering them when little, corrupt the principles of
nature in their children, and wonder afterwards to taste the bitter
waters, when they themselves have poisoned the fountain. For when
their children are grown up, and these ill habits with them; when
they are now too big to be dandled, and their parents can no longer
make use of them as playthings, then they complain that the brats
are untoward and perverse; then they are offended to see them willful,
and are troubled with those ill humors which they themselves in-
fused and fomented in them; and then, perhaps too late, would be
glad to get out those weeds which their own hands have planted,
and which now have taken too deep root to be easily extirpated.
For he that hath been used to have his will in everything, as long as
he was in coats, why should we think it strange that he should desire
it, and contend for it still, when he is in breeches? Indeed, as he
grows more towards a man, age shows his faults the more; so that
there be few parents then so blind as not to see them, few so insensible
as not to feel the ill effects of their own indulgence. He had the
will of his maid before he could speak or go; he had the mastery
of his parents ever since he could prattle; and why, now he is grown
up, is stronger and wiser than he was then, why now of a sudden
must he be restrained and curbed? Why must he at seven, fourteen,
or twenty years old, lose the privilege, which the parents' indulgence
till then so largely allowed him? Try it in a dog or a horse or any
other creature, and see whether the ill and resty tricks they have
learned when young are easily to be mended when they are knit;
and yet none of those creatures are half so willful and proud, or half
so desirous to be masters of themselves and others, as man.

36. We are generally wise enough to begin with them when they
are very young, and discipline betimes those other creatures we would
make useful and good for somewhat. They are only our own offspring that we neglect in this point; and having made them ill children, we foolishly expect they should be good men. For if the child
must have grapes or sugar-plums when he has a mind to them, rather
than make the poor baby cry or be out of humor; why, when he is
grown up, must he not be satisfied too, if his desires carry him to

wine or women? They are objects as suitable to the longing of one of more years as what he cried for, when little, was to the inclinations of a child. The having desires accommodated to the apprehensions and relish of those several ages is not the fault; but the not having them subject to the rules and restraints of reason: the difference lies not in having or not having appetites, but in the power to govern, and deny ourselves in them. He that is not used to submit his will to the reason of others when he is young, will scarce hearken to submit to his own reason when he is of an age to make use of it. And what kind of a man such a one is like to prove is easy to foresee.

37. These are oversights usually committed by those who seem to take the greatest care of their children's education. But if we look into the common management of children, we shall have reason to wonder, in the great dissoluteness of manners which the world complains of, that there are any footsteps at all left of virtue. I desire to know what vice can be named, which parents, and those about children, do not season them with, and drop into 'em the seeds of, as soon as they are capable to receive them? I do not mean by the examples they give, and the patterns they set before them, which is encouragement enough; but that which I would take notice of here is the downright teaching them vice, and actual putting them out of the way of virtue. Before they can go, they principle 'em with violence, revenge, and cruelty. Give me a blow, that I may beat him, is a lesson which most children every day hear; and it is thought nothing, because their hands have not strength to do any mischief. But I ask, does not this corrupt their mind? Is not this the way of force and violence, that they are set in? And if they have been taught when little to strike and hurt others by proxy, and encouraged to rejoice in the harm they have brought upon them, and see them suffer, are they not prepared to do it when they are strong enough to be felt themselves, and can strike to some purpose?

The coverings of our bodies which are for modesty, warmth, and defense, are by the folly or vice of parents recommended to their children for other uses. They are made matters of vanity and emulation. A child is set a-longing after a new suit, for the finery of it;

and when the little girl is tricked up in her new gown and commode,[c] how can her mother do less than teach her to admire herself, by calling her, 'her little queen' and 'her princess'? Thus the little ones are taught to be proud of their clothes before they can put them on. And why should they not continue to value themselves for their outside fashionableness of the tailor or tirewoman's making, when their parents have so early instructed them to do so?

Lying and equivocations, and excuses little different from lying, are put into the mouths of young people, and commended in apprentices and children, whilst they are for their master's or parents' advantage. And can it be thought that he that finds the straining of truth dispensed with, and encouraged, whilst it is for his godly master's turn, will not make use of that privilege for himself, when it may be for his own profit?

Those of the meaner sort are hindered, by the straitness of their fortunes, from encouraging intemperance in their children by the temptation of their diet, or invitations to eat or drink more than enough; but their own ill examples, whenever plenty comes in their way, show that 'tis not the dislike of drunkenness or gluttony that keeps them from excess, but want of materials. But if we look into the houses of those who are a little warmer in their fortunes, their eating and drinking are made so much the great business and happiness of life, that children are thought neglected, if they have not their share of it. Sauces and ragouts, and food disguised by all the arts of cookery, must tempt their palates, when their bellies are full; and then, for fear the stomach should be overcharged, a pretense is found for t'other glass of wine to help digestion, though it only serves to increase the surfeit.

Is my young master a little out of order, the first question is, 'What will my dear eat? What shall I get for thee?' Eating and drinking are instantly pressed; and everybody's invention is set on work, to find out something luscious and delicate enough to prevail over that want of appetite, which nature has wisely ordered in the beginning of distempers, as a defense against their increase; that being freed

[c] A ladies' cap, trimmed with ruffles and lace.

from the ordinary labor of digesting any new load in the stomach, she may be at leisure to correct and master the peccant humors.

And where children are so happy in the care of their parents, as by their prudence to be kept from the excess of their tables, to the sobriety of a plain and simple diet, yet there too they are scarce to be preserved from the contagion that poisons the mind; though, by a discreet management whilst they are under tuition, their healths perhaps may be pretty well secure, yet their desires must needs yield to the lessons which everywhere will be read to them upon this part of epicurism. The commendation that eating well has everywhere cannot fail to be a successful incentive to natural appetites, and bring them quickly to the liking and expense of a fashionable table. This shall have from everyone, even the reprovers of vice, the title of living well. And what shall sullen reason dare to say against the public testimony? Or can it hope to be heard, if it should call that luxury, which is so much owned and universally practiced by those of the best quality?

This is now so grown a vice, and has so great support, that I know not whether it do not put in for the name of virtue; and whether it will not be thought folly, or want of knowledge of the world, to open one's mouth against it? And truly I should suspect that what I have here said of it might be censured as a little satire out of my way, did I not mention it with this view, that it might awaken the care and watchfulness of parents in the education of their children, when they see how they are beset on every side, not only with temptations, but instructors to vice, and that, perhaps, in those they thought places of security.

I shall not dwell any longer on this subject, much less run over all the particulars that would show what pains are used to corrupt children, and instill principles of vice into them: but I desire parents soberly to consider what irregularity or vice there is which children are not visibly taught, and whether it be not their duty and wisdom to provide them other instructions.

38. It seems plain to me that the principle of all virtue and excellency lies in a power of denying ourselves the satisfaction of our own desires, where reason does not authorize them. This power is to be

got and improved by custom, made easy and familiar by an early practice. If therefore I might be heard, I would advise that, contrary to the ordinary way, children should be used to submit their desires, and go without their longings, even from their very cradles. The first thing they should learn to know should be that they were not to have anything because it pleased them, but because it was thought fit for them. If things suitable to their wants were supplied to them, so that they were never suffered to have what they once cried for, they would learn to be content without it, would never, with bawling and peevishness, contend for mastery, nor be half so uneasy to themselves and others as they are, because from the first beginning they are not thus handled. If they were never suffered to obtain their desire by the impatience they expressed for it, they would no more cry for another thing than they do for the moon.

39. I say not this, as if children were not to be indulged in anything, or that I expected they should in hanging sleeves have the reason and conduct of counsellors. I consider them as children, who must be tenderly used, who must play and have playthings. That which I mean, is, that whenever they craved what was not fit for them to have or do, they should not be permitted it because they were little, and desired it: nay, whatever they were importunate for, they should be sure, for that very reason, to be denied. I have seen children at a table, who, whatever was there, never asked for anything, but contentedly took what was given them: and at another place, I have seen others cry for everything they saw; must be served out of every dish, and that first too. What made this vast difference but this, that one was accustomed to have what they called or cried for, the other to go without it? The younger they are, the less I think are their unruly and disorderly appetites to be complied with; and the less reason they have of their own, the more are they to be under the absolute power and restraint of those in whose hands they are. From which I confess it will follow that none but discreet people should be about them. If the world commonly does otherwise, I cannot help that. I am saying what I think should be; which if it were already in fashion, I should not need to trouble the world with a discourse on this subject. But yet I doubt not but when it is con-

ﬁdered, there will be others of opinion with me, that the sooner this way is begun with children, the easier it will be for them and their governors too; and that this ought to be observed as an inviolable maxim, that whatever once is denied them, they are certainly not to obtain by crying or importunity, unless one has a mind to teach them to be impatient and troublesome by rewarding them for it when they are so.

40. Those therefore that intend ever to govern their children should begin it whilst they are very little, and look that they perfectly comply with the will of their parents. Would you have your son obedient to you when past a child, be sure then to establish the authority of a father as soon as he is capable of submission, and can understand in whose power he is. If you would have him stand in awe of you, imprint it in his infancy; and as he approaches more to a man, admit him nearer to your familiarity; so shall you have him your obedient subject (as is fit) whilst he is a child, and your affectionate friend when he is a man. For methinks they mightily misplace the treatment due to their children, who are indulgent and familiar when they are little, but severe to them, and keep them at a distance when they are grown up: for liberty and indulgence can do no good to children; their want of judgment makes them stand in need of restraint and discipline; and on the contrary, imperiousness and severity is but an ill way of treating men who have reason of their own to guide them; unless you have a mind to make your children, when grown up, weary of you, and secretly to say within themselves, 'When will you die, Father?'

41. I imagine everyone will judge it reasonable that their children, when little, should look upon their parents as their lords, their absolute governors, and as such stand in awe of them; and that when they come to riper years, they should look on them as their best, as their only sure friends, and as such love and reverence them. The way I have mentioned, if I mistake not, is the only one to obtain this. We must look upon our children, when grown up, to be like ourselves, with the same passions, the same desires. We would be thought rational creatures, and have our freedom; we love not to be uneasy under constant rebukes and browbeatings, nor can we bear

severe humors and great distance in those we converse with. Who-ever has such treatment when he is a man, will look out other company, other friends, other conversation, with whom he can be at ease. If therefore a strict hand be kept over children from the beginning, they will in that age be tractable, and quietly submit to it, as never having known any other: and if, as they grow up to the use of reason, the rigor of government be, as they deserve it, gently relaxed, the father's brow more smoothed to them, and the distance by degrees abated, his former restraints will increase their love, when they find it was only a kindness to them, and a care to make them capable to deserve the favor of their parents, and the esteem of everybody else.

42. Thus much for the settling your authority over your children in general. Fear and awe ought to give you the first power over their minds, and love and friendship in riper years to hold it: for the time must come, when they will be past the rod and correction; and then, if the love of you make them not obedient and dutiful, if the love of virtue and reputation keep them not in laudable courses, I ask, what hold will you have upon them to turn them to it? Indeed, fear of having a scanty portion if they displease you, may make them slaves to your estate, but they will be nevertheless ill and wicked in private; and that restraint will not last always. Every man must some time or other be trusted to himself and his own conduct; and he that is a good, a virtuous, and able man, must be made so within. And therefore what he is to receive from education, what is to sway and influence his life, must be something put into him betimes; habits woven into the very principles of his nature, and not a counterfeit carriage, and dissembled outside, put on by fear, only to avoid the present anger of a father who perhaps may disinherit him.

43. This being laid down in general, as the course that ought to be taken, 'tis fit we now come to consider the parts of the discipline to be used, a little more particularly. I have spoken so much of carrying a strict hand over children that perhaps I shall be suspected of not considering enough what is due to their tender age and constitutions. But that opinion will vanish when you have heard me a little farther: for I am very apt to think, that great severity of

punishment does but very little good, nay, great harm in education: and I believe it will be found that, *caeteris paribus,*[7] those children who have been most chastised seldom make the best men. All that I have hitherto contended for is that whatsoever rigor is necessary, it is more to be used, the younger children are; and having by a due application wrought its effect, it is to be relaxed, and changed into a milder sort of government.

44. A compliance and suppleness of their wills, being by a steady hand introduced by parents, before children have memories to retain the beginnings of it, will seem natural to them, and work afterwards in them as if it were so, preventing all occasions of struggling or repining. The only care is that it be begun early, and inflexibly kept to till awe and respect be grown familiar, and there appears not the least reluctancy in the submission, and ready obedience of their minds. When this reverence is once thus established (which it must be early, or else it will cost pains and blows to recover it, and the more the longer it is deferred), 'tis by it, still mixed with as much indulgence as they make not an ill use of, and not by beating, chiding, or other servile punishments, they are for the future to be governed as they grow up to more understanding.

45. That this is so will be easily allowed when it is but considered what is to be aimed at in an ingenuous education; and upon what it turns.

1. He that has not a mastery over his inclinations, he that knows not how to resist the importunity of present pleasure or pain, for the sake of what reason tells him is fit to be done, wants the true principle of virtue and industry, and is in danger never to be good for anything. This temper therefore, so contrary to unguided nature, is to be got betimes; and this habit, as the true foundation of future ability and happiness, is to be wrought into the mind as early as may be, even from the first dawnings of knowledge or apprehension in children, and so to be confirmed in them, by all the care and ways imaginable, by those who have the oversight of their education.

46. 2. On the other side, if the mind be curbed and humbled too

[7] Other things being equal.

much in children; if their spirits be abased and broken much, by too strict a hand over them, they lose all their vigor and industry, and are in a worse state than the former. For extravagant young fellows that have liveliness and spirit come sometimes to be set right, and so make able and great men; but dejected minds, timorous and tame, and low spirits, are hardly ever to be raised, and very seldom attain to anything. To avoid the danger that is on either hand is the great art; and he that has found a way how to keep up a child's spirit easy, active, and free, and yet at the same time to restrain him from many things he has a mind to, and to draw him to things that are uneasy to him; he, I say, that knows how to reconcile these seeming contradictions, has, in my opinion, got the true secret of education.

47. The usual lazy and short way by chastisement and the rod, which is the only instrument of government that tutors generally know or ever think of, is the most unfit of any to be used in education, because it tends to both those mischiefs; which, as we have shown, are the Scylla and Charybdis, which on the one hand or the other ruin all that miscarry.

48. 1. This kind of punishment contributes not at all to the mastery of our natural propensity to indulge corporal and present pleasure, and to avoid pain at any rate, but rather encourages it, and thereby strengthens that in us which is the root from whence spring all vicious actions and the irregularities of life. For what other motive, but of sensual pleasure and pain, does a child act by, who drudges at his book against his inclination, or abstains from eating unwholesome fruit that he takes pleasure in, only out of fear of whipping? He in this only prefers the greater corporal pleasure, or avoids the greater corporal pain. And what is it, to govern his actions, and direct his conduct by such motives as these? What is it, I say, but to cherish that principle in him, which it is our business to root out and destroy? And therefore I cannot think any correction useful to a child, where the shame of suffering for having done amiss does not work more upon him than the pain.

49. 2. This sort of correction naturally breeds an aversion to that which 'tis the tutor's business to create a liking to. How obvious is it to observe that children come to hate things which were at first

acceptable to them, when they find themselves whipped, and chid, and teased about them? And it is not to be wondered at in them, when grown men would not be able to be reconciled to anything by such ways. Who is there that would not be disgusted with any innocent recreation, in itself indifferent to him, if he should with blows or ill language be haled to it, when he had no mind? Or be constantly so treated, for some circumstances in his application to it? This is natural to be so. Offensive circumstances ordinarily infect innocent things which they are joined with; and the very sight of a cup wherein anyone uses to take nauseous physic, turns his stomach, so that nothing will relish well out of it, though the cup be never so clean and well shaped, and of the richest materials.

50. 3. Such a sort of slavish discipline makes a slavish temper. The child submits, and dissembles obedience, whilst the fear of the rod hangs over him; but when that is removed, and by being out of sight, he can promise himself impunity, he gives the greater scope to his natural inclination; which by this way is not at all altered, but, on the contrary, heightened and increased in him; and after such restraint, breaks out usually with the more violence; or,

51. 4. If severity carried to the highest pitch does prevail, and works a cure upon the present unruly distemper, it often brings in the room of it a worse and more dangerous disease, by breaking the mind; and then, in the place of a disorderly young fellow, you have a low-spirited moping creature, who, however with his unnatural sobriety he may please silly people, who commend tame unactive children, because they make no noise, nor give them any trouble; yet at last, will probably prove as uncomfortable a thing to his friends, as he will be all his life an useless thing to himself and others.

52. Beating them and all other sorts of slavish and corporal punishments are not the discipline fit to be used in the education of those we would have wise, good, and ingenuous men; and therefore very rarely to be applied, and that only in great occasions, and cases of extremity. On the other side, to flatter children by rewards of things that are pleasant to them is as carefully to be avoided. He that will give to his son apples or sugarplums, or what else of this kind he is most delighted with, to make him learn his book, does but author-

ize his love of pleasure, and cocker up that dangerous propensity, which he ought by all means to subdue and stifle in him. You can never hope to teach him to master it, whilst you compound for the check you gave his inclination in one place, by the satisfaction you propose to it in another. To make a good, a wise, and a virtuous man, 'tis fit he should learn to cross his appetite, and deny his inclination to riches, finery, or pleasing his palate, etc., whenever his reason advises the contrary, and his duty requires it. But when you draw him to do anything that is fit by the offer of money, or reward the pains of learning his book by the pleasure of a luscious morsel; when you promise him a lace cravat or a fine new suit upon performance of some of his little tasks; what do you by proposing these as rewards, but allow them to be the good things he should aim at, and thereby encourage his longing for 'em, and accustom him to place his happiness in them? Thus people, to prevail with children to be industrious about their grammar, dancing, or some other such matter, of no great moment to the happiness or usefulness of their lives, by misapplied rewards and punishments, sacrifice their virtue, invert the order of their education, and teach them luxury, pride, or covetousness, etc. For in this way, flattering those wrong inclinations which they should restrain and suppress, they lay the foundations of those future vices, which cannot be avoided but by curbing our desires and accustoming them early to submit to reason.

53. I say not this, that I would have children kept from the conveniences or pleasures of life that are not injurious to their health or virtue. On the contrary, I would have their lives made as pleasant and as agreeable to them as may be, in a plentiful enjoyment of whatsoever might innocently delight them; provided it be with this caution, that they have those enjoyments only as the consequences of the state of esteem and acceptation they are in with their parents and governors; but they should never be offered or bestowed on them, as the rewards of this or that particular performance that they show an aversion to, or to which they would not have applied themselves without that temptation.

54. But if you take away the rod, on one hand, and these little encouragements which they are taken with, on the other, how then

(will you say) shall children be governed? Remove hope and fear, and there is an end of all discipline. I grant that good and evil, reward and punishment, are the only motives to a rational creature: these are the spur and reins whereby all mankind are set on work and guided, and therefore they are to be made use of to children too. For I advise their parents and governors always to carry this in their minds, that children are to be treated as rational creatures.

55. Rewards, I grant, and punishments must be proposed to children, if we intend to work upon them. The mistake, I imagine, is that those that are generally made use of are ill chosen. The pains and pleasures of the body are, I think, of ill consequence, when made the rewards and punishments whereby men would prevail on their children; for, as I said before, they serve but to increase and strengthen those inclinations, which 'tis our business to subdue and master. What principle of virtue do you lay in a child, if you will redeem his desires of one pleasure by the proposal of another? This is but to enlarge his appetite, and instruct it to wander. If a child cries for an unwholesome and dangerous fruit, you purchase his quiet by giving him a less hurtful sweetmeat. This perhaps may preserve his health, but spoils his mind, and sets that farther out of order. For here you only change the object, but flatter still his *appetite,* and allow that must be satisfied, wherein, as I have showed, lies the root of the mischief; and till you bring him to be able to bear a denial of that satisfaction, the child may at present be quiet and orderly, but the disease is not cured. By this way of proceeding, you foment and cherish in him that which is the spring from whence all the evil flows, which will be sure on the next occasion to break out again with more violence, give him stronger longings, and you more trouble.

56. The rewards and punishments then, whereby we should keep children in order, are quite of another kind, and of that force that when we can get them once to work, the business, I think, is done, and the difficulty is over. *Esteem* and *disgrace* are, of all others, the most powerful incentives to the mind, when once it is brought to relish them. If you can once get into children a love of credit, and an apprehension of shame and disgrace, you have put into 'em the true

principle, which will constantly work and incline them to the right. But it will be asked, How shall this be done?

I confess it does not at first appearance want some difficulty; but yet I think it worth our while to seek the ways (and practice them when found) to attain this, which I look on as the great secret of education.

57. First, children (earlier perhaps than we think) are very sensible of praise and commendation. They find a pleasure in being esteemed and valued, especially by their parents and those whom they depend on. If therefore the father caress and commend them when they do well, show a cold and neglectful countenance to them upon doing ill, and this accompanied by a like carriage of the mother and all others that are about them, it will, in a little time, make them sensible of the difference; and this, if constantly observed, I doubt not but will of itself work more than threats or blows, which lose their force when once grown common, and are of no use when shame does not attend them; and therefore are to be forborne, and never to be used, but in the case hereafter-mentioned, when it is brought to extremity.

58. But secondly, to make the sense of esteem or disgrace sink the deeper, and be of the more weight, other agreeable or disagreeable things should constantly accompany these different states; not as particular rewards and punishments of this or that particular action, but as necessarily belonging to, and constantly attending one who by his carriage has brought himself into a state of disgrace or commendation. By which way of treating them, children may as much as possible be brought to conceive that those that are commended and in esteem for doing well will necessarily be beloved and cherished by everybody, and have all other good things as a consequence of it; and on the other side, when anyone by miscarriage falls into disesteem, and cares not to preserve his credit, he will unavoidably fall under neglect and contempt; and in that state, the want of whatever might satisfy or delight him will follow. In this way the objects of their desires are made assisting to virtue, when a settled experience from the beginning teaches children that the things they delight in, belong to, and are to be enjoyed by those only who are in a state of reputation. If by these

means you can come once to shame them out of their faults (for besides that, I would willingly have no punishment) and make them in love with the pleasure of being well thought on, you may turn them as you please, and they will be in love with all the ways of virtue.

59. The great difficulty here is, I imagine, from the folly and perverseness of servants, who are hardly to be hindered from crossing herein the design of the father and mother. Children discountenanced by their parents for any fault, find usually a refuge and relief in the caresses of those foolish flatterers, who thereby undo whatever the parents endeavor to establish. When the father or mother looks sour on the child, everybody else should put on the same coldness to him, and nobody give him countenance, till forgiveness asked, and a reformation of his fault has set him right again and restored him to his former credit. If this were constantly observed, I guess there would be little need of blows or chiding: their own ease and satisfaction would quickly teach children to court commendation and avoid doing that which they found everybody condemned and they were sure to suffer for, without being chid or beaten. This would teach them modesty and shame; and they would quickly come to have a natural abhorrence for that which they found made them slighted and neglected by everybody. But how this inconvenience from servants is to be remedied, I must leave to parents' care and consideration. Only I think it of great importance; and that they are very happy who can get discreet people about their children.

60. Frequent beating or chiding is therefore carefully to be avoided: because this sort of correction never produces any good, farther than it serves to raise shame and abhorrence of the miscarriage that brought it on them. And if the greatest part of the trouble be not the sense that they have done amiss, and the apprehension that they have drawn on themselves the just displeasure of their best friends, the pain of whipping will work but an imperfect cure. It only patches up for the present, and skins it over, but reaches not to the bottom of the sore; ingenuous shame, and the apprehensions of displeasure, are the only true restraint. These alone ought to hold the reins and keep the child in order. But corporal punishments must necessarily lose that effect, and wear out the sense of shame, where they frequently return. Shame

in children has the same place that modesty has in women, which cannot be kept and often transgressed against. And as to the apprehension of displeasure in the parents, that will come to be very insignificant, if the marks of that displeasure quickly cease, and a few blows fully expiate. Parents should well consider what faults in their children are weighty enough to deserve the declaration of their anger: but when their displeasure is once declared to a degree that carries any punishment with it, they ought not presently to lay by the severity of their brows, but to restore their children to their former grace with some difficulty and delay a full reconciliation till their conformity and more than ordinary merit make good their amendment. If this be not so ordered, punishment will, by familiarity, become a mere thing of course, and lose all its influence; offending, being chastised, and then forgiven, will be thought as natural and necessary, as noon, night, and morning following one another.

61. Concerning reputation, I shall only remark this one thing more of it, that though it be not the true principle and measure of virtue (for that is the knowledge of a man's duty, and the satisfaction it is to obey his maker, in following the dictates of that light God has given him, with the hopes of acceptation and reward), yet it is that which comes nearest to it: and being the testimony and applause that other people's reason, as it were by a common consent, gives to virtuous and well-ordered actions, it is the proper guide and encouragement of children, till they grow able to judge for themselves and to find what is right by their own reason.

62. This consideration may direct parents how to manage themselves in reproving and commending their children. The rebukes and chiding, which their faults will sometimes make hardly to be avoided, should not only be in sober, grave, and unpassionate words, but also alone and in private: but the commendations children deserve, they should receive before others. This doubles the reward, by spreading their praise; but the backwardness parents show in divulging their faults will make them set a greater value on their credit themselves, and teach them to be the more careful to preserve the good opinion of others, whilst they think they have it: but when being exposed to shame by publishing their miscarriages, they give it up for lost, that

check upon them is taken off, and they will be the less careful to preserve others' good thoughts of them, the more they suspect that their
reputation with them is already blemished.

63. But if a right course be taken with children, there will not be
so much need of the application of the common rewards and punishments as we imagine, and as the general practice has established. For
all their innocent folly, playing and childish actions, are to be left
perfectly free and unrestrained, as far as they can consist with the
respect due to those that are present; and that with the greatest allowance. If these faults of their age, rather than of the children themselves,
were, as they should be, left only to time and imitation and riper years
to cure, children would escape a great deal of misapplied and useless
correction, which either fails to overpower the natural disposition of
their childhood, and so by an ineffectual familiarity, makes correction
in other necessary cases of less use; or else if it be of force to restrain
the natural gaiety of that age, it serves only to spoil the temper both
of body and mind. If the noise and bustle of their play prove at any
time inconvenient, or unsuitable to the place or company they are in
(which can only be where their parents are), a look or a word from
the father or mother, if they have established the authority they should,
will be enough either to remove or quiet them for that time. But this
gamesome humor, which is wisely adapted by nature to their age and
temper, should rather be encouraged to keep up their spirits, and improve their strength and health, than curbed and restrained; and the
chief art is to make all that they have to do, sport and play too.

64. And here give me leave to take notice of one thing I think a
fault in the ordinary method of education; and that is, the charging
of children's memories, upon all occasions, with rules and precepts,
which they often do not understand, and constantly as soon forget as
given. If it be some action you would have done, or done otherwise,
whenever they forget, or do it awkwardly, make them do it over and
over again till they are perfect, whereby you will get these two advantages. First, to see whether it be an action they can do, or is fit to
be expected of them: for sometimes children are bid to do things
which upon trial they are found not able to do, and had need be taught
and exercised in before they are required to do them. But it is much

easier for a tutor to command than to teach. Secondly, another thing got by it will be this, that by repeating the same action till it be grown habitual in them, the performance will not depend on memory or reflection, the concomitant of prudence and age, and not of childhood, but will be natural in them. Thus bowing to a gentleman when he salutes him, and looking in his face when he speaks to him, is by constant use as natural to a well-bred man as breathing; it requires no thought, no reflection. Having this way cured in your child any fault, it is cured forever: and thus one by one you may weed them out all, and plant what habits you please.

65. I have seen parents so heap rules on their children that it was impossible for the poor little ones to remember a tenth part of them, much less to observe them. However, they were either by words or blows corrected for the breach of those multiplied and often very impertinent precepts. Whence it naturally followed that the children minded not what was said to them, when it was evident to them that no attention they were capable of was sufficient to preserve them from transgression, and the rebukes which followed it.

Let therefore your rules to your son be as few as possible, and rather fewer than more than seem absolutely necessary. For if you burden him with many rules, one of these two things must necessarily follow: that either he must be very often punished, which will be of ill consequence, by making punishment too frequent and familiar; or else you must let the transgressions of some of your rules go unpunished, whereby they will of course grow contemptible, and your authority become cheap to him. Make but few laws, but see they be well observed when once made. Few years require but few laws, and as his age increases, when one rule is by practice well established, you may add another.

66. But pray remember, children are not to be taught by rules which will be always slipping out of their memories. What you think necessary for them to do, settle in them by an indispensable practice, as often as the occasion returns; and if it be possible, make occasions. This will beget habits in them which being once established, operate of themselves easily and naturally, without the assistance of the memory. But here let me give two cautions. 1. The one is, that you keep

them to the practice of what you would have grow into a habit in them, by kind words and gentle admonitions, rather as minding them of what they forget, than by harsh rebukes and chiding, as if they were willfully guilty. 2. Another thing you are to take care of is not to endeavor to settle too many habits at once, lest by variety you confound them, and so perfect none. When constant custom has made any one thing easy and natural to 'em, and they practice it without reflection, you may then go on to another.

This method of teaching children by a repeated practice and the same action done over and over again, under the eye and direction of the tutor, till they have got the habit of doing it well, and not by relying on rules trusted to their memories, has so many advantages, which way soever we consider it, that I cannot but wonder (if ill customs could be wondered at in any thing) how it could possibly be so much neglected. I shall name one more that comes now in my way. By this method we shall see whether what is required of him be adapted to his capacity, and any way suited to the child's natural genius and constitution; for that too must be considered in a right education. We must not hope wholly to change their original tempers, or make the gay pensive and grave, or the melancholy sportive, without spoiling them. God has stamped certain characters upon men's minds, which like their shapes, may perhaps be a little mended, but can hardly be totally altered and transformed into the contrary.

He therefore that is about children should well study their natures and aptitudes, and see by often trials what turn they easily take, and what becomes them; observe what their native stock is, how it may be improved, and what it is fit for: he should consider what they want, whether they be capable of having it wrought into them by industry, and incorporated there by practice; and whether it be worth while to endeavor it. For in many cases, all that we can do, or should aim at, is to make the best of what nature has given, to prevent the vices and faults to which such a constitution is most inclined, and give it all the advantages it is capable of. Everyone's natural genius should be carried as far as it could; but to attempt the putting another upon him will be but labor in vain; and what is so plastered on will at best sit but untowardly, and have always hanging to it the ungracefulness of constraint and affectation.

Affectation is not, I confess, an early fault of childhood, or the product of untaught nature. It is of that sort of weeds which grow not in the wild uncultivated waste, but in garden-plots, under the negligent hand or unskillful care of a gardener. Management and instruction, and some sense of the necessity of breeding, are requisite to make anyone capable of affectation, which endeavors to correct natural defects, and has always the laudable aim of pleasing, though it always misses it; and the more it labors to put on gracefulness, the farther it is from it. For this reason, it is the more carefully to be watched, because it is the proper fault of education; a perverted education indeed, but such as young people often fall into, either by their own mistake, or the ill conduct of those about them.

He that will examine wherein that gracefulness lies, which always pleases, will find it arises from that natural coherence which appears between the thing done and such a temper of mind as cannot but be approved of as suitable to the occasion. We cannot but be pleased with a humane, friendly, civil temper wherever we meet with it. A mind free and master of itself and all its actions, not low and narrow, not haughty and insolent, not blemished with any great defect, is what everyone is taken with. The actions which naturally flow from such a well-formed mind, please us also, as the genuine marks of it, and being, as it were, natural emanations from the spirit and disposition within, cannot but be easy and unconstrained. This seems to me to be that beauty which shines through some men's actions, sets off all that they do, and takes all they come near; when by a constant practice, they have fashioned their carriage, and made all those little expressions of civility and respect, which nature or custom has established in conversation, so easy to themselves that they seem not artificial or studied, but naturally to follow from a sweetness of mind and a well-turned disposition.

On the other side, affectation is an awkward and forced imitation of what should be genuine and easy, wanting the beauty that accompanies what is natural; because there is always a disagreement between the outward action and the mind within, one of these two ways:

1. Either when a man would outwardly put on a disposition of mind, which then he really has not, but endeavors by a forced carriage to make show of; yet so that the constraint he is under discovers itself: and thus men affect sometimes to appear sad, merry, or kind, when in truth they are not so.

2. The other is, when they do not endeavor to make show of dispositions of mind, which they have not, but to express those they have by a carriage not suited to them. And such in conversation are all constrained motions, actions, words, or looks, which, though designed to show either their respect or civility to the company, or their satisfaction and easiness in it, are not yet natural or genuine marks of the one or the other, but rather of some defect or mistake within. Imitation of others, without discerning what is graceful in them, or what is peculiar to their characters, often makes a great part of this. But affectation of all kinds, whencesoever it proceeds, is always offensive, because we naturally hate whatever is counterfeit, and condemn those who have nothing better to recommend themselves by.

Plain and rough nature, left to itself, is much better than an artificial ungracefulness, and such studied ways of being ill-fashioned. The want of an accomplishment, or some defect in our behavior coming short of the utmost gracefulness, often escapes observation and censure. But affectation in any part of our carriage is lighting up a candle to our defects, and never fails to make us be taken notice of, either as wanting sense or wanting sincerity. This governors ought the more diligently to look after, because, as I above observed, 'tis an acquired ugliness, owing to mistaken education, few being guilty of it but those who pretend to breeding, and would not be thought ignorant of what is fashionable and becoming in conversation; and, if I mistake not, it has often its rise from the lazy admonitions of those who give rules and propose examples, without joining practice with their instructions and making their pupils repeat the action in their sight, that they may correct what is indecent or constrained in it, till it be perfected into an habitual and becoming easiness.

67. Manners, as they call it, about which children are so often perplexed, and have so many goodly exhortations made them by their wise maids and governesses, I think, are rather to be learnt by ex-

ample than rules; and then children, if kept out of ill company, will take a pride to behave themselves prettily, after the fashion of others, perceiving themselves esteemed and commended for it. But if by a little negligence in this part, the boy should not pull off his hat, nor make legs [8] very gracefully, a dancing-master will cure that defect, and wipe off all that plainness of nature, which the a-la-mode people call clownishness. And since nothing appears to me to give children so much becoming confidence and behavior, and so to raise them to the conversation of those above their age, as dancing, I think they should be taught to dance as soon as they are capable of learning it. For though this consist only in outward gracefulness of motion, yet, I know not how, it gives children manly thoughts and carriage more than anything. But otherwise, I would not have little children much tormented about punctilios or niceties of breeding.

Never trouble yourself about those faults in them which you know age will cure: and therefore want of well-fashioned civility in the carriage, whilst civility is not wanting in the mind (for there you must take care to plant it early), should be the parents' least care, whilst they are young. If his tender mind be filled with a veneration for his parents and teachers, which consists of love and esteem, and a fear to offend them, and with respect and good will to all people, that respect will of itself teach those ways of expressing it which he observes most acceptable. Be sure to keep up in him the principles of good nature and kindness; make them as habitual as you can, by credit and commendation, and the good things accompanying that state: and when they have taken root in his mind, and are settled there by a continued practice, fear not the ornaments of conversation and the outside of fashionable manners will come in their due time; if when they are removed out of their maid's care, they are put into the hands of a well-bred man to be their governor.

Whilst they are very young, any carelessness is to be borne with in children that carries not with it the marks of pride or ill nature; but those, whenever they appear in any action, are to be corrected immediately by the ways above-mentioned. What I have said concerning

[8] To make legs: to make bows.

manners, I would not have so understood, as if I meant that those who have the judgment to do it, should not gently fashion the motions and carriage of children, when they are very young. It would be of great advantage, if they had people about them from their being first able to go that had the skill, and would take the right way to do it. That which I complain of is the wrong course that is usually taken in this matter. Children who were never taught any such thing as behavior are often (especially when strangers are present) chid for having some way or other failed in good manners, and have thereupon reproofs and precepts heaped upon them, concerning putting off their hats, or making of legs, etc. Though in this, those concerned pretend to correct the child, yet in truth, for the most part, it is but to cover their own shame; and they lay the blame on the poor little ones, sometimes passionately enough to divert it from themselves, for fear the bystanders should impute to their want of care and skill the child's ill behavior.

For, as for the children themselves, they are never one jot bettered by such occasional lectures. They at other times should be shown what to do, and by reiterated actions be fashioned beforehand into the practice of what is fit and becoming, and not told and talked to do upon the spot of what they have never been accustomed nor know how to do as they should. To hare and rate [9] them thus at every turn is not to teach them, but to vex and torment them to no purpose. They should be let alone, rather than chid for a fault which is none of theirs, nor is in their power to mend for speaking to. And it were much better their natural childish negligence or plainness should be left to the care of riper years than that they should frequently have rebukes misplaced upon them, which neither do nor can give them graceful motions. If their minds are well-disposed and principled with inward civility, a great part of the roughness which sticks to the outside for want of better teaching, time and observation will rub off, as they grow up, if they are bred in good company; but if in ill, all the rules in the world, all the correction imaginable, will not be able to polish them. For you must take this for a certain truth, that let them have

[9] Hare and rate: harass and berate.

what instructions you will, and ever so learned lectures of breeding daily inculcated into them, that which will most influence their carriage will be the company they converse with and the fashion of those about them. Children (nay, and men too) do most by example. We are all a sort of chameleons, that still take a tincture from things near us; nor is it to be wondered at in children, who better understand what they see than what they hear.

68. I mentioned above one great mischief that came by servants to children, when by their flatteries they take off the edge and force of the parents' rebukes, and so lessen their authority: and here is another great inconvenience which children receive from the ill examples which they meet with amongst the meaner servants.

They are wholly, if possible, to be kept from such conversation; for the contagion of these ill precedents, both in civility and virtue, horribly infects children, as often as they come within reach of it. They frequently learn from unbred or debauched servants such language, untowardly tricks and vices, as otherwise they possibly would be ignorant of all their lives.

69. 'Tis a hard matter wholly to prevent this mischief. You will have very good luck if you never have a clownish or vicious servant, and if from them your children never get any infection: but yet as much must be done towards it as can be, and the children kept as much as may be [10] in the company of their parents, and those to whose care they are committed. To this purpose, their being in their presence should be made easy to them; they should be allowed the liberties and freedoms suitable to their ages, and not be held under unnecessary restraints, when in their parents' or governor's sight. If it be a prison to them, 'tis no wonder they should not like it. They must not be hindered from being children, or from playing, or doing as children, but from doing ill; all other liberty is to be allowed them. Next, to make them in love with the company of their parents, they should receive all their good things there, and from their hands. The servants

[10] How much the Romans thought the education of their children a business that properly belonged to the parents themselves, see in Suetonius, *August.* § 64. Plutarch, *Vita Catonis Censoris,* Diodorus Siculus, l. 2, cap. 3.

should be hindered from making court to them by giving them strong drink, wine, fruit, playthings, and other such matters, which may make them in love with their conversation.

70. Having named *company*, I am almost ready to throw away my pen, and trouble you no farther on this subject: for since that does more than all precepts, rules and instructions, methinks 'tis almost wholly in vain to make a long discourse of other things, and to talk of that almost to no purpose. For you will be ready to say, what shall I do with my son? If I keep him always at home, he will be in danger to be my young master; and if I send him abroad, how is it possible to keep him from the contagion of rudeness and vice, which is everywhere so in fashion? In my house he will perhaps be more innocent, but more ignorant too of the world; wanting there change of company and being used constantly to the same faces, he will, when he comes abroad, be a sheepish or conceited creature.

I confess both sides have their inconveniences. Being abroad, 'tis true, will make him bolder, and better able to bustle and shift among boys of his own age; and the emulation of schoolfellows often puts life and industry into young lads. But still you can find a school wherein it is possible for the master to look after the manners of his scholars, and can show as great effects of his care of forming their minds to virtue, and their carriage to good breeding, as of forming their tongues to the learned languages, you must confess, that you have a strange value for words, when preferring the languages of the ancient Greeks and Romans to that which made 'em such brave men, you think it worth while to hazard your son's innocence and virtue for a little Greek and Latin. For, as for that boldness and spirit which lads get amongst their playfellows at school, it has ordinarily such a mixture of rudeness and ill-turned confidence that those misbecoming and disingenuous ways of shifting in the world must be unlearnt, and all the tincture washed out again, to make way for better principles and such manners as make a truly worthy man. He that considers how diametrically opposite the skill of living well, and managing, as a man should do, his affairs in the world, is to that mal-pertness, tricking, or violence learnt amongst schoolboys, will think the faults of a privater education infinitely to be preferred to such improvements, and will take care to preserve his child's innocence and modesty at home, as being nearer of kin, and more in the way of those qualities which make a useful and able man. Nor does anyone find, or so much as suspect, that that retirement and bashfulness which their daughters are brought up in makes them less knowing or less able women. Conversation, when they come into the world, soon gives them a becoming assurance; and whatsoever, beyond that, there is of rough and boisterous, may in men be very well spared too; for courage and steadiness, as I take it, lie not in roughness and ill breeding.

Virtue is harder to be got than a knowledge of the world; and if lost in a young man, is seldom recovered. Sheepishness and ignorance of the world, the faults imputed to a private education, are neither the necessary consequences of being bred at home, nor if they were, are they incurable evils. Vice is the more stubborn, as well as the more dangerous evil of the two; and therefore in the first place to be fenced against. If that sheepish softness, which often enervates those who are bred like fondlings at home, be carefully to be avoided, it is principally so for virtue's sake; for fear lest such a yielding temper should be too susceptible of vicious impressions, and expose the novice too easily to be corrupted. A young man before he leaves the shelter of his father's house, and the guard of a tutor, should be fortified with resolution, and made acquainted with men, to secure his virtues, lest he should be led into some ruinous course, or fatal precipice, before he is sufficiently acquainted with the dangers of conversation, and has steadiness enough not to yield to every temptation. Were it not for this, a young man's bashfulness and ignorance in the world would not so much need an early care. Conversation would cure it in a great measure; or if that will not do it early enough, it is only a stronger reason for a good tutor at home. For if pains are to be taken to give him a manly air and assurance betimes, it is chiefly as a fence to his virtue when he goes into the world under his own conduct.

It is preposterous therefore to sacrifice his innocence to the attaining of confidence and some little skill of bustling for himself among others, by his conversation with ill-bred and vicious boys; when the chief use of that sturdiness and standing upon his own legs is only for the preservation of his virtue. For if confidence or cunning come once to mix with vice, and support his miscarriages, he is only the surer lost; and you must undo again, and strip him of that he has got from his companions, or give him up to ruin. Boys will unavoidably be taught assurance by conversation with men, when they are brought into it; and that is time enough. Modesty and submission, till then, better fits them for instruction; and therefore there needs not any great care to stock them with confidence beforehand. That which requires most time, pains, and assiduity is to work into them the principles and practice of virtue and good breeding. This is the seasoning they should be prepared with, so as not easily to be got out again. This they had need to be well provided with, for conversation, when they come into the world, will add to their knowledge and assurance, but be too apt to take from their virtue; which therefore they ought to be plentifully stored with, and have that tincture sunk deep into them.

How they should be fitted for conversation, and entered into the world, when they are ripe for it, we shall consider in another place. But how anyone's being put into a mixed herd of unruly boys, and there learning to wrangle at trap, or rook at span-farthing,[11] fits him for civil conversation or business, I do not see. And what qualities are ordinarily to be got from such a troop of playfellows as schools usually assemble together from parents of all kinds, that a father should so much covet, is hard to divine. I am sure he who is able to be at the charge of a tutor at home may there give his son a more genteel carriage, more manly thoughts, and a sense of what is worthy and becoming, with a greater proficiency in learning into the bargain, and ripen him up sooner into a man, than any at school can do. Not that I blame the schoolmaster in this, or think it to be laid to his charge. The difference is great between two or three pupils in the same house, and three or four score boys lodged up and down: for let the master's industry and skill be never so great, it is impossible he should have fifty or a hundred scholars under his eye any longer than they are in the school together, nor can it be expected that he should instruct them successfully in anything but their books; the

[11] Trap and span-farthing are old English children's games.

forming of their minds and manners requiring a constant attention,
and particular application to every single boy, which is impossible in
a numerous flock, and would be wholly in vain (could he have time
to study and correct everyone's particular defects and wrong inclinations) when the lad was to be left to himself, or the prevailing infection of his fellows, the greatest part of the four and twenty hours.

But fathers, observing that fortune is often most successfully courted
by bold and bustling men, are glad to see their sons pert and forward
betimes; take it for a happy omen that they will be thriving men,
and look on the tricks they play their schoolfellows, or learn from
them, as a proficiency in the art of living, and making their way
through the world. But I must take the liberty to say that he that lays
the foundation of his son's fortune in virtue and good breeding takes
the only sure and warrantable way. And 'tis not the waggeries or
cheats practiced amongst schoolboys, 'tis not their roughness one to
another, nor the well-laid plots of robbing an orchard together, that
make an able man; but the principles of justice, generosity, and
sobriety, joined with observation and industry, qualities which I
judge schoolboys do not learn much of one another. And if a young
gentleman bred at home be not taught more of them than he could
learn at school, his father has made a very ill choice of a tutor. Take
a boy from the top of a grammar-school and one of the same age bred
as he should be in his father's family, and bring them into good company together and then see which of the two will have the more manly
carriage, and address himself with the more becoming assurance to
strangers. Here I imagine the schoolboy's confidence will either fail
or discredit him; and if it be such as fits him only for the conversation
of boys, he were better to be without it.

Vice, if we may believe the general complaint, ripens so fast nowa-
days, and runs up to seed so early in young people, that it is impossible
to keep a lad from the spreading contagion, if you will venture him
abroad in the herd, and trust to chance or his own inclination for the
choice of his company at school. By what fate Vice has so thriven
amongst us these years past, and by what hands it has been nursed up
into so uncontrolled a dominion, I shall leave to others to inquire.
I wish that those who complain of the great decay of Christian piety

and virtue everywhere, and of learning and acquired improvements in the gentry of this generation, would consider how to retrieve them in the next. This I am sure, that if the foundation of it be not laid in the education and principling of the youth, all other endeavors will be in vain. And if the innocence, sobriety, and industry of those who are coming up, be not taken care of and preserved, 'twill be ridiculous to expect that those who are to succeed next on the stage, should abound in that virtue, ability, and learning which has hitherto made England considerable in the world. I was going to add courage too, though it has been looked on as the natural inheritance of Englishmen. What has been talked of some late actions at sea, of a kind unknown to our ancestors, gives me occasion to say that debauchery sinks the courage of men; and when dissoluteness has eaten out the sense of true honor, bravery seldom stays long after it. And I think it impossible to find an instance of any nation, however renowned for their valor, who ever kept their credit in arms, or made themselves redoubtable amongst their neighbors, after corruption had once broke through and dissolved the restraint of discipline, and vice was grown to such an head that it durst show itself barefaced without being out of countenance.

'Tis virtue then, direct virtue, which is the hard and valuable part to be aimed at in education, and not a forward pertness or any little arts of shifting. All other considerations and accomplishments should give way and be postponed to this. This is the solid and substantial good which tutors should not only read lectures and talk of, but the labor and art of education should furnish the mind with and fasten there, and never cease till the young man had a true relish of it, and placed his strength, his glory, and his pleasure in it.

The more this advances, the easier way will be made for other accomplishments in their turns. For he that is brought to submit to virtue will not be refractory, or restive, in anything that becomes him; and therefore I cannot but prefer breeding of a young gentleman at home in his father's sight, under a good governor, as much the best and safest way to this great and main end of education, when it can be had, and is ordered as it should be. Gentlemen's houses are seldom without variety of company. They should accustom their sons to all the strange faces that come here, and engage them in conversation with men of parts and breeding, as soon as they are capable of it. And why those who live in the country should not take them with them, when they make visits of civility to their neighbors, I know not. This I am sure, a father that breeds his son at home has the opportunity to have him more in his own company, and there give him what encouragement he thinks fit, and can keep him better from the taint of servants and the meaner sort of people than is possible to be done abroad. But what shall be resolved in the case must in great measure be left to the parents, to be determined by their circumstances and conveniences; only I think it the worst sort of good husbandry for a father not to strain himself a little for his son's breeding; which, let his condition be what it will, is the best portion he can leave him. But if, after all, it shall be thought by some, that the breeding at home has too little company, and that at ordinary schools, not such as it should be for a young gentleman, I think there might be ways found out to avoid the inconveniences on the one side and the other.

71. Having under consideration how great the influence of company is, and how prone we are all, especially children, to imitation, I must here take the liberty to mind parents of this one thing, viz., that he that will have his son have a respect for him and his orders, must himself have a great reverence for his son. *Maxima debetur pueris reverentia.*[12] You must do nothing before him which you would not have him imitate. If anything escape you which you would have pass for a fault in him, he will be sure to shelter himself under your example, and shelter himself so as that it will not be easy to come at him, to correct it in him the right way. If you punish him for what he sees you practice yourself, he will not think that severity to proceed from kindness in you, careful to amend a fault in him; but will be apt to interpret it the peevishness and arbitrary imperiousness of a father, who, without any ground for it, would deny his son the liberty and pleasures he takes himself. Or if you assume to yourself the liberty you have taken, as a privilege belonging to riper years, to which a child must not aspire, you do but add new force to your example, and

[12] We owe the greatest reverence to youth.

recommend the action the more powerfully to him. For you must always remember, that children affect to be men earlier than is thought; and they love breeches, not for their cut or ease, but because the having them is a mark or step towards manhood. What I say of the father's carriage before his children must extend itself to all those who have any authority over them, or for whom he would have them have any respect.

72. But to return to the business of rewards and punishments. All the actions of childishness, and unfashionable carriage, and whatever time and age will of itself be sure to reform, being (as I have said) exempt from the discipline of the rod, there will not be so much need of beating children as is generally made use of. To which if we add learning to read, write, dance, foreign languages, etc., as under the same privilege, there will be but very rarely an occasion for blows or force in an ingenuous education. The right way to teach them those things is to give them a liking and inclination to what you suppose to them to be learned, and that will engage their industry and application. This I think no hard matter to do, if children be handled as they should be, and the rewards and punishments above-mentioned be carefully applied, and with them these few rules observed in the method of instructing them.

73. 1. None of the things they are to learn should ever be made a burden to them, or imposed on them as a *task*. Whatever is so proposed presently becomes irksome; the mind takes an aversion to it, though before it were a thing of delight or indifferency. Let a child but be ordered to whip his top at a certain time every day, whether he has or has not a mind to it; let this be but required of him as a duty, wherein he must spend so many hours morning and afternoon, and see whether he will not soon be weary of any play at this rate. Is it not so with grown men? What they do cheerfully of themselves, do they not presently grow sick of and can no more endure, as soon as they find it is expected of them as a duty? Children have as much a mind to show that they are free, that their own good actions come from themselves, that they are absolute and independent, as any of the proudest of you grown men, think of them as you please.

74. 2. As a consequence of this, they should seldom be put about

doing even those things you have got an inclination in them to, but when they have a mind and disposition to it. He that loves reading, writing, music, etc., finds yet in himself certain seasons wherein those things have no relish to him, and if at that time he forces himself to it, he only pothers and wearies himself to no purpose. So it is with children. This change of temper should be carefully observed in them, and the favorable seasons of aptitude and inclination be heedfully laid hold of: and if they are not often enough forward of themselves, a good disposition should be talked into them, before they be set upon anything. This I think no hard matter for a discreet tutor to do, who has studied his pupil's temper, and will be at a little pains to fill his head with suitable ideas, such as may make him in love with the present business. By this means a great deal of time and tiring would be saved: for a child will learn three times as much when he is in tune, as he will with double the time and pains when he goes awkwardly or is dragged unwillingly to it. If this were minded as it should, children might be permitted to weary themselves with play, and yet have time enough to learn what is suited to the capacity of each age. But no such thing is considered in the ordinary way of education, nor can it well be. That rough discipline of the rod is built upon other principles, has no attraction in it, regards not what humor children are in, nor looks after favorable seasons of inclination. And indeed it would be ridiculous, when compulsion and blows have raised an aversion in the child to his task, to expect he should freely of his own accord leave his play, and with pleasure court the occasions of learning; whereas, were matters ordered right, learning anything they should be taught might be made as much a recreation to their play, as their play is to their learning. The pains are equal on both sides. Nor is it that which troubles them; for they love to be busy, and the change and variety is that which naturally delights them. The only odds is, in that which we call play they act at liberty, and employ their pains (whereof you may observe them never sparing) freely; but what they are to learn is forced upon them, they are called, compelled, and driven to it. This is that that at first entrance balks and cools them; they want their liberty. Get them but to ask their tutor to teach them, as they do often their playfellows, instead of his calling upon them to learn, and they being satisfied that they act as freely in this as they do in other things, they will go on with as much pleasure in it, and it will not differ from their other sports and play. By these ways, carefully pursued, a child may be brought to desire to be taught anything you have a mind he should learn. The hardest part, I confess, is with the first or eldest; but when once he is set right, it is easy by him to lead the rest whither one will.

75. Though it be past doubt that the fittest time for children to learn anything, is when their *minds* are *in tune, and well disposed* to it; when neither flagging of spirit, nor intentness of thought upon something else, makes them awkward and averse; yet two things are to be taken care of: 1. That these seasons either not being warily observed, and laid hold on as often as they return, or else, not returning as often as they should, the improvement of the child be not thereby neglected, and so he be let grow into an habitual idleness and confirmed in this disposition: 2. That though other things are ill learned, when the mind is either indisposed or otherwise taken up; yet it is of great moment, and worth our endeavors, to teach the mind to get the mastery over itself, and to be able, upon choice, to take itself off from the hot pursuit of one thing, and set itself upon another with facility and delight, or at any time to shake off its sluggishness, and vigorously employ itself about what reason, or the advice of another shall direct. This is to be done in children, by trying them sometimes, when they are by laziness unbent, or by avocation bent another way, and endeavoring to make them buckle to the thing proposed If by this means the mind can get an habitual dominion over itself, lay by ideas or business as occasion requires, and betake itself to new and less acceptable employments without reluctance or discomposure. it will be an advantage of more consequence than Latin or logic or most of those things children are usually required to learn.

76. Children being more active and busy in that age than in any other part of their life, and being indifferent to anything they can do, so they may be but doing; dancing and scotchhoppers [13] would be the same thing to them, were the encouragements and discouragements equal. But to things we would have them learn, the great and only

[13] Hopscotch.

discouragement I can observe is that they are called to it. 'tis made their business, they are teased and chid about it, and do it with trembling and apprehension; or, when they come willingly to it, are kept too long at it, till they are quite tired: all which intrenches too much on that natural freedom they extremely affect. And it is that liberty alone which gives the true relish and delight to their ordinary playgames. Turn the tables, and you will find they will soon change their application; especially if they see the examples of others whom they esteem and think above themselves. And if the things which they observe others to do be ordered so that they insinuate themselves into them as the privilege of an age or condition above theirs; then ambition, and the desire still to get forward and higher, and to be like those above them, will set them on work, and make them go on with vigor and pleasure; pleasure in what they have begun by their own desire, in which way the enjoyment of their dearly beloved freedom will be no small encouragement to them. To all which, if there be added the satisfaction of credit and reputation, I am apt to think there will need no other spur to excite their application and assiduity, as much as is necessary. I confess, there needs patience and skill, gentleness and attention, and a prudent conduct to attain this at first. But why have you a tutor, if there needed no pains? But when this is once established, all the rest will follow, more easily than in any more severe and imperious discipline. And I think it no hard matter to gain this point; I am sure it will not be, where children have no ill examples set before them. The great danger therefore, I apprehend, is only from servants and other ill-ordered children, or such other vicious or foolish people, who spoil children both by the ill pattern they set before them in their own ill manners, and by giving them together the two things they should never have at once; I mean vicious pleasures and commendation.

77. As children should very seldom be corrected by blows, so I think frequent, and especially passionate chiding of almost as ill consequence. It lessens the authority of the parents and the respect of the child; for I bid you still remember, they distinguish early betwixt passion and reason: and as they cannot but have a reverence for what comes from the latter, so they quickly grow into a contempt of the

former; or if it causes a present terror, yet it soon wears off, and natural inclination will easily learn to slight such scarecrows which make a noise, but are not animated by reason. Children are to be restrained by the parents only in vicious (which, in their tender years, are only a few) things, a look or nod only ought to correct them when they do amiss; or, if words are sometimes to be used, they ought to be grave, kind, and sober, representing the ill or unbecomingness of the faults, rather than a hasty rating of the child for it; which makes him not sufficiently distinguish, whether your dislike be not more directed to him than his fault. Passionate chiding usually carries rough and ill language with it, which has this farther ill effect, that it teaches and justifies it in children: and the names that their parents or preceptors give them, they will not be ashamed or backward to bestow on others, having so good authority for the use of them.

78. I foresee here it will be objected to me, what then, will you have children never beaten nor chid for any fault? This will be to let loose the reins to all kind of disorder. Not so much as is imagined, if a right course has been taken in the first seasoning of their minds, and implanting that awe of their parents above mentioned. For beating, by constant observation, is found to do little good, where the smart of it is all the punishment is feared or felt in it; for the influence of that quickly wears out, with the memory of it. But yet there is one, and but one, fault for which, I think, children should be beaten, and that is obstinacy or rebellion. And in this too, I would have it ordered so, if it can be, that the shame of the whipping and not the pain should be the greatest part of the punishment. Shame of doing amiss, and deserving chastisement, is the only true restraint belonging to virtue. The smart of the rod, if shame accompanies it not, soon ceases and is forgotten, and will quickly by use lose its terror. I have known the children of a person of quality kept in awe by the fear of having their shoes pulled off, as much as others by apprehensions of a rod hanging over them. Some such punishment I think better than beating; for 'tis shame of the fault, and the disgrace that attends it that they should stand in fear of, rather than pain, if you would have them have a temper truly ingenuous. But stubbornness, and an obstinate disobedience, must be mastered with force and blows; for

this there is no other remedy. Whatever particular action you bid him do, or forbear, you must be sure to see yourself obeyed; no quarter in this case, no resistance: for when once it comes to be a trial of skill, a contest for mastery betwixt you, as it is if you command and he refuses, you must be sure to carry it, whatever blows it costs, if a nod or words will not prevail; unless, forever after, you intend to live in obedience to your son. A prudent and kind mother of my acquaintance was, on such an occasion, forced to whip her little daughter, at her first coming home from nurse, eight times successively the same morning, before she could master her stubbornness, and obtain a compliance in a very easy and indifferent matter. If she had left off sooner, and stopped at the seventh whipping, she had spoiled the child forever, and, by her unprevailing blows, only confirmed her refractoriness, very hardly afterwards to be cured: but wisely persisting till she had bent her mind, and suppled her will, the only end of correction and chastisement, she established her authority thoroughly in the very first occasions, and had ever after a very ready compliance and obedience in all things from her daughter; for as this was the first time, so I think it was the last too she ever struck her.

The pain of the rod, the first occasion that requires it, continued and increased, without leaving off till it has thoroughly prevailed, should first bend the mind, and settle the parent's authority; and then gravity, mixed with kindness, should forever after keep it.

This, if well reflected on, would make people more wary in the use of the rod and the cudgel, and keep them from being so apt to think beating the safe and universal remedy to be applied at random on all occasions. This is certain, however, if it does no good, it does great harm; if it reaches not the mind, and makes not the will supple, it hardens the offender; and whatever pain he has suffered for it does but endear him to his beloved stubbornness, which has got him this time the victory, and prepares him to contest, and hope for it for the future. This I doubt not but by ill-ordered correction many have been taught to be obstinate and refractory who otherwise would have been very pliant and tractable. For if you punish a child so, as if it were only to revenge the past fault, which has raised your choler, what operation can this have upon his mind, which is the part to be amended? If there were no sturdy humor or willfulness mixed with his fault, there was nothing in it that required the severity of blows. A kind or grave admonition is enough to remedy the slips of frailty, forgetfulness, or inadvertency, and is as much as they will stand in need of. But if there were a perverseness in the will, if it were a designed, resolved disobedience, the punishment is not to be measured by the greatness or smallness of the matter wherein it appeared, but by the opposition it carries, and stands in, to that respect and submission is due to the father's orders; which must always be rigorously exacted, and the blows by pauses laid on, till they reach the mind, and you perceive the signs of a true sorrow, shame, and purpose of obedience.

This, I confess, requires something more than setting children a task, and whipping them without any more a-do if it be not done, and done to our fancy. This requires care, attention, observation, and a nice study of children's tempers, and weighing their faults well, before we come to this sort of punishment. But is not that better than always to have the rod in hand as the only instrument of government? And by frequent use of it on all occasions, misapply and render inefficacious this last and useful remedy, where there is need of it? For what else can be expected, when it is promiscuously used upon every little slip? When a mistake in concordance, or a wrong position in verse, shall have the severity of the lash in a well-tempered and industrious lad, as surely as a willful crime in an obstinate and perverse offender; how can such a way of correction be expected to do good on the mind, and set that right? Which is the only thing to be looked after, and when set right, brings all the rest that you can desire along with it.

79. Where a wrong bent of the will wants not amendment, there can be no need of blows. All other faults, where the mind is rightly disposed and refuses not the government and authority of the father or tutor, are but mistakes, and may often be overlooked; or when they are taken notice of, need no other but the gentle remedies of advice, direction, and reproof, till the repeated and willful neglect of those shows the fault to be in the mind, and that a manifest perverseness of the will lies at the root of their disobedience. But whenever obstinacy,

which is an open defiance, appears, *that* cannot be winked at or neglected, but must, in the first instance, be subdued and mastered; only care must be had that we mistake not and we must be sure it is obstinacy and nothing else.

80. But since the occasions of punishment, especially beating, are as much to be avoided as may be, I think it should not be often brought to this point. If the awe I spoke of be once got, a look will be sufficient in most cases. Nor indeed should the same carriage, seriousness, or application be expected from young children as from those of riper growth. They must be permitted, as I said, the foolish and childish actions suitable to their years, without taking notice of them. Inadvertency, carelessness, and gaiety, is the character of that age. I think the severity I spoke of is not to extend itself to such unseasonable restraints. Nor is that hastily to be interpreted obstinacy or willfulness, which is the natural product of their age or temper. In such miscarriages they are to be assisted and helped towards an amendment, as weak people under a natural infirmity; which, though they are warned of, yet every relapse must not be counted a perfect neglect, and they presently treated as obstinate. Faults of frailty, as they should never be neglected or let pass without minding, so, unless the will mix with them, they should never be exaggerated or very sharply reproved, but with a gentle hand set right, as time and age permit. By this means, children will come to see what 'tis in any miscarriage that is chiefly offensive, and so learn to avoid it. This will encourage them to keep their wills right; which is the great business, when they find that it preserves them from any great displeasure, and that in all their other failings they meet with the kind concern and help, rather than the anger and passionate reproaches of their tutor and parents. Keep them from vice and vicious dispositions, and such a kind of behavior in general will come with every degree of their age, as is suitable to that age and the company they ordinarily converse with; and as they grow in years, they will grow in attention and application. But that your words may always carry weight and authority with them, if it shall happen upon any occasion that you bid him leave off the doing of any even childish things, you must be sure to carry the point, and not let him have the mastery. But yet, I say, I

would have the father seldom interpose his authority and command in these cases, or in any other, but such as have a tendency to vicious habits. I think there are better ways of prevailing with them: and a gentle persuasion in reasoning, when the first point of submission to your will is got, will most times do much better.

81. It will perhaps be wondered that I mention *reasoning* with children; and yet I cannot but think that the true way of dealing with them. They understand it as early as they do language; and, if I misobserve not, they love to be treated as rational creatures sooner than is imagined. 'Tis a pride should be cherished in them, and, as much as can be, made the greatest instrument to turn them by.

But when I talk of reasoning, I do not intend any other but such as is suited to the child's capacity and apprehension. Nobody can think a boy of three or seven years old should be argued with as a grown man. Long discourses and philosophical reasonings, at best, amaze and confound but do not instruct children. When I say, therefore, that they must be *treated as rational creatures,* I mean that you should make them sensible, by the mildness of your carriage, and the composure even in your correction of them, that what you do is reasonable in you, and useful and necessary for them; and that it is not out of *caprichio,* passion, or fancy that you command or forbid them anything. This they are capable of understanding; and there is no virtue they should be excited to nor fault they should be kept from which I do not think they may be convinced of; but it must be by such reasons as their age and understandings are capable of, and those proposed always in very few and plain words. The foundations on which several duties are built, and the fountains of right and wrong from which they spring, are not perhaps easily to be let into the minds of grown men, not used to abstract their thoughts from common received opinions. Much less are children capable of reasonings from remote principles. They cannot conceive the force of long deductions. The reasons that move them must be obvious, and level to their thoughts, and such as may, if I may so say, be felt and touched. But yet, if their age, temper, and inclination be considered, there will never want such motives as may be sufficient to convince them. If there be no other more particular, yet these will always be intelligible, and of force, to deter them from any fault fit to be taken notice of in them, viz., that it will be a discredit and disgrace to them, and displease you.

82. But of all the ways whereby children are to be instructed, and their manners formed, the plainest, easiest, and most efficacious, is to set before their eyes the examples of those things you would have them do or avoid; which, when they are pointed out to them, in the practice of persons within their knowledge, with some reflections on their beauty and unbecomingness, are of more force to draw or deter their imitation than any discourses which can be made to them. Virtues and vices can by no words be so plainly set before their understandings as the actions of other men will show them, when you direct their observation, and bid them view this or that good or bad quality in their practice. And the beauty or uncomeliness of many things, in good and ill breeding, will be better learnt and make deeper impressions on them, in the examples of others, than from any rules or instructions can be given about them.

This is a method to be used, not only whilst they are young, but to be continued even as long as they shall be under another's tuition or conduct; nay, I know not whether it be not the best way to be used by a father, as long as he shall think fit, on any occasion, to reform anything he wishes mended in his son; nothing sinking so gently, and so deep, into men's minds, as example. And what ill they either overlook or indulge in themselves, they cannot but dislike and be ashamed of when it is set before them in another.

83. It may be doubted, concerning whipping, when as the last remedy it comes to be necessary, at what times and by whom it should be done; whether presently upon the committing the fault, whilst it is yet fresh and hot; and whether parents themselves should beat their children. As to the first, I think it should not be done presently, lest passion mingle with it; and so, though it exceed the just proportion, yet it lose of its due weight: for even children discern when we do things in passion. But, as I said before, that has most weight with them that appears sedately to come from their parents' reason; and they are not without this distinction. Next, if you have any discreet servant capable of it, and has the place of governing your child (for

if you have a tutor, there is no doubt) I think it is best the smart should come immediately from another's hand, though by the parent's order, who should see it done; whereby the parent's authority will be preserved, and the child's aversion, for the pain it suffers, rather to be turned on the person that immediately inflicts. For I would have a father seldom strike his child, but upon very urgent necessity and as the last remedy; and then perhaps it will be fit to do it so that the child should not quickly forget it.

84. But, as I said before, beating is the worst and therefore the last means to be used in the correction of children, and that only in cases of extremity, after all gentle ways have been tried, and proved unsuccessful; which, if well observed, there will be very seldom any need of blows. For, it not being to be imagined that a child will often, if ever, dispute his father's present command in any particular instance, and the father not interposing his absolute authority, in peremptory rules, concerning either childish or indifferent actions, wherein his son is to have his liberty, or concerning his learning or improvement, wherein there is no compulsion to be used: there remains only the prohibition of some vicious actions, wherein a child is capable of obstinacy, and consequently can deserve beating; and so there will be but very few occasions of that discipline to be used by anyone who considers well and orders his child's education as it should be. For the first seven years, what vices can a child be guilty of, but lying or some ill-natured tricks, the repeated commission whereof, after his father's direct command against it, shall bring him into the condemnation of obstinacy, and the chastisement of the rod? If any vicious inclination in him be, in the first appearance and instances of it, treated as it should be, first with your wonder, and then, if returning again, a second time discountenanced with the severe brow of a father, tutor, and all about him, and a treatment suitable to the state of discredit before-mentioned; and this continued till he be made sensible and ashamed of his fault, I imagine there will be no need of any other correction, nor ever any occasion to come to blows. The necessity of such chastisement is usually the consequence only of former indulgences or neglects: If vicious inclinations were watched from the beginning, and the first irregularities which they cause cor-

rected by those gentler ways, we should seldom have to do with more than one disorder at once; which would be easily set right without any stir or noise, and not require so harsh a discipline as beating. Thus one by one as they appeared, they might all be weeded out, without any signs or memory that ever they had been there. But letting their faults (by indulging and humoring our little ones) grow up, till they are sturdy and numerous and the deformity of them makes us ashamed and uneasy, we are fain to come to the plow and the harrow; the spade and the pick-ax must go deep to come at the roots; and all the force, skill, and diligence we can use is scarce enough to cleanse the vitiated seed-plat, overgrown with weeds, and restore us the hopes of fruits, to reward our pains in its season.

85. This course, if observed, will spare both father and child the trouble of repeated injunctions, and multiplied rules of doing and forbearing. For I am of opinion that of those actions which tend to vicious habits (which are those alone that a father should interpose his authority and commands in), none should be forbidden children till they are found guilty of them. For such untimely prohibitions, if they do nothing worse, do at least so much towards teaching and allowing 'em, that they suppose that children may be guilty of them, who would possibly be safer in the ignorance of any such faults. And the best remedy to stop them is, as I have said, to show wonder and amazement at any such action as hath a vicious tendency, when it is first taken notice of in a child. For example, when he is first found in a lie or any ill-natured trick, the first remedy should be to talk to him of it as a strange monstrous matter that it could not be imagined he would have done, and so shame him out of it.

86. It will be ('tis like) objected that whatsoever I fancy of the tractableness of children, and the prevalency of those softer ways of shame and commendation; yet there are many who will never apply themselves to their books and to what they ought to learn, unless they are scourged to it. This, I fear, is nothing but the language of ordinary schools and fashion, which have never suffered the other to be tried as it should be, in places where it could be taken notice of. Why, else, does the learning of Latin and Greek need the rod, when French and Italian need it not? Children learn to dance and fence

without whipping; nay, arithmetic, drawing, etc., they apply themselves well enough to without beating: which would make one suspect
that there is something strange, unnatural, and disagreeable to that
age, in the things required in grammar-schools, or in the methods used
there, that children cannot be brought to without the severity of the
lash, and hardly with that too; or else, that it is a mistake, that those
tongues could not be taught them without beating.

87. But let us suppose some so negligent or idle that they will
not be brought to learn by the gentle ways proposed (for we must
grant that there will be children found of all tempers), yet it does
not thence follow that the rough discipline of the cudgel is to be
used to all. Nor can anyone be concluded unmanageable by the milder
methods of government till they have been thoroughly tried upon
him; and if they will not prevail with him to use his endeavors, and
do what is in his power to do, we make no excuses for the obstinate.
Blows are the proper remedies for those; but blows laid on in a way
different from the ordinary. He that willfully neglects his book, and
stubbornly refuses anything he can do, required of him by his father,
expressing himself in a positive serious command, should not be corrected with two or three angry lashes for not performing his task,
and the same punishment repeated again and again upon every the
like default; but when it is brought to that pass, that willfulness
evidently shows itself, and makes blows necessary, I think the chastisement should be a little more sedate, and a little more severe, and the
whipping, mingled with admonition between, so continued, till the
impressions of it on the mind were found legible in the face, voice,
and submission of the child, not so sensible of the smart as of the
fault he has been guilty of, and melting in true sorrow under it. If
such a correction as this, tried some few times at fit distances and
carried to the utmost severity, with the visible displeasure of the
father all the while, will not work the effect, turn the mind, and
produce a future compliance, what can be hoped from blows, and to
what purpose should they be any more used? Beating, when you can
expect no good from it, will look more like the fury of an enraged
enemy, than the good will of a compassionate friend; and such
chastisement carries with it only provocation, without any prospect

of amendment. If it be any father's misfortune to have a son tnus perverse and untractable, I know not what more he can do but pray for him. But, I imagine, if a right course be taken with children from the beginning, very few will be found to be such; and when there are any such instances, they are not to be the rule for the education of those who are better natured, and may be managed with better usage.

88. If a tutor can be got, that, thinking himself in the father's place, charged with his care, and relishing these things, will at the beginning apply himself to put them in practice, he will afterwards find his work very easy; and you will, I guess, have your son in a little time a greater proficient in both learning and breeding than per-haps you imagine. But let him by no means beat him at any time without your consent and direction; at least till you have experience of his discretion and temper. But yet, to keep up his authority with his pupil, besides concealing that he has not the power of the rod, you must be sure to use him with great respect yourself, and cause all your family to do so too: for you cannot expect your son should have any regard for one whom he sees you, or his mother, or others slight. If you think him worthy of contempt, you have chosen amiss; and if you show any contempt of him, he will hardly escape it from your son: and whenever that happens, whatever worth he may have in himself, and abilities for this employment, they are all lost to your child, and can afterwards never be made useful to him.

89. As the father's example must teach the child respect for his tutor, so the tutor's example must lead the child into those actions he would have him do. His practice must by no means cross his pre-cepts, unless he intend to set him wrong. It will be to no purpose for the tutor to talk of the restraint of the passions whilst any of his own are let loose; and he will in vain endeavor to reform any vice or indecency in his pupil which he allows in himself. Ill patterns are sure to be followed more than good rules; and therefore he must always carefully preserve him from the influence of ill precedents, especially the most dangerous of all, the examples of the servants; from whose company he is to be kept, not by prohibitions, for that will but give him an itch after it, but by other ways I have mentioned.

90. In all the whole business of education, there is nothing like to be less hearkened to, or harder to be well observed, than what I am now going to say; and that is, that children should, from their first beginning to talk, have some discreet, sober, nay, wise person about them, whose care it should be to fashion them aright, and keep them from all ill, especially the infection of bad company. I think this province requires great sobriety, temperance, tenderness, diligence, and discretion; qualities hardly to be found united in persons that are to be had for ordinary salaries, nor easily to be found anywhere. As to the charge of it, I think it will be the money best laid out that can be, about our children; and therefore, though it may be expensive more than is ordinary, yet it cannot be thought dear. He that at any rate procures his child a good mind, well-principled, tempered to virtue and usefulness, and adorned with civility and good breed· ing, makes a better purchase for him than if he laid out the money for an addition of more earth to his former acres. Spare it in toys and play-games, in silk and ribbons, laces, and other useless expenses, as much as you please; but be not sparing in so necessary a part as this. 'Tis not good husbandry to make his fortune rich, and his mind poor. I have often with great admiration seen people lavish it profusely in tricking up their children in fine clothes, lodging, and feeding them sumptuously, allowing them more than enough of useless servants, and yet at the same time starve their minds, and not take sufficient care to cover that which is the most shameful nakedness, viz., their natural wrong inclinations and ignorance. This I can look on as no other than a sacrificing to their own vanity, it showing more their pride than true care of the good of their children; whatsoever you employ to the advantage of your son's mind, will show your true kindness, though it be to the lessening of his estate. A wise and good man can hardly want either the opinion or reality of being great and happy; but he that is foolish or vicious can be neither great nor happy, what estate soever you leave him: and I ask you whether there be not men in the world, whom you had rather have your son be with five hundred pounds per annum, than some other you know with five thousand pounds.

91. The consideration of charge ought not therefore to deter those

who are able. The great difficulty will be where to find a proper person: for those of small age, parts, and virtue, are unfit for this employment, and those that have greater, will hardly be got to undertake such a charge. You must therefore look out early, and inquire everywhere; for the world has people of all sorts. And I remember, Montaigne says in one of his essays that the learned Castalio was fain to make trenchers at Basle to keep himself from starving, when his father would have given any money for such a tutor for his son, and Castalio have willingly embraced such an employment upon very reasonable terms; but this was for want of intelligence.

92. If you find it difficult to meet with such a tutor as we desire, you are not to wonder. I only can say, spare no care or cost to get such a one. All things are to be had that way: and I dare assure you, that if you can get a good one, you will never repent the charge; but will always have the satisfaction to think it the money of all other the best laid out. But be sure take nobody upon friends, or charity, no, nor upon great commendations. Nay, if you will do as you ought, the reputation of a sober man, with a good stock of learning, which is all usually required in a tutor, will not be enough to serve your turn. In this choice be as curious as you would be in that of a wife for him; for you must not think of trial or changing afterwards: This will cause great inconvenience to you, and greater to your son. When I consider the scruples and cautions I here lay in your way, methinks it looks as if I advised you to something which I would have offered at, but in effect not done. But he that shall consider how much the business of a tutor, rightly employed, lies out of the road, and how remote it is from the thoughts of many, even of those who propose to themselves this employment, will perhaps be of my mind, that one fit to educate and form the mind of a young gentleman is not everywhere to be found, and that more than ordinary care is to be taken in the choice of him, or else you may fail of your end.

93. The character of a sober man and a scholar is, as I have above observed, what everyone expects in a tutor. This generally is thought enough, and is all that parents commonly look for; but when such a one has emptied out into his pupil all the Latin and logic he has brought from the university, will that furniture make him a fine gentle-

man? Or can it be expected that he should be better bred, better skilled in the world, better principled in the grounds and foundations of true virtue and generosity, than his young tutor is?

To form a young gentleman as he should be, 'tis fit his governor should himself be well-bred, understanding the ways of carriage and measures of civility in all the variety of persons, times, and places; and keep his pupil, as much as his age requires, constantly to the observation of them. This is an art not to be learnt or taught by books. Nothing can give it but good company and observation joined together. The tailor may make his clothes modish, and the dancing-master give fashion to his motions; yet neither of these, though they set off well, make a well-bred gentleman: no, though he have learning to boot, which, if not well managed, makes him more impertinent and intolerable in conversation. Breeding is that which sets a gloss upon all his other good qualities, and renders them useful to him, in procuring him the esteem and good will of all that he comes near. Without good breeding his other accomplishments make him pass but for proud, conceited, vain, or foolish.

Courage in an ill-bred man has the air and escapes not the opinion of brutality: Learning becomes pedantry; wit, buffoonery; plainness, rusticity; good nature, fawning. And there cannot be a good quality in him which want of breeding will not warp and disfigure to his disadvantage. Nay, virtue and parts, though they are allowed their due commendation, yet are not enough to procure a man a good reception, and make him welcome wherever he comes. Nobody contents himself with rough diamonds, and wears them so, who would appear with advantage. When they are polished and set, then they give a luster. Good qualities are the substantial riches of the mind, but 'tis good breeding sets them off: and he that will be acceptable must give beauty, as well as strength, to his actions. Solidity, or even usefulness, is not enough: a graceful way and fashion in everything, is that which gives the ornament and liking. And in most cases, the manner of doing is of more consequence than the thing done; and upon that depends the satisfaction or disgust wherewith it is received. This there- fore, which lies not in the putting off the hat, or making of compli- ments, but in a due and free composure of language, looks, motion, posture, place, etc., suited to persons and occasions, and can be learned only by habit and use, though it be above the capacity of children, and little ones should not be perplexed about it, yet it ought to be begun and in a good measure learned by a young gentleman whilst he is under a tutor, before he comes into the world upon his own legs: for then usually it is too late to hope to reform several habitual indecencies, which lie in little things. For the carriage is not as it should be, till it is become natural in every part, falling, as skillful musicians' fingers do, into harmonious order without care and without thought. If in conversation a man's mind be taken up with a solicitous watchfulness about any part of his behavior, instead of being mended by it, it will be constrained, uneasy, and ungraceful.

Besides, this part is most necessary to be formed by the hand and care of a governor, because, though the errors committed in breeding are the first that are taken notice of by others, yet they are the last that anyone is told of; not but that the malice of the world is forward enough to tattle of them; but it is always out of his hearing, who should make profit of their judgment and reform himself by their censure. And indeed, this is so nice a point to be meddled with, that even those who are friends, and wish it were mended, scarce ever dare mention it, and tell those they love that they are guilty in such or such cases of ill breeding. Errors in other things may often with civility be shown another; and 'tis no breach of good manners or friendship to set him right in other mistakes; but good breeding itself allows not a man to touch upon this, or to insinuate to another that he is guilty of want of breeding. Such information can come only from those who have authority over them; and from them too it comes very hardly and harshly to a grown man; and however softened, goes but ill down with anyone who has lived ever so little in the world. Wherefore it is necessary that this part should be the governor's principal care, that an habitual gracefulness, and politeness in all his carriage, may be settled in his charge, as much as may be, before he goes out of his hands; and that he may not need advice in this point when he has neither time nor disposition to receive it, nor has anybody left to give it him. The tutor therefore ought in the first place to be well-bred: and a young gentleman, who gets this one qualification from his governor, sets out with great advantage, and will find that this one accomplishment will more open his way to him, get him more friends, and carry him farther in the world, than all the hard words or real knowledge he has got from the liberal arts, or his tutor's learned encyclopaedia: not that those should be neglected, but by no means preferred, or suffered to thrust out the other.

94. Besides being well-bred, the tutor should know the world well; the ways, the humors, the follies, the cheats, the faults of the age he is fallen into, and particularly of the country he lives in. These he should be able to show to his pupil, as he finds him capable; teach him skill in men, and their manners; pull off the mask which their several callings and pretenses cover them with, and make his pupil discern what lies at the bottom under such appearances, that he may not, as unexperienced young men are apt to do if they are unwarned, take one thing for another, judge by the outside, and give himself up to show, and the insinuation of a fair carriage, or an obliging application. A governor should teach his scholar to guess at and beware of the designs of men he has to do with, neither with too much suspicion, nor too much confidence; but as the young man is by nature most inclined to either side, rectify him, and bend him the other way. He should accustom him to make, as much as is possible, a true judgment of men by those marks which serve best to show what they are, and give a prospect into their inside, which often shows itself in little things, especially when they are not in parade and upon their guard.

He should acquaint him with the true state of the world, and dispose him to think no man better or worse, wiser or foolisher, than he really is. Thus, by safe and insensible degrees, he will pass from a boy to a man; which is the most hazardous step in all the whole course of life. This therefore should be carefully watched, and a young man with great diligence handed over it; and not as now usually is done, be taken from a governor's conduct, and all at once thrown into the world under his own, not without manifest dangers of immediate spoiling; there being nothing more frequent than instances of the great looseness, extravagance, and debauchery which young men have run into as soon as they have been let loose from a severe and strict education: Which I think may be chiefly imputed to their wrong way of breeding, especially in this part; for having been bred up in a great ignorance of what the world truly is, and finding it a quite other thing, when they come into it, than what they were taught it should be and so imagined it was, are easily persuaded, by other kind of tutors, which they are sure to meet with, that the discipline they were kept under and the lectures read to them were but the formalities of education and the restraints of childhood; that the freedom belonging to men is to take their swing in a full enjoyment of what was before forbidden them. They show the young novice the world full of fashionable and glittering examples of this everywhere, and he is presently dazzled with them. My young master failing not to be willing to show himself a man, as much as any of the sparks of his years, lets himself loose to all the irregularities he finds in the most debauched; and thus courts credit and manliness in the casting off the modesty and sobriety he has till then been kept in; and thinks it brave, at his first setting out, to signalize himself in running counter to all the rules of virtue which have been preached to him by his tutor.

The showing him the world as really it is, before he comes wholly into it, is one of the best means, I think, to prevent this mischief. He should by degrees be informed of the vices in fashion, and warned of the applications and designs of those who will make it their business to corrupt him. He should be told the arts they use, and the trains they lay; and now and then have set before him the tragical or ridiculous examples of those who are ruining or ruined this way. The age is not like to want instances of this kind, which should be made landmarks to him, that by the disgraces, diseases, beggary, and shame of hopeful young men thus brought to ruin, he may be precautioned, and be made see how those join in the contempt and neglect of them that are undone, who, by pretenses of friendship and respect lead them to it, and help to prey upon them whilst they were undoing; that he may see, before he buys it by a too dear experience, that those who persuade him not to follow the sober advices he has received from his governors, and the counsel of his own reason, which they call being governed by others, do it only that they may have the government of him themselves; and make him believe he goes like a man of himself, by his own conduct, and for his own pleasure, when in truth he is wholly as a child led by them into those vices which best serve their purposes. This is a knowledge which upon all occasions a tutor should endeavor to instill, and by all methods try to make him comprehend and thoroughly relish.

I know it is often said that to discover to a young man the vices of the age is to teach them him. That, I confess, is a good deal so, according as it is done; and therefore requires a discreet man of parts who knows the world and can judge of the temper, inclination, and weak side of his pupil. This farther is to be remembered, that it is not possible now (as perhaps formerly it was) to keep a young gentleman from vice by a total ignorance of it, unless you will all his life mew him up in a closet, and never let him go into company. The longer he is kept thus hoodwinked, the less he will see when he comes abroad into open daylight, and be the more exposed to be a prey to himself and others. And an old boy, at his first appearance, with all the gravity of his ivy-bush about him, is sure to draw on him the eyes and chirping of the whole town volery; [14] amongst which there will not be wanting some birds of prey, that will presently be on the wing for him.

The only fence against the world is a thorough knowledge of it, into which a young gentleman should be entered by degrees, as he can bear it; and the earlier the better, so he be in safe and skillful hands to guide him. The scene should be gently opened, and his entrance made step by step, and the dangers pointed out that attend him from the several degrees, tempers, designs, and clubs of men. He should be prepared to be shocked by some and caressed by others; warned who are like to oppose, who to mislead, who to undermine him, and who to serve him. He should be instructed how to know and distinguish them; where he should let them see, and when dissemble the knowledge of them and their aims and workings. And if he be too forward to venture upon his own strength and skill, the perplexity and trouble of a misadventure now and then, that reaches not his innocence, his health, or reputation, may not be an ill way to teach him more caution.

[14] An ancient term for aviary; also, a flock of birds.

This, I confess, containing one great part of wisdom, is not the product of some superficial thoughts, or much reading; but the effect of experience and observation in a man who has lived in the world with his eyes open, and conversed with men of all sorts. And therefore I think it of most value to be instilled into a young man upon all occasions which offer themselves, that when he comes to launch into the deep himself, he may not be like one at sea without a line, compass or sea chart; but may have some notice beforehand of the rocks and shoals, the currents and quicksands, and know a little how to steer, that he sink not before he get experience. He that thinks not this of more moment to his son, and for which he more needs a governor, than the languages and learned sciences, forgets of how much more use it is to judge right of men, and manage his affairs wisely with them, than to speak Greek and Latin, or argue in mood and figure; or to have his head filled with the abstruse speculations of natural philosophy and metaphysics; nay, than to be well versed in Greek and Roman writers, though that be much better for a gentleman than to be a good Peripatetic or Cartesian,[15] because those ancient authors observed and painted mankind well, and give the best light into that kind of knowledge. He that goes into the eastern parts of Asia will find able and acceptable men without any of these; but without virtue, knowledge of the world, and civility, an accomplished and valuable man can be found nowhere.

A great part of the learning now in fashion in the schools of Europe, and that goes ordinarily into the round of education, a gentleman may in a good measure be unfurnished with, without any great disparagement to himself or prejudice to his affairs. But prudence and good breeding are in all the stations and occurrences of life necessary; and most young men suffer in the want of them, and come rawer and more awkward into the world than they should, for this very reason, because these qualities, which are of all other the most necessary to be taught, and stand most in need of the assistance and help of a teacher, are generally neglected and thought but a slight or no part of a tutor's business. Latin and learning make all the noise;

[15] Peripatetic: a follower of Aristotle; Cartesian, of Descartes.

and the main stress is laid upon his proficiency in things a great part whereof belong not to a gentleman's calling; which is to have the knowledge of a man of business, a carriage suitable to his rank, and to be eminent and useful in his country, according to his station. Whenever either spare hours from that, or an inclination to perfect himself in some parts of knowledge, which his tutor did but just enter him in, set him upon any study, the first rudiments of it, which he learned before, will open the way enough for his own industry to carry him as far as his fancy will prompt, or his parts enable him to go. Or, if he thinks it may save his time and pains to be helped over some difficulties by the hand of a master, he may then take a man that is perfectly well skilled in it, or choose such an one as he thinks fittest for his purpose. But to initiate his pupil in any part of learning, as far as is necessary for a young man in the ordinary course of his studies, an ordinary skill in the governor is enough. Nor is it requisite that he should be a thorough scholar, or possess in perfection all those sciences which 'tis convenient a young gentleman should have a taste of in some general view, or short system. A gentleman that would penetrate deeper must do it by his own genius and industry afterwards: For nobody ever went far in knowledge, or became eminent in any of the sciences, by the discipline and constraint of a master.

The great work of a governor is to fashion the carriage and form the mind; to settle in his pupil good habits and the principles of virtue and wisdom; to give him by little and little a view of mankind, and work him into a love and imitation of what is excellent and praiseworthy; and, in the prosecution of it, to give him vigor, activity, and industry. The studies which he sets him upon are but, as it were, the exercises of his faculties, and employment of his time, to keep him from sauntering and idleness, to teach him application, and accustom him to take pains, and to give him some little taste of what his own industry must perfect. For who expects that under a tutor a young gentleman should be an accomplished critic, orator, or logician? go to the bottom of metaphysics, natural philosophy, or mathematics, or be a master in history or chronology? though something of each of these is to be taught him. But it is only to open the door, that he may look in, and as it were begin an acquaintance, but not to dwell there. And a governor would be much blamed that should keep his pupil too long and lead him too far in most of them. But of good breeding, knowledge of the world, virtue, industry, and a love of reputation, he cannot have too much; and if he have these, he will not long want what he needs or desires of the other.

And since it cannot be hoped he should have time and strength to learn all things, most pains should be taken about that which is most necessary; and that principally looked after which will be of most and frequentest use to him in the world.

Seneca complains of the contrary practice in his time; and yet the Burgursdicius's and the Scheiblers did not swarm in those days as they do now in these. What would he have thought if he had lived now, when the tutors think it their great business to fill the studies and heads of their pupils with such authors as these? He would have had much more reason to say, as he does, *non vitae sed scholae discimus,* we learn not to live, but to dispute; and our education fits us rather for the university than the world. But 'tis no wonder if those who make the fashion suit it to what they have, and not to what their pupils want. The fashion being once established, who can think it strange that in this, as well as in all other things, it should prevail? And that the greatest part of those who find their account in an easy submission to it should be ready to cry out, *Heresy,* when anyone departs from it? 'Tis nevertheless matter of astonishment that men of quality and parts should suffer themselves to be so far misled by custom and implicit faith. Reason, if consulted with, would advise that their children's time should be spent in acquiring what might be useful to them when they come to be men, rather than to have their heads stuffed with a deal of trash, a great part whereof they usually never do ('tis certain they never need to) think on again as long as they live: and so much of it as does stick by them they are only the worse for. This is so well known that I appeal to parents them-selves, who have been at cost to have their young heirs taught it, whether it be not ridiculous for their sons to have any tincture of that sort of learning, when they come abroad into the world, whether any appearance of it would not lessen and disgrace them in company? And that certainly must be an admirable acquisition, and deserves well to make a part in education, which men are ashamed of where they are most concerned to show their parts and breeding.

There is yet another reason why politeness of manners and knowledge of the world should principally be looked after in a tutor; and that is because a man of parts and years may enter a lad far enough in any of those sciences, which he has no deep insight into himself. Books in these will be able to furnish him, and give him light and precedency enough to go before a young follower: but he will never be able to set another right in the knowledge of the world, and above all in breeding, who is a novice in them himself.

This is a knowledge he must have about him, worn into him by use and conversation and a long forming himself by what he has observed to be practiced and allowed in the best company. This, if he has it not of his own, is nowhere to be borrowed for the use of his pupil; or if he could find pertinent treatises of it in books that would reach all the particulars of an English gentleman's behavior, his own ill-fashioned example, if he be not well-bred himself, would spoil all his lectures; it being impossible that anyone should come forth well-fashioned out of unpolished, ill-bred company.

I say this not that I think such a tutor is every day to be met with, or to be had at the ordinary rates, but that those who are able may not be sparing of inquiry or cost in what is of so great moment; and that other parents, whose estates will not reach to greater salaries, may yet remember what they should principally have an eye to in the choice of one to whom they would commit the education of their children; and what part they should chiefly look after themselves, whilst they are under their care, and as often as they come within their observation; and not think that all lies in Latin and French or some dry systems of logic and philosophy.

95. But to return to our method again. Though I have mentioned the severity of the father's brow, and the awe settled thereby in the mind of children when young, as one main instrument whereby their education is to be managed; yet I am far from being of an opinion that it should be continued all along to them, whilst they are under the discipline and government of pupilage; I think it should be relaxed as fast as their age, discretion and good behavior could allow

it; even to that degree that a father will do well, as his son grows up, and is capable of it, to talk familiarly with him; nay, ask his advice, and consult with him about those things wherein he has any knowledge or understanding. By this, the father will gain two things, both of great moment. The one is, that it will put serious considerations into his son's thoughts, better than any rules or advices he can give him. The sooner you *treat him as a man*, the sooner he will begin to be one: and if you admit him into serious discourses sometimes with you, you will insensibly raise his mind above the usual amusements of youth, and those trifling occupations which it is commonly wasted in. For it is easy to observe that many young men continue longer in the thought and conversation of schoolboys than otherwise they would, because their parents keep them at that distance and in that low rank, by all their carriage to them.

96. Another thing of greater consequence which you will obtain by such a way of treating him will be *his friendship*. Many fathers, though they proportion to their sons liberal allowances, according to their age and condition, yet they keep the knowledge of their estates and concerns from them with as much reservedness as if they were guarding a secret of state from a spy or an enemy. This, if it looks not like jealousy, yet it wants those marks of kindness and intimacy which a father should show to his son, and no doubt often hinders or abates that cheerfulness and satisfaction wherewith a son should address himself to and rely upon his father. And I cannot but often wonder to see fathers who love their sons very well, yet so order the matter by a constant stiffness and a mien of authority and distance to them all their lives, as if they were never to enjoy, or have any comfort from those they love best in the world, till they had lost them by being removed into another. Nothing cements and establishes friendship and good will so much as confident communication of concernments and affairs. Other kindnesses, without this, leave still some doubts: but when your son sees you open your mind to him, when he finds that you interest him in your affairs, as things you are willing should in their turn come into his hands, he will be concerned for them as for his own, wait his season with patience, and love you in the meantime, who keep him not at the distance of a stranger. This will also make him

see that the enjoyment you have is not without care; which the more he is sensible of, the less will he envy you the possession, and the more think himself happy under the management of so favorable a friend and so careful a father. There is scarce any young man of so little thought or so void of sense that would not be glad of a sure friend, that he might have recourse to and freely consult on occasion. The reservedness and distance that fathers keep often deprive their sons of that refuge which would be of more advantage to them than a hundred rebukes and chidings. Would your son engage in some frolic or take a vagary, were it not much better he should do it with than without your knowledge? For since allowances for such things must be made to young men, the more you know of his intrigues and designs, the better will you be able to prevent great mischiefs; and by letting him see what is like to follow, take the right way of prevailing with him to avoid less inconveniences.[16] Would you have him open his heart to you, and ask your advice? You must begin to do so with him first, and by your carriage beget that confidence.

97. But whatever he consults you about, unless it lead to some fatal and irremediable mischief, be sure you advise only as a friend of more experience; but with your advice mingle nothing of command or authority, nor more than you would to your equal or a stranger. That would be to drive him forever from any farther demanding or receiving advantage from your counsel. You must consider that he is a young man, and has pleasures and fancies which you are past. You must not expect his inclination should be just as yours, nor that at twenty he should have the same thoughts you have at fifty. All that you can wish is that since youth must have some liberty, some outleaps, they might be with the ingenuity of a son, and under the eye of a father, and then no very great harm can come of it. The way to obtain this, as I said before, is (according as you find him capable) to talk with him about your affairs, propose matters to him familiarly, and ask his advice; and when he ever lights on the right, follow it as his; and if it succeed well, let him have the commendation. This will not at all lessen your authority, but increase

[16] Improprieties.

his love and esteem of you. Whilst you keep your estate, the staff will be in your own hands; and your authority the surer, the more it is strengthened with confidence and kindness. For you have not that power you ought to have over him, till he comes to be more afraid of offending so good a friend than of losing some part of his future expectation.

98. Familiarity of discourse, if it can become a father to his son, may much more be condescended to by a tutor to his pupil. All their time together should not be spent in reading of lectures, and magisterially dictating to him what he is to observe and follow. Hearing him in his turn, and using him to reason about what is proposed, will make the rules go down the easier and sink the deeper, and will give him a liking to study and instruction. And he will then begin to value knowledge, when he sees that it enables him to discourse, and he finds the pleasure and credit of bearing a part in the conversation, and of having his reasons sometimes approved and hearkened to; particularly in morality, prudence, and breeding, cases should be put to him, and his judgment asked. This opens the understanding better than maxims, how well soever explained, and settles the rules better in the memory for practice. This way lets things into the mind which stick there, and retain their evidence with them; whereas words at best are faint representations, being not so much as the true shadows of things, and are much sooner forgotten. He will better comprehend the foundations and measures of decency and justice, and have livelier and more lasting impressions of what he ought to do, by giving his opinion on cases proposed and reasoning with his tutor on fit instances than by giving a silent, negligent, sleepy audience to his tutor's lectures; and much more than by captious logical disputes, or set declamations of his own, upon any question. The one sets the thoughts upon wit and false colors, and not upon truth; the other teaches fallacy, wrangling, and opiniatry; and they are both of them things that spoil the judgment, and put a man out of the way of right and fair reasoning; and therefore carefully to be avoided by one who would improve himself, and be acceptable to others.

99. When by making your son sensible that he depends on you, and is in your power, you have established your authority; and by

peing inflexibly severe in your carriage to him when obstinately persisting in any ill-natured trick which you have forbidden, especially
lying, you have imprinted on his mind that awe which is necessary;
and, on the other side, when (by permitting him the full liberty due
to his age, and laying no restraint in your presence to those childish
actions and gaiety of carriage, which, whilst he is very young, is as
necessary to him as meat or sleep) you have reconciled him to your
company, and made him sensible of your care and love of him, by
indulgence and tenderness, especially caressing him on all occasions
wherein he does anything well, and being kind to him after a thousand fashions suitable to his age, which nature teaches parents better
than I can: When, I say, by these ways of tenderness and affection,
which parents never want for their children, you have also planted in
him a particular affection for you; he is then in the state you could
desire, and you have formed in his mind that true reverence which is
always afterwards carefully to be continued and maintained in both
parts of it, love and fear, as the great principles whereby you will
always have hold upon him, to turn his mind to the ways of virtue
and honor.

100. When this foundation is once well laid, and you find this
reverence begin to work in him, the next thing to be done is carefully to consider his temper, and the particular constitution of his
mind. Stubbornness, lying, and ill-natured actions, are not, as has
been said, to be permitted in him from the beginning, whatever his
temper be. Those seeds of vices are not to be suffered to take any
root, but must be carefully weeded out as soon as ever they begin
to show themselves in him; and your authority is to take place and
influence his mind, from the very dawning of any knowledge in him,
that it may operate as a natural principle, whereof he never perceived
the beginning, never knew that it was, or could be otherwise. By
this, if the reverence he owes you be established early, it will always
be sacred to him, and it will be as hard for him to resist as the principles of his nature.

101. Having thus very early set up your authority, and by the
gentler applications of it shamed him out of what leads towards an
immoral habit, as soon as you have observed it in him (for I would

by no means have chiding used, much less blows, till obstinacy and incorrigibleness make it absolutely necessary), it will be fit to consider which way the natural make of his mind inclines him. Some men by the unalterable frame of their constitutions, are stout, others timorous, some confident, others modest, tractable, or obstinate, curious or careless, quick or slow. There are not more differences in men's faces, and the outward lineaments of their bodies than there are in the makes and tempers of their minds; only there is this difference, that the distinguishing characters of the face and the lineaments of the body grow more plain and visible with time and age; but the peculiar physiognomy of the mind is most discernible in children, before art and cunning have taught them to hide their deformities, and conceal their ill inclinations under a dissembled outside.

102. Begin therefore betimes nicely to observe your son's temper; and that when he is under least restraint, in his play, and as he thinks out of your sight. See what are his predominate passions and prevailing inclinations; whether he be fierce or mild, bold or bashful, compassionate or cruel, open or reserved, etc. For as these are different in him, so are your methods to be different, and your authority must hence take measures to apply itself different ways to him. These native propensities, these prevalencies of constitution, are not to be cured by rules or a direct contest, especially those of them that are the humbler and meaner sort, which proceed from fear and lowness of spirit; though with art they may be much mended and turned to good purposes. But this be sure, after all is done, the bias will always hang on that side that nature first placed it. And if you carefully observe the characters of his mind, now in the first scenes of his life, you will ever after be able to judge which way his thoughts lean, and what he aims at even hereafter, when, as he grows up, the plot thickens, and he puts on several shapes to act it.

103. I told you before that children love liberty; and therefore they should be brought to do the things are fit for them, without feeling any restraint laid upon them. I now tell you they love something more, and that is dominion: And this is the first original of most vicious habits that are ordinary and natural. This love of power and dominion shows itself very early, and that in these two things.

104. 1. We see children, as soon almost as they are born (I am sure long before they can speak) cry, grow peevish, sullen, and out of humor, for nothing but to have their *wills*. They would have their desires submitted to by others; they contend for a ready compliance from all about them, especially from those that stand near or beneath them in age or degree, as soon as they come to consider others with those distinctions.

105. 2. Another thing wherein they show their love of dominion is their desire to have things to be theirs: They would have propriety and possession, pleasing themselves with the power which that seems to give, and the right they thereby have, to dispose of them as they please. He that has not observed these two humors working very betimes in children has taken little notice of their actions: And he who thinks that these two roots of almost all the injustice and contention that so disturb human life are not early to be weeded out, and contrary habits introduced, neglects the proper season to lay the foundations of a good and worthy man. To do this, I imagine these following things may somewhat conduce.

106. 1. That a child should never be suffered to have what he craves, much less what he cries for, I had said, or so much as speaks for: But that being apt to be misunderstood, and interpreted as if I meant a child should never speak to his parents for anything, which will perhaps be thought to lay too great a curb on the minds of chil-dren, to the prejudice of that love and affection which should be between them and their parents; I shall explain myself a little more particularly. It is fit that they should have liberty to declare their wants to their parents, and that with all tenderness they should be hearkened to, and supplied, at least whilst they are very little. But 'tis one thing to say, 'I am hungry,' another to say, 'I would have roast meat.' Having declared their wants, their natural wants, the pain they feel from hunger, thirst, cold, or any other necessity of nature, 'tis the duty of their parents and those about them to relieve them; but children must leave it to the choice and ordering of their parents, what they think properest for them, and how much; and must not be permitted to choose for themselves, and say, 'I would have wine, or white bread'; the very naming of it should make them lose it.

107. That which parents should take care of here is to distinguish between the wants of fancy and those of nature; which Horace has well taught them to do in this verse:

Queis humana sibi doleat natura negatis.[17]

Those are truly natural wants which reason alone, without some other help, is not able to fence against, nor keep from disturbing us. The pains of sickness and hurts, hunger, thirst, and cold, want of sleep and rest or relaxation of the part wearied with labor, are what all men feel and the best disposed minds cannot but be sensible of their uneasiness; and therefore ought, by fit applications, to seek their removal, though not with impatience, or over-great haste, upon the first approaches of them, where delay does not threaten some irreparable harm. The pains that come from the necessities of nature are monitors to us to beware of greater mischiefs, which they are the forerunners of; and therefore they must not be wholly neglected, nor strained too far. But yet the more children can be inured to hardships of this kind, by a wise care to make them stronger in body and mind, the better it will be for them. I need not here give any caution to keep within the bounds of doing them good, and to take care that what children are made to suffer should neither break their spirits nor injure their health, parents being but too apt of themselves to incline more than they should to the softer side.

But whatever compliance the necessities of nature may require, the wants of fancy children should never be gratified in, nor suffered to mention. The very *speaking* for any such thing should make them lose it. Clothes, when they need, they must have; but if they speak for this stuff or that color, they should be sure to go without it. Not that I would have parents purposely cross the desires of their children in matters of indifference; on the contrary, where their carriage deserves it, and one is sure it will not corrupt or effeminate their minds, and make them fond of trifles, I think all things should be contrived, as much as could be, to their satisfaction, that they may find the ease and pleasure of doing well. The best for children is that they should

[17] Denying which brings distress to our human nature.

not place any pleasure in such things at all, nor regulate their delight by their fancies, but be indifferent to all that nature has made so. This is what their parents and teachers should chiefly aim at; but till this be obtained, all that I oppose here is the liberty of asking, which in these things of conceit ought to be restrained by a constant for-feiture annexed to it.

This may perhaps be thought a little too severe by the natural in-dulgence of tender parents; but yet it is no more than necessary. For since the method I propose is to banish the rod, this restraint of their tongues will be of great use to settle that awe we have elsewhere spoken of, and to keep up in them the respect and reverence due to their parents. Next, it will teach to keep in and so master their inclina-tions. By this means they will be brought to learn the art of stifling their desires as soon as they rise up in them, when they are easiest to be subdued. For giving vent gives life and strength to our appetites; and he that has the confidence to turn his wishes into demands, will be but a little way from thinking he ought to obtain them. This, I am sure, everyone can more easily bear a denial from himself, than from anybody else. They should therefore be accustomed betimes to consult, and make use of their reason, before they give allowance to their in-clinations. 'Tis a great step towards the mastery of our desires to give this stop to them, and shut them up in silence. This habit got by chil-dren, of staying the forwardness of their fancies, and deliberating whether it be fit or no, before they speak, will be of no small advan-tage to them in matters of greater consequence, in the future course of their lives. For that which I cannot too often inculcate, is that whatever the matter be about which it is conversant, whether great or small, the main (I had almost said only) thing to be considered in every action of a child is what influence it will have upon his mind; what habit it tends to, and is like to settle in him; how it will become him when he is bigger; and if it be encouraged, whither it will lead him when he is grown up.

My meaning therefore is not that children should purposely be made uneasy. This would relish too much of inhumanity and ill-nature, and be apt to infect them with it. They should be brought to deny their appetites; and their minds, as well as bodies, be made vigorous, easy, and strong, by the custom of having their inclinations in subjection, and their bodies exercised with hardships: But all this, without giving them any mark or apprehension of ill-will towards them. The constant loss of what they craved or carved to themselves, should teach them modesty, submission, and a power to forbear: But the rewarding their modesty, and silence, by giving them what they liked, should also assure them of the love of those who rigorously exacted this obedience. The contenting themselves now in the want of what they wished for is a virtue that another time should be rewarded with what is suited and acceptable to them; which should be bestowed on them as if it were a natural consequence of their good behavior, and not a bargain about it. But you will lose your labor, and what is more, their love and reverence too, if they can receive from others what you deny them. This is to be kept very staunch, and carefully to be watched. And here the servants come again my way.

108. If this be begun betimes, and they accustom themselves early to silence their desires, this useful habit will settle them; and as they come to grow up in age and discretion, they may be allowed greater liberty when reason comes to speak in 'em, and not passion: For whenever reason would speak, it should be hearkened to. But as they should never be heard, when they speak for any particular thing they would have, unless it be first proposed to them; so they should always be heard, and fairly and kindly answered, when they ask after anything they would know, and desire to be informed about. Curiosity should be as carefully cherished in children as other appetites suppressed.

However strict a hand is to be kept upon all desires of fancy, yet there is one case wherein fancy must be permitted to speak, and be hearkened to also. Recreation is as necessary as labor or food. But because there can be no recreation without delight, which depends not always on reason, but oftener fancy, it must be permitted children not only to divert themselves, but to do it after their own fashion, provided it be innocently and without prejudice to their health; and therefore in this case they should not be denied, if they proposed any particular kind of recreation. Though I think in a well-ordered education, they will seldom be brought to the necessity of asking any such liberty. Care should be taken that what is of advantage to them they should always do with delight; and before they are wearied with one, they should be timely diverted to some other useful employment. But if they are not yet brought to that degree of perfection, that one way of improvement can be made a recreation to them, they must be let loose to the childish play they fancy; which they should be weaned from by being made to surfeit of it. But from things of use, that they are employed in, they should always be sent away with an appetite; at least be dismissed before they are tired, and grow quite sick of it, that so they may return to it again as to a pleasure that diverts them. For you must never think them set right, till they can find delight in the practice of laudable things; and the useful exercises of the body and mind, taking their turns, make their lives and improvement pleasant in a continued train of *recreations,* wherein the wearied part is constantly relieved and refreshed. Whether this can be done in every temper, or whether tutors and parents will be at the pains and have the discretion and patience to bring them to this, I know not; but that it may be done in most children, if a right course be taken to raise in them the desire of credit, esteem, and reputation, I do not at all doubt. And when they have so much true life put into them, they may freely be talked with about what most delights them, and be directed or let loose to it; so that they may perceive that they are beloved and cherished, and that those under whose tuition they are are not enemies to their satisfaction. Such a management will make them in love with the hand that directs them, and the virtue they are directed to.

This farther advantage may be made by a free liberty permitted them in their recreations, that it will discover their natural tempers, show their inclinations and aptitudes, and thereby direct wise parents in the choice both of the course of life and employment they shall design them for, and of fit remedies, in the meantime, to be applied to whatever bent of nature they may observe most likely to mislead any of their children.

109. 2. Children who live together often strive for mastery whose wills shall carry it over the rest: whoever begins the contest, should be sure to be crossed in it. But not only that, but they should be

taught to have all the deference, complaisance, and civility one for the other imaginable. This, when they see it procures them respect, love, and esteem, and that they lose no superiority by it, they will take more pleasure in than in insolent domineering; for so plainly is the other.

The accusations of children one against another, which usually are but the clamors of anger and revenge desiring aid, should not be favorably received nor hearkened to. It weakens and effeminates their minds to suffer them to complain; and if they endure sometimes crossing or pain from others without being permitted to think it strange or intolerable, it will do them no harm to learn sufferance, and harden them early. But though you give no countenance to the complaints of the querulous, yet take care to curb the insolence and ill nature of the injurious. When you observe it yourself, reprove it before the injured party: but if the complaint be of something really worth your notice and prevention another time, then reprove the offender by himself alone, out of sight of him that complained and make him go and ask pardon, and make reparation: which coming thus, as it were from himself, will be the more cheerfully performed, and more kindly received, the love strengthened between them, and a custom of civility grow familiar amongst your children.

110. 3. As to the having and possessing of things, teach them to part with what they have, easily and freely to their friends, and let them find by experience that the most liberal has always the most plenty, with esteem and commendation to boot, and they will quickly learn to practice it. This, I imagine, will make brothers and sisters kinder and civiler to one another, and consequently to others, than twenty rules about good manners, with which children are ordinarily perplexed and cumbered. Covetousness, and the desire of having in our possession and under our dominion more than we have need of, being the root of all evil, should be early and carefully weeded out, and the contrary quality of a readiness to impart to others, implanted. This should be encouraged by great commendation and credit, and constantly taking care that he loses nothing by his liberality. Let all the instances he gives of such freeness be always repaid, and with interest; and let him sensibly perceive that the kindness he shows to others is

no ill husbandry for himself; but that it brings a return of kindness both from those that receive it and those who look on. Make this a contest among children, who shall out-do one another this way; and by this means, by a constant practice, children having made it easy to themselves to part with what they have, good nature may be settled in them into a habit, and they may take pleasure, and pique themselves in being kind, liberal and civil, to others.

If liberality ought to be encouraged, certainly great care is to be taken that children transgress not the rules of justice; and whenever they do, they should be set right, and if there be occasion for it, severely rebuked.

Our first actions being guided more by self-love than reason or reflection, 'tis no wonder that in children they should be very apt to deviate from the just measures of right and wrong; which are in the mind the result of improved reason and serious meditation. This the more they are apt to mistake, the more careful guard ought to be kept over them; and every least slip in this great social virtue taken notice of and rectified; and that in things of the least weight and moment, both to instruct their ignorance and prevent ill habits; which from small beginnings in pins and cherry-stones, will, if let alone, grow up to higher frauds, and be in danger to end at last in downright hardened dishonesty. The first tendency to any injustice that appears, must be suppressed with a show of wonder and abhorrence in the parents and governors. But because children cannot well comprehend what injustice is till they understand property, and how particular persons come by it, the safest way to secure honesty is to lay the foundations of it early in liberality, and an easiness to part with to others whatever they have or like themselves. This may be taught them early, before they have language and understanding enough to form distinct notions of property, and to know what is theirs by a peculiar right exclusive of others. And since children seldom have anything but by gift, and that for the most part from their parents, they may be at first taught not to take or keep anything but what is given them by those whom they take to have power over it. And as their capacities enlarge, other rules and cases of justice, and rights concerning *Meum* and *Tuum*, may be proposed and inculcated. If any act of injustice in them appears to proceed, not from mistake, but a perverseness in their wills, when a gentle rebuke and shame will not reform this irregular and covetous inclination, rougher remedies must be applied. And 'tis but for the father and tutor to take and keep from them something that they value and think their own, or order somebody else to do it; and by such instances, make them sensible what little advantage they are like to make by possessing themselves unjustly of what is another's, whilst there are in the world stronger and more men than they. But if an ingenuous detestation of this shameful vice be but carefully and early instilled into 'em, as I think it may, that is the true and genuine method to obviate this crime, and will be a better guard against dishonesty than any considerations drawn from interest; habits working more constantly, and with greater facility, than reason, which, when we have most need of it, is seldom fairly consulted, and more rarely obeyed.

111. Crying is a fault that should not be tolerated in children; not only for the unpleasant and unbecoming noise it fills the house with, but for more considerable reasons, in reference to the children themselves; which is to be our aim in education.

Their crying is of two sorts; either stubborn and domineering, or querulous and whining.

1. Their crying is very often a striving for mastery and an open declaration of their insolence or obstinacy; when they have not the power to obtain their desire, they will, by their clamor and sobbing, maintain their title and right to it. This is an avowed continuing their claim, and a sort of remonstrance against the oppression and injustice of those who deny them what they have a mind to.

112. 2. Sometimes their crying is the effect of pain, or true sorrow, and a bemoaning themselves under it.

These two, if carefully observed, may, by the mien, looks, actions, and particularly by the tone of their crying be easily distinguished; but neither of them must be suffered, much less encouraged.

1. The obstinate or stomachful crying should by no means be permitted, because it is but another way of flattering their desires, and encouraging those passions which 'tis our main business to subdue: and if it be, as often it is, upon the receiving any correction, it quite

defeats all the good effects of it; for any chastisement which leaves them in this declared opposition only serves to make them worse. The restraints and punishments laid on children are all misapplied and lost, as far as they do not prevail over their wills, teach them to submit their passions, and make their minds supple and pliant to what their parents' reason advises them now, and so prepare them to obey what their own reason shall advise hereafter. But if in anything wherein they are crossed, they may be suffered to go away crying, they confirm themselves in their desires, and cherish the ill humor, with a declaration of their right, and a resolution to satisfy their inclination the first opportunity. This therefore is another argument against the frequent use of blows: for, whenever you come to that extremity, 'tis not enough to whip or beat them, you must do it till you find you have subdued their minds, till with submission and patience they yield to the correction; which you shall best discover by their crying, and their ceasing from it upon your bidding. Without this, the beating of children is but a passionate tyranny over them; and it is mere cruelty, and not correction, to put their bodies in pain, without doing their minds any good. As this gives us a reason why children should seldom be corrected, so it also prevents their being so. For if, whenever they are chastised, it were done thus without passion, soberly, and yet effectually too, laying on the blows and smart not furiously, and all at once, but slowly, with reasoning between, and with observation how it wrought, stopping when it had made them pliant, penitent, and yielding, they would seldom need the like punishment again, being made careful to avoid the fault that deserved it. Besides, by this means, as the punishment would not be lost for being too little, and not effectual, so it would be kept from being too much, if we gave off as soon as we perceived that it reached the mind, and that was bettered. For since the chiding or beating of children should be always the least that possibly may be, that which is laid on in the heat of anger, seldom observes that measure, but is commonly more than it should be, though it prove less than enough.

113. 2. Many children are apt to cry upon any little pain they suffer, and the least harm that befalls them puts them into complaints

and bawling. This few children avoid: for it being the first and
natural way to declare their sufferings or wants, before they can speak,
the compassion that is thought due to that tender age foolishly encourages, and continues it in them long after they can speak. 'Tis the
duty, I confess, of those about children, to compassionate them, whenever they suffer any hurt, but not to show it in pitying them. Help
and ease them the best you can, but by no means bemoan them.
This softens their minds, and makes them yield to the little harms
that happen to them; whereby they sink deeper into that part which
alone feels, and makes larger wounds there than otherwise they
would. They should be hardened against all sufferings, especially of
the body, and have no tenderness but what rises from an ingenuous
shame and a quick sense of reputation. The many inconveniences
this life is exposed to require we should not be too sensible of every
little hurt. What our minds yield not to makes but a slight impression, and does us but very little harm. 'Tis the suffering of our spirits
that gives and continues the pain. This brawniness and insensibility
of mind is the best armor we can have against the common evils and
accidents of life; and being a temper that is to be got by exercise and
custom more than any other way, the practice of it should be begun
betimes; and happy is he that is taught it early. That effeminacy of
spirit, which is to be prevented or cured, as nothing that I know so
much increases in children as crying; so nothing, on the other side,
so much checks and restrains as their being hindered from that sort
of complaining. In the little harms they suffer from knocks and falls,
they should not be pitied for falling, but bid do so again; which
besides that it stops their crying, is a better way to cure their heed-
lessness, and prevent their tumbling another time, than either chiding
or bemoaning them. But let the hurts they receive be what they will,
stop their crying, and that will give them more quiet and ease at
present, and harden them for the future.

114. The former sort of crying requires severity to silence it; and
where a look or a positive command will not do it, blows must: for
it proceeding from pride, obstinacy, and stomach, the will, where the
fault lies, must be bent, and made to comply, by a rigor sufficient to
master it. But this latter being ordinarily from softness of mind,

a quite contrary cause ought to be treated with a gentler hand. Persuasion, or diverting the thoughts another way, or laughing at their whining, may perhaps be at first the proper method: but for this, the circumstances of the thing, and the particular temper of the child, must be considered. No certain unvariable rules can be given about it; but it must be left to the prudence of the parents or tutor. But this, I think, I may say in general, that there should be a constant discountenancing of this sort of crying also; and that the father, by his authority, should always stop it, mixing a greater degree of roughness in his looks or words, proportionately as the child is of a greater age, or a sturdier temper: But always let it be enough to silence their whimpering and put an end to the disorder.

115. Cowardice and courage are so nearly related to the fore-mentioned tempers that it may not be amiss here to take notice of them. Fear is a passion that, if rightly governed, has its use. And though self-love seldom fails to keep it watchful and high enough in us, yet there may be an excess on the daring side; foolhardiness and insensibility of danger being as little reasonable as trembling and shrinking at the approach of every little evil. Fear was given us as a monitor to quicken our industry, and keep us upon our guard against the approaches of evil; and therefore to have no apprehension of mischief at hand, not to make a just estimate of the danger, but heedlessly to run into it, be the hazard what it will, without considering of what use or consequence it may be, is not the resolution of a rational creature, but brutish fury. Those who have children of this temper have nothing to do but a little to awaken their reason, which self-preservation will quickly dispose them to hearken to, unless (which is usually the case) some other passion hurries them on headlong, without sense and without consideration. A dislike of evil is so natural to mankind that nobody, I think, can be without fear of it: fear being nothing but an uneasiness under the apprehension of that coming upon us which we dislike. And therefore, whenever anyone runs into danger, we may say, 'tis under the conduct of ignorance, or the command of some more imperious passion, nobody being so much an enemy to himself, as to come within the reach of evil, out of free choice, and court danger for danger's sake If it

be therefore pride, vainglory, or rage, that silences a child's fear, or makes him not hearken to its advice, those are by fit means to be abated, that a little consideration may allay his heat, and make him bethink himself, whether this attempt be worth the venture. But this being a fault that children are not so often guilty of, I shall not be more particular in its cure. Weakness of spirit is the more common defect, and therefore will require the greater care.

Fortitude is the guard and support of the other virtues; and without courage a man will scarce keep steady to his duty, and fill up the character of a truly worthy man.

Courage, that makes us bear up against dangers that we fear and evils that we feel, is of great use in an estate, as ours is in this life, exposed to assaults on all hands: and therefore it is very advisable to get children into this armor as early as we can. Natural temper, I confess, does here a great deal; but even where that is defective, and the heart is in itself weak and timorous, it may, by a right management, be brought to a better resolution. What is to be done to prevent breaking children's spirits by frightful apprehensions instilled into them when young, or bemoaning themselves under every little suffering, I have already taken notice; how to harden their tempers, and raise their courage, if we find them too much subject to fear, is farther to be considered.

True fortitude I take to be the quiet possession of a man's self and an undisturbed doing his duty, whatever evil besets or danger lies in his way. This there are so few men attain to that we are not to expect it from children. But yet something may be done: and a wise conduct by insensible degrees may carry them farther than one expects.

The neglect of this great care of them, whilst they are young, is the reason, perhaps, why there are so few that have this virtue in its full latitude when they are men. I should not say this in a nation so naturally brave, as ours is, did I think that true fortitude required nothing but courage in the field, and a contempt of life in the face of an enemy. This, I confess, is not the least part of it, nor can be denied the laurels and honors always justly due to the valor of those who venture their lives for their country. But yet this is not all. Dangers attack us in other places besides the field of battle; and though death be the king of terrors, yet pain, disgrace and poverty have frightful looks, able to discompose most men whom they seem ready to seize on: and there are those who contemn some of these, and yet are heartily frighted with the other. True fortitude is pre-pared for dangers of all kinds, and unmoved, whatsoever evil it be that threatens. I do not mean unmoved with any fear at all. Where danger shows itself, apprehension cannot, without stupidity, be wanting; where danger is, sense of danger should be; and so much fear as should keep us awake, and excite our attention, industry, and vigor, but not disturb the calm use of our reason, nor hinder the execution of what that dictates.

The first step to get this noble and manly steadiness is what I have above mentioned, carefully to keep children from frights of all kinds when they are young. Let not any fearful apprehensions be talked into them, nor terrible objects surprise them. This often so shatters and discomposes the spirits that they never recover it again, but during their whole life, upon the first suggestion or appearance of any terrifying idea, are scattered and confounded; the body is en-ervated, and the mind disturbed, and the man scarce himself, or capable of any composed or rational action. Whether this be from an habitual motion of the animal spirits, introduced by the first strong impression, or from the alteration of the constitution by some more unaccountable way, this is certain, that so it is. Instances of such who in a weak timorous mind have borne, all their whole lives through, the effects of a fright when they were young, are everywhere to be seen, and therefore as much as may be to be prevented.

The next thing is by gentle degrees to accustom children to those things they are too much afraid of. But here great caution is to be used, that you do not make too much haste, nor attempt this cure too early, for fear lest you increase the mischief instead of remedying it. Little ones in arms may be easily kept out of the way of terrifying objects, and till they can talk and understand what is said to them are scarce capable of that reasoning and discourse which should be used to let them know there is no harm in those frightful objects which we would make them familiar with, and do to that purpose by gentle degrees bring nearer and nearer to them. And therefore 'tis seldom there is need of any application to them of this kind till after they can run about and talk. But yet, if it should happen that infants should have taken offense at anything which cannot be easily kept out of their way, and that they show marks of terror as often as it comes in sight; all the allays of fright, by diverting their thoughts, or mixing pleasant and agreeable appearances with it, must be used till it be grown familiar and inoffensive to them.

I think we may observe that, when children are first born, all objects of sight that do not hurt the eyes are indifferent to them; and they are no more afraid of a blackamoor or a lion than of their nurse or a cat. What is it, then, that afterwards, in certain mixtures of shape and color, comes to affright them? Nothing but the apprehensions of harm that accompanies those things. Did a child suck every day a new nurse, I make account it would be no more affrighted with the change of faces at six months old than at sixty. The reason then why it will not come to a stranger is because having been accustomed to receive its food and kind usage only from one or two that are about it, the child apprehends, by coming into the arms of a stranger, the being taken from what delights and feeds it and every moment supplies its wants, which it often feels, and therefore fears when the nurse is away.

The only thing we naturally are afraid of is pain, or loss of pleasure. And because these are not annexed to any shape, color, or size of visible objects, we are frighted with none of them till either we have felt pain from them, or have notions put into us that they will do us harm. The pleasant brightness and luster of flame and fire so delights children that at first they always desire to be handling of it: but when constant experience has convinced them, by the exquisite pain it has put them to, how cruel and unmerciful it is, they are afraid to touch it and carefully avoid it. This being the ground of fear, 'tis not hard to find whence it arises, and how it is to be cured in all mistaken objects of terror. And when the mind is confirmed against them, and has got a mastery over itself and its usual fears in lighter occasions, it is in good preparation to meet more real dangers. Your child shrieks, and runs away at the sight of a frog; let another catch it, and lay it down at a good distance from him: at first accustom

￼im to look upon it; when he can do that, then to come nearer to it, and see it leap without emotion; then to touch it lightly, when it is held fast in another's hand; and so on, till he can come to handle it as confidently as a butterfly or a sparrow. By the same way any other vain terrors may be removed; if care be taken that you go not too fast, and push not the child on to a new degree of assurance till he be thoroughly confirmed in the former. And thus the young soldier is to be trained on to the warfare of life; wherein care is to be taken that more things be not represented as dangerous than really are so; and then, that whatever you observe him to be more frighted at than he should, you be sure to tole him on to by insensible degrees, till he at last, quitting his fears, masters the difficulty, and comes off with applause. Successes of this kind, often repeated, will make him find that evils are not always so certain or so great as our fears represent them; and that the way to avoid them is not to run away, or be discomposed, dejected, and deterred by fear, where either our credit or duty requires us to go on.

But since the great foundation of fear in children is pain, the way to harden and fortify children against fear and danger is to accustom them to suffer pain. This 'tis possible will be thought by kind parents a very unnatural thing towards their children; and by most, unreasonable, to endeavor to reconcile anyone to the sense of pain, by bringing it upon him. 'Twill be said: 'It may perhaps give the child an aversion for him that makes him suffer, but can never recommend to him suffering itself. This is a strange method. You will not have children whipped and punished for their faults, but you would have them tormented for doing well, or for tormenting sake.' I doubt not but such objections as these will be made, and I shall be thought inconsistent with myself, or fantastical, in proposing it. I confess it is a thing to be managed with great discretion, and therefore it falls not out amiss that it will not be received or relished, but by those who consider well and look into the reason of things. I would not have children much beaten for their faults, because I would not have them think bodily pain the greatest punishment: and I would have them, when they do well, be sometimes put in pain, for the same reason that they might be accustomed to bear it, without looking on it as the greatest evil. How much education may reconcile young people to pain and sufferance, the examples of Sparta do sufficiently show: and they who have once brought themselves not to think bodily pain the greatest of evils, or that which they ought to stand most in fear of, have made no small advance towards virtue. But I am not so foolish to propose the Lacedæmonian discipline in our age or constitution. But yet I do say that inuring children gently to suffer some degrees of pain without shrinking is a way to gain firmness to their minds, and lay a foundation for courage and resolution in the future part of their lives.

Not to bemoan them, or permit them to bemoan themselves, on every little pain they suffer, is the first step to be made. But of this I have spoken elsewhere.

The next thing is, sometimes designedly, to put them in pain: but care must be taken that this be done when the child is in good humor, and satisfied of the good will and kindness of him that hurts him, at the time that he does it. There must no marks of anger or displeasure on the one side, or compassion or repenting on the other, go along with it; and it must be sure to be no more than the child can bear without repining or taking it amiss, or for a punishment. Managed by these degrees, and with such circumstances, I have seen a child run away laughing with good smart blows of a wand on his back, who would have cried for an unkind word, and have been very sensible of the chastisement of a cold look, from the same person. Satisfy a child by a constant course of your care and kindness that you perfectly love him, and he may by degrees be accustomed to bear very painful and rough usage from you, without flinching or complaining: and this we see children do every day in play one with another. The softer you find your child is, the more you are to seek occasions, at fit times, thus to harden him. The great art in this is to begin with what is but very little painful, and to proceed by insensible degrees, when you are playing, and in good humor with him, and speaking well of him: and when you have once got him to think himself made amends for his suffering by the praise given him for his courage; when he can take pride in giving such marks of his manliness, and can prefer the reputation of being brave and stout to the avoiding a little pain or the shrinking under it; you need not despair in time and by the assistance of his growing reason, to master his timorousness, and mend the weakness of his constitution. As he grows bigger, he is to be set upon bolder attempts than his natural temper carries him to; and whenever he is observed to flinch from what one has reason to think he would come off well in, if he had but courage to undertake, *that* he should be assisted in at first, and by degrees shamed to, till at last practice has given more assurance, and with it a mastery; which must be rewarded with great praise and the good opinion of others, for his performance. When by these steps he has got resolution enough not to be deterred from what he ought to do, by the apprehension of danger; when fear does not, in sudden or hazardous occurrences, discompose his mind, set his body a-trembling, and make him unfit for action, or run away from it, he has then the courage of a rational creature: and such a hardiness we should endeavor by custom and use to bring children to, as proper occasions come in our way.

116. One thing I have frequently observed in children, that when they have got possession of any poor creature, they are apt to use it ill: they often torment, and treat very roughly, young birds, butterflies, and such other poor animals which fall into their hands, and that with a seeming kind of pleasure. This I think should be watched in them, and if they incline to any such cruelty, they should be taught the contrary usage. For the custom of tormenting and killing of beasts, will, by degrees, harden their minds even towards men; and they who delight in the suffering and destruction of inferior creatures will not be apt to be very compassionate or benign to those of their own kind. Our practice takes notice of this in the exclusion of butchers from juries of life and death. Children should from the beginning be bred up in abhorrence of killing or tormenting any living creature; and be taught not to spoil or destroy anything, unless it be for the preservation or advantage of some other that is nobler. And truly, if the preservation of all mankind, as much as in him lies, were everyone's persuasion, as indeed it is everyone's duty, and the true principle to regulate our religion, politics, and morality by, the world would be much quieter and better natured than it is. But to

return to our present business; I cannot but commend both the kind-ness and prudence of a mother I knew, who was wont always to indulge her daughters, when any of them desired dogs, squirrels, birds, or any such things as young girls use to be delighted with: but then, when they had them, they must be sure to keep them well, and look diligently after them, that they wanted nothing, or were not ill used. For if they were negligent in their care of them, it was counted a great fault, which often forfeited their possession, or at least they failed not to be rebuked for it; whereby they were early taught diligence and good nature. And indeed, I think people should be accustomed, from their cradles, to be tender to all sensible creatures, and to spoil or waste nothing at all.

This delight they take in doing of mischief, whereby I mean spoil-ing of anything to no purpose, but more especially the pleasure they take to put anything in pain, that is capable of it, I cannot persuade myself to be any other than a foreign and introduced disposition, a habit borrowed from custom and conversation. People teach chil-dren to strike, and laugh when they hurt or see harm come to others; and they have the examples of most about them to confirm them in it. All the entertainment and talk of history is nothing almost but fight-ing and killing: and the honor and renown that is bestowed on conquerors (who for the most part are but the great butchers of mankind) farther mislead growing youth, who by this means come to think slaughter the laudable business of mankind, and the most heroic of virtues. By these steps unnatural cruelty is planted in us; and what humanity abhors, custom reconciles and recommends to us, by laying it in the way to honor. Thus, by fashion and opinion, that comes to be a pleasure which in itself neither is nor can be any. This ought carefully to be watched, and early remedied; so as to settle and cherish the contrary and more natural temper of benignity and com-passion in the room of it; but still by the same gentle methods which are to be applied to the other two faults before mentioned. It may not perhaps be unreasonable here to add this farther caution, viz., that the mischiefs or harms that come by play, inadvertency, or ig-norance, and were not known to be harms, or designed for mischief's sake, though they may perhaps be sometimes of considerable damage, yet are not at all, or but very gently, to be taken notice of. For this, I think, I cannot too often inculcate that whatever miscarriage a child is guilty of, and whatever be the consequence of it, the thing to be regarded in taking notice of it is only what root it springs from and what habit it is like to establish: and to that the correction ought to be directed, and the child not to suffer any punishment for any harm which may have come by his play or inadvertency. The faults to be amended lie in the mind, and if they are such as either age will cure or no ill habits will follow from, the present action, whatever displeasing circumstances it may have, is to be passed by without any animadversion.

117. Another way to instill sentiments of humanity, and to keep them lively in young folks, will be to accustom them to civility in their language and deportment towards their inferiors and the meaner sort of people, particularly servants. It is not unusual to observe the children in gentlemen's families treat the servants of the house with domineering words, names of contempt, and an imperious carriage; as if they were of another race and species beneath them. Whether ill example, the advantage of fortune, or their natural vanity, inspire this haughtiness, it should be prevented, or weeded out; and a gentle, courteous, affable carriage towards the lower ranks of men, placed in the room of it. No part of their superiority will be hereby lost, but the distinction increased and their authority strengthened, when love in inferiors is joined to outward respect, and an esteem of the person has a share in their submission; and domestics will pay a more ready and cheerful service, when they find themselves not spurned because fortune has laid them below the level of others at their master's feet. Children should not be suffered to lose the consideration of human nature in the shufflings of outward conditions. The more they have, the better humored they should be taught to be, and the more compassionate and gentle to those of their brethren who are placed lower, and have scantier portions. If they are suffered from their cradles to treat men ill and rudely, because, by their father's title, they think they have a little power over them, at best it is ill-bred; and if care be not taken, will by degrees nurse up their natural pride into an

habitual contempt of those beneath them. And where will that probably end but in oppression and cruelty?

118. Curiosity in children (which I had occasion just to mention, 108) is but an appetite after knowledge; and therefore ought to be encouraged in them, not only as a good sign, but as the great instrument nature has provided to remove that ignorance they were born with; and which, without this busy inquisitiveness, will make them dull and useless creatures. The ways to encourage it, and keep it active and busy, are, I suppose, these following:

1. Not to check or discountenance any inquiries he shall make, nor suffer them to be laughed at; but to answer all his questions, and explain the matter he desires to know, so as to make them as much intelligible to him as suits the capacity of his age and knowledge. But confound not his understanding with explications or notions that are above it, or with the variety or number of things that are not to his present purpose. Mark what 'tis his mind aims at in the question, and not what words he expresses it in: and when you have informed and satisfied him in that, you shall see how his thoughts will enlarge themselves, and how by fit answers he may be led on farther than perhaps you could imagine. For knowledge is grateful to the understanding, as light to the eyes: children are pleased and delighted with it exceedingly, especially if they see that their inquiries are regarded, and that their desire of knowing is encouraged and commended. And I doubt not but one great reason why many children abandon themselves wholly to silly sports, and trifle away all their time insipidly is because they have found their curiosity balked, and their inquiries neglected. But had they been treated with more kindness and respect, and their questions answered, as they should, to their satisfaction; I doubt not but they would have taken more pleasure in learning, and improving their knowledge, wherein there would be still newness and variety, which is what they are delighted with, than in returning over and over to the same play and playthings.

119. 2. To this serious answering their questions and informing their understandings in what they desire, as if it were a matter that needed it, should be added some peculiar ways of commendation. Let others whom they esteem be told before their faces of the knowledge

they have in such and such things; and since we are all, even from our cradles, vain and proud creatures, let their vanity be flattered with things that will do them good; and let their pride set them on work on something which may turn to their advantage. Upon this ground you shall find that there cannot be a greater spur to the attaining what you would have the eldest learn and know himself than to set him upon teaching it his younger brothers and sisters.

120. 3. As children's inquiries are not to be slighted, so also great care is to be taken that they never receive deceitful and eluding answers. They easily perceive when they are slighted or deceived, and quickly learn the trick of neglect, dissimulation and falsehood, which they observe others to make use of. We are not to intrench upon truth in any conversation, but least of all with children; since if we play false with them, we not only deceive their expectation and hinder their knowledge, but corrupt their innocence and teach them the worst of vices. They are travelers newly arrived in a strange country, of which they know nothing; we should therefore make conscience not to mislead them. And though their questions seem sometimes not very material, yet they should be seriously answered; for however they may appear to us (to whom they are long since known) inquiries not worth the making, they are of moment to those who are wholly ignorant. Children are strangers to all we are acquainted with; and all the things they meet with are at first unknown to them, as they once were to us; and happy are they who meet with civil people that will comply with their ignorance and help them to get out of it.

If you or I now should be set down in Japan, with all our prudence and knowledge about us, a conceit whereof makes us, perhaps, so apt to slight the thoughts and inquiries of children—should we, I say, be set down in Japan, we should, no doubt (if we would inform ourselves of what is there to be known) ask a thousand questions, which, to a supercilious or inconsiderate Japaner, would seem very idle and impertinent, though to us they would be very material and of importance to be resolved; and we should be glad to find a man so complaisant and courteous as to satisfy our demands and instruct our ignorance.

When any new thing comes in their way, children usually ask the common question of a stranger: *What is it?* Whereby they ordinarily mean nothing but the name; and therefore to tell them how it is called, is usually the proper answer to that demand. And the next question usually is, *What is it for?* And to this it should be answered truly and directly. The use of the thing should be told, and the way explained, how it serves to such a purpose, as far as their capacities can comprehend it. And so of any other circumstances they shall ask about it; not turning them going till you have given them all the satisfaction they are capable of; and so leading them by your answers into farther questions. And perhaps to a grown man such conversation will not be altogether so idle and insignificant as we are apt to imagine. The native and untaught suggestions of inquisitive children do often offer things that may set a considering man's thoughts on work. And I think there is frequently more to be learned from the unexpected questions of a child than the discourses of men who talk in a road, according to the notions they have borrowed and the prejudices of their education.

121. 4. Perhaps it may not sometimes be amiss to excite their curiosity by bringing strange and new things in their way, on purpose to engage their inquiry, and give them occasion to inform themselves about them; and if by chance their curiosity leads them to ask what they should not know, it is a great deal better to tell them plainly that it is a thing that belongs not to them to know than to pop them off with a falsehood or a frivolous answer.

122. Pertness, that appears sometimes so early, proceeds from a principle that seldom accompanies a strong constitution of body, or ripens into a strong judgment of mind. If it were desirable to have a child a more brisk talker, I believe there might be ways found to make him so: But I suppose a wise father had rather that his son should be able and useful, when a man, than pretty company and a diversion to others, whilst a child; though if that too were to be considered, I think I may say there is not so much pleasure to have a child prattle agreeably as to reason well. Encourage therefore his inquisitiveness all you can by satisfying his demands and informing his judgment as far as it is capable. When his reasons are any way tolerable, let him find the credit and commendation of it: and when

they are quite out of the way, let him, without being laughed at for his mistake, be gently put into the right; and if he show a forwardness to be reasoning about things that come in his way, take care, as much as you can, that nobody check this inclination in him, or mislead it by captious or fallacious ways of talking with him. For when all is done, this, as the highest and most important faculty of our minds, deserves the greatest care and attention in cultivating it: the right improvement and exercise of our reason being the highest perfection that a man can attain to in this life.

123. Contrary to this busy inquisitive temper, there is sometimes observable in children a listless carelessness, a want of regard to anything, and a sort of trifling, even at their business. This sauntering humor I look on as one of the worst qualities can appear in a child, as well as one of the hardest to be cured, where it is natural. But it being liable to be mistaken in some cases, care must be taken to make a right judgment concerning that trifling at their books or business, which may sometimes be complained of in a child. Upon the first suspicion a father has that his son is of a sauntering temper, he must carefully observe him, whether he be listless and indifferent in all his actions, or whether in some things alone he be slow and sluggish, but in others vigorous and eager. For though we find that he does loiter at his book, and let a good deal of the time he spends in his chamber or study run idly away, he must not presently conclude that this is from a sauntering humor in his temper. It may be childishness, and a preferring something to his study, which his thoughts run on; and he dislikes his book, as is natural, because it is forced upon him as a task. To know this perfectly, you must watch him at play when he is out of his place and time of study, following his own inclination, and see there whether he be stirring and active; whether he designs anything, and with labor and eagerness pursues it, till he has accomplished what he aimed at, or whether he lazily and listlessly dreams away his time. If this sloth be only when he is about his book, I think it may be easily cured. If it be in his temper, it will require a little more pains and attention to remedy it.

124. If you are satisfied by his earnestness at play or anything else he sets his mind on in the intervals between his hours of business, that

he is not of himself inclined to laziness, but that only want of relish of
his book makes him negligent and sluggish in his application to it,
the first step is to try by talking to him kindly of the folly and inconvenience of it, whereby he loses a good part of his time, which he
might have for his diversion; but be sure to talk calmly and kindly,
and not much at first, but only these plain reasons in short. If this
prevails, you have gained the point in the most desirable way, which
is that of reason and kindness. If this softer application prevails not,
try to shame him out of it by laughing at him for it, asking every day,
when he comes to table, if there be no strangers there, how long he
was that day about his business. And if he has not done it in the time
he might be well supposed to have dispatched it, expose and turn him
into ridicule for it; but mix no chiding, only put on a pretty cold
brow towards him, and keep it till he reform; and let his mother, tutor,
and all about him do so too. If this work not the effect you desire, then
tell him he shall be no longer troubled with a tutor to take care of
his education, you will not be at the charge to have him spend his
time idly with him; but since he prefers this or that (whatever play
he delights in) to his book, that only he shall do; and so in earnest
set him to work on his beloved play, and keep him steadily, and in
earnest, to it morning and afternoon, till he be fully surfeited, and
would, at any rate, change it for some hours at his book again. But
when you thus set him his task of play, you must be sure to look
after him yourself or set somebody else to do it, that may constantly
see him employed in it, and that he be not permitted to be idle at
that too. I say, yourself look after him, for it is worth a father's while,
whatever business he has, to bestow two or three days upon his son,
to cure so great a mischief as his sauntering at his business.

125. This is what I propose, if it be idleness, not from his general
temper, but a peculiar or acquired aversion to learning, which you
must be careful to examine and distinguish. But though you have
your eyes upon him, to watch what he does with the time which he
has at his own disposal, yet you must not let him perceive that you or
anybody else do so; for that may hinder him from following his own
inclination, which he being full of, and not daring, for fear of you,
to prosecute what his head and heart are set upon, he may neglect

all other things, which then he relishes not, and so may seem to be idle and listless, when in truth it is nothing but being intent on that, which the fear of your eye or knowledge keeps him from executing. To be clear in this point, the observation must be made when you are out of the way, and he not so much as under the restraint of a suspicion that anybody has an eye upon him. In those seasons of perfect freedom, let somebody you can trust mark how he spends his time, whether he unactively loiters it away, when without any check he is left to his own inclination. Thus, by his employing of such times of liberty, you will easily discern, whether it be listlessness in his temper, or aversion to his book, that makes him saunter away his time of study.

126. If some defect in his constitution has cast a damp on his mind, and he be naturally listless and dreaming, this unpromising disposition is none of the easiest to be dealt with, because, generally carrying with it an unconcernedness for the future, it wants the two great springs of action, foresight and desire; which how to plant and increase, where nature has given a cold and contrary temper, will be the question. As soon as you are satisfied that this is the case, you must carefully inquire whether there be nothing he delights in. Inform yourself what it is he is most pleased with, and if you can find any particular tendency his mind has, increase it all you can, and make use of that to set him on work, and to excite his industry. If he loves praise, or play, or fine clothes, etc., or, on the other side, dreads pain, disgrace, or your displeasure, etc., whatever it be that he loves most, except it be sloth (for that will never set him on work), let that be made use of to quicken him and make him bestir himself. For in this listless temper you are not to fear an excess of appetite (as in all other cases) by cherishing it. 'Tis that which you want, and therefore must labor to raise and increase; for where there is no desire, there will be no industry.

127. If you have not hold enough upon him this way to stir up vigor and activity in him, you must employ him in some constant bodily labor, whereby he may get a habit of doing something. The keeping him hard to some study were the better way to get him a habit of exercising and applying his mind. But because this is an invisible attention, and nobody can tell when he is or is not idle at it,

you must find bodily employments for him, which he must be con-stantly busied in, and kept to; and if they have some little hardship and shame in them, it may not be the worse that they may the sooner weary him and make him desire to return to his book. But be sure, when you exchange his book for his other labor, set him such a task, to be done in such a time as may allow him no opportunity to be idle. Only after you have by this way brought him to be attentive and indus-trious at his book, you may, upon his dispatching his study within the time set him, give him as a reward some respite from his other labor; which you may diminish as you find him grow more and more steady in his application, and at last wholly take off when his saunter-ing at his book is cured.

128. We formerly observed that variety and freedom was that that delighted children, and recommended their plays to them; and that therefore their book or anything we would have them learn should not be enjoined them as *business*. This their parents, tutors, and teachers are apt to forget; and their impatience to have them busied in what is fit for them to do suffers them not to deceive them into it, but by the repeated injunctions they meet with, children quickly distinguish between what is required of them, and what not. When this mistake has once made his book uneasy to him, the cure is to be applied at the other end. And since it will be then too late to endeavor to make it a play to him, you must take the contrary course: observe what play he is most delighted with; enjoin that, and make him play so many hours every day, not as a punishment for playing, but as if it were the business required of him. This, if I mistake not, will in a few days make him so weary of his most beloved sport that he will prefer his book, or anything to it, especially if it may redeem him from any part of the task of play set him, and he may be suffered to employ some part of the time destined to his *task of play* in his book, or such other exercise as is really useful to him. This I at least think a better cure than that forbidding, which usually increases the desire, or any other punishment should be made use of to remedy it; for when you have once glutted his appetite, which may safely be done in all things but eating and drinking, and made him surfeit of what you would have him avoid, you have put into him a principle of aversion, and you

need not so much fear afterwards his longing for the same thing again.

129. This I think is sufficiently evident, that children generally hate to be idle. All the care then is that their busy humor should be constantly employed in something of use to them; which, if you will attain, you must make what you would have them do a recreation to them, and not a business. The way to do this, so that they may not perceive you have any hand in it, is this proposed here, viz., to make them weary of that which you would not have them do, by enjoining and making them under some pretense or other do it, till they are surfeited. For example: Does your son play at top and scourge too much? Enjoin him to play so many hours every day, and look that he do it; and you shall see he will quickly be sick of it, and willing to leave it. By this means making the recreations you dislike a business to him, he will of himself with delight betake himself to those things you would have him do, especially if they be proposed as rewards for having performed his task in that play which is commanded him. For if he be ordered every day to whip his top so long as to make him sufficiently weary, do you not think he will apply himself with eagerness to his book, and wish for it, if you promise it him as a reward of having whipped his top lustily, quite out all the time that is set him? Children, in the things they do, if they comport with their age, find little difference so they may be doing: the esteem they have for one thing above another they borrow from others, so that what those about them make to be a reward to them will really be so. By this art it is in their governor's choice, whether scotchhoppers shall reward their dancing, or dancing their scotchhoppers; whether peg-top, or reading; playing at trap, or studying the globes, shall be more acceptable and pleasing to them; all that they desire being to be busy, and busy, as they imagine, in things of their own choice, and which they receive as favors from their parents or others for whom they have respect and with whom they would be in credit. A set of children thus ordered and kept from the ill example of others would all of them, I suppose, with as much earnestness and delight learn to read, write, and what else one would have them, as others do their ordinary plays: and the eldest being thus entered, and this made the fashion of the place, it would be as

impossible to hinder them from learning the one, as it is ordinarily to keep them from the other.

130. Playthings I think children should have, and of divers sorts; but still to be in the custody of their tutors or somebody else, whereof the child should have in his power but one at once, and should not be suffered to have another but when he restored that. This teaches them betimes to be careful of not losing or spoiling the things they have; whereas plenty and variety in their own keeping makes them wanton and careless, and teaches them from the beginning to be squanderers and wasters. These, I confess, are little things, and such as will seem beneath the care of a governor; but nothing that may form children's minds is to be overlooked and neglected, and whatsoever introduces habits, and settles customs in them, deserves the care and attention of their governors, and is not a small thing in its consequences.

One thing more about children's playthings may be worth their parents' care. Though it be agreed they should have of several sorts, yet, I think, they should have none bought for them. This will hinder that great variety they are often overcharged with, which serves only to teach the mind to wander after change and superfluity, to be unquiet, and perpetually stretching itself after something more still, though it knows not what, and never to be satisfied with what it has. The court that is made to people of condition in such kind of presents to their children, does the little ones great harm. By it they are taught pride, vanity, and covetousness, almost before they can speak. And I have known a young child so distracted with the number and variety of his play games that he tired his maid every day to look them over; and was so accustomed to abundance that he never thought he had enough, but was always asking, "What more? What more? What new thing shall I have?" A good introduction to moderate desires, and the ready way to make a contented happy man!

How then shall they have the play games you allow them, if none must be bought for them? I answer, they should make them themselves, or at least endeavor it, and set themselves about it; till then they should have none, and till then they will want none of any great artifice. A smooth pebble, a piece of paper, the mother's bunch of keys, or anything they cannot hurt themselves with, serves as much to divert little children as those more chargeable and curious toys from the shops, which are presently put out of order and broken. Children are never dull, or out of humor, for want of such playthings, unless they have been used to them; when they are little, whatever occurs serves the turn; and as they grow bigger, if they are not stored by the expensive folly of others, they will make them themselves. Indeed, when they once begin to set themselves to work about any of their inventions, they should be taught and assisted; but should have nothing whilst they lazily sit still, expecting to be furnished from other hands, without employing their own. And if you help them where they are at a stand, it will more endear you to them than any chargeable toys you shall buy for them. Playthings which are above their skill to make, as tops, gigs, battledores, and the like, which are to be used with labor, should indeed be procured them. These 'tis convenient they should have, not for variety but exercise; but these too should be given them as bare as might be. If they had a top, the scourge-stick and leather strap should be left to their own making and fitting. If they sit gaping to have such things drop into their mouths, they should go without them. This will accustom them to seek for what they want, in themselves and in their own endeavors; whereby they will be taught moderation in their desires, application, industry, thought, contrivance, and good husbandry: qualities that will be useful to them when they are men, and therefore cannot be learned too soon, or fixed too deep. All the plays and diversions of children should be directed towards good and useful habits, or else they will introduce ill ones. Whatever they do leaves some impression on that tender age, and from thence they receive a tendency to good or evil: and whatever has such an influence ought not to be neglected.

131. Lying is so ready and cheap a cover for any miscarriage, and so much in fashion among all sorts of people, that a child can hardly avoid observing the use is made of it on all occasions, and so can scarce be kept without great care from getting into it. But it is so ill a quality, and the mother of so many ill ones that spawn from it and take shelter under it, that a child should be brought up in the greatest abhorrence of it imaginable. It should be always (when occasionally it comes to be mentioned) spoke of before him with the utmost de-

testation, as a quality so wholly inconsistent with the name and character of a gentleman that nobody of any credit can bear the imputation of a lie; a mark that is judged the utmost disgrace, which debases
a man to the lowest degree of a shameful meanness, and ranks him
with the most contemptible part of mankind and the abhorred ras-
cality; and is not to be endured in anyone who would converse with
people of condition, or have any esteem or reputation in the world.
The first time he is found in a lie, it should rather be wondered at
as a monstrous thing in him, than reproved as an ordinary fault. If
that keeps him not from relapsing, the next time he must be sharply
rebuked, and fall into the state of great displeasure of his father and
mother and all about him who take notice of it. And if this way work
not the cure, you must come to blows; for after he has been thus
warned, a premeditated lie must always be looked upon as obstinacy,
and never be permitted to escape unpunished.

132. Children, afraid to have their faults seen in their naked
colors, will, like the rest of the sons of Adam, be apt to make excuses.
This is a fault usually bordering upon and leading to untruth, and
is not to be indulged in them; but yet it ought to be cured rather with
shame than roughness. If therefore, when a child is questioned for
anything, his first answer be an excuse, warn him soberly to tell the
truth; and then if he persists to shuffle it off with a falsehood, he
must be chastised; but if he directly confess, you must commend his
ingenuity,[18] and pardon the fault, be it what it will; and pardon it
so that you never so much as reproach him with it, or mention it to
him again: for if you would have him in love with ingenuity, and by
a constant practice make it habitual to him, you must take care that it
never procure him the least inconvenience; but on the contrary, his
own confession bringing always with it perfect impunity, should be
besides encouraged by some marks of approbation. If his excuse be
such at any time that you cannot prove it to have any falsehood in it,
let it pass for true, and be sure not to show any suspicion of it. Let
him keep up his reputation with you as high as is possible; for when
once he finds he has lost that, you have lost a great and your best

[18] Sense of honor, ingenuousness.

hold upon him. Therefore let him not think he has the character of a liar with you, as long as you can avoid it without flattering him in it. Thus some slips in truth may be overlooked. But after he has once been corrected for a lie, you must be sure never after to pardon it in him, whenever you find and take notice to him that he is guilty of it: for it being a fault which he has been forbid, and may, unless he be willful, avoid, the repeating of it is perfect perverseness, and must have the chastisement due to that offense.

133. This is what I have thought concerning the general method of educating a young gentleman; which, though I am apt to suppose may have some influence on the whole course of his education, yet I am far from imagining it contains all those particulars which his growing years or peculiar temper may require. But this being premised in general, we shall in the next place descend to a more particular consideration of the several parts of his education.

134. That which every gentleman (that takes any care of his education) desires for his son, besides the estate he leaves him, is contained, I suppose, in these four things, *virtue, wisdom, breeding* and *learning*. I will not trouble myself whether these names do not some of them sometimes stand for the same thing, or really include one another. It serves my turn here to follow the popular use of these words, which, I presume, is clear enough to make me be understood, and I hope there will be no difficulty to comprehend my meaning.

135. I place *virtue* as the first and most necessary of those endowments that belong to a man or a gentleman; as absolutely requisite to make him valued and beloved by others, acceptable or tolerable to himself. Without that, I think, he will be happy neither in this nor the other world.

136. As the foundation of this, there ought very early to be imprinted on his mind a true notion of God, as of the independent Supreme Being, Author and Maker of all things, from Whom we receive all our good, Who loves us, and gives us all things. And consequent to this, instill into him a love and reverence of this Supreme Being. This is enough to begin with, without going to explain this matter any farther; for fear lest by talking too early to him of spirits, and being unseasonably forward to make him understand the incom-

prehensible nature of that Infinite Being, his head be either filled with false or perplexed with unintelligible notions of Him. Let him only be told upon occasion, that God made and governs all things, hears and sees everything, and does all manner of good to those that love and obey Him; you will find, that being told of such a God, other thoughts will be apt to rise up fast enough in his mind about Him; which, as you observe them to have any mistakes, you must set right. And I think it would be better if men generally rested in such an idea of God, without being too curious in their notions about a Being which all must acknowledge incomprehensible; whereby many, who have not strength and clearness of thought to distinguish between what they can and what they cannot know, run themselves in super-stitions or atheism, making God like themselves, or, because they can-not comprehend anything else, none at all. And I am apt to think the keeping children constantly morning and evening to acts of devotion to God, as to their Maker, Preserver and Benefactor, in some plain and short form of prayer, suitable to their age and capacity, will be of much more use to them in religion, knowledge, and virtue, than to distract their thoughts with curious inquiries into His inscrutable essence and being.

137. Having by gentle degrees, as you find him capable of it, settled such an idea of God in his mind, and taught him to pray to Him, and praise Him as the Author of his being, and of all the good he does or can enjoy, forbear any discourse of other spirits, till the mention of them coming in his way, upon occasion hereafter to be set down, and his reading the scripture history, put him upon that inquiry.

138. But even then, and always whilst he is young, be sure to preserve his tender mind from all impressions and notions of spirits and goblins, or any fearful apprehensions in the dark. This he will be in danger of from the indiscretion of servants, whose usual method is to awe children, and keep them in subjection, by telling them of raw-head and bloody-bones, and such other names as carry with them the ideas of something terrible and hurtful, which they have reason to be afraid of when alone, especially in the dark. This must be care-fully prevented, for though by this foolish way, they may keep them

from little faults, yet the remedy is much worse than the disease; and there are stamped upon their imaginations ideas that follow them with terror and affrightment. Such bugbear thoughts once got into the tender minds of children, and being set on with a strong impression from the dread that accompanies such apprehensions, sink deep, and fasten themselves so as not easily, if ever, to be got out again; and whilst they are there, frequently haunt them with strange visions, making children dastards when alone, and afraid of their shadows and darkness all their lives after. I have had those complain to me, when men, who had been thus used when young, that though their reason corrected the wrong ideas they had taken in, and they were satisfied that there was no cause to fear invisible beings more in the dark than in the light, yet that these notions were apt still upon any occasion to start up first in their prepossessed fancies, and not to be removed without some pains.

And to let you see how lasting and frightful images are that take place in the mind early, I shall here tell you a pretty remarkable but true story. There was in a town in the west a man of a disturbed brain, whom the boys used to tease when he came in their way. This fellow one day seeing in the street one of those lads that used to vex him stepped into a cutler's shop he was near, and there seizing on a naked sword, made after the boy; who seeing him coming so armed, betook himself to his feet, and ran for his life, and by good luck had strength and heels enough to reach his father's house before the madman could get up to him. The door was only latched, and when he had the latch in his hand, he turned about his head to see how near his pursuer was, who was at the entrance of the porch, with his sword up ready to strike; and he had just time to get in, and clap to the door to avoid the blow, which, though his body escaped, his mind did not. This frightening idea made so deep an impression there that it lasted many years, if not all his life after. For, telling this story when he was a man, he said that after that time till then, he never went in at that door (that he could remember) at any time without looking back, whatever business he had in his head, or how little soever before he came thither he thought of this madman.

If children were let alone, they would be no more afraid in the dark than in broad sunshine; they would in their turns as much welcome the one for sleep as the other to play in. There should be no distinction made to them by any discourse of more danger or terrible things in the one than the other: but if the folly of anyone about them should do them this harm, and make them think there is any difference between being in the dark and winking, you must get it out of their minds as soon as you can; and let them know that God, who made all things good for them, made the night that they might sleep the better and the quieter; and that they being under his protection, there is nothing in the dark to hurt them. What is to be known more of God and good spirits is to be deferred till the time we shall hereafter mention; and of evil spirits, 'twill be well if you can keep him from wrong fancies about them till he is ripe for that sort of knowledge.

139. Having laid the foundations of virtue in a true notion of a God, such as the creed wisely teaches, as far as his age is capable, and by accustoming him to pray to Him, the next thing to be taken care of is to keep him exactly to speaking of truth, and by all the ways imaginable inclining him to be good-natured. Let him know that twenty faults are sooner to be forgiven than the straining of truth to cover anyone by an excuse. And to teach him betimes to love and be good-natured to others is to lay early the true foundation of an honest man; all injustice generally springing from too great love of ourselves and too little of others.

This is all I shall say of this matter in general, and is enough for laying the first foundations of virtue in a child. As he grows up, the tendency of his natural inclination must be observed; which, as it inclines him more than is convenient on one or t'other side from the right path of virtue, ought to have proper remedies applied. For few of Adam's children are so happy, as not to be born with some bias in their natural temper, which it is the business of education either to take off or counterbalance. But to enter into particulars of this would be beyond the design of this short treatise of education. I intend not a discourse of all the virtues and vices, how each virtue is to be attained, and every particular vice by its peculiar remedies cured, though

I have mentioned some of the most ordinary faults, and the ways to be used in correcting them.

140. *Wisdom* I take in the popular acceptation, for a man's managing his business ably and with foresight in this world. This is the product of a good natural temper, application of mind, and experience together, and so above the reach of children. The greatest thing that in them can be done towards it is to hinder them, as much as may be, from being cunning; which, being the ape of wisdom, is the most distant from it that can be: and as an ape for the likeness it has to a man, wanting what really should make him so, is by so much the uglier; cunning is only the want of understanding, which, because it cannot compass its ends by direct ways, would do it by a trick and circumvention; and the mischief of it is, a cunning trick helps but once, but hinders ever after. No cover was ever made so big or so fine as to hide itself: nobody was ever so cunning as to conceal their being so; and when they are once discovered, everybody is shy, everybody distrustful of crafty men; and all the world forwardly join to oppose and defeat them; whilst the open, fair, wise man has everybody to make way for him, and goes directly to his business. To accustom a child to have true notions of things, and not to be satisfied till he has them, to raise his mind to great and worthy thoughts, and to keep him at a distance from falsehood and cunning, which has always a broad mixture of falsehood in it, is the fittest preparation of a child for wisdom. The rest, which is to be learned from time, experience, and observation, and an acquaintance with men, their tempers, and designs, is not to be expected in the ignorance and inadvertency of childhood, or the inconsiderate heat and unweariness of youth. All that can be done towards it, during this unripe age, is, as I have said, to accustom them to truth and sincerity, to a submission to reason, and as much as may be to reflection on their own actions.

141. The next good quality belonging to a gentleman is *good breeding*. There are two sorts of ill breeding: the one a sheepish bashfulness, and the other a misbecoming negligence and disrespect in our carriage; both which are avoided by duly observing this one rule, *not to think meanly of ourselves, and not to think meanly of others.*

142. The first part of this rule must not be understood in opposition to humility but to assurance. We ought not to think so well of ourselves as to stand upon our own value; and assume to ourselves a preference before others, because of any advantage we may imagine we have over them; but modestly to take what is offered, when it is our due. But yet we ought to think so well of ourselves as to perform those actions which are incumbent on and expected of us without discomposure or disorder, in whose presence soever we are; keeping that respect and distance which is due to everyone's rank and quality. There is often in people, especially children, a clownish shamefacedness before strangers or those above them: they are confounded in their thoughts, words, and looks; and so lose themselves in that confusion as not to be able to do anything, or at least not to do it with that freedom and gracefulness which pleases and makes them be acceptable. The only cure for this, as for any other miscarriage, is by use to introduce the contrary habit. But since we cannot accustom ourselves to converse with strangers and persons of quality without being in their company, nothing can cure this part of ill breeding but change and variety of company, and that of persons above us.

143. As the before-mentioned consists in too great a concern how to behave ourselves towards others; so the other part of ill breeding lies in the appearance of too little care of pleasing or showing respect to those we have to do with. To avoid this these two things are requisite: first, a disposition of the mind not to offend others; and secondly, the most acceptable and agreeable way of expressing that disposition. From the one men are called *civil;* from the other *well-fashioned.* The latter of these is that decency and gracefulness of looks, voice, words, motions, gestures, and of all the whole outward demeanor, which takes in company, and makes those with whom we may converse easy and well pleased. This is, as it were, the language whereby that internal civility of the mind is expressed; which, as other languages are, being very much governed by the fashion and custom of every country, must, in the rules and practice of it, be learned chiefly from observation, and the carriage of those who are allowed to be exactly well-bred. The other part, which lies deeper than the outside, is that general good will and regard for all people, which

makes anyone have a care not to show in his carriage any contempt, disrespect, or neglect of them; but to express, according to the fashion and way of that country, a respect and value for them according to their rank and condition. It is a disposition of the mind that shows itself in the carriage, whereby a man avoids making anyone uneasy in conversation.

I shall take notice of four qualities, that are most directly opposite to this first and most taking of all the social virtues. And from some one of these four it is that incivility commonly has its rise. I shall set them down, that children may be preserved or recovered from their ill influence.

1. The first is a natural *roughness,* which makes a man uncomplaisant to others, so that he has no deference for their inclinations, tempers, or conditions. 'Tis the sure badge of a clown not to mind what pleases or displeases those he is with; and yet one may often find a man in fashionable clothes give an unbounded swing to his own humor and suffer it to jostle or overrun anyone that stands in its way, with a perfect indifference how they take it. This is a brutality that everyone sees and abhors, and nobody can be easy with: and therefore this finds no place in anyone who would be thought to have the least tincture of good breeding. For the very end and business of good breeding is to supple the natural stiffness and so soften men's tempers, that they may bend to a compliance, and accommodate themselves to those they have to do with.

2. *Contempt,* or want of due respect, discovered either in looks, words, or gesture: this, from whomsoever it comes, brings always uneasiness with it. For nobody can contentedly bear being slighted.

3. *Censoriousness,* and finding fault with others, has a direct opposition to civility. Men, whatever they are or are not guilty of, would not have their faults displayed and set in open view and broad daylight, before their own or other people's eyes. Blemishes affixed to anyone always carry shame with them: and the discovery, or even bare imputation of any defect is not borne without some uneasiness. *Raillery* is the most refined way of exposing the faults of others: but, because it is usually done with wit and good language, and gives entertainment to the company, people are led into a mistake, that where it

keeps within fair bounds there is no incivility in it. And so the pleasantry of this sort of conversation often introduces it amongst people of the better rank; and such talkers are favorably heard and generally applauded by the laughter of the bystanders on their side. But they ought to consider that the entertainment of the rest of the company is at the cost of that one who is set out in their burlesque colors, who therefore is not without uneasiness, unless the subject for which he is rallied be really in itself matter of commendation. For then the pleasant images and representations which make the raillery carrying praise as well as sport with them, the rallied person also finds his account, and takes part in the diversion. But because the right management of so nice and ticklish a business, wherein a little slip may spoil all, is not everybody's talent, I think those who would secure themselves from provoking others, especially all young people, should carefully abstain from raillery, which by a small mistake or any wrong turn, may leave upon the mind of those who are made uneasy by it, the lasting memory of having been piquantly, though wittily, taunted for something censurable in them.

Besides raillery, *contradiction* is a sort of censoriousness wherein ill breeding often shows itself. Complaisance does not require that we should always admit all the reasonings or relations that the company is entertained with, no, nor silently to let pass all that is vented in our hearing. The opposing the opinions, and rectifying the mistakes of others, is what truth and charity sometimes require of us, and civility does not oppose, if it be done with due caution and care of circumstances. But there are some people that one may observe, possessed as it were with the spirit of contradiction, that steadily, and without regard to right or wrong, oppose someone, or, perhaps, everyone of the company, whatever they say. This is so visible and outrageous a way of censuring that nobody can avoid thinking himself injured by it. All opposition to what another man has said is so apt to be suspected of censoriousness, and is so seldom received without some sort of humiliation, that it ought to be made in the gentlest manner, and softest words can be found, and such as with the whole deportment may express no forwardness to contradict. All marks of respect and good will ought to accompany it, that whilst we gain the argument we may not lose the esteem of those that hear us.

4. *Captiousness* is another fault opposite to civility; not only because it often produces misbecoming and provoking expressions and carriage, but because it is a tacit accusation and reproach of some incivility taken notice of in those whom we are angry with. Such a suspicion or intimation cannot be borne by anyone without uneasiness. Besides, one angry body discomposes the whole company, and the harmony ceases upon any such jarring.

The happiness that all men so steadily pursue consisting in pleasure, it is easy to see why the civil are more acceptable than the useful. The ability, sincerity, and good intention of a man of weight and worth, or a real friend, seldom atones for the uneasiness that is produced by his grave and solid representations. Power and riches, nay virtue itself, are valued only as conducing to our happiness. And therefore he recommends himself ill to another as aiming at his happiness, who, in the services he does him, makes him uneasy in the manner of doing them. He that knows how to make those he converses with easy, without debasing himself to low and servile flattery, has found the true art of living in the world, and being both welcome and valued everywhere. Civility, therefore, is what in the first place should with great care be made habitual to children and young people.

144. There is another fault in good manners, and that is *excess of ceremony,* and an obstinate persisting to force upon another what is not his due, and what he cannot take without folly or shame. This seems rather a design to expose than oblige: or at least looks like a contest for mastery, and at best is but troublesome and so can be no part of good breeding, which has no other use or end but to make people easy and satisfied in their conversation with us. This is a fault few young people are apt to fall into, but yet if they are ever guilty of it or are suspected to incline that way, they should be told of it and warned of this mistaken civility. The thing they should endeavor and aim at in conversation should be to show respect, esteem, and good will, by paying to everyone that common ceremony and regard which is in civility due to them. To do this without

a suspicion of flattery, dissimulation, or meanness, is a great skill, which good sense, reason, and good company can only teach; but is of so much use in civil life that it is well worth the studying.

145. Though the managing ourselves well in this part of our behavior has the name of good breeding, as if peculiarly the effect of education; yet, as I have said, young children should not be much perplexed about it; I mean, about putting off their hats and making legs modishly. Teach them humility and to be good-natured, if you can, and this sort of manners will not be wanting; civility being in truth nothing but a care not to show any slighting or contempt of anyone in conversation. What are the most allowed and esteemed ways of expressing this, we have above observed. It is as peculiar and different, in several countries of the world, as their languages; and therefore, if it be rightly considered, rules and discourses made to children about it are as useless and impertinent as it would be now and then to give a rule or two of the Spanish tongue to one that converses only with Englishmen. Be as busy as you please with discourses of civility to your son, such as is his company, such will be his manners. A plowman of your neighborhood that has never been out of his parish, read what lectures you please to him, will be as soon in his language as his carriage a courtier; that is, in neither will be more polite than those he uses to converse with: and therefore, of this no other care can be taken till he be of an age to have a tutor put to him, who must not fail to be a well-bred man. And, in good earnest, if I were to speak my mind freely, so children do nothing out of obstinacy, pride, and ill-nature, 'tis no great matter how they put off their hats or make legs. If you can teach them to love and respect other people, they will, as their age requires it, find ways to express it acceptably to everyone, according to the fashions they have been used to: and as to their motions and carriage of their bodies, a dancing-master, as has been said, when it is fit, will teach them what is most becoming. In the meantime, when they are young, people expect not that children should be overmindful of these ceremonies; carelessness is allowed to that age, and becomes them as well as compliments do grown people: or, at least, if some very nice people will think it a fault, I am sure it is a fault that should be overlooked, and

left to time, a tutor, and conversation to cure. And therefore I think it not worth your while to have your son, as I often see children are, molested or chid about it: but where there is pride or ill-nature appearing in his carriage, there he must be persuaded or shamed out of it.

Though children, when little, should not be much perplexed with rules and ceremonious parts of breeding, yet there is a sort of unmannerliness very apt to grow up with young people, if not early restrained, and that is a forwardness to interrupt others that are speaking, and to stop them with some contradiction. Whether the custom of disputing, and the reputation of parts and learning usually given to it as if it were the only standard and evidence of knowledge, make young men so forward to watch occasions to correct others in their discourse, and not to slip any opportunity of showing their talents: so it is, that I have found scholars most blamed in this point. There cannot be a greater rudeness than to interrupt another in the current of his discourse; for if there be not impertinent folly in answering a man before we know what he will say, yet it is a plain declaration that we are weary to hear him talk any longer, and have a dis-esteem of what he says; which we judging not fit to entertain the company, desire them to give audience to us, who have something to produce worth their attention. This shows a very great disrespect, and cannot but be offensive: and yet this is what almost all interruption constantly carries with it. To which, if there be added, as is usual, a correcting of any mistake, or a contradiction of what has been said, it is a mark of yet greater pride and self-conceitedness, when we thus intrude ourselves for teachers, and take upon us either to set another right in his story, or show the mistakes of his judgment.

I do not say this, that I think there should be no difference of opinions in conversation, or opposition in men's discourses: this would be to take away the greatest advantage of society, and the improvements are to be made by ingenious company; where the light is to be got from the opposite arguings of men of parts, showing the different sides of things and their various aspects and probabilities, would be quite lost, if everyone were obliged to assent to and say after the first speaker. 'Tis not the owning one's dissent from another that I speak against, but the manner of doing it. Young men should be taught not to be forward to interpose their opinions unless asked, or when others have done and are silent; and then only by way of inquiry, not instruction. The positive asserting and the magisterial air should be avoided; and when a general pause of the whole company affords an opportunity, they may modestly put in their question as learners.

This becoming decency will not cloud their parts, or weaken the strength of their reason; but bespeak the more favorable attention, and give what they say the greater advantage. An ill argument, or ordinary observation, thus introduced, with some civil preface of deference and respect to the opinions of others, will procure them more credit and esteem than the sharpest wit, or profoundest science, with a rough, insolent, or noisy management, which always shocks the hearers, leaves an ill opinion of the man, though he get the better of it in the argument.

This therefore should be carefully watched in young people, stopped in the beginning, and the contrary habit introduced in all their conversation. And the rather, because forwardness to talk, frequent interruptions in arguing, and loud wrangling, are too often observable amongst grown people, even of rank, amongst us. The Indians, whom we call barbarous, observe much more decency and civility in their discourses and conversation, giving one another a fair silent hearing till they have quite done; and then answering them calmly, and without noise or passion. And if it be not so in this civilized part of the world, we must impute it to a neglect in education, which has not yet reformed this ancient piece of barbarity amongst us.

Was it not, think you, an entertaining spectacle, to see two ladies of quality accidentally seated on the opposite sides of a room, set round with company, fall into a dispute, and grow so eager in it, that in the heat of the controversy, edging by degrees their chairs forwards, they were in a little time got up close to one another in the middle of the room; where they for a good while managed the dispute as fiercely as two gamecocks in the pit, without minding or taking any notice of the circle, which could not all the while forbear smiling? This I was told by a person of quality, who was present at the combat, and did not omit to reflect upon the indecencies that warmth in dispute often runs people into; which, since custom makes too frequent, education should take the more care of. There is nobody but condemns this in others, though they overlook it in themselves; and many who are sensible of it in themselves, and resolve against it, cannot yet get rid of an ill custom, which neglect in their education has suffered to settle into an habit.

146. What has been above said concerning company would perhaps, if it were well reflected on, give us a larger prospect, and let us see how much farther its influence reaches. 'Tis not the modes of civility alone that are imprinted by conversation: the tincture of company sinks deeper than the outside; and possibly, if a true estimate were made of the morality and religions of the world, we should find that the far greater part of mankind received even those opinions and ceremonies they would die for, rather from the fashions of their countries, and the constant practice of those about them, than from any conviction of their reasons. I mention this only to let you see of what moment I think *company* is to your son in all the parts of his life, and therefore how much that one part is to be weighed and provided for; it being of greater force to work upon him than all you can do besides.

147. You will wonder, perhaps, that I put *learning* last, especially if I tell you I think it the least part. This may seem strange in the mouth of a bookish man; and this making usually the chief, if not only bustle and stir about children, this being almost that alone which is thought on, when people talk of education, makes it the greater paradox. When I consider what ado is made about a little Latin and Greek, how many years are spent in it, and what a noise and business it makes to no purpose, I can hardly forbear thinking that the parents of children still live in fear of the schoolmaster's rod, which they look on as the only instrument of education; as a language or two to be its whole business. How else is it possible that a child should be chained to the oar seven, eight, or ten of the best years of his life, to get a language or two, which, I think, might be had at a great deal cheaper rate of pains and time, and be learned almost in playing?

Forgive me, therefore, if I say I cannot with patience think that a young gentleman should be put into the herd, and be driven with a whip and scourge, as if he were to run the gantlet through the several classes, *ad capiendum ingenii cultum.*[19] What then, say you, would you not have him write and read? Shall he be more ignorant than the clerk of our parish, who takes Hopkins and Sternhold for the best poets in the world, whom yet he makes worse than they are by his ill reading? Not so, not so fast, I beseech you. Reading and writing and learning I allow to be necessary, but yet not the chief business. I imagine you would think him a very foolish fellow that should not value a virtuous or a wise man infinitely before a great scholar. Not but that I think learning a great help to both in well-disposed minds; but yet it must be confessed also that in others not so disposed, it helps them only to be the more foolish or worse men. I say this that when you consider the breeding of your son, and are looking out for a schoolmaster or a tutor, you would not have (as is usual) Latin and logic only in your thoughts. Learning must be had, but in the second place, as subservient only to greater qualities. Seek out somebody that may know how discreetly to frame his manners; place him in hands where you may, as much as possible, secure his innocence, cherish and nurse up the good, and gently correct and weed out any bad inclinations, and settle in him good habits. This is the main point, and this being provided for, learning may be had into the bargain, and that, as I think, at a very easy rate, by methods that may be thought on.

148. When he can talk, 'tis time he should begin to learn to read. But as to this, give me leave here to inculcate again what is very apt to be forgotten, viz., that great care is to be taken that it be never made as a business to him, nor he look on it as a task. We naturally, as I said, even from our cradles, love liberty, and have therefore an aversion to many things for no other reason but because they are enjoined us. I have always had a fancy that learning might be made a play and recreation to children: and that they might be brought to desire to be taught, if it were proposed to them as a thing of honor, credit, delight, and recreation, or as a reward for doing something else; and if they were never chid or corrected for the neglect of it.

[19] To seize hold of culture for his mind.

That which confirms me in this opinion is that amongst the Portuguese, 'tis so much a fashion and emulation amongst their children
to learn to read and write that they cannot hinder them from it: they
will learn it one from another and are as intent on it as if it were
forbidden them. I remember that being at a friend's house, whose
younger son, a child in coats, was not easily brought to his book (being taught to read at home by his mother) I advised to try another
way, than requiring it of him as his duty; we therefore, in a discourse on purpose amongst ourselves, in his hearing but without taking
any notice of him, declared that it was the privilege and advantage of
heirs and elder brothers to be scholars; that this made them fine
gentlemen and beloved by everybody: and that for younger brothers,
'twas a favor to admit them to breeding; to be taught to read and
write was more than came to their share; they might be ignorant
bumpkins and clowns, if they pleased. This so wrought upon the child
that afterwards he desired to be taught; would come himself to his
mother to learn, and would not let his maid be quiet till she heard
him his lesson. I doubt not but some way like this might be taken
with other children; and when their tempers are found, some thoughts
be instilled into them that might set them upon desiring of learning
themselves, and make them seek it as another sort of play or recreation. But then, as I said before, it must never be imposed as a task,
or made a trouble to them. There may be dice and playthings, with the
letters on them to teach children the alphabet by playing; and twenty
other ways may be found, suitable to their particular tempers, to make
this kind of learning a sport to them.

149. Thus children may be cozened into a knowledge of the letters; be taught to read, without perceiving it to be anything but a
sport, and play themselves into that which others are whipped for.
Children should not have anything like work, or serious, laid on them;
neither their minds nor bodies will bear it. It injures their health;
and their being forced and tied down to their books in an age at
enmity with all such restraint, has, I doubt not, been the reason why
a great many have hated books and learning all their lives after. 'Tis
like a surfeit that leaves an aversion behind not to be removed.

150. I have therefore thought that if playthings were fitted to

this purpose, as they are usually to none, contrivances might be made to teach children to read, whilst they thought they were only playing. For example, what if an ivory-ball were made like that of the royal-oak lottery, with thirty-two sides, or one rather of twenty-four or twenty-five sides; and upon several of those sides pasted on an A, upon several others B, on others C, and on others D? I would have you begin with but these four letters, or perhaps only two at first; and when he is perfect in them, then add another; and so on till each side having one letter, there be on it the whole alphabet. This I would have others play with before him, it being as good a sort of play to lay a stake who shall first throw an A or B, as who upon dice shall throw six or seven. This being a play amongst you, tempt him not to it, lest you make it business; for I would not have him understand 'tis anything but a play of older people, and I doubt not but he will take to it of himself. And that he may have the more reason to think it is a play that he is sometimes in favor admitted to, when the play is done the ball should be laid up safe out of his reach, that so it may not, by his having it in his keeping at any time, grow stale to him.

151. To keep up his eagerness to it, let him think it a game belonging to those above him: and when, by this means, he knows the letters, by changing them into syllables, he may learn to read, without knowing how he did so, and never have any chiding or trouble about it, nor fall out with books because of the hard usage and vexation they have caused him. Children, if you observe them, take abundance of pains to learn several games, which, if they should be enjoined them, they would abhor as a task and business. I know a person of great quality (more yet to be honored for his learning and virtue than for his rank and high place) who by pasting on the six vowels (for in our language Y is one) on the six sides of a die, and the remaining eighteen consonants on the sides of three other dice, has made this a play for his children that he shall win who, at one cast, throws most words on these four dice; whereby his eldest son, yet in coats, has played himself into spelling, with great eagerness, and without once having been chid for it or forced to it.

152. I have seen little girls exercise whole hours together and take abundance of pains to be expert at dibstones, as they call it. Whilst

I have been looking on, I have thought it wanted only some good contrivance to make them employ all that industry about something that might be more useful to them; and methinks 'tis only the fault and negligence of elder people that it is not so. Children are much less apt to be idle than men; and men are to be blamed if some part of that busy humor be not turned to useful things; which might be made usually as delightful to them as those they are employed in, if men would be but half so forward to lead the way as these little apes would be to follow. I imagine some wise Portuguese heretofore began this fashion amongst the children of his country, where I have been told, as I said, it is impossible to hinder the children from learning to read and write: and in some parts of France they teach one another to sing and dance from the cradle.

153. The letters pasted upon the sides of the dice, or polygon, were best to be of the size of those of the folio Bible, to begin with, and none of them capital letters; when once he can read what is printed in such letters, he will not long be ignorant of the great ones; and in the beginning he should not be perplexed with variety. With this die also, you might have a play just like the royal oak, which would be another variety, and play for cherries or apples, etc.

154. Besides these, twenty other plays might be invented depending on letters, which those who like this way may easily contrive and get made to this use if they will. But the four dice above-mentioned I think so easy and useful that it will be hard to find any better, and there will be scarce need of any other.

155. Thus much for learning to read, which let him never be driven to, nor chid for; cheat him into it if you can, but make it not a business for him. 'Tis better it be a year later before he can read, than that he should this way get an aversion to learning. If you have any contest with him, let it be in matters of moment, of truth, and good nature; but lay no task on him about A B C. Use your skill to make his will supple and pliant to reason; teach him to love credit and commendation, to abhor being thought ill or meanly of, especially by you and his mother, and then the rest will come all easily. But I think if you will do that, you must not shackle and tie him up with rules about indifferent matters, or rebuke him for every little

fault, or perhaps some that to others would seem great ones; but of this I have said enough already.

156. When by these gentle ways he begins to read, some easy pleasant book, suited to his capacity, should be put into his hands, wherein the entertainment that he finds might draw him on and reward his pains in reading, and yet not such as should fill his head with perfectly useless trumpery, or lay the principles of vice and folly. To this purpose, I think *Aesop's Fables* the best, which, being stories apt to delight and entertain a child, may yet afford useful reflections to a grown man; and if his memory retain them all his life after, he will not repent to find them there, amongst his manly thoughts and serious business. If his Aesop has pictures in it, it will entertain him much the better, and encourage him to read, when it carries the increase of knowledge with it: For such visible objects children hear talked of in vain and without any satisfaction whilst they have no ideas of them; those ideas being not to be had from sounds, but from the things themselves or their pictures. And therefore I think as soon as he begins to spell, as many pictures of animals should be got him as can be found, with the printed names to them, which at the same time will invite him to read and afford him matter of inquiry and knowledge. *Reynard the Fox* is another book I think may be made use of to the same purpose. And if those about him will talk to him often about the stories he has read, and hear him tell them, it will, besides other advantages, add encouragement and delight to his reading, when he finds there is some use and pleasure in it. These baits seem wholly neglected in the ordinary method; and 'tis usually long before learners find any use or pleasure in reading, which may tempt them to it, and so take books only for fashionable amusements, or impertinent troubles, good for nothing.

157. The Lord's Prayer, the Creeds, and Ten Commandments, 'tis necessary he should learn perfectly by heart; but, I think, not by reading them himself in his primer, but by somebody's repeating them to him, even before he can read. But learning by heart, and learning to read, should not I think be mixed, and so one made to clog the other. But his learning to read should be made as little trouble or business to him as might be.

What other books there are in English of the kind of those above-mentioned, fit to engage the liking of children and tempt them to *read,* I do not know, but am apt to think that children being generally delivered over to the method of schools, where the fear of the rod is to enforce, and not any pleasure of the employment to invite them to learn, this sort of useful books, amongst the number of silly ones that are of all sorts, have yet had the fate to be neglected; and nothing that I know has been considered of this kind out of the ordinary road of the horn-book, primer, psalter, Testament, and Bible.

158. As for the Bible, which children are usually employed in to exercise and improve their talent in reading, I think the promiscuous reading of it through by chapters as they lie in order is so far from being of any advantage to children, either for the perfecting their reading or principling their religion, that perhaps a worse could not be found. For what pleasure or encouragement can it be to a child to exercise himself in reading those parts of a book where he understands nothing? And how little are the law of Moses, the song of Solomon, the prophecies in the Old, and the Epistles and Apocalypse in the New Testament, suited to a child's capacity! And though the history of the Evangelists and the Acts have something easier, yet, taken altogether, it is very disproportional to the understanding of childhood. I grant that the principles of religion are to be drawn from thence, and in the words of the Scripture; yet none should be proposed to a child, but such as are suited to a child's capacity and notions. But 'tis far from this to read through *the whole Bible,* and that for reading's sake. And what an odd jumble of thoughts must a child have in his head, if he have any at all, such as he should have concerning religion, who in his tender age reads all the parts of the Bible indifferently as the word of God, without any other distinction! I am apt to think that this, in some men, has been the very reason why they never had clear and distinct thoughts of it all their lifetime.

159. And now I am by chance fallen on this subject, give me leave to say that there are some parts of the Scripture which may be proper to be put into the hands of a child to engage him to read; such as are the story of Joseph and his brethren, of David and Go-

liath, of David and Jonathan, etc. and others that he should be made to read for his instruction, as that, *What you would have others do unto you, do you the same unto them;* and such other easy and plain moral rules, which being fitly chosen, might often be made use of, both for reading and instruction together; and so often read till they are throughly fixed in the memory; and then afterwards, as he grows ripe for them, may in their turns on fit occasions be inculcated as the standing and sacred rules of his life and actions. But the reading of the whole Scripture indifferently is what I think very inconvenient for children, till after having been made acquainted with the plainest fundamental parts of it, they have got some kind of general view of what they ought principally to believe and practice; which yet, I think, they ought to receive in the very words of the Scripture, and not in such as men prepossessed by systems and analogies are apt in this case to make use of and force upon them. Dr. Worthington, to avoid this, has made a catechism which has all its answers in the precise words of the Scripture; a thing of good example, and such a sound form of words as no Christian can except against as not fit for his child to learn. Of this, as soon as he can say the Lord's Prayer, Creed, the Ten Commandments, by heart, it may be fit for him to learn a question every day, or every week, as his understanding is able to receive and his memory to retain them. And when he has this catechism perfectly by heart, so as readily and roundly to answer to any question in the whole book, it may be convenient to lodge in his mind the remaining moral rules scattered up and down in the Bible, as the best exercise of his memory, and that which may be always a rule to him, ready at hand, in the whole conduct of his life.

160. When he can read English well, it will be seasonable to enter him in writing: and here the first thing should be taught him is to hold his pen right; and this he should be perfect in before he should be suffered to put it to paper: for not only children but anybody else that would do anything well, should never be put upon too much of it at once, or be set to perfect themselves in two parts of an action at the same time, if they can possibly be separated. I think the Italian way of holding the pen between the thumb and the fore-

finger alone, may be best; but in this you may consult some good writing-master, or any other person who writes well and quick. When he has learned to hold his pen right, in the next place he should learn how to lay his paper, and place his arm and body to it. These practices being got over, the way to teach him to write without much trouble is to get a plate graved with the characters of such a hand as you like best: but you must remember to have them a pretty deal bigger than he should ordinarily write; for everyone naturally comes by degrees to write a less hand than he at first was taught, but never a bigger. Such a plate being graved, let several sheets of good writing-paper be printed off with red ink, which he has nothing to do but go over with a good pen filled with black ink, which will quickly bring his hand to the formation of those characters, being at first showed where to begin, and how to form every letter. And when he can do that well, he must then exercise on fair paper; and so may easily be brought to write the hand you desire.

161. When he can write well and quick, I think it may be convenient not only to continue the exercise of his hand in writing, but also to improve the use of it further in drawing; a thing very useful to a gentleman in several occasions; but especially if he travel, as that which helps a man often to express, in a few lines well put together, what a whole sheet of paper in writing would not be able to represent and make intelligible. How many buildings may a man see, how many machines and habits meet with, the ideas whereof would be easily retained and communicated by a little skill in drawing; which being committed to words, are in danger to be lost, or at best but ill retained in the most exact descriptions. I do not mean that I would have your son a perfect painter; to be that to any tolerable degree will require more time than a young gentleman can spare from his other improvements of greater moment. But so much insight into perspective and skill in drawing as will enable him to represent tolerably on paper anything he sees, except faces, may, I think, be got in a little time, especially if he have a genius to it; but where that is wanting, unless it be in the things absolutely necessary, it is better to let him pass them by quietly than to vex him about them to no pur-

pose: and therefore in this, as in all other things not absolutely necessary, the rule holds, *nil invita Minerva*.[20]

1. Shorthand, an art, as I have been told, known only in England, may perhaps be thought worth the learning, both for dispatch in what men write for their own memory, and concealment of what they would not have lie open to every eye. For he that has once learned any sort of character may easily vary it to his own private use or fancy, and with more contraction suit it to the business he would employ it in. Mr. Rich's, the best contrived of any I have seen, may, as I think, by one who knows and considers grammar well, be made much easier and shorter. But for the learning this compendious way of writing, there will be no need hastily to look out a master; it will be early enough when any convenient opportunity offers itself at any time, after his hand is well settled in fair and quick writing. For boys have but little use of shorthand, and should by no means practice it till they write perfectly well, and have thoroughly fixed the habit of doing so.

162. As soon as he can speak English, 'tis time for him to learn some other language. This nobody doubts of, when French is proposed. And the reason is, because people are accustomed to the right way of teaching that language, which is by talking it into children in constant conversation, and not by grammatical rules. The Latin tongue would easily be taught the same way, if his tutor, being constantly with him, would talk nothing else to him, and make him answer still in the same language. But because French is a living language, and to be used more in speaking, that should be first learned, that the yet pliant organs of speech might be accustomed to a due formation of those sounds, and he get the habit of pronouncing French well, which is the harder to be done the longer it is delayed.

163. When he can speak and read French well, which in this method is usually in a year or two, he should proceed to Latin, which 'tis a wonder parents, when they have had the experiment in French, should not think ought to be learned the same way, by talking and reading. Only care is to be taken whilst he is learning these foreign

[20] Nothing against Minerva's will; or, freely translated, a mind should not be forced.

languages, by speaking and reading nothing else with his tutor, that he do not forget to read English, which may be preserved by his mother or somebody else hearing him read some chosen parts of the Scripture or other English book every day.

164. Latin I look upon as absolutely necessary to a gentleman; and indeed custom, which prevails over everything, has made it so much a part of education that even those children are whipped to it, and made spend many hours of their precious time uneasily in Latin, who after they are once gone from school, are never to have more to do with it as long as they live. Can there be anything more ridiculous than that a father should waste his own money and his son's time in setting him to learn the Roman language, when at the same time he designs him for a trade, wherein he having no use of Latin, fails not to forget that little which he brought from school, and which 'tis ten to one he abhors for the ill usage it procured him? Could it be believed, unless we had everywhere amongst us examples of it, that a child should be forced to learn the rudiments of a language which he is never to use in the course of life that he is designed to, and neglect all the while the writing a good hand and casting accounts, which are of great advantage in all conditions of life, and to most trades indispensably necessary? But though these qualifications, requisite to trade and commerce and the business of the world, are seldom or never to be had at grammar-schools, yet thither not only gentlemen send their younger sons, intended for trades, but even tradesmen and farmers fail not to send their children, though they have neither intention nor ability to make them scholars. If you ask them why they do this, they think it as strange a question as if you should ask them why they go to church. Custom serves for reason, and has, to those who take it for reason, so consecrated this method, that it is almost religiously observed by them, and they stick to it, as if their children had scarce an orthodox education unless they learned Lilly's grammar.

165. But how necessary soever Latin be to some, and is thought to be to others to whom it is of no manner of use and service; yet the ordinary way of learning it in a grammar-school is that which having had thoughts about I cannot be forward to encourage. The reasons against it are so evident and cogent that they have prevailed with some

intelligent persons to quit the ordinary road, not without success, though the method made use of was not exactly what I imagine the easiest, and in short is this. To trouble the child with no grammar at all, but to have Latin, as English has been, without the perplexity of rules, talked into him; for if you will consider it, Latin is no more unknown to a child, when he comes into the world, than English: and yet he learns English without master, rule, or grammar; and so might he Latin too, as Tully did, if he had somebody always to talk to him in this language. And when we so often see a Frenchwoman teach an English girl to speak and read French perfectly in a year or two, without any rule of grammar, or anything else but prattling to her, I cannot but wonder how gentlemen have overseen this way for their sons, and thought them more dull or incapable than their daughters.

166. If therefore a man could be got, who himself speaking good Latin, would always be about your son, talk constantly to him, and suffer him to speak or read nothing else, this would be the true and genuine way, and that which I would propose, not only as the easiest and best, wherein a child might, without pains or chiding, get a language, which others are wont to be whipped for at school six or seven years together: but also as that, wherein at the same time he might have his mind and manners formed, and he be instructed to boot in several sciences, such as are a good part of geography, astronomy, chronology, anatomy, besides some parts of history, and all other parts of knowledge of things that fall under the senses and require little more than memory. For there, if we would take the true way, our knowledge should begin, and in those things be laid the foundation; and not in the abstract notions of logic and metaphysics, which are fitter to amuse than inform the understanding in its first setting out towards knowledge. When young men have had their heads employed a while in those abstract speculations without finding the success and improvement, or that use of them, which they expected, they are apt to have mean thoughts either of learning or themselves; they are tempted to quit their studies, and throw away their books as containing nothing but hard words and empty sounds; or else, to conclude that if there be any real knowledge in them, they

themselves have not understandings capable of it. That this is so, perhaps I could assure you upon my own experience. Amongst other
things to be learned by a young gentleman in this method, whilst
others of his age are wholly taken up with Latin and languages, I may
also set down geometry for one; having known a young gentleman,
bred something after this way, able to demonstrate several propositions in Euclid before he was thirteen.

167. But if such a man cannot be got, who speaks good Latin, and
being able to instruct your son in all these parts of knowledge, will
undertake it by this method, the next best is to have him taught as
near this way as may be, which is by taking some easy and pleasant
book, such as *Aesop's Fables,* and writing the English translation
(made as literal as it can be) in one line, and the Latin words which
answer each of them, just over it in another. These let him read every
day over and over again, till he perfectly understands the Latin; and
then go on to another fable, till he be also perfect in that, not omitting
what he is already perfect in, but sometimes reviewing that, to keep
it in his memory. And when he comes to write, let these be set him
for copies, which with the exercise of his hand will also advance him
to Latin. This being a more imperfect way than by talking Latin unto
him; the formation of the verbs first, and afterwards the declensions
of the nouns and pronouns perfectly learned by heart, may facilitate his
acquaintance with the genius and manner of the Latin tongue, which
varies the signification of verbs and nouns, not as the modern languages do by particles prefixed, but by changing the last syllables.
More than this of grammar, I think he need not have, till he can
read himself *Sanctii Minerva,* with Scioppius' and Perizonius' notes.

In teaching of children, this too, I think, is to be observed, that in
most cases where they stick, they are not to be farther puzzled by
putting them upon finding it out themselves, as by asking such questions as these, viz., which is the nominative case, in the sentence they
are to construe; or demanding what *aufero* signifies, to lead them to
the knowledge what *abstlere* signifies, etc., when they cannot readily
tell. This wastes time only in disturbing them; for whilst they are
learning, and apply themselves with attention, they are to be kept in
good humor, and everything made easy to them, and as pleasant as

possible. Therefore, wherever they are at a stand, and are willing to go forwards, help them presently over the difficulty, without any rebuke or chiding, remembering, that where harsher ways are taken, they are the effect only of pride and peevishness in the teacher, who expects children should instantly be masters of as much as he knows; whereas he should rather consider that his business is to settle in them habits, not angrily to inculcate rules, which serve for little in the conduct of our lives; at least are of no use to children, who forget them as soon as given. In sciences where their reason is to be exercised, I will not deny but this method may sometimes be varied, and difficulties proposed on purpose to excite industry and accustom the mind to employ its own strength and sagacity in reasoning. But yet, I guess, this is not to be done to children, whilst very young, nor at their entrance upon any sort of knowledge. Then everything of itself is difficult, and the great use and skill of a teacher is to make all as easy as he can, but particularly in learning of languages there is least occasion for posing of children. For languages being to be learned by rote, custom, and memory, are then spoken in greatest perfection, when all rules of grammar are utterly forgotten. I grant the grammar of a language is sometimes very carefully to be studied, but it is not to be studied but by a grown man, when he applies himself to the understanding of any language critically, which is seldom the business of any but professed scholars. This I think will be agreed to, that if a gentleman is to study any language, it ought to be that of his own country, that he may understand the language which he has constant use of with the utmost accuracy.

There is yet a further reason why masters and teachers should raise no difficulties to their scholars, but on the contrary should smooth their way and readily help them forwards, where they find them stop. Children's minds are narrow and weak, and usually susceptible but of one thought at once. Whatever is in a child's head, fills it for the time, especially if set on with any passion. It should therefore be the skill and art of the teacher to clear their heads of all other thoughts whilst they are learning of anything, the better to make room for what he would instill into them, that it may be received with attention and application, without which it leaves no impression. The natural temper of children disposes their minds to wander. Novelty alone takes them; whatever that presents, they are presently eager to have a taste of, and are as soon satiated with it. They quickly grow weary of the same thing, and so have almost their whole delight in change and variety. It is a contradiction to the natural state of childhood for them to fix their fleeting thoughts. Whether this be owing to the temper of their brains, or the quickness or instability of their animal spirits, over which the mind has not yet got a full command, this is visible, that it is a pain to children to keep their thoughts steady to anything. A lasting continued attention is one of the hardest tasks can be imposed on them; and therefore, he that requires their application, should endeavor to make what he proposes as grateful and agreeable as possible; at least he ought to take care not to join any displeasing or frightful idea with it. If they come not to their books with some kind of liking and relish, 'tis no wonder their thoughts should be perpetually shifting from what disgusts them; and seek better entertainment in more pleasing objects, after which they will unavoidably be gadding.

'Tis, I know, the usual method of tutors to endeavor to procure attention in their scholars, and to fix their minds to the business in hand by rebukes and corrections, if they find them ever so little wandering. But such treatment is sure to produce the quite contrary effect. Passionate words or blows from the tutor fill the child's mind with terror and affrightment, which immediately takes it wholly up and leaves no room for other impressions. I believe there is nobody that reads this, but may recollect what disorder hasty or imperious words from his parents or teachers have caused in his thoughts; how for the time it has turned his brains, so that he scarce knew what was said by or to him. He presently lost the sight of what he was upon, his mind was filled with disorder and confusion, and in that state was no longer capable of attention to anything else.

'Tis true, parents and governors ought to settle and establish their authority by an awe over the minds of those under their tuition, and to rule them by that; but when they have got an ascendant over them, they should use it with great moderation, and not make themselves such scarecrows that their scholars should always tremble in their sight. Such an austerity may make their government easy to themselves, but of very little use to their pupils. 'Tis impossible children should learn anything whilst their thoughts are possessed and disturbed with any passion, especially fear, which makes the strongest impression on their yet tender and weak spirits. Keep the mind in an easy calm temper, when you would have it receive your instructions or any increase of knowledge. 'Tis as impossible to draw fair and regular characters on a trembling mind as on a shaking paper.

The great skill of a teacher is to get and keep the attention of his scholar; whilst he has that, he is sure to advance as fast as the learner's abilities will carry him; and without that, all his bustle and pother will be to little or no purpose. To attain this, he should make the child comprehend, as much as may be, the usefulness of what he teaches him, and let him see, by what he has learned, that he can do something which he could not do before; something which gives him some power and real advantage above others who are ignorant of it. To this he should add sweetness in all his instructions, and by a certain tenderness in his whole carriage make the child sensible that he loves him and designs nothing but his good, the only way to beget love in the child, which will make him hearken to his lessons, and relish what he teaches him.

Nothing but obstinacy should meet with any imperiousness or rough usage. All other faults should be corrected with a gentle hand; and kind engaging words will work better and more effectually upon a willing mind, and even prevent a good deal of that perverseness which rough and imperious usage often produces in well disposed and generous minds. 'Tis true, obstinacy and willful neglects must be mastered, even though it cost blows to do it, but I am apt to think perverseness in the pupils is often the effect of frowardness in the tutor; and that most children would seldom have deserved blows, if needless and misapplied roughness had not taught them ill-nature, and given them an aversion for their teacher and all that comes from him.

Inadvertency, forgetfulness, unsteadiness, and wandering of thought, are the natural faults of childhood; and therefore, where they are not observed to be willful, are to be mentioned softly, and gained upon by time. If every slip of this kind produces anger and rating, the occasions of rebuke and corrections will return so often that the tutor will be a constant terror and uneasiness to his pupils. Which one thing is enough to hinder their profiting by his lessons, and to defeat all his methods of instruction.

Let the awe he has got upon their minds be so tempered with the constant marks of tenderness and good will that affection may spur them to their duty, and make them find a pleasure in complying with his dictates. This will bring them with satisfaction to their tutor; make them hearken to him, as to one who is their friend, that cherishes them, and takes pains for their good. This will keep their thoughts easy and free whilst they are with him, the only temper wherein the mind is capable of receiving new informations, and of admitting into itself those impressions, which, if not taken and retained, all that they and their teachers do together is lost labor; there is much uneasiness and little learning.

168. When by this way of interlining Latin and English one with another, he has got a moderate knowledge of the Latin tongue, he may then be advanced a little farther to the reading of some other easy Latin book, such as Justin or Eutropius; and to make the reading and understanding of it the less tedious and difficult to him, let him help himself if he pleases with the English translation. Nor let the objection that he will then know it only by rote fright anyone. This, when well considered, is not of any moment against, but plainly for this way of learning a language. For languages are only to be learned by rote; and a man who does not speak English or Latin perfectly by rote, so that having thought of the thing he would speak of, his tongue of course, without thought of rule or grammar, falls into the proper expression and idiom of that language, does not speak it well, nor is master of it. And I would fain have anyone name to me that tongue that anyone can learn, or speak as he should do, by the rules of grammar. Languages were made not by rules or art, but by accident and the common use of the people. And he that will speak them well has no other rule but that; nor anything to trust to but his memory, and the habit of speaking after the fashion learned from those that are allowed to speak properly, which in other words is only to speak by rote.

It will possibly be asked here, is grammar then of no use? And have those who have taken so much pains in reducing several languages to rules and observations, who have writ so much about declensions and conjugations, about concords and syntaxis, lost their labor, and been learned to no purpose? I say not so; grammar has its place too. But this I think I may say, there is more stir a great deal made with it than there needs, and those are tormented about it, to whom it does not at all belong; I mean children, at the age wherein they are usually perplexed with it in grammar-schools.

There is nothing more evident than that languages learned by rote serve well enough for the common affairs of life and ordinary commerce. Nay, persons of quality of the softer sex, and such of them as have spent their time in well-bred company, show us that this plain natural way, without the least study or knowledge of grammar, can carry them to a great degree of elegance and politeness in their language: and there are ladies who, without knowing what tenses and participles, adverbs and prepositions are, speak as properly and as correctly (they might take it for an ill compliment if I said as any country schoolmaster) as most gentlemen who have been bred up in the ordinary methods of grammar-schools. Grammar, therefore, we see may be spared in some cases. The question then will be, to whom should it be taught, and when? To this I answer:

1. Men learn languages for the ordinary intercourse of society and communication of thoughts in common life, without any farther design in the use of them. And for this purpose, the original way of learning a language by conversation not only serves well enough, but is to be preferred as the most expedite, proper, and natural. Therefore, to this use of language one may answer that grammar is not necessary. This so many of my readers must be forced to allow, as understand what I here say, and who conversing with others, understand them without having ever been taught the grammar of the English tongue. Which I suppose is the case of incomparably the greatest part of English men, of whom I have never yet known anyone who learned his mother-tongue by rules.

2. Others there are, the greatest part of whose business in this world is to be done with their tongues and with their pens; and to these it is convenient, if not necessary, that they should speak properly

and correctly, whereby they may let their thoughts into other men's minds the more easily, and with the greater impression. Upon this account it is that any sort of speaking, so as will make him be understood, is not thought enough for a gentleman. He ought to study grammar amongst the other helps of speaking well, but it must be the grammar of his own tongue, of the language he uses, that he may understand his own country speech nicely, and speak it properly, without shocking the ears of those it is addressed to, with solecisms and offensive irregularities. And to this purpose grammar is necessary; but it is the grammar only of their own proper tongues, and to those only who would take pains in cultivating their language, and in perfecting their styles. Whether all gentlemen should not do this, I leave to be considered, since the want of propriety and grammatical exactness is thought very misbecoming one of that rank, and usually draws on one guilty of such faults the censure of having had a lower breeding and worse company than suits with his quality. If this be so, as I suppose it is, it will be matter of wonder why young gentlemen are forced to learn the grammars of foreign and dead languages, and are never once told of the grammar of their own tongues, they do not so much as know there is any such thing, much less is it made their business to be instructed in it. Nor is their own language ever proposed to them as worthy their care and cultivating, though they have daily use of it, and are not seldom, in the future course of their lives, judged of by their handsome or awkward way of expressing themselves in it. Whereas the languages whose grammars they have been so much employed in are such as probably they shall scarce ever speak or write; or if, upon occasion, this should happen, they should be excused for the mistakes and faults they make in it. Would not a Chinese, who took notice of this way of breeding, be apt to imagine that all our young gentlemen were designed to be teachers and professors of the dead languages of foreign countries, and not to be men of business in their own?

3. There is a third sort of men who apply themselves to two or three foreign, dead, and (which amongst us are called the) learned languages, make them their study, and pique themselves upon their skill in them. No doubt, those who propose to themselves the learn-

ing of any language with this view, and would be critically exact in it, ought carefully to study the grammar of it. I would not be mistaken here, as if this were to undervalue Greek and Latin. I grant these are languages of great use and excellency, and a man can have no place among the learned in this part of the world, who is a stranger to them. But the knowledge a gentleman would ordinarily draw for his use out of the Roman and Greek writers, I think he may attain without studying the grammars of those tongues, and by bare reading may come to understand them sufficiently for all his purposes. How much farther he shall at any time be concerned to look into the grammar and critical niceties of either of these tongues, he himself will be able to determine when he comes to propose to himself the study of anything that shall require it. Which brings me to the other part of the inquiry, viz., When grammar should be taught?

To which, upon the premised grounds, the answer is obvious: That if grammar ought to be taught at any time, it must be to one that can speak the language already; how else can he be taught the grammar of it? This at least is evident from the practice of the wise and learned nations amongst the ancients. They made it a part of education to cultivate their own, not foreign tongues. The Greeks counted all other nations barbarous, and had a contempt for their languages. And though the Greek learning grew in credit amongst the Romans, towards the end of their commonwealth, yet it was the Roman tongue that was made the study of their youth: their own language they were to make use of, and therefore it was their own language they were instructed and exercised in.

But, more particularly to determine the proper season for grammar, I do not see how it can reasonably be made anyone's study, but as an introduction to rhetoric; when it is thought time to put anyone upon the care of polishing his tongue, and of speaking better than the illiterate, then is the time for him to be instructed in the rules of grammar, and not before. For grammar being to teach men not to speak, but to speak correctly and according to the exact rules of the tongue, which is one part of elegance, there is little use of the one to him that has no need of the other; where rhetoric is not necessary, grammar may be spared. I know not why anyone should waste his time and beat his head about the Latin grammar, who does not intend to be a critic, or make speeches and write dispatches in it. When anyone finds in himself a necessity or disposition to study any foreign language to the bottom, and to be nicely exact in the knowledge of it, it will be time enough to take a grammatical survey of it. If his use of it be only to understand some books writ in it, without a critical knowledge of the tongue itself, reading alone, as I have said, will attain this end, without charging the mind with the multiplied rules and intricacies of grammar.

169. For the exercise of his writing, let him sometimes translate Latin into English; but the learning of Latin being nothing but the learning of words, a very unpleasant business both to young and old, join as much other real knowledge with it as you can, beginning still with that which lies most obvious to the senses, such as is the knowledge of minerals, plants and animals, and particularly timber and fruit-trees, their parts, and ways of propagation, wherein a great deal may be taught a child which will not be useless to the man; but more especially geography, astronomy, and anatomy. But whatever you are teaching him, have a care still that you do not clog him with too much at once, or make anything his business but downright virtue, or reprove him for anything but vice, or some apparent tendency to it.

170. But if, after all, his fate be to go to school to get the Latin tongue, 'twill be in vain to talk to you concerning the method I think best to be observed in schools; you must submit to that you find there, not expect to have it changed for your son; but yet by all means obtain, if you can, that he be not employed in making Latin themes and declamations, and least of all, verses of any kind. You may insist on it, if it will do any good, that you have no design to make him either a Latin orator or poet, but barely would have him understand perfectly a Latin author; and that you observe those who teach any of the modern languages, and that with success, never amuse their scholars to make speeches or verses either in French or Italian, their business being language barely, and not invention.

171. But to tell you a little more fully why I would not have him exercised in making of themes and verses. 1. As to themes, they have, I confess, the pretense of something useful, which is to teach people

to speak handsomely and well on any subject; which, if it could be attained this way, I own would be a great advantage, there being nothing more becoming a gentleman, or more useful in all the occurrences of life, than to be able on any occasion to speak well and to the purpose. But this I say, that the making of themes, as is usual at schools, helps not one jot towards it, for do but consider what it is, in making a theme, that a young lad is employed about. It is to make a speech on some Latin saying, as *Omnia vincit amor;* or *Non licet in bello bis peccare,* etc.[21] And here the poor lad, who wants knowledge of those things he is to speak of, which is to be had only from time and observation, must set his invention on the rack, to say something where he knows nothing; which is a sort of Egyptian tyranny, to bid them make bricks who have not yet any of the materials. And therefore it is usual in such cases for the poor children to go to those of higher forms with this petition, *Pray give me a little sense;* which, whether it be more reasonable or more ridiculous, it is not easy to determine. Before a man can be in any capacity to speak on any subject, 'tis necessary he be acquainted with it; or else it is as foolish to set him to discourse of it as to set a blind man to talk of colors, or a deaf man of music. And would you not think him a little cracked, who would require another to make an argument on a moot point, who understands nothing of our laws? And what, I pray, do schoolboys understand concerning those matters which are used to be proposed to them in their themes as subjects to discourse on, to whet and exercise their fancies?

172. In the next place, consider the language that their themes are made in: 'tis Latin, a language foreign in their country and long since dead everywhere; a language which your son, 'tis a thousand to one, shall never have an occasion once to make a speech in as long as he lives after he comes to be a man; and a language wherein the manner of expressing oneself is so far different from ours, that to be perfect in that would very little improve the purity and facility of his English style. Besides that, there is now so little room or use for set speeches in our own language in any part of our English business, that I can

[21] Love conquers all; and, A man may not make two mistakes in war.

see no pretense for this sort of exercise in our schools, unless it can be supposed that the making of set Latin speeches should be the way to teach men to speak well in English *extempore*. The way to that, I should think rather to be this: that there should be proposed to young gentlemen rational and useful questions, suited to their age and capacities, and on subjects not wholly unknown to them nor out of their way: such as these, when they are ripe for exercises of this nature, they should *extempore*, or after a little meditation upon the spot, speak to, without penning of anything: for I ask, if we will examine the effects of this way of learning to speak well, who speak best in any business, when occasion calls them to it upon any debate, either those who have accustomed themselves to compose and write down beforehand what they would say, or those, who thinking only of the matter, to understand that as well as they can, use themselves only to speak *extempore*? And he that shall judge by this will be little apt to think that the accustoming him to studied speeches and set compositions is the way to fit a young gentleman for business.

173. But perhaps we shall be told, 'tis to improve and perfect them in the Latin tongue. 'Tis true, that is their proper business at school; but the making of themes is not the way to it. That perplexes their brains about invention of things to be said, not about the signification of words to be learned; and when they are making a theme, 'tis thoughts they search and sweat for, and not language. But the learning and mastery of a tongue being uneasy and unpleasant enough in itself, should not be cumbered with any other difficulties, as is done in this way of proceeding. In fine, it boys' invention is to be quickened by such exercise, let them make themes in English, where they have facility and a command of words, and will better see what kind of thoughts they have, when put into their own language. And if the Latin tongue is to be learned, let it be done the easiest way, without toiling and disgusting the mind by so uneasy an employment as that of making speeches joined to it.

174. If these may be any reasons against children's making Latin themes at school, I have much more to say, and of more weight, against their making verses; verses of any sort: for if he has no genius to poetry, 'tis the most unreasonable thing in the world to torment a

child and waste his time about that which can never succeed; and
if he have a poetic vein, 'tis to me the strangest thing in the world
that the father should desire or suffer it to be cherished or improved.
Methinks the parents should labor to have it stifled and suppressed as
much as may be; and I know not what reason a father can have to
wish his son a poet, who does not desire to have him bid defiance to
all other callings and business; which is not yet the worst of the case;
for if he proves a successful rhymer, and gets once the reputation
of a wit, I desire it may be considered what company and places he
is like to spend his time in, nay, and estate too; for it is very seldom
seen that anyone discovers mines of gold or silver in Parnassus. 'Tis
a pleasant air, but a barren soil; and there are very few instances of
those who have added to their patrimony by anything they have reaped
from thence. Poetry and gaming, which usually go together, are alike
in this too, that they seldom bring any advantage but to those who
have nothing else to live on. Men of estates almost constantly go
away losers; and 'tis well if they escape at a cheaper rate than their
whole estates, or the greatest part of them. If therefore you would
not have your son the fiddle to every jovial company, without whom
the sparks could not relish their wine or know how to pass an afternoon idly; if you would not have him to waste his time and estate
to divert others, and contemn the dirty acres left him by his ancestors,
I do not think you will much care he should be a poet, or that his
schoolmaster should enter him in versifying. But yet, if anyone will
think poetry a desirable quality in his son, and that the study of it
would raise his fancy and parts, he must needs yet confess, that to
that end reading the excellent Greek and Roman poets is of more use
than making bad verses of his own, in a language that is not his own.
And he whose design it is to excel in English poetry, would not, I
guess, think the way to it were to make his first essays in Latin verses.

175. Another thing very ordinary in the vulgar method of grammar-schools there is, of which I see no use at all, unless it be to balk
young lads in the way to learning languages, which, in my opinion,
should be made as easy and pleasant as may be; and that which was
painful in it, as much as possible quite removed. That which I mean,
and here complain of, is their being forced to learn by heart great

parcels of the authors which are taught them; wherein I can discover no advantage at all, especially to the business they are upon. Languages are to be learned only by reading and talking, and not by scraps of authors got by heart; which when a man's head is stuffed with, he has got the just furniture of a pedant, and 'tis the ready way to make him one; than which there is nothing less becoming a gentleman. For what can be more ridiculous than to mix the rich and handsome thoughts and sayings of others with a deal of poor stuff of his own; which is thereby the more exposed, and has no other grace in it, nor will otherwise recommend the speaker than a threadbare russet coat would, that was set off with large patches of scarlet and glittering brocade. Indeed, where a passage comes in the way, whose matter is worth remembrance, and the expression of it very close and excellent (as there are many such in the ancient authors), it may not be amiss to lodge it in the mind of young scholars, and with such admirable strokes of those great masters sometimes exercise the memories of schoolboys. But their learning of their lessons by heart, as they happen to fall out in their books, without choice or distinction, I know not what it serves for, but to misspend their time and pains, and give them a disgust and aversion to their books, wherein they find nothing but useless trouble.

176. I hear it is said that children should be employed in getting things by heart, to exercise and improve their memories. I could wish this were said with as much authority of reason as it is with forwardness of assurance, and that this practice were established upon good observation more than old custom: for it is evident that strength of memory is owing to a happy constitution, and not to any habitual improvement got by exercise. 'Tis true what the mind is intent upon, and, for fear of letting it slip, often imprints afresh on itself by frequent reflection, that it is apt to retain, but still according to its own natural strength of retention. An impression made on beeswax or lead will not last so long as on brass or steel. Indeed, if it be renewed often, it may last the longer; but every new reflecting on it is a new impression; and 'tis from thence one is to reckon, if one would know how long the mind retains it. But the learning pages of Latin by heart no more fits the memory for retention of anything else than the graving

of one sentence in lead makes it the more capable of retaining firmly any other characters. If such a sort of exercise of the memory were able to give it strength and improve our parts, players of all other people must needs have the best memories and be the best company. But whether the scraps they have got into their heads this way make them remember other things the better; and whether their parts be improved proportionably to the pains they have taken in getting by heart others' sayings, experience will show.

Memory is so necessary to all parts and conditions of life, and so little is to be done without it, that we are not to fear it should grow dull and useless for want of exercise, if exercise would make it grow stronger. But I fear this faculty of the mind is not capable of much help and amendment in general by any exercise or endeavor of ours, at least not by that used upon this pretense in grammar-schools. And if Xerxes was able to call every common soldier by name in his army that consisted of no less than a hundred thousand men, I think it may be guessed he got not this wonderful ability by learning his lessons by heart when he was a boy. This method of exercising and improving the memory by toilsome repetitions without book of what they read, is, I think, little used in the education of princes, which if it had that advantage is talked of, should be as little neglected in them as in the meanest schoolboys: princes having as much need of good memories as any men living, and have generally an equal share in this faculty with other men; though it has never been taken care of this way. What the mind is intent upon and careful of, that it remembers best, and for the reason above-mentioned: to which, if method and order be joined, all is done, I think, that can be, for the help of a weak memory; and he that will take any other way to do it, especially that of charging it with a train of other peoples' words, which he that learns cares not for, will, I guess, scarce find the profit answer half the time and pains employed in it.

I do not mean hereby that there should be no exercise given to children's memories. I think their memories should be employed, but not in learning by rote whole pages out of books, which, the lesson being once said, and that task over, are delivered up again to oblivion and neglected forever. This mends neither the memory nor the mind.

What they should learn by heart out of authors, I have above mentioned: and such wise and useful sentences being once given in charge to their memories, they should never be suffered to forget again, but be often called to account for them: whereby, besides the use those sayings may be to them in their future life, as so many good rules and observations, they will be taught to reflect often, and bethink themselves what they have to remember, which is the only way to make the memory quick and useful. The custom of frequent reflection will keep their minds from running adrift, and call their thoughts home from useless unattentive roving; and therefore I think it may do well to give them something every day to remember, but something still that is in itself worth the remembering, and what you would never have out of mind, whenever you call, or they themselves search for it. This will oblige them often to turn their thoughts inwards, than which you cannot wish them a better intellectual habit.

177. But under whose care soever a child is put to be taught during the tender and flexible years of his life, this is certain, it should be one who thinks *Latin* and *language* the least part of education; one who knowing how much virtue and a well-tempered soul is to be preferred to any sort of learning or language, makes it his chief business to form the mind of his scholars, and give that a right disposition; which if once got, though all the rest should be neglected, would in due time produce all the rest; and which, if it be not got and settled so as to keep out ill and vicious habits, languages and sciences, and all the other accomplishments of education, will be to no purpose but to make the worse or more dangerous man. And indeed whatever stir there is made about getting of Latin as the great and difficult business, his mother may teach it him herself, if she will but spend two or three hours in a day with him, and make him read the Evangelists in Latin to her: for she need but buy a Latin Testament, and having got somebody to mark the last syllable but one where it is long in words above two syllables (which is enough to regulate her pronunciation, and accenting the words), read daily in the Gospels, and then let her avoid understanding them in Latin if she can. And when she understands the Evangelists in Latin, let her, in the same manner, read *Aesop's Fables,* and so proceed on to

Eutropius, Justin, and other such books. I do not mention this, as an imagination of what I fancy may do, but as of a thing I have known done, and the Latin tongue with ease got this way.

But, to return to what I was saying: he that takes on him the charge of bringing up young men, especially young gentlemen, should have something more in him than Latin, more than even a knowledge in the liberal sciences: he should be a person of eminent virtue and prudence, and with good sense, have good humor, and the skill to carry himself with gravity, ease and kindness, in a constant conversation with his pupils. But of this I have spoken at large in another place.

178. At the same time that he is learning French and Latin, a child, as has been said, may also be entered in arithmetic, geography, chronology, history, and geometry too. For if these be taught him in French or Latin, when he begins once to understand either of these tongues, he will get a knowledge in these sciences, and the language to boot.

Geography I think should be begun with: for the learning of the figure of the globe, the situation and boundaries of the four parts of the world, and that of particular kingdoms and countries, being only an exercise of the eyes and memory, a child with pleasure will learn and retain them. And this is so certain that I now live in the house with a child whom his mother has so well instructed this way in geography, that he knew the limits of the four parts of the world, could readily point, being asked, to any country upon the globe, or any county in the map of England; knew all the great rivers, promontories, straits, and bays in the world, and could find the longitude and latitude of any place, before he was six years old. These things, that he will thus learn by sight, and have by rote in his memory, are not all, I confess, that he is to learn upon the globes. But yet it is a good step and preparation to it, and will make the remainder much easier, when his judgment is grown ripe enough for it; besides that, it gets so much time now, and by the pleasure of knowing things, leads him on insensibly to the gaining of languages.

179. When he has the natural parts of the globe well fixed in his memory, it may then be time to begin arithmetic. By the natural parts of the globe, I mean the several positions of the parts of the earth and sea, under different names and distinctions of countries, not com-

ing yet to those artificial and imaginary lines which have been invented, and are only supposed for the better improvement of that
science.

180. Arithmetic is the easiest and consequently the first sort of
abstract reasoning which the mind commonly bears or accustoms itself
to; and is of so general use in all parts of life and business, that
scarce anything is to be done without it. This is certain, a man cannot
have too much of it, nor too perfectly. He should, therefore, begin
to be exercised in counting as soon, and as far, as he is capable of it;
and do something in it every day, till he is master of the art of numbers.
When he understands addition and subtraction, he then may be
advanced farther in geography, after he is acquainted with the poles,
zones, parallel circles, and meridians, be taught longitude and latitude,
and by them be made to understand the use of maps, and by the
numbers placed on their sides, to know the respective situation of
countries, and how to find them out on the terrestrial globe. Which
when he can readily do, he may then be entered in the celestial; and
there going over all the circles again, with a more particular observation of the ecliptic, or zodiac, to fix them all very clearly and distinctly in his mind, he may be taught the figure and position of the
several constellations, which may be showed him first upon the globe,
and then in the heavens.

When that is done, and he knows pretty well the constellations of
this our hemisphere, it may be time to give him some notions of this
our planetary world; and to that purpose, it may not be amiss to
make him a draught of the Copernican system, and therein explain
to him the situation of the planets, their respective distances from the
sun, the center of their revolutions. This will prepare him to understand the motion and theory of the planets the most easy and natural
way. For since astronomers no longer doubt of the motion of the
planets about the sun, it is fit he should proceed upon that hypothesis,
which is not only the simplest and least perplexed for a learner, but
also the likeliest to be true in itself. But in this, as in all other parts
of instruction, great care must be taken with children, to begin with
that which is plain and simple, and to teach them as little as can be
at once, and settle that well in their heads before you proceed to the

next, or anything new in that science. Give them first one simple idea, and see that they take it right, and perfectly comprehend it before you go any farther, and then add some other simple idea which lies next in your way to what you aim at; and so proceeding by gentle and insensible steps, children without confusion and amazement will have their understandings opened and their thoughts extended farther than could have been expected. And when anyone has learned anything himself, there is no such way to fix it in his memory, and to encourage him to go on, as to set him to teach it others.

181. When he has once got such an acquaintance with the globes, as is above mentioned, he may be fit to be tried in a little geometry; wherein I think the first six books of Euclid enough for him to be taught. For I am in some doubt whether more, to a man of business, be necessary or useful. At least, if he have a genius and inclination to it, being entered so far by his tutor, he will be able to go on of himself without a teacher.

The globes therefore must be studied, and that diligently; and I think may be begun betimes, if the tutor will be but careful to distinguish what the child is capable of knowing, and what not; for which this may be a rule that perhaps will go a pretty way, viz., that children may be taught anything that falls under their senses, especially their sight, as far as their memories only are exercised: and thus a child very young may learn which is the equator, which the meridian, etc., which Europe, and which England, upon the globes, as soon almost as he knows the rooms of the house he lives in, if care be taken not to teach him too much at once, or to set him upon a new part till that which he is upon be perfectly learned and fixed in his memory.

182. With geography, chronology ought to go hand in hand. I mean the general part of it, so that he may have in his mind a view of the whole current of time, and the several considerable epochs that are made use of in history. Without these two, history, which is the great mistress of prudence and civil knowledge, and ought to be the proper study of a gentleman or man of business in the world; without geography and chronology, I say, history will be very ill retained, and very little useful; but be only a jumble of matters of fact. con-

fusedly heaped together without order or instruction. 'Tis by these two that the actions of mankind are ranked into their proper places of time and countries, under which circumstances they are not only much easier kept in the memory, but in that natural order are only capable to afford those observations which make a man the better and the abler for reading them.

183. When I speak of chronology as a science he should be perfect in, I do not mean the little controversies that are in it. These are endless, and most of them of so little importance to a gentleman as not to deserve to be inquired into, were they capable of an easy decision. And therefore all that learned noise and dust of the chronologist is wholly to be avoided. The most useful book I have seen in that part of learning, is a small treatise of Strauchius, which is printed in twelves, under the title of *Breviarium Chronologicum*, out of which may be selected all that is necessary to be taught a young gentleman concerning chronology; for all that is in that treatise a learner need not be cumbered with. He has in him the most remarkable or useful epochs reduced all to that of the Julian Period, which is the easiest and plainest and surest method that can be made use of in chronology. To this treatise of Strauchius, Helvicus' *Tables* may be added, as a book to be turned to on all occasions.

184. As nothing teaches, so nothing delights more than history. The first of these recommends it to the study of grown men, the latter makes me think it the fittest for a young lad, who as soon as he is instructed in chronology, and acquainted with the several epochs in use in this part of the world, and can reduce them to the Julian Period, should then have some Latin history put into his hand. The choice should be directed by the easiness of the style; for wherever he begins, chronology will keep it from confusion; and the pleasantness of the subject inviting him to read, the language will insensibly be got without that terrible vexation and uneasiness which children suffer where they are put into books beyond their capacity; such as are the Roman orators and poets, only to learn the Roman language. When he has by reading mastered the easier, such perhaps as Justin, Eutropius, Quintius Curtius, etc., the next degree to these will give him no great trouble; and thus by a gradual progress from the plainest

and easiest historians, he may at last come to read the most difficult and sublime of the Latin authors, such as are Tully,[22] Vergil, and Horace.

185. The knowledge of *virtue*, all along from the beginning, in all the instances he is capable of, being taught him more by practice than rules; and the love of reputation, instead of satisfying his appetite, being made habitual in him, I know not whether he should read any other discourses of morality but what he finds in the Bible; or have any system of ethics put into his hand till he can read Tully's *Offices*, not as a schoolboy to learn Latin, but as one that would be informed in the principles and precepts of virtue for the conduct of his life.

186. When he has pretty well digested Tully's *Offices*, and added to it, Puffendorf, *de Officio Hominis et Civis*, it may be seasonable to set him upon Grotius, *de Jure Belli et Pacis*, or, which perhaps is the better of the two, Puffendorf, *de Jure naturali et Gentium;* wherein he will be instructed in the natural rights of men, and the origin and foundations of society, and the duties resulting from thence. This general part of civil law and history are studies which a gentleman should not barely touch at, but constantly dwell upon, and never have done with. A virtuous and well-behaved young man, that is well-versed in the general part of the civil law (which concerns not the chicane of private cases, but the affairs and intercourse of civilized nations in general, grounded upon principles of reason) understands Latin well, and can write a good hand, one may turn loose into the world with great assurance that he will find employment and esteem everywhere.

187. It would be strange to suppose an English gentleman should be ignorant of the law of his country. This, whatever station he is in, is so requisite, that from a Justice of the Peace to a Minister of State I know no place he can well fill without. I do not mean the chicane or wrangling and captious part of the law: a gentleman, whose business is to seek the true measures of right and wrong, and not the arts how to avoid doing the one and secure himself in doing the other,

[22] Marcus Tullius Cicero.

ought to be as far from such a study of the law, as he is concerned diligently to apply himself to that wherein he may be serviceable to his country. And to that purpose, I think the right way for a gentleman to study our law, which he does not design for his calling, is to take a view of our English constitution and government in the ancient books of the common law, and some more modern writers, who out of them have given an account of this government. And having got a true idea of that, then to read our history, and with it join in every king's reign the laws then made. This will give an insight into the reason of our statutes, and show the true ground upon which they came to be made, and what weight they ought to have.

188. Rhetoric and logic being the arts that in the ordinary method usually follow immediately after grammar, it may perhaps be wondered that I have said so little of them. The reason is because of the little advantage young people receive by them: for I have seldom or never observed anyone to get the skill of reasoning well, or speaking handsomely, by studying those rules which pretend to reach it; and therefore I would have a young gentleman take a view of them in the shortest systems could be found, without dwelling long on the contemplation and study of those formalities. Right reasoning is founded on something else than the *predicaments* and *predicables,* and does not consist in talking in *mode* and *figure* itself. But 'tis beside my present business to enlarge upon this speculation. To come therefore to what we have in hand; if you would have your son reason well, let him read Chillingworth; [23] and if you would have him speak well, let him be conversant in Tully, to give him the true idea of eloquence; and let him read those things that are well writ in English, to perfect his style in the purity of our language.

189. If the use and end of right reasoning be to have right notions and a right judgment of things, to distinguish betwixt truth and falsehood, right and wrong, and to act accordingly, be sure not to let your son be bred up in the art and formality of disputing, either practicing it himself, or admiring it in others; unless instead of an able man, you desire to have him an insignificant wrangler, opiniator in dis-

[23] William Chillingworth, an English theologian of the seventeenth century.

course, and priding himself in contradicting others; or, which is worse, questioning everything, and thinking there is no such thing as truth to be sought, but only victory, in disputing. There cannot be anything so disingenuous, so misbecoming a gentleman or anyone who pretends to be a rational creature, as not to yield to plain reason and the conviction of clear arguments. Is there anything more consistent with civil conversation, and the end of all debate, than not to take an answer, though never so full and satisfactory, but still to go on with the dispute as long as equivocal sounds can furnish (a *medius terminus*) a term to wrangle with on the one side, or a distinction on the other; whether pertinent or impertinent, sense or nonsense, agreeing with or contrary to what he had said before, it matters not. For this, in short, is the way and perfection of logical disputes, that the opponent never takes any answer, nor the respondent ever yields to any argument. This neither of them must do, whatever becomes of truth or knowledge, unless he will pass for a poor baffled wretch, and lie under the disgrace of not being able to maintain whatever he has once affirmed, which is the great aim and glory in disputing. Truth is to be found and supported by a mature and due consideration of things themselves, and not by artificial terms and ways of arguing: these lead not men so much into the discovery of truth as into a captious and fallacious use of doubtful words, which is the most useless and most offensive way of talking, and such as least suits a gentleman or a lover of truth of anything in the world.

There can scarce be a greater defect in a gentleman than not to express himself well either in writing or speaking. But yet I think I may ask my reader whether he doth not know a great many who live upon their estates, and so with the name should have the qualities of gentlemen, who cannot so much as tell a story as they should, much less speak clearly and persuasively in any business. This I think not to be so much their fault as the fault of their education; for I must, without partiality, do my countrymen this right, that where they apply themselves, I see none of their neighbors outgo them. They have been taught rhetoric, but yet never taught how to express themselves handsomely with their tongues or pens in the language they are always to use; as if the names of the figures that embellished the discourses of those who understood the art of speaking were the very art and skill of speaking well. This, as all other things of practice, is to be learned not by a few or a great many rules given, but by exercise and application according to good rules, or rather patterns, till habits are got, and a facility of doing it well.

Agreeable hereunto, perhaps it might not be amiss to make children, as soon as they are capable of it, often to tell a story of anything they know; and to correct at first the most remarkable fault they are guilty of in their way of putting it together. When that fault is cured, then to show them the next, and so on, till one after another, all, at least the gross ones, are mended. When they can tell tales pretty well, then it may be the time to make them write them. The *Fables* of Aesop, the only book almost that I know fit for children, may afford them matter for this exercise of writing English, as well as for reading and translating, to enter them in the Latin tongue. When they have got past the faults of grammar, and can join in a continued coherent discourse the several parts of a story, without bald and unhandsome forms of transition (as is usual) often repeated, he that desires to perfect them yet further in this, which is the first step to speaking well and needs no invention, may have recourse to Tully, and by putting in practice those rules which that master of eloquence gives in his first book, *De inventione,* make them know wherein the skill and graces of a handsome narrative, according to the several subjects and designs of it, lie. Of each of which rules fit examples may be found out, and therein they may be shown how others have practiced them. The ancient classic authors afford plenty of such examples, which they should be made not only to translate, but have set before them as patterns for their daily imitation.

When they understand how to write English with due connection, propriety, and order, and are pretty well masters of a tolerable narrative style, they may be advanced to writing of letters; wherein they should not be put upon any strains of wit or compliment, but taught to express their own plain easy sense, without any incoherence, confusion or roughness. And when they are perfect in this, they may, to raise their thoughts, have set before them the examples of *Voitures,*[24] for the entertainment of their friends at a distance, with letters of compliment, mirth, raillery, or diversion; and Tully's *Epistles,* as the best pattern whether for business or conversation. The writing of letters has so much to do in all the occurrences of human life that no gentleman can avoid showing himself in this kind of writing. Occasions will daily force him to make this use of his pen, which, besides the consequences that, in his affairs, his well or ill managing of it often draws after it, always lays him open to a severer examination of his breeding, sense, and abilities, than oral discourses; whose transient faults dying for the most part with the sound that gives them life, and so not subject to a strict review, more easily escape observation and censure.

Had the methods of education been directed to their right end, one would have thought this so necessary a part could not have been neglected whilst themes and verses in Latin, of no use at all, were so constantly everywhere pressed, to the racking of children's inventions beyond their strength and hindering their cheerful progress in learning the tongues by unnatural difficulties. But custom has so ordained it, and who dares disobey? And would it not be very unreasonable to require of a learned country schoolmaster (who has all the tropes and figures in Farnaby's *Rhetoric* at his fingers' ends) to teach his scholar to express himself handsomely in English, when it appears to be so little his business or thought that the boy's mother (despised, 'tis like, as illiterate for not having read a system of logic and rhetoric) outdoes him in it?

To write and speak correctly gives a grace and gains a favorable attention to what one has to say: and since 'tis English that an *English* gentleman will have constant use of, that is the language he should chiefly cultivate, and wherein most care should be taken to polish and perfect his style. To speak or write better Latin than English may make a man be talked of, but he would find it more to his purpose to express himself well in his own tongue, that he uses every moment, than to have the vain commendation of others for a very insignificant

[24] Vincent Voiture, a French poet of the early seventeenth century.

quality. This I find universally neglected, and no care taken anywhere to improve young men in their own language, that they may thoroughly understand and be masters of it. If anyone among us have a facility or purity more than ordinary in his mother tongue, it is owing to chance, or his genius, or anything rather than to his education or any care of his teacher. To mind what English his pupil speaks or writes is below the dignity of one bred up amongst Greek and Latin, though he have but little of them himself. These are the learned languages fit only for learned men to meddle with and teach; English is the language of the illiterate vulgar: though yet we see the polity of some of our neighbors has not thought it beneath the public care to promote and reward the improvement of their own language. Polishing and enriching their tongue is no small business amongst them; it has colleges and stipends appointed it, and there is raised amongst them a great ambition and emulation of writing correctly: and we see what they are come to by it, and how far they have spread one of the worst languages possibly in this part of the world, if we look upon it as it was in some few reigns backwards, whatever it be now. The great men among the Romans were daily exercising themselves in their own language; and we find yet upon record the names of orators, who taught some of their emperors Latin, though it were their mother tongue.

'Tis plain the Greeks were yet more nice in theirs. All other speech was barbarous to them but their own, and no foreign language appears to have been studied or valued amongst that learned and acute people, though it be past doubt that they borrowed their learning and philosophy from abroad.

I am not here speaking against Greek and Latin; I think they ought to be studied, and the Latin at least understood well by every gentleman. But whatever foreign languages a young man meddles with (and the more he knows the better) that which he should critically study, and labor to get a facility, clearness, and elegance to express himself in, should be his own; and to this purpose he should daily be exercised in it.

190. Natural philosophy, as a speculative science, I imagine we have none, and perhaps I may think I have reason to say we never shall be able to make a science of it. The works of nature are contrived

by a wisdom, and operate by ways too far surpassing our faculties to discover or capacities to conceive, for us ever to be able to reduce them into a science. Natural philosophy being the knowledge of the principles, properties, and operations of things as they are in themselves, I imagine there are two parts of it, one comprehending *spirits,* with their nature and qualities, and the other *bodies.* The first of these is usually referred to metaphysics: but under what title soever the consideration of spirits comes, I think it ought to go before the study of matter and body, not as a science that can be methodized into a system, and treated of upon principles of knowledge; but as an enlargement of our minds towards a truer and fuller comprehension of the intellectual world to which we are led both by reason and revelation. And since the clearest and largest discoveries we have of other spirits, besides God and our own souls, is imparted to us from heaven by revelation, I think the information that at least young people should have of them should be taken from that revelation. To this purpose, I conclude, it would be well, if there were made a good history of the Bible for young people to read; wherein if everything that is fit to be put into it, were laid down in its due order of time, and several things omitted which are suited only to riper age, that confusion which is usually produced by promiscuous reading of the Scripture, as it lies now bound up in our Bibles, would be avoided. And also this other good obtained, that by reading of it constantly, there would be instilled into the minds of children a notion and belief of spirits, they having so much to do in all the transactions of that history, which will be a good preparation to the study of bodies. For without the notion and allowance of spirit, our philosophy will be lame and defective in one main part of it, when it leaves out the contemplation of the most excellent and powerful part of the creation.

191. Of this History of the Bible, I think too it would be well if there were a short and plain epitome made, containing the chief and most material heads, for children to be conversant in as soon as they can read. This, though it will lead them early into some notion of spirits, yet it is not contrary to what I said above, that I would not have children troubled, whilst young, with notions of spirits; whereby my meaning was, that I think it inconvenient that their yet tender

minds should receive early impressions of goblins, specters, and apparitions, wherewith their maids and those about them are apt to fright them into a compliance with their orders, which often proves a great inconvenience to them all their lives after, by subjecting their minds to frights, fearful apprehensions, weakness, and superstition; which when coming abroad into the world and conversation they grow weary and ashamed of, it not seldom happens, that to make, as they think, a thorough cure, and ease themselves of a load which has sat so heavy on them, they throw away the thoughts of all spirits together, and so run into the other, but worse, extreme.

192. The reason why I would have this premised to the study of bodies, and the Doctrine of the Scriptures well imbibed before young men be entered in natural philosophy, is because matter, being a thing that all our senses are constantly conversant with, it is so apt to possess the mind and exclude all other beings but matter, that prejudice, grounded on such principles, often leaves no room for the admittance of spirits, or the allowing any such things as immaterial beings *in rerum natura;* [25] when yet it is evident that by mere matter and motion none of the great phenomena of nature can be resolved, to instance but in that common one of gravity, which I think impossible to be explained by any natural operation of matter, or any other law of motion, but the positive will of a superior being so ordering it. And therefore since the deluge cannot be well explained without admitting something out of the ordinary course of nature, I propose it to be considered whether God's altering the center of gravity in the earth for a time (a thing as intelligible as gravity itself, which perhaps a little variation of causes unknown to us would produce) will not more easily account for Noah's Flood than any hypothesis yet made use of to solve it. I hear the great objection to this is that it would produce but a partial deluge. But the alteration of the center of gravity once allowed, 'tis no hard matter to conceive that the divine power might make the center of gravity, placed at a due distance from the center of the earth, move round it in a convenient space of time, whereby the flood would become universal, and, as I think, answer all the

[25] In the nature of things.

phenomena of the deluge as delivered by Moses, at an easier rate than those many hard suppositions that are made use of to explain it. But this is not a place for that argument, which is here only mentioned by the by, to show the necessity of having recourse to something beyond bare matter and its motion in the explication of nature; to which the notions of spirits and their power, as delivered in the Bible, where so much is attributed to their operation, may be a fit preparative, reserving to a fitter opportunity a fuller explication of this hypothesis, and the application of it to all the parts of the deluge, and any difficulties can be supposed in the history of the flood, as recorded in the Scripture.

193. But to return to the study of natural philosophy. Though the world be full of systems of it, yet I cannot say I know any one which can be taught a young man as a science wherein he may be sure to find truth and certainty, which is what all sciences give an expectation of. I do not hence conclude that none of them are to be read. It is necessary for a gentleman in this learned age to look into some of them to fit himself for conversation: but whether that of Descartes be put into his hands, as that which is most in fashion, or it be thought fit to give him a short view of that and several others also, I think the systems of natural philosophy that have obtained in this part of the world are to be read more to know the hypotheses, and to understand the terms and ways of talking of the several sects, than with hopes to gain thereby a comprehensive, scientific, and satisfactory knowledge of the works of nature. Only this may be said, that the modern Corpuscularians [26] talk in most things more intelligibly than the Peripatetics, who possessed the schools immediately before them. He that would look further back, and acquaint himself with the several opinions of the ancients, may consult Dr. Cudworth's [27] *Intellectual System,* wherein that very learned author has with such accurateness and judgment collected and explained the opinions of the Greek philosophers, that

[26] Believers in the corpuscular philosophy, which attempted to account for the phenomena of nature by the motion, position, etc. of minute particles of matter.

[27] Dr. Cudworth, a prominent theologian of the day, was one of Locke's associates, and his daughter Damaris Cudworth, later Lady Masham, was a lifelong friend.

what principles they built on, and what were the chief hypotheses that divided them, is better to be seen in him than anywhere else that I know. But I would not deter anyone from the study of nature because all the knowledge we have or possibly can have of it cannot be brought into a science. There are very many things in it that are convenient and necessary to be known to a gentleman; and a great many others that will abundantly reward the pains of the curious with delight and advantage. But these, I think, are rather to be found amongst such writers as have employed themselves in making rational experiments and observations than in starting barely speculative systems. Such writings therefore, as many of Mr. Boyle's [28] are, with others that have writ of husbandry, planting, gardening, and the like, may be fit for a gentleman, when he has a little acquainted himself with some of the systems of the natural philosophy in fashion.

194. Though the systems of physics that I have met with afford little encouragement to look for certainty or science in any treatise which shall pretend to give us a body of natural philosophy from the first principles of bodies in general, yet the incomparable Mr. Newton [29] has shown how far mathematics applied to some parts of nature may, upon principles that matter of fact justify, carry us in the knowledge of some, as I may so call them, particular provinces of the incomprehensible universe. And if others could give us so good and clear an account of other parts of nature, as he has of this our planetary world, and the most considerable phenomena observable in it, in his admirable book, *Philosophiae naturalis Principia Mathematica,* we might in time hope to be furnished with more true and certain knowledge in several parts of this stupendous machine than hitherto we could have expected. And though there are very few that have mathe-

[28] Robert Boyle, the great English chemist, had known Locke at Oxford, and a common interest in science kept the friendship alive until the death of Boyle. Locke was one of his literary executors.

[29] Sir Isaac Newton was another friend, and a fellow-member of the Royal Academy, where Newton's *Principia Mathematica* was first presented. The final volume of this great work was published six years before the present treatise was written. Locke was instrumental in securing for Newton a lucrative government appointment.

matics enough to understand his demonstrations, yet the most accurate mathematicians who have examined them allowing them to be such, his book will deserve to be read, and give no small light and pleasure to those, who, willing to understand the motions, properties, and operations of the great masses of matter, in this our solar system, will but carefully mind his conclusions, which may be depended on as propositions well proved.

195. This is, in short, what I have thought concerning a young gentleman's studies; wherein it will possibly be wondered that I should omit Greek, since amongst the Grecians is to be found the original, as it were, and foundation of all that learning which we have in this part of the world. I grant it so; and will add that no man can pass for a scholar that is ignorant of the Greek tongue. But I am not here considering the education of a professed scholar, but of a gentleman, to whom Latin and French, as the world now goes, is by everyone acknowledged to be necessary. When he comes to be a man, if he has a mind to carry his studies further, and look into the Greek learning, he will then easily get that tongue himself: and if he has not that inclination, his learning of it under a tutor will be but lost labor, and much of his time and pains spent in that which will be neglected and thrown away as soon as he is at liberty. For how many are there of a hundred, even amongst scholars themselves, who retain the Greek they carried from school; or ever improve it to a familiar reading and perfect understanding of Greek authors?

To conclude this part, which concerns a young gentleman's studies, his tutor should remember that his business is not so much to teach him all that is knowable as to raise in him a love and esteem of knowledge; and to put him in the right way of knowing and improving himself when he has a mind to it.

The thoughts of a judicious author on the subject of languages I shall here give the reader, as near as I can, in his own way of expressing them. He says, "One can scarce burden children too much with the knowledge of languages. They are useful to men of all conditions, and they equally open them the entrance, either to the most profound, or the more easy and entertaining parts of learning. If this irksome study be put off to a little more advanced age, young men either have not resolution enough to apply it out of choice or steadiness to carry it on. And if anyone has the gift of perseverance, it is not without the inconvenience of spending that time upon languages, which is destined to other uses: and he confines to the study of words that age of his life that is above it, and requires things; at least it is the losing the best and beautifulest season of one's life. This large foundation of languages cannot be well laid but when everything makes an easy and deep impression on the mind; when the memory is fresh, ready, and tenacious; when the head and heart are as yet free from cares, passions, and designs; and those on whom the child depends have authority enough to keep him close to a long continued application. I am persuaded that the small number of truly learned, and the multitude of superficial pretenders, is owing to the neglect of this."

I think everybody will agree with this observing gentleman that languages are the proper study of our first years. But 'tis to be considered by the parents and tutors, what tongues 'tis fit the child should learn. For it must be confessed that it is fruitless pains and loss of time to learn a language which in the course of life that he is designed to he is never like to make use of, or which one may guess by his temper he will wholly neglect and lose again as soon as an approach to manhood, setting him free from a governor, shall put him into the hands of his own inclination, which is not likely to allot any of his time to the cultivating the learned tongues, or dispose him to mind any other language but what daily use or some particular necessity shall force upon him.

But yet for the sake of those who are designed to be scholars, I will add what the same author subjoins to make good his foregoing remark. It will deserve to be considered by all who desire to be truly learned, and therefore may be a fit rule for tutors to inculcate and leave with their pupils to guide their future studies.

"The study," says he, "of the original text can never be sufficiently recommended.[30] 'Tis the shortest, surest, and most agreeable way to

[30] This section gains interest in view of the current trend in American higher education to replace textbooks by original texts. Some colleges base their entire curriculum on the study and discussion of the great works of philosophy, science, and literature.

all sorts of learning. Draw from the spring-head, and take not things at second hand. Let the writings of the great masters be never laid aside, dwell upon them, settle them in your mind, and cite them upon occasion; make it your business thoroughly to understand them in their full extent and all their circumstances; acquaint yourself fully with the principles of original authors; bring them to a consistency, and then do you yourself make your deductions. In this state were the first commentators, and do not you rest till you bring yourself to the same. Content not yourself with those borrowed lights, nor guide yourself by their views but where your own fails you and leaves you in the dark. Their explications are not yours, and will give you the slip. On the contrary, your own observations are the product of your own mind, where they will abide and be ready at hand upon all occasions in converse, consultation, and dispute. Lose not the pleasure it is to see that you are not stopped in your reading but by difficulties that are invincible; where the commentators and scholiasts themselves are at a stand and have nothing to say. Those copious expositors of other places, who with a vain and pompous overflow of learning poured out on passages plain and easy in themselves, are very free of their words and pains, where there is no need. Convince yourself fully by thus ordering your studies, that 'tis nothing but men's laziness which has encouraged pedantry to cram rather than enrich libraries, and to bury good authors under heaps of notes and commentaries, and you will perceive that sloth herein has acted against itself and its own interest by multiplying reading and inquiries, and increasing the pains it endeavored to avoid."

This, though it may seem to concern none but direct scholars, is of so great moment for the right ordering of their education and studies that I hope I shall not be blamed for inserting of it here; especially if it be considered that it may be of use to gentlemen too, when at any time they have a mind to go deeper than the surface, and get to themselves a solid, satisfactory, and masterly insight in any part of learning.

Order and constancy are said to make the great difference between one man and another: this I am sure, nothing so much clears a learner's way, helps him so much on in it, and makes him go so easy and so far in any inquiry, as a good *method*. His governor should take pains to make him sensible of this, accustom him to order, and teach him *method* in all the applications of his thoughts; show him wherein it lies, and the advantages of it; acquaint him with the several sorts of it, either from general to particulars, or from particulars to what is more general; exercise him in both of them, and make him see in what cases each different method is most proper, and to what ends it best serves.

In history the order of time should govern, in philosophical inquiries that of nature, which in all progression is to go from the place one is then in to that which joins and lies next to it; and so it is in the mind, from the knowledge it stands possessed of already, to that which lies next, and is coherent to it, and so on to what it aims at, by the simplest and most uncompounded parts it can divide the matter into. To this purpose, it will be of great use to his pupil to accustom him to distinguish well, that is, to have distinct notions, wherever the mind can find any real difference; but as carefully to avoid distinctions in terms, where he has not distinct and different clear ideas.

196. Besides what is to be had from study and books, there are other accomplishments necessary for a gentleman, to be got by exercise, and to which time is to be allowed, and for which masters must be had.

Dancing being that which gives graceful motions all the life, and above all things manliness, and a becoming confidence to young children, I think it cannot be learned too early, after they are once of an age and strength capable of it. But you must be sure to have a good master, that knows, and can teach, what is graceful and becoming, and what gives a freedom and easiness to all the motions of the body. One that teaches not this is worse than none at all: natural unfashionableness being much better than apish affected postures; and I think it much more passable, to put off the hat and make a leg like an honest country gentleman than like an ill-fashioned dancing-master. For as for the jigging part, and the figures of dances, I count that little or nothing, farther than as it tends to perfect graceful carriage.

197. Music is thought to have some affinity with dancing, and a good hand upon some instruments is by many people mightily valued. But it wastes so much of a young man's time to gain but a moderate

skill in it; and engages often in such odd company that many think it much better spared: and I have amongst men of parts and business so seldom heard anyone commended or esteemed for having an excellency in music, that amongst all those things that ever came into the list of accomplishments, I think I may give it the last place. Our short lives will not serve us for the attainment of all things; nor can our minds be always intent on something to be learned. The weakness of our constitutions, both of mind and body, requires that we should be often unbent: and he that will make a good use of any part of his life, must allow a large portion of it to recreation. At least, this must not be denied to young people; unless whilst you with too much haste make them old, you have the displeasure to set them in their graves or a second childhood sooner than you could wish. And therefore, I think, that the time and pains allotted to serious improvements should be employed about things of most use and consequence, and that too in the methods the most easy and short that could be at any rate obtained: and perhaps, as I have above said, it would be none of the least secrets of education to make the exercises of the body and the mind the recreation one to another. I doubt not but that something might be done in it, by a prudent man, that would well consider the temper and inclination of his pupil. For he that is wearied either with study or dancing does not desire presently to go to sleep, but to do something else which may divert and delight him. But this must be always remembered, that nothing can come into the account of *recreation,* that is not done with delight.

198. Fencing and riding the great horse are looked upon so necessary parts of breeding that it would be thought a great omission to neglect them; the latter of the two, being for the most part to be learned only in great towns, is one of the best exercises for health, which is to be had in those places of ease and luxury: and upon that account makes a fit part of a young gentleman's employment during his abode there. And as far as it conduces to give a man a firm and graceful seat on horseback, and to make him able to teach his horse to stop and turn quick, and to rest on his haunches, is of use to a gentleman both in peace and war. But whether it be of moment enough to be made a business of, and deserve to take up more of his time

than should barely for his health be employed at due intervals in some such vigorous exercise, I shall leave to the discretion of parents and tutors; who will do well to remember in all the parts of education, that most time and application is to be bestowed on that which is like to be of greatest consequence and frequentest use in the ordinary course and occurrences of that life the young man is designed for.

199. As for fencing, it seems to me a good exercise for health, but dangerous to the life; the confidence of their skill being apt to engage in quarrels those that think they have learned to use their swords. This presumption makes them often more touchy than needs on point of honor and slight or no provocations. Young men, in their warm blood, are forward to think they have in vain learned to fence, if they never show their skill and courage in a duel; and they seem to have reason. But how many sad tragedies that reason has been the occasion of, the tears of many a mother can witness. A man that cannot fence will be more careful to keep out of bullies' and gamesters' company, and will not be half so apt to stand upon punctilios, or to give affronts, or fiercely justify them when given, which is that which usually makes the quarrel. And when a man is in the field, a moderate skill in fencing rather exposes him to the sword of his enemy than secures him from it. And certainly a man of courage who cannot fence at all and therefore will put all upon one thrust and not stand parrying, has the odds against a moderate fencer, especially if he has skill in wrestling. And therefore, if any provision be to be made against such accidents, and a man be to prepare his son for duels, I had much rather mine should be a good wrestler than an ordinary fencer, which is the most a gentle-man can attain to in it, unless he will be constantly in the fencing-school and every day exercising. But since fencing and riding the great horse are so generally looked upon as necessary qualifications in the breeding of a gentleman, it will be hard wholly to deny anyone of that rank these marks of distinction. I shall leave it therefore to the father to consider how far the temper of his son and the station he is like to be in will allow or encourage him to comply with fashions which, having very little to do with civil life, were yet formerly un-known to the most warlike nations, and seem to have added little of force or courage to those who have received them; unless we will

think martial skill or prowess have been improved by dueling, with which fencing came into, and with which I presume it will go out of the world.

200. These are my present thoughts concerning *learning* and *accom-plishments*. The great business of all is *virtue* and *wisdom*:

> *Nullum numen abest si sit Prudentia.*[31]

Teach him to get a mastery over his inclinations, and *submit his appe-tite to reason*. This being obtained, and by constant practice settled into habit, the hardest part of the task is over. To bring a young man to this, I know nothing which so much contributes as the love of praise and commendation, which should therefore be instilled into him by all arts imaginable. Make his mind as sensible of credit and shame as may be; and when you have done that, you have put a principle into him which will influence his actions when you are not by, to which the fear of a little smart of a rod is not comparable, and which will be the proper stock whereon afterwards to graft the true principles of morality and religion.

201. I have one thing more to add, which as soon as I mention I shall run the danger of being suspected to have forgot what I am about, and what I have above written concerning education all tending to-wards a gentleman's calling, with which a trade seems wholly incon-sistent. And yet I cannot forbear to say, I would have him learn a trade, a manual trade; nay two or three, but one more particularly.

202. The busy inclination of children being always to be directed to something that may be useful to them, the advantages proposed from what they are set about may be considered of two kinds: 1. Where the skill itself that is got by exercise is worth the having. Thus skill not only in languages and learned sciences, but in painting, turning, gardening, tempering and working in iron, and all other useful arts is worth the having. 2. Where the exercise itself, without any considera-tion, is necessary or useful for health. Knowledge in some things is so necessary to be got by children whilst they are young, that some

[31] No divinity is absent provided good sense is present; a proverb from Juvenal.

part of their time is to be allotted to their improvement in them, though those employments contribute nothing at all to their health. Such are reading and writing and all other sedentary studies for the cultivating of the mind, which unavoidably take up a great part of a gentleman's time, quite from their cradles. Other manual arts, which are both got and exercised by labor, do many of them by that exercise not only increase our dexterity and skill, but contribute to our health too, especially such as employ us in the open air. In these, then, health and improvement may be joined together; and of these should some fit ones be chosen, to be made the recreations of one whose chief business is with books and study. In this choice the age and inclination of the person is to be considered, and constraint always to be avoided in bringing him to it. For command and force may often create, but can never cure, an aversion: and whatever anyone is brought to by compulsion, he will leave as soon as he can, and be little profited and less recreated by, whilst he is at it.

203. That which of all others would please me best would be a painter, were there not an argument or two against it not easy to be answered. First, ill painting is one of the worst things in the world; and to attain a tolerable degree of skill in it requires too much of a man's time. If he has a natural inclination to it, it will endanger the neglect of all other more useful studies to give way to that; and if he have no inclination to it, all the time, pains, and money shall be employed in it, will be thrown away to no purpose. Another reason why I am not for painting in a gentleman is because it is a sedentary recreation, which more employs the mind than the body. A gentleman's more serious employment I look on to be study; and when that demands relaxation and refreshment, it should be in some exercise of the body, which unbends the thought and confirms the health and strength. For these two reasons I am not for painting.

204. In the next place, for a country gentleman I should propose one, or rather both these, viz., gardening or husbandry in general, and working in wood, as a carpenter, joiner, or turner, these being fit and healthy recreations for a man of study or business. For since the mind endures not to be constantly employed in the same thing or way, and sedentary or studious men should have some exercise that at the

same time might divert their minds and employ their bodies, I know none that could do it better for a country gentleman than these two; the one of them affording him exercise when the weather or season keeps him from the other. Besides that, by being skilled in the one of them, he will be able to govern and teach his gardener; by the other, contrive and make a great many things both of delight and use: though these I propose not as the chief end of his labor, but as temptations to it; diversion from his other more serious thoughts and employments by useful and healthy manual exercise being what I chiefly aim at in it.

205. The great men among the ancients understood very well how to reconcile manual labor with affairs of state, and thought it no lessening to their dignity to make the one the recreation to the other. That indeed which seems most generally to have employed and diverted their spare hours was agriculture. Gideon among the Jews was taken from threshing, as well as Cincinnatus amongst the Romans from the plow, to command the armies of their countries against their enemies; and 'tis plain their dextrous handling of the flail or the plow, and being good workmen with these tools, did not hinder their skill in arms, or make them less able in the arts of war or government. They were great captains and statesmen as well as husbandmen. Cato Major, who had with great reputation borne all the great offices of the commonwealth, has left us an evidence under his own hand how much he was versed in country affairs; and, as I remember, Cyrus thought gardening so little beneath the dignity and grandeur of a throne that he showed Xenophon a large field of fruit trees all of his own planting. The records of antiquity, both among Jews and Gentiles, are full of instances of this kind, if it were necessary to recommend useful recreations by examples.

206. Nor let it be thought that I mistake, when I call these or the like exercises of manual arts, diversions, or recreations: for recreation is not being idle (as everyone may observe) but easing the wearied part by change of business: and he that thinks diversion may not lie in hard and painful labor, forgets the early rising, hard riding, heat, cold and hunger of huntsmen, which is yet known to be the constant recreation of men of the greatest condition. Delving, planting, inoculating, or any the like profitable employments, would be no less a

diversion than any of the idle sports in fashion, if men could but be brought to delight in them, which custom and skill in a trade will quickly bring anyone to do. And I doubt not but there are to be found those who, being frequently called to cards or any other play by those they could not refuse, have been more tired with these recreations than with any the most serious employment of life, though the play has been such as they have naturally had no aversion to, and with which they could willingly sometimes divert themselves.

207. Play, wherein persons of condition, especially ladies, waste so much of their time, is a plain instance to me that men cannot be perfectly idle; they must be doing something; for how else could they sit so many hours toiling at that which generally gives more vexation than delight to people whilst they are actually engaged in it? 'Tis certain gaming leaves no satisfaction behind it to those who reflect when it is over, and it no way profits either body or mind: as to their estates, if it strike so deep as to concern them, it is a *trade* then, and not a *recreation,* wherein few that have anything else to live on thrive: and at best, a thriving gamester has but a poor trade on't, who fills his pockets at the price of his reputation.

Recreation belongs not to people who are strangers to business, and are not wasted and wearied with the employment of their calling. The skill should be, so to order their time of recreation that it may relax and refresh the part that has been exercised and is tired, and yet do something which, besides the present delight and ease, may produce what will afterwards be profitable. It has been nothing but the vanity and pride of greatness and riches that has brought unprofitable and dangerous *pastimes,* as they are called, into fashion, and persuaded people into a belief that the learning or putting their hands to anything that was useful could not be a diversion fit for a gentleman. This has been that which has given cards, dice, and drinking so much credit in the world; and a great many throw away their spare hours in them, through the prevalency of custom, and want of some better employment to fill up the vacancy of leisure, more than from any real delight is to be found in them. They cannot bear the dead weight of unemployed time lying upon their hands, nor the uneasiness it is to do nothing at all; and having never learned any laudable manual art

wherewith to divert themselves, they have recourse to those foolish
or ill ways in use, to help off their time, which a rational man, till
corrupted by custom, could find very little pleasure in.

208. I say not this, that I would never have a young gentleman
accommodate himself to the innocent diversions in fashion amongst
those of his age and condition. I am so far from having him austere
and morose to that degree that I would persuade him to more than
ordinary complaisance for all the gaieties and diversions of those he
converses with, and be averse or testy in nothing they should desire
of him that might become a gentleman and an honest man. Though
as to cards and dice, I think the safest and best way is never to learn
any play upon them, and so to be incapacitated for those dangerous
temptations and encroaching wasters of useful time. But allowance
being made for idle and jovial conversation and all fashionable becoming recreations I say, a young man will have time enough from
his serious and main business to learn almost any trade. 'Tis want of
application, and not of leisure, that men are not skillful in more arts
than one; and an hour in a day, constantly employed in such a way
of diversion, will carry a man in a short time a great deal further than
he can imagine: which, if it were of no other use but to drive the
common, vicious, useless, and dangerous pastimes out of fashion, and
to show there was no need of them, would deserve to be encouraged.
If men from their youth were weaned from that sauntering humor
wherein some out of custom let a good part of their lives run uselessly
away, without either business or recreation, they would find time
enough to acquire dexterity and skill in hundreds of things, which,
though remote from their proper callings, would not at all interfere
with them. And therefore, I think, for this, as well as other reasons
before-mentioned, a lazy, listless humor that idly dreams away the
days, is of all others the least to be indulged or permitted in young
people. It is the proper state of one sick and out of order in his health,
and is tolerable in nobody else of what age or condition soever.

209. To the arts above-mentioned may be added perfuming, var-
nishing, graving, and several sorts of working in iron, brass, and silver;
and if, as it happens to most young gentlemen, that a considerable part
of his time be spent in a great town, he may learn to cut, polish, and

set precious stones, or employ himself in grinding and polishing optical glasses. Amongst the great variety there is of ingenious manual arts, 'twill be impossible that no one should be found to please and delight him, unless he be either idle or debauched, which is not to be supposed in a right way of education. And since he cannot be always employed in study, reading, and conversation, there will be many an hour, besides what his exercises will take up, which, if not spent this way, will be spent worse. For, I conclude, a young man will seldom desire to sit perfectly still and idle; or, if he does, 'tis a fault that ought to be mended.

210. But if his mistaken parents, frightened with the disgraceful names of *mechanic* and *trade*, shall have an aversion to anything of this kind in their children, yet there is one thing relating to trade, which, when they consider, they will think absolutely necessary for their sons to learn.

Merchants' accounts, though a science not likely to help a gentleman to get an estate, yet possibly there is not anything of more use and efficacy to make him preserve the estate he has. 'Tis seldom observed that he keeps an account of his income and expenses, and thereby not having constantly under view the course of his domestic affairs, lets them run to ruin; and I doubt not but many a man gets behind-hand before he is aware, or runs farther on when he is once in, for want of this care, or the skill to do it. I would therefore advise all gentlemen to learn perfectly merchants' accounts, and not to think it is a skill that belongs not to them, because it has received its name from and has been chiefly practiced by men of traffic.

211. When my young master has once got the skill of keeping accounts (which is a business of reason more than arithmetic) perhaps it will not be amiss that his father from thenceforth require him to do it in all his concernments. Not that I would have him set down every pint of wine or play that costs him money; the general name of expenses will serve for such things well enough: nor would I have his father look so narrowly into these accounts, as to take occasion from thence to criticize his expenses; he must remember that he himself was once a young man, and not forget the thoughts he had then, nor the right his son has to have the same, and to have allowance

made for them. If therefore I would have the young gentleman obliged to keep an account, it is not at all to have that way a check upon his expenses (for what the father allows him, he ought to let him be fully master of) but only that he might be brought early into the custom of doing it, and that it might be made familiar and habitual to him betimes, which will be so useful and necessary to be constantly practiced the whole course of his life. A noble Venetian, whose son wallowed in the plenty of his father's riches, finding his son's expenses grow very high and extravagant, ordered his cashier to let him have for the future no more money than what he should count when he received it. This one would think no great restraint to a young gentleman's expenses; who could freely have as much money as he would tell. But yet this, to one that was used to nothing but the pursuit of his pleasures, proved a very great trouble, which at last ended in this sober and advantageous reflection: if it be so much pains to me barely to count the money I would spend, what labor and pains did it cost my ancestors, not only to count, but get it? This rational thought, suggested by this little pains imposed upon him, wrought so effectually upon his mind that it made him take up, and from that time forwards prove a good husband. This, at least, everybody must allow, that nothing is likelier to keep a man within compass than the having constantly before his eyes the state of his affairs in a regular course of *accounting*.

212. The last part usually in education is travel, which is commonly thought to finish the work, and complete the gentleman. I confess travel into foreign countries has great advantages, but the time usually chosen to send young men abroad is, I think, of all other, that which renders them least capable of reaping those advantages. Those which are proposed, as to the main of them, may be reduced to these two: first, language, secondly, an improvement in wisdom and prudence, by seeing men, and conversing with people of tempers, customs, and ways of living different from one another, and especially from those of his parish and neighborhood. But from sixteen to one and twenty, which is the ordinary time of travel, men are, of all their lives, the least suited to these improvements. The first season to get foreign languages, and form the tongue to their

true accents, I should think, should be from seven to fourteen or sixteen, and then too a tutor with them is useful and necessary, who may with those languages teach them other things. But to put them out of their parents' view at a great distance under a governor, when they think themselves to be too much men to be governed by others, and yet have not prudence and experience enough to govern themselves, what is it, but to expose them to all the greatest dangers of their whole life, when they have the least fence and guard against them? 'Till that boiling boisterous part of life comes in, it may be hoped the tutor may have some authority: neither the stubbornness of age nor the temptation or examples of others can take him from his tutor's conduct till fifteen or sixteen; but then, when he begins to comfort himself with men, and thinks himself one; when he comes to relish and pride himself in manly vices, and thinks it a shame to be any longer under the control and conduct of another, what can be hoped from even the most careful and discreet governor, when neither he has power to compel nor his pupil a disposition to be persuaded; but on the contrary, has the advice of warm blood and prevailing fashion to hearken to the temptations of his companions, just as wise as himself, rather than to the persuasions of his tutor, who is now looked on as an enemy to his freedom? And when is a man so like to miscarry, as when at the same time he is both raw and unruly?

This is the season of all his life that most requires the eye and authority of his parents and friends to govern it. The flexibleness of the former part of a man's age, not yet grown up to be headstrong, makes it more governable and safe; and in the afterpart, reason and foresight begin a little to take place, and mind a man of his safety and improvement. The time therefore I should think the fittest for a young gentleman to be sent abroad, would be, either when he is younger, under a tutor, when he might be the better for; or when he is some years older, without a governor; when he is of age to govern himself, and make observations of what he finds in other countries worthy his notice, and that might be of use to him after his return; and when too, being throughly acquainted with the laws and fashions, the natural and moral advantages and defects of his own country, he has something to exchange with those abroad, from whose conversation he hoped to reap any knowledge.

213. [Wanting].

214. The ordering of travel otherwise is that, I imagine, which makes so many young gentlemen come back so little improved by it. And if they do bring home with them any knowledge of the places and people they have seen, it is often an admiration of the worst and vainest practices they met with abroad; retaining a relish and memory of those things wherein their liberty took its first swing, rather than of what should make them better and wiser after their return. And indeed how can it be otherwise, going abroad at the age they do under the care of another, who is to provide their necessaries and make their observations for them? Thus under the shelter and pretense of a governor, thinking themselves excused from standing upon their own legs or being accountable for their own conduct, they very seldom trouble themselves with inquiries or making useful observations of their own. Their thoughts run after play and pleasure, wherein they take it as a lessening to be controlled; but seldom trouble themselves to examine the designs, observe the address, and consider the arts, tempers, and inclinations of men they meet with; that so they may know how to comport themselves towards them. Here he that travels with them is to screen them; get them out when they have run themselves into the briars; and in all their miscarriages be answerable for them.

215. I confess the knowledge of men is so great a skill that it is not to be expected a young man should presently be perfect in it. But yet his going abroad is to little purpose, if travel does not sometimes open his eyes, make him cautious and wary, and accustom him to look beyond the outside, and, under the inoffensive guard of a civil and obliging carriage, keep himself free and safe in his conversation with strangers and all sorts of people without forfeiting their good opinion. He that is sent out to travel, at the age and with the thoughts of a man designing to improve himself, may get into the conversation and acquaintance of persons of condition where he comes; which, though a thing of most advantage to a gentleman that travels. yet I ask, amongst our young men that go abroad under

tutors, what one is there of a hundred that ever visits any person of quality? Much less makes an acquaintance with such, from whose conversation he may learn what is good breeding in that country, and what is worth observation in it; though from such persons it is one may learn more in one day than in a year's rambling from one inn to another. Nor indeed, is it to be wondered; for men of worth and parts will not easily admit the familiarity of boys who yet need the care of a tutor; though a young gentleman and stranger, appearing like a man, and showing a desire to inform himself in the customs, manners, laws, and government of the country he is in, will find welcome assistance and entertainment amongst the best and most knowing persons everywhere, who will be ready to receive, encourage, and countenance an ingenuous and inquisitive foreigner.

216. This, how true soever it be, will not, I fear, alter the custom, which has cast the time of travel upon the worst part of a man's life; but for reasons not taken from their improvement. The young lad must not be ventured abroad at eight or ten, for fear of what may happen to the tender child, though he then runs ten times less risk than at sixteen or eighteen. Nor must he stay at home till that danger-ous, heady age be over, because he must be back again by one and twenty, to marry and propagate. The father cannot stay any longer for the portion, or the mother for a new set of babies to play with; and so my young master, whatever comes on it, must have a wife looked out for him by that time he is of age; though it would be no prejudice to his strength, his parts, or his issue, if it were respited for some time, and he had leave to get, in years and knowledge, the start a little of his children, who are often found to tread too near upon the heels of their fathers, to the no great satisfaction either of son or father. But the young gentleman being got within view of matrimony, 'tis time to leave him to his mistress.

217. Though I am now come to a conclusion of what obvious remarks have suggested to me concerning education, I would not have it thought that I look on it as a just treatise on this subject. There are a thousand other things that may need consideration; especially if one should take in the various tempers, different inclina-tions, and particular defaults that are to be found in children, and

prescribe proper remedies. The variety is so great that it would require a volume; nor would that reach it. Each man's mind has some peculiarity, as well as his face, that distinguishes him from all others; and there are possibly scarce two children who can be conducted by exactly the same method. Besides that, I think a prince, a nobleman, and an ordinary gentleman's son, should have different ways of breeding. But having had here only some general views in reference to the main end and aims in education, and those designed for a gentleman's son, whom, being then very little, I considered only as white paper, or wax, to be molded and fashioned as one pleases; I have touched little more than those heads which I judged necessary for the breeding of a young gentleman of his condition in general; and have now published these my occasional thoughts with this hope, that though this be far from being a complete treatise on this subject, or such as that everyone may find what will just fit his child in it, yet it may give some small light to those whose concern for their dear little ones makes them so irregularly bold, that they dare venture to consult their own reason in the education of their children, rather than wholly to rely upon old custom.

APPENDIX

THE FUNDAMENTAL CONSTITUTIONS OF CAROLINA

LOCKE'S CONTRIBUTION to the *Constitutions of Carolina*, of which there is at least one copy in Locke's hand, is confined to Articles XCV-CX, dealing with religious freedom. The remainder of the *Constitutions* is so at variance with his political views that it is doubtful if Locke had any influence except perhaps in style. Lord Ashley, whom Locke advised, shared many of Locke's beliefs concerning religious toleration, but neither Ashley nor the other proprietors of the new colony accepted Locke's more democratic political doctrines. The proprietors, therefore, and not Locke were undoubtedly responsible for the major portion of the document.

Articles XCV, CIII, and CVIII, which restricted civil rights to free-men who believed in God, denied the privilege of seditious pronunciations against the government, and refused the right to disobey any provisions of the Constitutions on the ground of religious beliefs, were, as we have seen in *A Letter Concerning Toleration,* acceptable to Locke and even advocated by him. These provisions he thought were necessary for the preservation of the state.

Article XCVI, calling for public financial support of the Church of England, however, was inserted over his protests. (See note 4).

Aside from the articles devoted to religious toleration, the *Constitutions* are interesting as an attempt to write into the fundamental law of a New World colony the English system of local government, as well as many of the feudal customs of seventeenth century England. As the reader of history will remember, the *Constitutions of Carolina* were never very effective. Several modifications were made in the document before it was finally discarded in 1690. The sections on religious liberty nevertheless continued to guide the people of the colony. Carolina remained one of the few American colonies which placed only minor restrictions on freeholders who were adherents of other than the dominant church in the colony.

THE FUNDAMENTAL CONSTITUTIONS
OF CAROLINA

OUR SOVEREIGN lord the king having, out of his royal grace and bounty, granted unto us the province of Carolina, with all the royalties, properties, jurisdictions, and privileges, of a county palatine,[1] as large and ample as the county palatine of Durham, with other great privileges, for the better settlement of the government of the said place, and establishing the interest of the lords proprietors with equality, and without confusion; and that the government of this province may be made most agreeable to the monarchy under which we live, and of which this province is a part; and that we may avoid erecting a numerous democracy: we, the lords and proprietors of the province aforesaid, have agreed to this following form of government, to be perpetually established amongst us, unto which we do oblige ourselves, our heirs, and successors, in the most binding ways that can be devised.

I. The eldest of the lords proprietors shall be palatine;[1] and, upon the decease of the palatine, the eldest of the seven surviving proprietors shall always succeed him.

II. There shall be seven other chief offices erected, viz., the admiral's, chamberlain's, chancellor's, constable's, chief justice's, high steward's, and treasurer's; which places shall be enjoyed by none but the lords proprietors, to be assigned at first by lot; and upon the vacancy of any one of the seven great offices by death, or otherwise, the eldest proprietor shall have his choice of the said place.

III. The whole province shall be divided into counties; each county

[1] In Medieval Europe a palatine was a lord having sovereign power in a royal province or dependency.

shall consist of eight signiories, eight baronies, and four precincts; each precinct shall consist of six colonies.

IV. Each signiory, barony, and colony, shall consist of twelve thousand acres; the eight signiories being the share of the eight proprietors, and the eight baronies of the nobility; both which shares, being each of them one fifth part of the whole, are to be perpetually annexed, the one to the proprietors, the other to the hereditary nobility, leaving the colonies, being three-fifths, amongst the people: that so in setting out, and planting the lands, the balance of the government may be preserved.

V. At any time before the year one thousand seven hundred and one, any of the lords proprietors shall have power to relinquish, alienate, and dispose to any other person, his proprietorship, and all the signiories, powers, and interest thereunto belonging, wholly and entirely together, and not otherwise. But, after the year one thousand seven hundred, those, who are then lords proprietors, shall not have the power to alienate or make over their proprietorship, with the signiories and privileges thereunto belonging, or any part thereof, to any person whatsoever, otherwise than as in Sec. XVIII, but it shall all descend unto their heirs-male; and, for want of heirs-male, it shall all descend on that landgrave, or cassique,[2] of Carolina, who is descended of the next heirs-female of the proprietor; and, for want of such heirs, it shall descend on the next heir-general; and, for want of such heirs, the remaining seven proprietors shall, upon the vacancy, choose a landgrave to succeed the deceased proprietor, who being chosen by the majority of the seven surviving proprietors, he and his heirs, successively, shall be proprietors, as fully, to all intents and purposes, as any of the rest.

VI. That the number of eight proprietors may be constantly kept; if, upon the vacancy of any proprietorship, the seven surviving proprietors shall not choose a landgrave to be a proprietor, before the second biennial parliament after the vacancy; then the next biennial

---

[2] Landgrave, a county noble, having territorial jurisdiction. The word is of German origin. Cassique, or cacique, a chief among the natives of the West Indies and Mexico.

parliament but one after such vacancy shall have the power to choose any landgrave to be a proprietor.

VII. Whosoever after the year one thousand seven hundred, either by inheritance or choice, shall succeed any proprietor in his proprietorship, and signiories thereunto belonging, shall be obliged to take the name and arms of that proprietor, whom he succeeds; which from thenceforth shall be the name and arms of his family and their posterity.

VIII. Whatsoever landgrave or cassique shall any way come to be a proprietor, shall take the signiories annexed to the said proprietorship; but his former dignity, with the baronies annexed, shall devolve into the hands of the lords proprietors.

IX. There shall be just as many landgraves as there are counties, and twice as many cassiques, and no more. These shall be the hereditary nobility of the province, and by right of their dignity be members of parliament. Each landgrave shall have four baronies, and each cassique two baronies, hereditarily and unalterably annexed to, and settled upon, the said dignity.

X. The first landgraves and cassiques of the twelve first counties to be planted, shall be nominated thus; that is to say, of the twelve landgraves, the lords proprietors shall each of them, separately for himself, nominate and choose one; and the remaining four landgraves of the first twelve shall be nominated and chosen by the palatine's court. In like manner, of the twenty-four first cassiques, each proprietor for himself shall nominate and choose two, and the remaining eight shall be nominated and chosen by the palatine's court; and when the twelve first counties shall be planted, the lords proprietors shall again in the same manner nominate and choose twelve more landgraves, and twenty-four cassiques for the next twelve counties to be planted; that is to say, two-thirds of each number by the single nomination of each proprietor for himself and the remaining one-third by the joint election of the palatine's court, and so proceed in the same manner till the whole province of Carolina be set out and planted, according to the proportions in these Fundamental Constitutions.

XI. Any landgrave or cassique, at any time before the year one thousand seven hundred and one, shall have power to alienate, sell, or make over to any other person, his dignity, with the baronies thereunto belonging, all entirely together. But after the year one thousand seven hundred, no landgrave or cassique shall have power to alienate, sell, make over, or let the hereditary baronies of his dignity, or any part thereof, otherwise than as in Sec. XVIII; but they shall all entirely with the dignity thereunto belonging, descend unto his heirs-male; and for want of heirs-male, all entirely and undivided, to the next heir-general; and for want of such heirs, shall devolve into the hands of the lords proprietors.

XII. That the due number of landgraves and cassiques may be always kept up; if, upon the devolution of any landgraveship and cassiqueship, the palatine's court shall not settle the devolved dignity, with the baronies thereunto annexed, before the second biennial parliament after such devolution; the next biennial parliament but one after such devolution shall have power to make any one landgrave or cassique, in the room of him, who dying without heirs, his dignity and baronies devolved.

XIII. No one person shall have more than one dignity, with the signiories or baronies thereunto belonging. But whensoever it shall happen, that anyone, who is already proprietor, landgrave, or cassique, shall have any of these dignities descend to him by inheritance, it shall be at his choice to keep which of the dignities, with the lands annexed, he shall like best; but shall leave the other, with the lands annexed, to be enjoyed by him, who not being his heir-apparent, and certain successor to his present dignity, is next of blood.

XIV. Whosoever, by right of inheritance, shall come to be landgrave or cassique, shall take the name and arms of his predecessor in that dignity, to be thenceforth the name and arms of his family and their posterity.

XV. Since the dignity of proprietor, landgrave, or cassique, cannot be divided, and the signiories and baronies thereunto annexed must forever all entirely descend with, and accompany that dignity; whensoever for want of heirs-male it shall descend on the issue female, the eldest daughter and her heirs shall be preferred; and in the inheritance of those dignities, and in the signiories or baronies annexed, there shall be no coheirs.

XVI. In every signiory, barony, and manor, the respective lord shall have power in his own name to hold court-leet [3] there, for trying of all causes both civil and criminal; but where it shall concern any person being no inhabitant, vassal, or leet-man of the said signiory, barony, or manor, he, upon paying down of forty shillings to the lords proprietors' use, shall have an appeal from the signiory or barony-court to the precinct-court.

XVII. Every manor shall consist of not less than three thousand acres, and not above twelve thousand acres in one entire piece and colony: but any three thousand acres or more in one piece, and the possession of one man, shall not be a manor, unless it be constituted a manor by the grant of the palatine's court.

XVIII. The lords of signiories and baronies shall have power only of granting estates not exceeding three lives, or thirty-one years, in two-thirds of the said signiories or baronies, and the remaining third shall be always demesne.[4]

XIX. Any lord of a manor may alienate, sell, or dispose to any other person and his heirs forever, his manor, all entirely together, with all the privileges and leet-men thereunto belonging, so far forth as any colony lands; but no grant of any part thereof, either in fee, or for any longer term than three lives, or one and twenty years, shall be good against the next heir.

XX. No manor, for want of issue-male shall be divided amongst coheirs; but the manor, if there be but one, shall all entirely descend to the eldest daughter and her heirs. If there be more manors than one, the eldest daughter first shall have her choice, the second next, and so on, beginning again at the eldest, till all the manors be taken up; so that the privileges, which belong to manors being indivisible, the lands of the manors, to which they are annexed, may be kept entire,

---

[3] Court-leet, a court in which the noble, or in this case the proprietor, exercised his private jurisdiction; leet-man, any person under the jurisdiction of a court-leet.

[4] Controlled by state, in contrast to privately owned.

and the manor not lose those privileges, which, upon parceling out to several owners, must necessarily cease.

XXI. Every lord of a manor, within his manor, shall have all the powers, jurisdictions, and privileges, which a landgrave or cassique hath in his baronies.

XXII. In every signiory, barony, or manor, all the leet-men shall be under the jurisdiction of the respective lords of the said signiory, barony, or manor, without appeal from him. Nor shall any leet-man, or leet-woman, have liberty to go off from the land of their particular lord, and live anywhere else, without license obtained from their said lord, under hand and seal.

XXIII. All the children of leet-men shall be leet-men, and so to all generations.

XXIV. No man shall be capable of having a court-leet, or leet-men, but a proprietor, landgrave, cassique, or lord of a manor.

XXV. Whoever shall voluntarily enter himself a leet-man, in the registry of the county-court, shall be a leet-man.

XXVI. Whoever is lord of leet-men, shall upon the marriage of a leet-man or leet-woman of his, give them ten acres of land for their lives; they paying to him therefor not more than one-eighth part of all the yearly produce and growth of the said ten acres.

XXVII. No landgrave or cassique shall be tried for any criminal cause, in any but the chief-justice's court, and that by a jury of his peers.

XXVIII. There shall be eight supreme courts. The first called the palatine's court, consisting of the palatine, and the other seven proprietors. The other seven courts of the other seven great officers, shall consist each of them of a proprietor, and six counsellors added to him. Under each of these latter seven courts, shall be a college of twelve assistants. The twelve assistants of the several colleges shall be chosen, two out of the landgraves, cassiques, or eldest sons of the proprietors, by the palatine's court; two out of the landgraves, by the landgraves' chamber; two out of the cassiques, by the cassiques' chamber; four more of the twelve shall be chosen by the commons' chamber, out of such as have been or are members of parliament, sheriffs, or justices of the county-court, or the younger sons of proprietors, or the eldest sons of landgraves or cassiques; the two other shall be chosen by the palatine's court, out of the same sort of persons, out of which the commons' chamber is to choose.

XXIX. Out of these colleges shall be chosen at first by the palatine's court, six counsellors, to be joined with each proprietor in his court; of which six, one shall be of those who were chosen into any of the colleges by the palatine's court, out of the landgraves, cassiques, or eldest sons of the proprietors; one out of those who were chosen by the cassiques' chamber; two out of those who were chosen by the commons' chamber; and one out of those who were chosen by the palatine's court, out of the proprietors' younger sons, or eldest of the landgraves, cassiques, or commons, qualified as aforesaid.

XXX. When it shall happen that any counsellor dies, and thereby there is a vacancy, the grand council shall have power to remove any counsellor that is willing to be removed out of any of the proprietors' courts to fill up the vacancy; provided they take a man of the same degree and choice the other was of, whose vacant place is to be filled up. But if no counsellor consent to be removed, or upon such remove the last remaining vacant place, in any of the proprietors' courts, shall be filled up by the choice of the grand council, who shall have power to remove out of any of the colleges any assistant, who is of the same degree and choice that counsellor was of, into whose vacant place he is to succeed. The grand council also shall have power to remove any assistant, that is willing, out of one college into another, provided he be of the same degree and choice. But the last remaining vacant place in any college shall be filled up by the same choice, and out of the same degree of persons the assistant was of who is dead, or removed. No place shall be vacant in any proprietors' court above six months. No place shall be vacant in any college longer than the next session of parliament.

XXXI. No man, being a member of the grand council, or of any of the seven colleges, shall be turned out, but for misdemeanor, of which the grand council shall be judge; and the vacancy of the person so put out shall be filled, not by the election of the grand council, but by those who first chose him, and out of the same degree he was of, who is expelled. But it is not hereby to be understood that the grand council hath any power to turn out any one of the lords proprietors having in themselves an inherent original right.

XXXII. All elections in the parliament, in the several chambers of the parliament, and in the grand council, shall be passed by balloting.

XXXIII. The palatine's court shall consist of the palatine, and seven proprietors, wherein shall be acted without the presence and consent of the palatine or his deputy, and three others of the proprietors or their deputies. This court shall have power to call parliaments, to pardon all offenses, to make elections of all officers in the proprietors' dispose, and to nominate and appoint port-towns; and also shall have power, by their order to the treasurer, to dispose of all public treasure, excepting money granted by the parliament, and by them directed to some particular public use; and also shall have a negative upon all acts, orders, votes, and judgments, of the grand council and the parliament, except only as in Sec. VI and XII, and shall have all the powers granted to the lords proprietors, by their patent from our sovereign lord the king, except in such things as are limited by these Fundamental Constitutions.

XXXIV. The palatine himself, when he in person shall be either in the army, or in any of the proprietors' courts, shall then have the powers of general, or of that proprietor, in whose court he is then present; and the proprietor, in whose court the palatine then presides, shall during his presence there be but as one of the council.

XXXV. The chancellor's court, consisting of one of the proprietors, and his six counsellors, who shall be called vice-chancellors, shall have the custody of the seal of the palatine, under which charters of lands or otherwise, commissions and grants of the palatine's court, shall pass. And it shall not be lawful to put the seal of the palatinate to any writing, which is not signed by the palatinate or his deputy, and three other proprietors or their deputies. To this court also belong all state matters, despatches, and treaties with the neighbor Indians. To this court also belong all invasions of the law, of liberty of conscience, and all disturbances of the public peace, upon pretense of religion, as also the license of printing. The twelve assistants belonging to this court shall be called recorders.

XXXVI. Whatever passes under the seal of the palatinate, shall be registered in that proprietor's court, to which the matter therein contained belongs.

XXXVII. The chancellor, or his deputy, shall be always speaker in parliament, and president of the grand council; and in his and his deputy's absence, one of his vice-chancellors.

XXXVIII. The chief justice's court, consisting of one of the proprietors and his six counsellors, who shall be called justices of the bench, shall judge all appeals in cases both civil and criminal, except all such cases as shall be under the jurisdiction and cognizance of any other of the proprietors' courts, which shall be tried in those courts respectively. The government and regulation of the registries of writings and contracts shall belong to the jurisdiction of this court. The twelve assistants of this court shall be called masters.

XXXIX. The constable's court, consisting of one of the proprietors and his six counsellors, who shall be called marshals, shall order and determine of all military affairs by land, and all land-forces, arms, ammunition, artillery, garrisons and forts, etc., and whatever belongs unto war. His twelve assistants shall be called lieutenant-generals.

XL. In time of actual war, the constable, whilst he is in the army, shall be general of the army; and the six counsellors, or such of them as the palatine's court shall for that time or service appoint, shall be the immediate great officers under him, and the lieutenant-generals next to them.

XLI. The admiral's court, consisting of one of the proprietors, and his six counsellors, called consuls, shall have the care and inspection over all ports, moles, and navigable rivers, so far as the tide flows, and also all the public shipping of Carolina, and stores thereunto belonging, and all maritime affairs. This court also shall have the power of the court of admiralty; and shall have power to constitute judges in port-towns, to try cases belonging to law-merchant, as shall be most convenient for trade. The twelve assistants, belonging to this court, shall be called pro-consuls.

XLII. In time of actual war, the admiral, whilst he is at sea, shall command in chief, and his six counsellors, or such of them as the palatine's court shall for that time and service appoint, shall be the immediate great officers under him, and the pro-consuls next to them.

XLIII. The treasurer's court, consisting of a proprietor and his six counsellors, called under-treasurers, shall take care of all matters that concern the public revenues and treasury. The twelve assistants shall be called auditors.

XLIV. The high steward's court, consisting of a proprietor and his six counsellors, called comptrollers, shall have the care of all foreign and domestic trade, manufactures, public buildings, work-houses, highways, passages by water above the flood of the tide, drains, sewers, and banks against inundations, bridges, post, carriers, fairs, markets. corruption or infection of the common air or water, and all things in order to the public commerce and health; also setting out and surveying of lands; and also setting out and appointing places for towns to be built on in the precincts, and the prescribing and determining the figure and bigness of the said towns, according to such models as the said court shall order; contrary or differing from which models it shall not be lawful for anyone to build in any town. This court shall have power also to make any public building, or any new highway, or enlarge any old highway, upon any man's land whatsoever; as also to make cuts, channels, banks, locks, and bridges, for making rivers navigable, or for draining fens, or any other public use. The damage the owner of such lands (on or through which any such public things shall be made) shall receive thereby, shall be valued, and satisfaction made by such ways as the grand council shall appoint. The twelve assistants, belonging to this court, shall be called surveyors.

XLV. The chamberlain's court, consisting of a proprietor and his six counsellors, called vice-chamberlains, shall have the care of all ceremonies, precedency, heraldry, reception of public messengers, pedigrees, the registry of all births, burials, and marriages, legitimation, and all cases concerning matrimony, or arising from it; and shall also have power to regulate all fashions, habits, badges, games, and sports. To this court also it shall belong to convocate the grand council. The twelve assistants belonging to this court shall be called provosts.

XLVI. All causes belonging to, or under the jurisdiction of, any of the proprietors' courts, shall in them respectively be tried, and ultimately determined without any farther appeal.

XLVII. The proprietors' courts shall have a power to mitigate all fines, and suspend all executions in criminal causes, either before or after sentence, in any of the other inferior courts respectively.

XLVIII. In all debates, hearings, or trials, in any of the proprietors' courts, the twelve assistants belonging to the said courts, respectively shall have liberty to be present, but shall not interpose, unless their opinions be required, nor have any vote at all; but their business shall be, by the direction of the respective courts, to prepare such business as shall be committed to them; as also to bear such offices, and despatch such affairs, either where the court is kept, or elsewhere, as the court shall think fit.

XLIX. In all the proprietors' courts, the proprietor, and any three of his counsellors, shall make a quorum; provided always, that for the better despatch of business, it shall be in the power of the palatine's court to direct what sort of causes shall be heard and determined by a quorum of any three.

L. The grand council shall consist of the palatine and seven proprietors, and the forty-two counsellors of the several proprietors' courts, who shall have power to determine any controversies that may arise between any of the proprietors' courts about their respective jurisdictions, or between the members of the same court about their manner and methods of proceeding; to make peace and war, leagues, treaties, etc., with any of the neighbor Indians; to issue out their general orders to the constable's and admiral's courts, for the raising, disposing, or disbanding the forces, by land or by sea.

LI. The grand council shall prepare all matters to be proposed in parliament. Nor shall any matter whatsoever be proposed in parliament, but what hath first passed the grand council; which, after having been read three several days in parliament, shall by majority of votes be passed or rejected.

LII. The grand council shall always be judges of all causes and appeals that concern the palatine, or any of the lords proprietors, or any counsellor of any proprietor's court, in any cause, which otherwise should have been tried in the court in which the said counsellor is judge himself.

LIII. The grand council, by their warrants to the treasurer's court, shall dispose of all the money given by the parliament, and by them directed to any particular public use.

LIV. The quorum of the grand council shall be thirteen, whereof a proprietor, or his deputy, shall be always one.

LV. The grand council shall meet the first Tuesday in every month, and as much oftener as either they shall think fit, or they shall be convocated by the chamberlain's court.

LVI. The palatine, or any of the lords proprietors, shall have power, under hand and seal, to be registered in the grand council, to make a deputy, who shall have the same power, to all intents and purposes, as he himself who deputes him; except in confirming acts of parliament, as in Sec. LXXVI, and except also in nominating and choosing landgraves and cassiques, as in Sec. X. All such deputations shall cease and determine at the end of four years, and at any time shall be revocable at the pleasure of the deputator.

LVII. No deputy of any proprietor shall have any power, whilst the deputator is in any part of Carolina, except the proprietor, whose deputy he is, be a minor.

LVIII. During the minority of any proprietor, his guardian shall have power to constitute and appoint his deputy.

LIX. The eldest of the lords proprietors, who shall be personally in Carolina, shall of course be the palatine's deputy, and if no proprietor be in Carolina, he shall choose his deputy out of the heirs-apparent of any of the proprietors, if any such be there; and if there be no heir-apparent of any of the lords proprietors above one-and-twenty years old, in Carolina, then he shall choose for deputy any one of the landgraves of the grand council: till he have, by deputation, under hand and seal, chosen any one of the fore-mentioned heirs apparent, or landgraves, to be his deputy, the eldest man of the landgraves, and for want of a landgrave, the eldest man of the cassiques, who shall be personally in Carolina, shall of course be his deputy.

LX. Each proprietor's deputy shall be always one of his own six counsellors respectively; and in case any of the proprietors hath not, in his absence out of Carolina, a deputy, commissioned under his hand and seal, the eldest nobleman of his court shall of course be his deputy.

LXI. In every county there shall be a court, consisting of a sheriff and four justices of the county, for every precinct one. The sheriff shall be an inhabitant of the county, and have at least five hundred acres of freehold within the said county; and the justices shall be inhabitants, and have each of them five hundred acres apiece freehold within the precinct for which they serve respectively. These five shall be chosen and commissioned from time to time by the palatine's court.

LXII. For any personal causes exceeding the value of two hundred pounds sterling, or in title of land, or in any criminal cause, either party, upon paying twenty pounds sterling to the lords proprietors' use, shall have liberty of appeal from the county-court unto the respective proprietor's court.

LXIII. In every precinct there shall be a court, consisting of a steward and four justices of the precinct, being inhabitants, and having three hundred acres of freehold within the said precinct, who shall judge all criminal causes, except for treason, murder, and any other offenses punishable with death, and except all criminal causes of the nobility; and shall judge also all civil causes whatsoever; and in all personal actions, not exceeding fifty pounds sterling, without appeal; but where the cause shall exceed that value, or concern a title of land, and in all criminal causes, there either party, upon paying five pounds sterling to the lords proprietors' use, shall have liberty of appeal to the county-court.

LXIV. No cause shall be twice tried in any one court, upon any reason or pretense whatsoever.

LXV. For treason, murder, and all other offenses punishable with death, there shall be a commission, twice a year at least, granted unto one or more members of the grand council, or colleges, who shall come as itinerant judges to the several counties, and, with the sheriff and four justices, shall hold assizes to judge such causes; but, upon paying of fifty pounds sterling to the lords proprietors' use, there shall be liberty of appeal to the respective proprietor's court.

LXVI. The grand jury at the several assizes shall, upon their oaths, and under their hands and seals, deliver in to the itinerant judges a presentment of such grievances, misdemeanors, exigencies, or defects, which they think necessary for the public good of the country; which presentments shall, by the itinerant judges, at the end of their circuit, be delivered in to the grand council at their next sitting. And whatsoever therein concerns the execution of laws already made, the several proprietors' courts, in the matters belonging to each of them respectively, shall take cognizance of it, and give such order about it as shall be effectual for the due execution of the laws. But whatever concerns the making of any new law shall be referred to the several respective courts to which the matter belongs, and be by them prepared and brought to the grand council.

LXVII. For terms, there shall be quarterly such a certain number of days, not exceeding one-and-twenty at any one time, as the several respective courts shall appoint. The time for the beginning of the term, in the precinct-court, shall be the first Monday in January, April, July, and October; in the county-court, the first Monday in February, May, August, and November; and in the proprietors' courts, the first Monday in March, June, September, and December.

LXVIII. In the precinct-court no man shall be a juryman under fifty acres of freehold. In the county-court, or at the assizes, no man shall be a grand juryman under three hundred acres of freehold; and no man shall be a petty juryman under two hundred acres of freehold. In the proprietors' courts no man shall be a juryman under five hundred acres of freehold.

LXIX. Every jury shall consist of twelve men; and it shall not be necessary they should all agree, but the verdict shall be according to the consent of the majority.

LXX. It shall be a base and vile thing to plead for money or reward; nor shall anyone (except he be a near kinsman, not farther off than cousin-german to the party concerned) be permitted to plead another man's cause, till before the judge, in open court, he hath taken an oath that he doth not plead for money or reward, nor hath, nor will receive, nor directly, nor indirectly, bargained with the party whose cause he is going to plead, for money or any other reward, for pleading his cause.

LXXI. There shall be a parliament, consisting of the proprietors, or their deputies, the landgraves and cassiques, and one freeholder out of every precinct, to be chosen by the freeholders of the said precinct respectively. They shall sit all together in one room, and have every member one vote.

LXXII. No man shall be chosen a member of parliament who hath less than five hundred acres of freehold within the precinct for which he is chosen; nor shall any have a vote in choosing the said member that hath less than fifty acres of freehold within the said precinct.

LXXIII. A new parliament shall be assembled the first Monday of the month of November every second year, and shall meet and sit in the town they last sat in, without any summons, unless, by the palatine's court, they be summoned to meet at any other place. And if there shall be any occasion of a parliament in these intervals, it shall be in the power of the palatine's court to assemble them in forty days' notice, and at such time and place as the said court shall think fit; and the palatine's court shall have power to dissolve the said parliament when they shall think fit.

LXXIV. At the opening of every parliament, the first thing that shall be done shall be the reading of these Fundamental Constitutions, which the palatine and proprietors, and the rest of the members then present, shall subscribe. Nor shall any person whatsoever sit or vote in the parliament, till he hath that session subscribed these Fundamental Constitutions, in a book kept for the purpose by the clerk of the parliament.

LXXV. In order to the due election of members for the biennial parliament, it shall be lawful for the freeholders of the respective precincts to meet the first Tuesday in September every two years, in the same town or place that they last met in to choose parliament-men; and there choose those members that are to sit the next November following, unless the steward of the precinct shall, by sufficient notice thirty days before, appoint some other place for their meeting, in order to the election.

LXXVI. No act or order of parliament shall be of any force, unless it be ratified in open parliament, during the same session, by the palatine or his deputy, and three more of the lords proprietors, or their deputies; and then not to continue longer in force but until the next biennial parliament, unless, in the meantime, it be ratified under the hands and seals of the palatine himself, and three more of the lords proprietors themselves, and by their order published at the next biennial parliament.

LXXVII. Any proprietor, or his deputy, may enter his protestation against any act of the parliament, before the palatine or his deputy's consent be given as aforesaid, if he shall conceive the said act to be contrary to this establishment, or any of these Fundamental Constitutions of the government. And in such case, after full and free debate, the several estates shall retire into four several chambers: the palatine and the proprietors into one; the landgraves into another; the cassiques into another; and those chosen by the precincts into a fourth; and if the major part of any of the four estates shall vote that the law is not agreeable to this establishment, and these Fundamental Constitutions of the government, then it shall pass no farther, but be as if it had never been proposed.

LXXVIII. The quorum of the parliament shall be one half of those who are members, and capable of sitting in the house that present session of parliament. The quorum of each of the chambers of parliament shall be one half of the members of that chamber.

LXXIX. To avoid multiplicity of laws, which by degrees always change the right foundations of the original government, all acts of parliament whatsoever, in whatsoever form passed or enacted, shall at the end of an hundred years after their enacting, respectively cease and determine of themselves, and without any repeal become null and void, as if no such acts or laws had ever been made.

LXXX. Since multiplicity of comments, as well as of laws, have great inconveniences, and serve only to obscure and perplex, all manner of comments and expositions, on any part of these Fundamental Constitutions, or any part of the common or statute law of Carolina, are absolutely prohibited.

LXXXI. There shall be a registry in every precinct, wherein shall be enrolled all deeds, leases, judgments, mortgages, and other conveyances, which may concern any of the land within the said precinct; and all such conveyances, not so entered or registered, shall not be of force against any person or party to the said contract or conveyance.

LXXXII. No man shall be register of any precinct who hath not at least three hundred acres of freehold within the said precinct.

LXXXIII. The freeholders of every precinct shall nominate three men; out of which three, the chief justice's court shall choose and commission one to be register of the said precinct, whilst he shall well behave himself.

LXXXIV. There shall be a registry in every signiory, barony, and colony, wherein shall be recorded all the births, marriages, and deaths, that shall happen within the respective signiories, baronies, and colonies.

LXXXV. No man shall be register of a colony that hath not above fifty acres of freehold within the said colony.

LXXXVI. The time of everyone's age that is born in Carolina shall be reckoned from the day that his birth is entered in the registry, and not before.

LXXXVII. No marriage shall be lawful, whatever contract and ceremony they have used, till both the parties mutually own it before the register of the place where they were married, and he register it, with the names of the father and mother of each party.

LXXXVIII. No man shall administer to the goods, or have right to them, or enter upon the estate of any person deceased, till his death be registered in the respective registry.

LXXXIX. He that doth not enter, in the respective registry, the birth or death of any person that is born, or dies, in his house or ground, shall pay to the said register one shilling per week for each such neglect, reckoning from the time of each birth, or death, respectively, to the time of registering it.

XC. In like manner the births, marriages, and deaths, of the lords proprietors, landgraves, and cassiques, shall be registered in the chamberlain's court.

XCI. There shall be in every colony one constable, to be chosen annually by the freeholders of the colony; his estate shall be above a hundred acres of freehold within the said colony, and such subordinate officers as shall be appointed for his assistance, as the county-court shall find requisite. and shall be established by the said county-court. The election of the subordinate annual officers shall be also in the free-holders of the colony.

XCII. All towns incorporate shall be governed by a mayor, twelve aldermen, and twenty-four of the common-council. The said common-council shall be chosen by the present householders of the said town; the aldermen shall be chosen out of the common-council; and the mayor out of the aldermen, by the palatine's court.

XCIII. It being of great consequence to the plantation that port-towns should be built and preserved; therefore whosoever shall lade or unlade any commodity at any other place but a port-town, shall forfeit to the lords proprietors, for each tun so laden or unladen, the sum of ten pounds sterling; except only such goods as the palatine's court shall license to be laden or unladen elsewhere.

XCIV. The first port-town upon every river shall be in a colony, and be a port-town forever.

XCV. No man shall be permitted to be a freeman of Carolina, or to have any estate or habitation within it, that doth not acknowledge a God; and that God is publicly and solemnly to be worshiped.

XCVI. [As the country comes to be sufficiently planted and dis-tributed into fit divisions, it shall belong to the parliament to take care of the building of churches, and the public maintenance of di-vines, to be employed in the exercise of religion, according to the Church of England; which being the only true and orthodox, and the national religion of all the king's dominions, is so also of Carolina; and therefore it alone shall be allowed to receive public maintenance, by grant of parliament.[5]]

XCVII. But since the natives of that place, who will be concerned in our plantation, are utterly strangers to Christianity, whose idolatry, ignorance, or mistake, gives us no right to expel, or use them ill; and those who remove from other parts to plant there, will unavoidably be of different opinions concerning matters of religion, the liberty whereof they will expect to have allowed them, and it will not be reasonable for us on this account to keep them out: the civil peace

[5] This article was not drawn up by Locke, but inserted by some of the chief proprietors, against his judgment, as Mr. Locke himself informed one of his friends, to whom he presented a copy of these constitutions.

may be maintained amidst the diversity of opinions, and our agreement and compact with all men may be duly and faithfully observed; the violation whereof, upon what pretense soever, cannot be without great offense to Almighty God, and great scandal to the true religion, which we profess; and also that Jews, heathens, and other dissenters from the purity of the Christian religion, may not be scared and kept at a distance from it, but by having an opportunity of acquainting themselves with the truth and reasonableness of its doctrines, and the peaceableness and inoffensiveness of its professors, may by good usage and persuasion, and all those convincing methods of gentleness and meekness, suitable to the rules and design of the gospel, be won over to embrace and unfeignedly receive the truth; therefore any seven or more persons, agreeing in any religion, shall constitute a church or profession, to which they shall give some name, to distinguish it from others.

XCVIII. The terms of admittance and communion with any church or profession shall be written in a book, and therein be subscribed by all the members of the said church or profession; which book shall be kept by the public register of the precinct where they reside.

XCIX. The time of everyone's subscription and submittance shall be dated in the said book or religious record.

C. In the terms of communion of every church or profession, these following shall be three; without which no agreement or assembly of men, upon pretense of religion, shall be accounted a church or profession within these rules:

1. "That there is a GOD.

2. "That GOD is publicly to be worshiped.

3. "That it is lawful, and the duty of every man, being thereunto called by those that govern, to bear witness to truth; and that every church or profession shall in their terms of communion set down the external way whereby they witness a truth as in the presence of GOD, whether it be by laying hands on, or kissing the Bible, as in the Church of England, or by holding up the hand, or any other sensible way."

CI. No person above seventeen years of age shall have any benefit or protection of the law, or be capable of any place of profit or honor, who is not a member of some church or profession, having his name recorded in some one, and but one religious record at once.

CII. No person of any other church or profession shall disturb or molest any religious assembly.

CIII. No person whatsoever shall speak anything in their religious assembly, irreverently or seditiously of the government or governors, or state matters.

CIV. Any person subscribing the terms of communion in the record of the said church or profession, before the precinct register, and any five members of the said church or profession, shall be thereby made a member of the said church or profession.

CV. Any person striking out his own name out of any religious record, or his name being struck out by any officer thereunto, authorized by each church or profession respectively, shall cease to be a member of that church or profession.

CVI. No man shall use any reproachful, reviling or abusive language, against any religion of any church or profession; that being the certain way of disturbing the peace, and of hindering the conversion of any to the truth, by engaging them in quarrels and animosities, to the hatred of the professors and that profession, which otherwise they might be brought to assent to.

CVII. Since charity obliges us to wish well to the souls of all men, and religion ought to alter nothing in any man's civil estate or right, it shall be lawful for slaves, as well as others, to enter themselves, and be of what church or profession any of them shall think best, and thereof be as fully members as any freeman. But yet no slave shall hereby be exempted from that civil dominion his master hath over him, but be in all other things in the same state and conditions he was in before.

CVIII. Assemblies, upon what pretense soever of religion, not observing and performing the abovesaid rules, shall not be esteemed as churches, but unlawful meetings, and be punished as other riots.

CIX. No person whatsoever shall disturb, molest, or persecute another for his speculative opinions in religion, or his way of worship.

CX. Every freeman of Carolina shall have absolute power and authority over his negro slaves, of what opinion or religion soever.

CXI. No cause, whether civil or criminal, of any freeman, shall be tried in any court of judicature, without a jury of his peers.

CXII. No person whatsoever shall hold or claim any land in Carolina by purchase or gift, or otherwise, from the natives or any other whatsoever; but merely from the lords proprietors; upon pain of forfeiture of all his estate, moveable or immoveable, and perpetual banishment.

CXIII. Whosoever shall possess any freehold in Carolina, upon what title or grant soever, shall, at the farthest from and after the year one thousand six hundred eighty-nine, pay yearly unto the lords proprietors, for each acre of land, English measure, as much fine silver as is at this present in one English penny, or the value thereof, to be as a chief rent and acknowledgment to the lords proprietors, their heirs and successors forever. And it shall be lawful for the palatine's court by their officers, at any time, to take a new survey of any man's land, not to out him of any part of his possession, but that by such a survey the just number of acres he possesseth may be known, and the rent thereupon due may be paid by him.

CXIV. All wrecks, mines, minerals, quarries of gems, and precious stones, with pearl-fishing, whale-fishing, and one half of all ambergris, by whomsoever found, shall wholly belong to the lords proprietors.

CXV. All revenues and profits belonging to the lords proprietors, in common, shall be divided into ten parts, whereof the palatine shall have three, and each proprietor one; but if the palatine shall govern by a deputy, his deputy shall have one of those three tenths, and the palatine the other two tenths.

CXVI. All inhabitants and freemen of Carolina above seventeen years of age, and under sixty, shall be bound to bear arms, and serve as soldiers wherever the grand council shall find it necessary.

CXVII. A true copy of these Fundamental Constitutions shall be kept in a great book by the register of every precinct, to be subscribed before the said register. Nor shall any person of what condition or degree soever, above seventeen years old, have any estate or possession in Carolina, or protection or benefit of the law there, who hath not before a precinct register, subscribed these Fundamental Constitutions in this form:

"I A. B. do promise to bear faith and true allegiance to our sovereign lord King Charles the Second, his heirs and successors; and will be true and faithful to the palatine and lords proprietors of Carolina, their heirs and successors; and with my utmost power will defend them, and maintain the government according to this establishment in these Fundamental Constitutions."

CXVIII. Whatsoever alien shall, in this form, before any precinct register, subscribe these Fundamental Constitutions, shall be thereby naturalized.

CXIX. In the same manner shall every person, at his admittance into any office, subscribe these Fundamental Constitutions.

CXX. These Fundamental Constitutions, in number a hundred and twenty, and every part thereof, shall be and remain the sacred and unalterable form and rule of government of Carolina forever. Witness our hands and seals, the first day of March, 1669.

LOCKE'S PRINCIPAL WORKS

An Essay Concerning Human Understanding: In Four Books.

Two Treatises of Civil Government.

Essay for the Understanding of St. Paul's Epistles by consulting St. Paul himself.

A Letter concerning Toleration (translation by Wm. Popple).

> *A Second Letter concerning Toleration.*

> *A Third Letter for Toleration.*

The Reasonableness of Christianity, as delivered in the Scriptures.

Short Observations on a printed Paper, entitled For Encouraging the Coinage of Silver Money in England and after for keeping it here.

Some Considerations of the Consequences of the Lowering of Interest and the Raising of the Value of Money.

> *Further Considerations Concerning Raising the Value of Money Etc.*

Some Thoughts Concerning Education.

PARTIAL BIBLIOGRAPHY

Aaron, R. I., *John Locke,* New York, 1937.

Bourne, R. H. Fox, *The Life of John Locke,* London, 1876. 2 Vols.

Driver, C. H., "John Locke," in F. J. C. Hearnshaw, ed., *Social and Political Ideas of Some English Thinkers of the Augustan Age, A.D. 1650–1750.* London, 1928.

Gibson, James, *John Locke,* London, 1933.

Griswold, A. Whitney, "The Agrarian Democracy of Thomas Jefferson," *American Political Science Review,* Vol. XL, pp. 657–81. (August 1946.)

Kendall, Willmoore, *John Locke and the Doctrine of Majority-Rule,* Urbana, 1940.

Lord King, *The Life of John Locke, with Extracts from his Correspondence, Journals, and Common Place Books* (2nd ed.) 1830. 2 Vols.

Laski, Harold J., *Political Thought from Locke to Bentham,* London, 1920.

Santayana, George, "Locke and the Frontiers of Common Sense," *Some Turns of Thought in Modern Philosophy,* Cambridge, 1933.

Smith, Norman Kemp, *John Locke,* Manchester, 1933.